WAR, PEACE, AND ALLIANCE IN DEMOSTHENES' ATHENS

Every Athenian alliance, every declaration of war, and every peace treaty was instituted by a decision of the assembly, where citizens voted after listening to speeches that presented varied and often opposing arguments about the best course of action. The fifteen preserved assembly speeches of the mid fourth century BC thus provide an unparalleled body of evidence for the way that Athenians thought and felt about interstate relations: to understand this body of oratory is to understand how the Athenians of that period made decisions about war and peace. This is the first book to provide a comprehensive treatment of this subject. It deploys insights from a range of fields, from anthropology to international relations theory, in order not only to describe Athenian thinking, but also to explain it. Athenian thinking turns out to have been complex, sophisticated, and surprisingly familiar in both its virtues and its flaws.

PETER HUNT is Associate Professor of Classics at the University of Colorado at Boulder. He has also taught at Vassar and Davidson Colleges, and Harvard University. His publications include articles in top academic journals and edited collections. His first book was *Slaves, Warfare, and Ideology in the Greek Historians* (Cambridge, 1998).

WAR, PEACE, AND ALLIANCE IN DEMOSTHENES' ATHENS

PETER HUNT

University of Colorado

CAMBRIDGE UNIVERSITY PRESS
Cambridge, New York, Melbourne, Madrid, Cape Town, Singapore,
São Paulo, Delhi, Dubai, Tokyo

Cambridge University Press
The Edinburgh Building, Cambridge CB2 8RU, UK

Published in the United States of America by Cambridge University Press, New York

www.cambridge.org
Information on this title: www.cambridge.org/9780521835510

First published 2010

Printed in the United Kingdom at the University Press, Cambridge

A catalogue record for this publication is available from the British Library

Library of Congress Cataloguing in Publication data
Hunt, Peter, 1961–
War, peace, and alliance in Demosthenes' Athens :
debate and the process of decision-making / Peter Hunt.
p.   cm.
Includes index.
ISBN 978-0-521-83551-0 (hardback)
1. Athens (Greece) – Politics and government.   2. Athens (Greece) – Intellectual life.
3. Greece – Foreign relations – To 146 B.C.   4. Greece – Politics and government – To 146 B.C.
5. War and society – Greece – Athens – History.   6. War (Philosophy)   7. Peace (Philosophy)
8. Alliances – Philosophy.   I. Title.
DF233.2.H86   2010
938'.507 – dc22   2009047112

ISBN 978-0-521-83551-0 Hardback

For Mitzi

Contents

Acknowledgments

This book has been the work of a decade, during which time I have incurred many and deep debts to institutions, colleagues, fellow scholars, and friends.

I was able to work on this project without interruption during two years of fellowship. The first was at the Center for Hellenic Studies, where I profited from the friendly and stimulating atmosphere fostered by its then directors, Kurt Raaflaub and Deborah Boedeker, as well as from the intellectual companionship of a wonderful group of Fellows in 1999/2000. A faculty fellowship from the University of Colorado supported me during another year of work in 2007. Charles Lipson, organizer of the Program on International Policy, Economics, and Security (PIPES) at the University of Chicago, kindly allowed me to sit in on lectures and discussions for a semester and to receive PIPES papers by e-mail for several years; this was an invaluable resource for an outsider to the field of International Relations.

I presented ideas from this book and benefited from the lively discussions and insightful suggestions at a wide variety of venues: "Democratic Deliberations in and out of Attica: An International Symposium" at the University of Crete (2002); a panel in honor of Michael Jameson at the Annual Meeting of the American Philological Association in San Francisco (2004); a panel on "Social Structure and Interstate Structure in the Ancient Mediterranean," which I organized at the European Social Science History Conference in Berlin (2004); an "International Colloquium on War, Culture, and Democracy in Classical Athens" at the University of Sydney (2006); and lectures at Dartmouth College (1999), the University of Virginia (2002), and the University of Illinois, Chicago (2003).

Several scholars were kind enough to show me pre-publication versions of their books and papers, timely access to which was extremely helpful: I thank Ted Lendon, Polly Low, Judson Herrman, Ryan Balot, and Jonathan Hall. Ted Lendon and Judson Herrman also read, commented on, and improved various chapters. David Pritchard did the same with exemplary thoroughness for a paper (Hunt forthcoming) closely related to Chapter 3. My wife, Mitzi Lee, read the whole manuscript and made many valuable suggestions on several levels.

I thank all the readers at Cambridge University Press, both those who commented on the original proposal and sample chapters and those whose suggestions and criticisms helped me improve the final manuscript. At Cambridge I am also most grateful to Michael Sharp, Liz Hanlon, and especially my copy-editor, Jan Chapman. Amanda Sherpe did exemplary work for me as a research assistant. Several other individuals helped me in various ways more difficult to categorize – from a reading suggestion to a provocative query to proof-reading – but which deserve acknowledgment and for which I am grateful: Art Eckstein, Carol King, Stacey King, Stephanie Owings, Frank Russell, Paul Cartledge, and Ciaran Cronin.

I have been most fortunate in all my colleagues at the University of Colorado, who are wonderful people to work with and have been supportive of my research in ways both great and small. Discussions with and suggestions from my fellow Hellenists here – John Gibert, Susan Prince (now University of Cincinnati), and Eckart Schütrumpf – and our Roman historian, Noel Lenski, have over the years shaped my thinking and helped my research.

One never stops benefiting from one's teachers, so I am happy again to acknowledge my debts to all of mine and especially to Richard Saller, Josiah Ober, Victor Hanson, Susan Treggiari, and above all the late Michael Jameson.

Abbreviations, translations, and inscriptions

Abbreviations

FGrH Jacoby *et al.*, eds. (1923–) *Fragmente der griechischen Historiker.* Leiden.

Ha Harding, P. (1985) *Translated Documents of Greece and Rome*, vol. ii: *From the End of the Peloponnesian War to the Battle of Ipsus.* Cambridge.

HCT Gomme, A. W., A. Andrewes, and K. J. Dover (1945–81) *A Historical Commentary on Thucydides.* Oxford.

IG (1873–) *Inscriptiones Graecae.*

LIMC (1981–99) *Lexicon Iconographicum Mythologiae Classicae.* Zurich.

RO Rhodes, P. J. and R. Osborne (2003) *Greek Historical Inscriptions 403–323.* Oxford.

Translations

Aeneias the Tactician, *How to Survive under Siege: A Historical Commentary with Introduction and Translation*, trans. and ed. D. Whitehead. London: Oxford University Press, 1990.

Aeschines, *Aeschines, with an English Translation*, trans. C. D. Adams. Cambridge, MA: Harvard University Press, 1919.

Andocides, *Andocides*, trans. and ed. M. Edwards. Warminster: Aris and Phillips, 1995.

Aristotle, *History of Animals* (trans. d'A. W. Thompson), *Politics* (trans. B. Jowett), *Rhetoric* (trans. W. Roberts), *Rhetoric to Alexander* (trans. E. S. Forster) in Jonathan Barnes, ed., *The Complete Works of Aristotle.* 2 vols. Princeton University Press, 1984.

Demosthenes, *Demosthenes*, vol. I: *Olynthiacs, Philippics, Minor Public Speeches, Speech against Leptines, I–XVII, XX*, trans. J. H. Vince. Cambridge, MA: Harvard University Press, 1930.

Demosthenes, *Demosthenes*, vol. II: *De Corona, De Falsa Legatione*, trans. C. A. Vince and J. H. Vince. Cambridge, MA: Harvard University Press, 1926.

Demosthenes, *Demosthenes*, vol. III: *Meidias, Andotion, Aristocrates, Timocrates, Aristogeiton*, trans. J. H. Vince. Cambridge, MA: Harvard University Press, 1935.

Demosthenes, *On the False Embassy (Oration 19)*, trans. and ed. D. M. MacDowell. Oxford University Press, 2000.

Diodorus, *Diodorus of Sicily in Twelve Volumes*, vol. IX, trans. Russell M. Geer. Cambridge, MA: Harvard University Press, 1984.

Euripides, *Children of Heracles; Hippolytus; Andomache; Hecuba*, trans D. Kovacs. Cambridge, MA: Harvard University Press, 1995.

Homer, *The Iliad of Homer*, trans. R. Lattimore. University of Chicago Press, 1951.

Isocrates, *Isocrates, with an English Translation*, vols. I–III, trans. G. Norlin. Cambridge, MA: Harvard University Press, 1954–6.

Lysias, *Lysias, with an English Translation*, trans. W. R. M. Lamb. Cambridge, MA: Harvard University Press, 1930.

Minor Attic Orators, vol. II: *Lycurgus, Dinarchus, Demades, Hyperides*, trans. J. O. Burtt. Cambridge, MA: Harvard University Press, 1954.

Plato, *Alcibiades* (trans. D. S. Hutchinson), *Gorgias* (trans D. J. Zeyl), and *Republic* (trans. G. M. A. Grube, rev. C. D. C. Reeve), in J. Cooper and D. S. Hutchinson, eds., *Plato: Complete Works*. Indianapolis: Hackett 1997.

Plutarch, *The Age of Alexander: Nine Greek Lives*, trans. I. Scott-Kilvert. Harmondsworth: Penguin, 1973.

Thucydides, *The History of the Peloponnesian War*, trans. S. Lattimore. Indianapolis: Hackett 1998.

Xenophon, *The Persian Expedition*, trans. Rex Warner. Harmondsworth: Penguin 1949.

Xenophon, *Xenophon in Seven Volumes*, vols. I–II: *Hellenica*, trans. Carleton Brownson. Cambridge, MA: Harvard University Press, 1968.

Xenophon, *Xenophon in Seven Volumes*, vol. VII: *Scripta Minora*, trans. E. C. Marchant. Cambridge, MA: Harvard University Press, 1925.

Inscriptions

In order to make this book accessible to scholars without classical Greek, I have included cross-references to the translated collections of Fornara 1983, Harding 1985 (abbreviated Ha), and Rhodes and Osborne 2003 (abbreviated RO) whenever such translations existed. The cross-references lend a cumbersome appearance to some footnotes, but it should be easy for the non-specialist to find a translation of most of the inscriptions cited.

CHAPTER I

Introduction

INTRODUCTION

Every Athenian alliance, every declaration of war, and every peace treaty was instituted by a decision of the assembly. The assembled citizens voted after listening to speeches that presented varied and often opposing arguments about the best course of action for the state to take. For this reason, the fifteen preserved assembly speeches of the mid fourth century BC provide an unparalleled body of evidence for the way that Athenians thought and felt about interstate relations in general and about issues of war and peace in particular. To understand this body of oratory, its emotional appeals, its moral and legalistic arguments, and its invocation of state interests, is to understand how the Athenians of that period made decisions about war and peace. That is the goal of this book.

No one type of argument or single factor determined Athenian decisions. Rather, various considerations could play independent and important roles. As a result no single overarching thesis about Athenian thinking unites my chapters on, for example, "Legalism," "Household metaphors," and "Calculations of interest." My investigations are united rather by an attitude towards Athenian thinking, a charitable and empathetic one, and my methodological preference for the evidence of assembly speeches. This attitude and methodology are best illustrated by contrasting them first with scholarship that portrays Athenian thinking as simple and deplorable and second with *unmasking* methodologies, according to which the stated grounds for war – as found in assembly speeches – only mask the truth and thus need to be stripped away rather than examined.

Scholars have often underrated the richness and variety of Athenian thinking. Arnaldo Momigliano exemplifies this tendency in modern scholarship when he argues that Greek thinking about foreign policy "can never assess achievement except by reference to success and therefore can never teach more than prudence."[1] I argue against such representations of the Athenians as political Realists, that is, as amoral and seeking only advantage.[2] While concerned about the interests and security of their city, the Athenians do not reveal in the assembly speeches a foreign policy entirely determined by calculations of interest. They rather invoke a variety of moral criteria for action. Cynics may argue that assembly speakers' professions of morality reveal nothing more than their hypocrisy. Even were we to grant such an extreme view of Athenian politicians, hypocrisy is only advantageous, only makes sense, in a world in which moral judgments matter. Athens was such a world.

A contrary, but equally critical, tendency in recent scholarship focuses on the warlike, emotional side of Athenian decision-making. On this view, Athenian policies flowed from an irrational belligerence derived from Athenian culture and society. This enthusiasm for war is portrayed as resurfacing sporadically throughout the fourth century despite Athens' fading powers.[3] Scholars find two basic ways in which Athens' culture and society gave rise to its putative belligerence.

First, Athens' militarism, the high value placed on military service and prowess, cannot be denied. It probably did make Athens more prone to resort to war. Such militarism, however, was and is extremely common in a wide variety of cultures and societies. Athens was not a special case either in its militarism or in the reasons for which it went to war. Nor was Athenian culture overwhelmingly militarist: Athenians prized many things besides martial prowess. The claim that militarism ceaselessly propelled Athens into irrational and otherwise inexplicable wars is hyperbole.

Second, the moral and emotional component of Athenian thought was strongly structured by what is termed the "domestic analogy," an explicit or implicit parallel between the relations among states and relationships within the state. Scholars such as J. E. Lendon argue that atavistic individual values were applied to the realm of states and encouraged the recourse to war: for example, Athenians saw their city as a Homeric warrior writ large, dedicated to violent revenge and possessed of a touchy sense of honor. Such a state might well be as prone to fighting as the characters in Homer are.[4] But, again, the larger picture is more complex. Ritualized friendship, the relations between slaves and masters, the relations between men and women, and brotherhood – all these different relationships provided a

---

[1] Momigliano 1978: 22–3 on historiographical evidence for foreign policy thinking. See also, e.g., M. Finley 1985b: 70, and Sage 1996: 66.
[2] See pp. 155–7 for the meanings of Realism in foreign policy thinking.
[3] E.g. Badian 1995.   [4] Lendon 2000.

complex set of values and a cognitive framework for Athenian thinking about the relationship of city-states. Since conflict and competition were not alone of value within Athenian society, there is no reason to expect that the deployment of domestic analogies to states should lead only to war. In particular, the legal analogy, according to which states, like individuals within the state, should resolve their disputes without recourse to war, tended to curb Athenian belligerence.

Notwithstanding the laudable goal of supplementing the older view of the Athenians as calculating and amoral in their foreign policy, these two theories risk making them uncalculating only in a belligerence deriving either from militarism or from primitive and violent mores. As we shall see, such views gloss over the difficulties of connecting a society's values and its tendency to go to war and oversimplify a rich and complex moral discourse based largely on a wide variety of domestic analogies.

Such critics of Athenian thinking often adopt an *unmasking* approach to Athenian pronouncements: they seek to unmask, to debunk, the stated grounds for war – and hence evidence such as the assembly speeches – and locate the real causes of war elsewhere: for example, in amoral calculations of interest, in economic advantage, or in a militaristic culture.[5] Such factors cannot be neglected, but they should supplement rather than replace the Athenians' own deliberations about questions of war and peace; for this book finds there a richer understanding of the relationship of states than the sideways glances of scholars rushing to true and hidden causes would suggest.

For example, two of the most influential, theoretically inclined ancient historians of recent decades, Yvon Garlan and Moses Finley, have approached Greek warfare with a focus on its material results.[6] Garlan begins his analysis with a consideration of Plato and Aristotle, whom he characterizes as adherents of an economic view of Greek warfare.[7] His own view is Marxian and thus materialist: it was the limits of internal production that drove the Greek states to violent appropriation and thus war.[8] Finley, too, endorses Marx's view that in early societies such as Greece and Rome warfare rather than technological advance "was the basic factor in economic growth."[9] He concedes that wars were fought for mixed motives but emphasizes the economic ones: "the hard fact remains that successful ancient wars produced profits, and that ancient political leaders were fully

---

[5] In the first of these, they can justly claim to be following Thucydides; see pp. 156–7.
[6] Garlan 1989; M. Finley 1978b and 1985b.   [7] Garlan 1989: 31.
[8] Garlan 1989: 38.   [9] M. Finley 1985b: 74.

aware of that possibility."¹⁰ This consideration leads him to take a skeptical approach to ancient justifications of warfare. He argues that modern historians who have neglected the material reasons for war tend to present "a continuous succession of diplomatic and political events ending, for no sufficient reason, in a resort to arms."¹¹ Thus, the sequence of events, the claims, and the counterclaims of the antagonists are merely a smokescreen beneath which the historian must discern the fundamental and presumably "sufficient" cause of war, which derives from the nature of the classical Greek economy.

Finley's approach is typical of a number of modern unmasking theories of warfare. While he dismisses the "claims and counterclaims" in favor of concrete profits of war, the theorists of militarism point out that grounds for war are superfluous if a state or a powerful class is predisposed, as it were, to fight wars. Unmasking theories need not focus on internal factors. For example, political Realists take the same approach to the application of ethics to foreign policy: moral arguments are merely screens to justify decisions already made on the basis of power politics. All these unmasking theories hold that the stated reasons for war are just screens for some other *real* reason for war; their goal is to rip away or see through the mask to discern this reason.

Finley buttresses his claim that our evidence for the decision-making process is insufficient with the further observation that, based on modern experience – for example the later publication of statesmen's journals and internal memos – public pronouncements are often false to the actual motives of the actors concerned.¹² Nor, one might add, need orators always be fully aware of the real reasons for their policies. As J. A. Hobson put it: "politicians, in particular, acquire so strong a habit of setting their projects in the most favourable light that they soon convince themselves that the finest result which they think may conceivably accrue from any policy is the actual motive of that policy."¹³ Finally, one can imagine cases where, by tacit agreement, the real reasons for a war cannot be mentioned publicly.¹⁴

Unmasking theories borrow some of their appeal from cynicism, often amply justified, about the official and stated grounds for war. In

---

¹⁰ M. Finley 1985b: 76. See also M. Finley 1978b: 2–3.
¹¹ M. Finley 1985b: 77, cf. 75, 80–1. Garlan 1989: 21–2 contains a similar statement, but he concludes with a more complex Marxian analysis of the contradiction between Plato's and Aristotle's theories of economic motivations and the political reasons contained in accounts of the beginnings of Greek wars (32–40); so too in Garlan 1995: 56–9.
¹² M. Finley 1978b: 3.   ¹³ E.g. Hobson 1938: 198
¹⁴ E.g. Greenspan 2007: 463: "I am saddened that it is politically inconvenient to acknowledge what everyone knows: the Iraq war is largely about oil."

particular pro-war oratory in every age tends to exaggerate injuries suffered, to rouse ethnic, national, or city-state jingoism, to make compromise seem weak, to associate killing with manhood, and to valorize death in war as a noble and willing self-sacrifice. When successful, war rhetoric results in war with its hates, grief, maiming, destruction, and death. Since World War I such appeals and arguments, often treated as the manipulation of a gullible populace by unscrupulous politicians, have been particularly suspect.[15] A significant strain of twentieth-century thinking about war oratory is typified by Wilfred Owen's attack on "The Old Lie | Dulce et decorum est | Pro patria mori." Not only the nobility of dying for one's country, but even the whole just-war tradition has been attacked as a cover for other more sinister motives.[16] The same hostile, skeptical approach that many intellectuals have taken to the justification of wars since World War I seems to inform many treatments of Athenian assembly speeches. In some cases, the parallel is explicit: W. R. Connor discusses the arguments of Demosthenes: "his characterization of Macedon passes from exaggeration and simple misunderstanding into a melodramatic phantasia . . . " and seems "strangely familiar . . . reveal[ing] some of the most unfortunate and recurring illusion of commentators on foreign policy."[17]

In addition such attributions of hidden motivation make slippery targets. To return to M. I. Finley and fourth-century Athens, if an orator justified a war in terms of both justice and profit, the appeal to profit revealed its true motivation and the invocation of justice merely provided a specious pretext. If a war ended profitably for Athens, we are asked to judge its motivation on its results rather than on its justification or the events that led up to it.[18] If a war ended in disaster or wasted expense, it may still have been the result of a mistaken expectation of profit. We are, in this case, required to ignore the results of the war in judging its motivation.

The subject of this book would be less important and have to be approached from a different perspective if we were to accept such a complete separation between the stated causes of war – what we read in assembly speeches – and its real reasons. But we are not in an either-or situation. On the one hand, it is naïve to think that actors always state or are even fully conscious of the reasons for their actions. Nor do the actors' motivations

---

[15] Gaubatz 1999: 2. E.g. Russell 1951: 43. Cf. Russell 1916: 23. [16] E.g. Wells 1969 and Santoni 1991.
[17] Connor 1966: 57. The date of publication suggests that Connor is thinking of Cold War rhetoric in the United States. Given the importance of the Vietnam War to his intellectual development (Connor 1984: 6–7), the justifications of this war and contradictory pictures of Soviet power and fragility are perhaps the specific parallels that he had in mind.
[18] M. Finley 1985b: 75–6.

always provide an exhaustive explanation for the recourse to war. Some unmasking theories – most famously those of Marx, Darwin, and Freud – can provide persuasive explanations for the actions of states or individuals, explanations often unsuspected by the actors themselves.[19] Similarly, Finley's emphasis on the hope for economic gain as a motivation for war in ancient Greece is not entirely misplaced. This did sometimes play a role in the complex of motivations that led the Athenians to go to war. On the other hand, only an absolute certainty that the stated reasons are negligible and that the hypothetical real reasons are compelling and exhaustive could justify dismissing the former for the latter. In the case of classical Athens we manifestly lack this certainty.

A contrast between classical Athens and the modern world is telling against an excessively unmasking approach. Skepticism about the stated grounds of war makes the most sense when applied to modern representative democracies in which considerable power is delegated to the government – not to mention undemocratic states. In these cases, historians may and often do find a chasm between the considerations accorded weight by, for example, a president and his advisors in private and the public pronouncements about the reasons for war. As one eminent scholar of international relations puts it:

[Public] foreign policy discourse in the United States often sounds as if it has been lifted right out of a Liberalism 101 lecture ... Behind closed doors, however, the elite who make national security policy speak mostly the language of power, not that of principle.[20]

In a direct, participatory democracy such as Athens no such clear distinction can be made between the people and their representatives or executors. It is far more difficult to explain how important motivations for war could leave no trace in the arguments and appeals of war oratory. At Athens decision-making and the appeal to public opinion were one and the same process. Decisions were based on public opinion, the assembly's vote. They were not justified to a public after having been made on some other basis. And, in contrast to modern pictures of elite incitement of a peaceful but perhaps gullible people, it turns out that the rich at Athens tended to favor a less aggressive foreign policy; indeed, it was from their ranks that the few critics of Athenian militarism emerged.[21]

Finally, the arguments and appeals of deliberative oratory can provide insight and allow us to evaluate the importance even to the "real causes" of unmasking theories. Orators made reference, albeit rarely, to the potential

---

[19] McCullagh 1991.   [20] Mearsheimer 2001: 23–5.   [21] See pp. 39–48 and 256–7.

profits of war. They appealed directly to state interest as the basis for policy; some even took an unmasking position towards the moral professions of their opponents. They invoked the internal values of Athenian society in their appeals to act like real men, to avoid slavish behavior, and, in general, to avoid the shame of yielding. In Athens the stated grounds for war were not radically divorced from its real motivation. This is hardly surprising. A skilled orator who hoped to sway the assembly on a close vote could hardly afford to ignore the true motivations, feelings, and thinking of his audience.[22] One cannot assume a perfect proportionality between the importance of a motive and its appearance in assembly speeches, but there does not seem to be much scope left for important hidden motives.

So, if something was a factor in causing a war, it was usually present in the arguments upon which Athenian decisions were based. Just as important to our argument is the converse principle: arguments for war that successfully persuaded the audience should be regarded as genuine causal factors in the origins of a war. If an orator appealed to the justice of a course of action, it was because this was likely to affect the assembly. Orators did not make moral claims – which they did often – to waste time, but to win people over to their sides. If an argument based on justice, for example, convinced a majority of the citizens present at the assembly to vote for war, it can quite precisely be called a cause of war.

To sum up, the assembly speeches include a large variety of types of arguments, expected to be persuasive, about the relations of states. They need to be taken seriously rather than dismissed as some sort of façade; thus Athenian thinking is complex. That it is sophisticated is something that the reader will have to judge from my detailed investigations, but one final but crucial point requires emphasis here: behind some of the dismissals that we have been examining lies the smug and sterile assumption that correct views about war and peace are simple and straightforward, something that "we moderns" understand. Such a view strikes me as false as far as the present is concerned. It also contributes to a dismissive and superficial attitude towards Athenian thinking about the relationship of states, one not conducive to understanding it.

METHODOLOGY

In recent decades studies of forensic oratory and the funeral oration have proven fruitful for understanding Athenian social and political attitudes.[23]

---

[22] Raaflaub 1994: 135.
[23] E.g. Dover 1974; Loraux 1986; Ober 1989; D. Cohen 1995; Herman 1996; *pace* Worthington 1994: 111.

The need for orators to take into account their audiences, whether the large juries of the Athenian justice system or the people assembled to mourn the war dead, makes such studies of Athenian popular thought persuasive. So too, preserved deliberative speeches can be the best source of evidence for popular attitudes about war and interstate relations.[24]

One must grant, however, the occasional inaccuracy and even the self-serving mendacity of assembly speakers. References to the past in the Attic orators have been carefully studied and generally show a low level of historical accuracy.[25] When the orators discussed their own time, their partiality seems to have outweighed their more detailed and accurate knowledge. The discrepancies between the accounts of recent events by Demosthenes and Aeschines are notorious.[26] But even the lies of a dishonest orator can reveal shared standards by which actions are judged. For example, Demosthenes' claim that Athens had always come to the aid of weaker cities whose liberty or safety was in danger represents a distortion at best.[27] Nevertheless, we learn that Athenians considered aid to the weak a sufficient reason for going to war – and had an exaggerated opinion of their own altruism. The parallel to the use of forensic speeches is again apt. Courtroom speeches, often written for lying, guilty defendants or to convict the innocent, have provided the evidence for persuasive investigations of Athenian social and political attitudes. So too, can assembly speeches reveal much about foreign policy thinking, despite their ubiquitous partiality and occasional dishonesty.

Sometimes a speaker explicitly concedes the basic principles of his opponents. For example, in his attack on Aeschines and the Peace of Philocrates, Demosthenes repeatedly admits that peace is a good thing in itself, but he argues that the merits of peace in general are not at stake in Aeschines' trial.[28] Both sides assumed the desirability of peace in principle. Such passages, which occur with some frequency, provide perhaps the best opportunity to ascertain common beliefs.

The risk still exists of placing too much weight on arguments that, in the event, fell flat and failed to persuade; it is also crucial never to mistake an orator's straw-man for the opinion it misrepresents.[29] It is always dangerous

---

[24] Harding 1987: esp. 38–9. R. Thomas 1989: esp. 203–8. Cf. Todd 1990 and Herman 1996: 13–14 on forensic speeches.

[25] Pearson 1941; Worthington 1994; and Milns 1995. Cf. Missiou 1992: 59 on Andocides' inaccuracy.

[26] E.g. Cawkwell 1969: 163. Cf. Cawkwell 1978a: 117–19 and Cawkwell 1963b: 200 on Demosthenes' mendacity.

[27] Dem. 18.99.   [28] Dem. 19.88–9, 92, 96–7, 336.

[29] For an oratorical misstep see Dem. 19.16, 305–7; cf. Aeschin. 2.63–4, 74–8. That Demosthenes misrepresents the position of his opponents, especially Eubulus, is the thesis of a seminal article by Cawkwell (1963c).

to base too much on a single passage, but when we find a number of passages in different speeches depending on the same suppositions, these are likely to have been widely accepted. Furthermore, other types of evidence also admit of miscommunication and contain idiosyncratic passages; they often involve other complicating factors, such as the atypical, elite readership of philosophy or the mythical setting of tragedy.

The subject of this study is Athenian thinking about interstate relations; to some extent this focus requires us to ignore or put aside questions about how a speech works as a whole or how it related to its specific historical context. An orator may bring up a particular argument about proper interstate conduct because of the artistic or rhetorical imperatives of a well-fashioned speech.[30] An orator may stress one consideration rather than another, because of the particular details of the interstate situation or internal politics at that point in time.[31] But he could only make use of that consideration because it was already part of a shared system of thinking and of values concerning interstate relations. Some scholars argue that personal ambitions, ties, or enmities largely determined the political positions of Athenian politicians.[32] I do not find such arguments persuasive.[33] But even if the motivations of politicians were, in some sense or another, personal, the arguments that were expected to convince the assembly were invariably political and focused on the issue at hand. My relative neglect of an argument's connection to its rhetorical and historical context or to the personal motivations of the speaker allows us to focus on the connections between arguments and permits us to understand the overall structure of Athenian thinking about war and peace.

This aim has not only required me to neglect certain traditional approaches and questions but has also led to forays beyond the traditional confines of history. In particular, the knowledge that the Athenians thought about foreign affairs according to a particular model often prompts the question, "Why this model and not some other?" An explanation in terms of historical development – the Athenians believed *B* because they

---

[30] The third volume of F. Blass, *Die Attische Beredsamkeit*, 1877, mainly takes this approach to the speeches in our period. Modern scholarship in this vein includes Pearson 1964; Rowe 1966, 1968; Wooten 1977; Slater 1988; Tuplin 1998; Usher 1999: 209–43, 270–6.

[31] This is the dominant approach in Schäfer's monumental and still influential *Demosthenes und seine Zeit*, 1885–7. Important recent works with this primary concern include the following: Cawkwell 1962a, 1962b, 1969; Burke 1977; Strauss 1985; Cargill 1985; Sealey 1993; E. Harris 1995; Sawada 1996; Fox 1997; Badian 2000; Ryder 2000; Worthington 2000; Lambert 2001. Most commentaries on individual speeches treat the speeches both in their historical context and as works of rhetoric, e.g. Wankel 1976; Edwards 1995: 105–13; MacDowell 2000: 1–30; Yunis 2001: 1–26.

[32] E.g. Sealey 1956: 179; Perlman 1963: 351; Sealey 1993: 5 and *passim*; Sawada 1996; Badian 2000.

[33] See the critique of Konstan 1997a: esp. 62–7.

had previously believed A – is only occasionally satisfying. But to go further sometimes requires going beyond the bounds of traditional history. At the very least such investigations require a comparative-historical approach. Only the knowledge of other cultures' thinking about war and peace allows us accurately to judge what is unique about Athenian thinking and requires an explanation specific to Athens, and to judge what it has in common with other cultures, in which case a general explanation is often more appropriate. I have sought such general explanations by drawing upon theories and ideas from a variety of fields, namely cognitive psychology, Game Theory, international relations theory, and the sociology, anthropology, and comparative history of war and peace. Despite the perils of wading into the unfamiliar waters of these various disciplines – some of which are regarded with suspicion and hostility by scholars of ancient Greek history – I believe that, by casting our nets widely, we will gain immeasurably in our understanding not only of the *what* of Athenian thinking but also of the *why*.

EXPERIENCE AND INTEREST

Several factors at Athens favored well-informed thinking about foreign affairs. Athenians were proud of their high level of political participation and knowledge, which was certainly much higher in Athens than it is today among the citizens of a modern nation.[34] A term on the boule, the Council of Five Hundred, lasted for a full year and included the vetting of treaties, the official reception of foreign embassies, the preparation of proposals, and attendance at all assembly meetings. Such service was widespread: Mogens Hansen concludes that "over a third of all citizens over eighteen, and about two thirds of all citizens over forty, became councilors, some of them twice."[35] Sundry evidence suggests that foreign policy decisions were widely discussed away from the official meetings of the assembly and the boule.[36] In short, the intended audience of war oratory was well informed and often possessed active political experience.

The high level of popular involvement in issues of war and peace derived both from democratic practices and from the huge impact such decisions had on the Athenian population. In the late fifth century, during the course

---

[34] E.g. Thuc. 2.40.2; I follow here the arguments of Harding 1987: 37.
[35] Hansen 1991: 249. Whether we quarrel with Hansen's exact figures does not influence their basic force. See also Dem. 19.17.
[36] E.g. Ar. *Lys.* 506–28; Thuc. 3.36.4–6; Dem. 4.10–11, 48–9 (contra Dem. 10.1); 19.288; Theophr. *Char.* 26.6.

of the Peloponnesian War, the vast majority of Athens' male citizens saw military service. The demographic effect of this war on Athens was greater than that of almost any modern war – including the effect of World War II on Germany and the Soviet Union: estimates of the decline in Athens' citizen population during the Peloponnesian War range from 45 to 75 percent, a staggering loss in either case.[37] After its defeat, Athens' enemies considered enslaving its entire population. Even in the fourth century, when Athenian warfare was less intense, major campaigns could require the personal service of more than a quarter of the citizen population. The one thousand deaths and two thousand captured at Chaeronea in 338 were at least 10 percent of the male citizen population; the effect of this single day is comparable in percentage terms to the losses of the main combatants during the whole of World War I.[38] The Athenians had every reason to sit up and pay attention when war was on the agenda – and all indications suggest that they did.

Athenian politicians sometimes held the elected position of *stratēgos*, general, but their political power depended mainly on their ability to persuade the assembly. Foreign policy was one of the most common topics for deliberation. In a fourth-century, pseudo-Platonic dialogue Socrates assumes that Alcibiades' entrance to political life will involve giving the assembly advice on "who they should make peace with and who they should go to war with and how."[39] Although the discussion in the *Alcibiades* moves on to his knowledge of the just and the advantageous, Aristotle's *Rhetoric* details the range of specific knowledge required of the deliberative orator:

As to Peace and War, he must know the extent of the military strength of his country, both actual and potential, and also the nature of that actual and potential strength; and further, what wars his county has waged, and how it has waged them. He must know these facts not only about his own country, but also about neighboring countries; and also about countries with which war is likely, in order that peace may be maintained with those stronger than his own, and that his own may have power to make war or not against those that are weaker. He should know, too, whether the military power of another country is like or unlike that

---

[37] Aron 1964: 378–9; Strauss 1986: 81, 86 n. 54.

[38] Gaubatz 1999: 167–70. N. Ferguson 1999: 299 table 35 shows that WWI deaths for France were 13.3 percent of males aged 15–49, Britain and Ireland together lost 6.3 percent, and Germany 12.5 percent. For the number of male Athenian citizens I have used 30,000, the high estimate of Hansen 1991: 92–3 (see also Hansen 1985). Lower estimates, such as the 20,000 favored by, for example, A. H. M. Jones 1957: 75–96 and Sekunda 1992: 312, 316–18, would make the casualties at Chaeronea proportionally even more significant.

[39] [Pl.] *Alc.* I 107d. Denyer 2001: 14–26 has recently defended the authenticity of this dialogue, but see the criticisms of Joyal 2003. Even if this dialogue is not Platonic, it was probably written shortly after Plato's death by an Academic philosopher (Cooper and Hutchinson 1997: 558).

of his own; for this is a matter that may affect their relative strength. With that end in view he must, besides, have studied the wars of other countries as well as those of his own, and the way they ended; similar causes are likely to have similar results.[40]

Thus even a work on rhetoric emphasizes that not just oratorical skill but a detailed knowledge of foreign affairs and of war was crucial for a deliberative speaker. In addition to this factual knowledge, speakers needed to be familiar with the types of arguments that carried conviction. This knowledge encompassed more than rhetorical techniques.[41] It required speakers to understand and to be able to explain the motivations behind the actions of city-states. It involved knowing the grounds on which Athenians judged the actions of cities, both their own and others.

Aspiring statesmen may have acquired this knowledge from more experienced friends or relatives, by regular attendance at the assembly or the boule, by serving on the jury at political trials, by acting as a *proxenos* for another state, or by reading works of history. Last but not least, most important politicians, including all the authors of our core speeches, had served on diplomatic missions to other states.[42] These delegations extended over weeks, if not months, of travel, shared meals, and conversation. They could involve the making of individual speeches by every member of the embassy – sometimes to another city's assembly. Participation on an embassy could be taken to imply special knowledge and thus culpability in the event of a bad outcome.[43] Conversely, speakers such as Demosthenes could claim expertise on foreign policy matters: according to him the crisis of Philip's seizure of Elatea required not just a rich and patriotic man, but one who had followed the course of affairs from the beginning and understood why Philip had acted as he did.[44] On other occasions too, Demosthenes made claims for superior insight and inside information.

---

[40] Arist. *Rh.* 1.4.1359b34–1360a5. Cf. Arist. *Rh.* 2.22.1396a5–15; Xen. *Mem.* 3.6.8–10; Thuc. 1.80–1, 141–3.

[41] Contra Lewis 1996: 108–11.

[42] See Mosley 1973: 43–7. The embassy service of the known deliberative orators are as follows: (1) Andocides' speech *On the Peace* resulted from his participation on an embassy to Sparta. (2) and (3) Aeschines and Demosthenes had been on embassies to Philip, two of which provide the subject of their speeches *On the False Embassy*. Aeschines had also addressed the Arcadian assembly (Dem. 19.303–6). Demosthenes was a member of at least six embassies from 346 to 338 (Mosley 1973: 46–7), including three to the Peloponnese (Yunis 2001: 155 on Dem. 18.79; cf. 9.72) and his emergency mission to Thebes (Dem. 18.178–9). (4) Hegesippus, possibly the author of *On Halonnesus*, went on an embassy that visited a number of Peloponnesian cities (Dem. 9.72) and on another embassy to Philip (Dem. 19.331). (5) Hyperides, author of *Against Diondas* and perhaps of *On the Treaty with Alexander* was on embassies to Rhodes and perhaps Cos and Chios (Ryder 2000: 78 on Diod. 16.77.2; Hyp. frs. 5, 6). We also hear that Callistratos addressed the Messenian assembly (Ar. *Rh.* 3.17.1418b7–11). Aeschin. 3.242 assumes that service as an ambassador implies skill in speaking.

[43] Dem. 19.5.   [44] Dem. 18.172. Cf. Dem. 1.21 and 5.4–12.

But, although he often berated his audience for their contentiousness, indulgence of traitors, and their apathy, he never chided them for simple ignorance.[45]

THE STRUCTURE OF ATHENIAN THINKING

Thus deliberative speeches were typically delivered by experts to a well-informed and interested audience. But to what extent do their myriad appeals and varied arguments derive from a coherent way of understanding and judging the actions of states? Extreme positions on this question are untenable: neither is a fully developed theory of international affairs attested nor do our speeches reveal an incoherent jumble of possible arguments. Rather, we have to come to grips with something that is structured and generally coherent, but not rigorously developed or logically consistent.

The only possible candidate for a comprehensive, philosophical treatment of interstate relations is a work by Demetrius of Phaleron, a work dating well after our surviving speeches and which is no longer extant.[46] Earlier philosophical treatments of the subject were cursory. What we do possess in deliberative speeches are arguments whose primary criterion is their appeal to the common sense of the Athenian assembly. These arguments were not always consistent when brought face to face with each other – as they are in this study. An ancient philosopher attempting to educate and change the opinions of a small circle of elite students could often ignore or contradict popular presuppositions to maintain consistency; an orator could not.[47] For this reason, rather than a straightforward history of ideas, on occasion we shall find ourselves engaged in the elucidation of vague, unexamined, and sometimes contradictory notions.

Nevertheless, three considerations suggest that the arguments of war oratory did derive from a structured and coherent body of thought and feeling, albeit not a tightly systematic one. The first consideration is an ahistorical truth about human thought and culture: it is highly structured both in systems of opposed categories and by means of simplifying analogies. The second is a historical observation: behind the fifth-century speeches

---

[45] The exchange between Demosthenes and Aeschines about Demosthenes' references to several small Thracian towns reveals the limits of popular knowledge; the people had not known where these places were, but they had learned (Dem. 8.64; 9.15; 10.8; 18.27; 19.156; Aeschin. 3.82).

[46] Scala 1890: 156–8 argues that Demetrius produced a wide-ranging and coherent body of work on interstate relations. Wehrli 1949: 62 accepts a general, ethical essay in favor of peace but does not believe in a treatise on justice between states (71).

[47] Aristotle's typical method begins with popular perceptions, but involves their critical analysis (E.g. Arist. *Eth. Nic.* 1.4–5.1095a14–1096a10).

in Thucydides lie coherent systems of thinking; we should at least look for such coherence in fourth-century speeches. Third, it turns out that many apparent contradictions between speakers – or among the speeches of a single speaker – are merely a matter of speakers placing more or less weight on different types of arguments in different circumstances.

Crucial to our investigation is the simplicity and "apparent systematicity of cultural knowledge."[48] In particular, it is the use of a small number of simplifying analogies that accounts for much of the coherence of Greek thinking about interstate relations. Although systems of analogies do not constitute a developed theory, neither are they an unorganized mass.[49] Especially in recent years, a variety of scholars have treated aspects of Athenian politics and foreign policy in terms of relationships or value systems within the state.[50]

The use of these analogies was sometimes completely unselfconscious, but from the archaic period onwards, people had also argued about, rationalized, and justified the behavior of states. For example, the so-called "Athenian Theses" found in a number of Athenian speeches in Thucydides and in the Melian dialogue provide a relatively consistent and still influential outline of political Realism. Other scholars have persuasively argued that the contrary view of state relations as based on reciprocity was older and more prevalent and that it can also be detected in the speeches in Thucydides.[51] Although these two systems of thought often conflict, each is anything but random and unorganized. To the extent that Thucydides depicts the types of arguments actually presented, we can say that speakers in the fifth century made arguments deriving from systematic ways of understanding the world of the city-states. This yields an *a priori* likelihood that the speeches of the fourth century, too, operated within a context of systematic thinking about issues of interstate relation.

Like speakers in Thucydides, fourth-century orators were prone to invoke general laws: property belongs to those who are active and on

[48] Quinn and Holland 1987: 3, 35.
[49] Quinn and Holland 1987: 10. See also Lakoff and Johnson 1980 and the essays collected in Quinn and Holland 1987 and Fernandez 1991.
[50] Herman 1987 and Mitchell 1997 treat the way that the relationship of states interacted and were based on the relationship of aristocratic, ritualized friends. Lendon 2000 interprets Spartan foreign policy in terms of the reciprocal ethics of Homeric heroes. Davidson 1990: 26–9 examines Isocrates' portrait of imperial Athens as a tyrant lacking self-control. Strauss 1993a: 10 considers "the influence of relationships within the domestic domain on concepts and constructs in the politico-jural domain." Crane 1996: 140 discusses how the relationships of the *oikos*, though repressed, shape Thucydides' history. Raaflaub 1985 and O. Patterson 1991 discuss how the ideal of a state's freedom grew out of the experience of chattel slavery.
[51] Sealey 1957 and Crane 1998.

the spot; free men should be motivated by a sense of shame; to pre-empt an attack is the same as self-defense; democracies and oligarchies are natural enemies. In addition, arguments for or against particular wars often imply a moral framework. In many cases the elucidation of such a framework is relatively trivial. If Demosthenes, in arguing that Athens must prosecute a war with vigor, stresses that Athens is being attacked, we do not require an explicit statement that self-defense was an accepted ground for war. I hope to show that the rules invoked by the orators belong to systems of thinking just as surely as those in Thucydides have been shown to do.

Finally we find apparent contradictions between the arguments employed by a speaker at different times: most conspicuously Demosthenes is sometime moralizing and sometimes calculating in his arguments. These inconsistencies may, but do not necessarily, signal an incoherent way of thinking. Rather a different weight may be placed on one way of thinking or another in different situations. A concern of security and advantage, for example, may be more or less exigent according to the specific circumstances. Only extremists would argue that one or another consideration must determine policy in absolutely every situation; and, in this respect, the Athenians were not extremists.

THE EVIDENCE

Our core evidence consists of nineteen speeches.[52] Fifteen of these were delivered in the Athenian assembly; we have already noted their particular value. Four were delivered in a law court. Forensic orations share many of the advantages of deliberative speeches for our investigation. The large Athenian jury panels, five hundred and one or more men, are likely to have differed little, if at all, in composition from the assembly as a whole.[53] The need to appeal to shared values and not to offend was even more exigent for litigants than for speakers in the assembly. In most cases, individual disputes, and not the relationships of states, were their main focus. Even such speeches are valuable for the evidence they provide for the penetration of militarism into Athenian life: no case was too strong or too weak on its own merits, or so unrelated to war, that a reference to the litigants' military service might not prove useful. Even more important are two pairs of opposing trial speeches focusing largely on interstate affairs: first, Demosthenes' and Aeschines' speeches, *On the False Embassy*, and then

---

[52] The authenticity of specific speeches and the relationship of our texts to what was actually said in the assembly are treated in Appendix 1: Speeches and texts.

[53] Ober 1989: 141–8; cf. Todd 2007: 350–5.

Aeschines' *Against Ctesiphon* and Demosthenes' *On the Crown*. These two trials are pre-eminent in their relevance and thus must be added to the assembly speeches to constitute our core of nineteen speeches.[54]

The usefulness of this set of speeches lies in the wide variety of their subjects and historical contexts. A short survey will illustrate the range of issues addressed and provide some basic historical background. The first of these speeches, Andocides' *On the Peace*, unsuccessfully advocated a peace treaty with Sparta that would have ended the Corinthian War in 391. Unfortunately, Andocides' speech is chronologically isolated; we do not possess another assembly speech on foreign affairs for thirty-six years. The main group of speeches begins just after the disastrous Social War, which ended in 355. In this war Athens was unable to prevent the most powerful members of the Second Athenian League from leaving the alliance. In the aftermath of the Social War, Athens was left impoverished and leading a much less powerful group of allies. In 354 Demosthenes' first assembly speech, *On the Navy-Boards*, argues for a different method of financing the navy but also discusses the threat of war with Persia. His next two preserved speeches, *For the Megalopolitans* and *For the Liberty of the Rhodians*, concern respectively the risks and rewards of different alliances and a proposed intervention in another state's political conflicts. They also include several Realist pronouncements.

Beginning with the *First Philippic* in 350, the conflict with Philip II of Macedonia came to dominate Demosthenes' speeches and Athenian foreign policy. Despite the exhortations to vigorous action in Demosthenes' three *Olynthiacs*, Athenian assistance did not succeed in saving Olynthus, which fell to Philip in 348. In 346 Athens agreed to a peace treaty with Philip, the Peace of Philocrates. Demosthenes at first supported the peace and argued against provoking another war in *On the Peace*. This speech is particularly valuable as a complement to those in which he argued for war. Soon afterwards, however, Demosthenes took advantage of discontent with the Peace of Philocrates to prosecute Aeschines for accepting bribes during the negotiations with Macedonia. Aeschines was acquitted in 343: the trial speeches of Demosthenes and Aeschines, both entitled *On the False Embassy*, are preserved. These speeches deal as much with the complex interstate politics leading up to the Peace of Philocrates as with the charge of bribery. The Peace broke down in the late 340s, as Demosthenes argued for intransigence towards Macedonia in a series of speeches beginning

---

[54] Several other courtroom speeches touch upon foreign policy and provide additional evidence: Dem. 20, 22, 23, 24; Lycurg. *Against Leocrates*, and the recently discovered *Against Diondas* by Hyperides in Carey *et al.* (2008).

in 344: the *Second Philippic*, the *Third Philippic*, the *Fourth Philippic*, and *On the Chersonese*. In addition, we possess another speech from this period, *On Halonnesus*, which seems to be by another anti-Macedonian statesman, possibly Hegesippus. In 339 Demosthenes arranged an alliance with Athens' long-time enemy Thebes, which possessed a powerful and prestigious army to complement Athenian naval power in the fight against Philip. These two cities and their allies went down in defeat at Chaeronea in 338, a battle which established Macedonian dominance over mainland Greece. The speech *On the Treaty with Alexander* is set in this context and advocates war against Macedonia. Although not by Demosthenes, it is by a contemporary orator. Finally, we possess two speeches – Aeschines' *Against Ctesiphon* and Demosthenes' *On the Crown* – from the trial of Ctesiphon in 330 on the charge of proposing an illegal motion: that Demosthenes should be honored with a crown for his patriotism. Although Aeschines' case had a technical aspect, the main issue was Demosthenes' conduct of foreign policy throughout his career and especially his advocacy of the anti-Macedonian stance that led to Chaeronea.

Thus, we possess speeches both in favor of and against various alliances and peace treaties. Our speeches argue for wars, against wars, and for the more vigorous prosecution of existing wars. We certainly possess in them the raw material to delineate Athenian attitudes about war, peace, and alliances for the quarter century after the Social War. But questions remain and the limits to our evidence need to be acknowledged. How typical are these orations of all the many speeches delivered during this period? How much will this study tell us about other Greek states? How much about the rest of the classical period?

Of this core of nineteen speeches, fourteen are by Demosthenes. Our speeches do not reflect the variety of speakers in the Athenian assembly. Nevertheless, it is unlikely that our evidence is seriously misleading. First, the five speeches by other orators confirm the basic picture we find in Demosthenes.[55] This impression is confirmed in *Against Diondas* by the anti-Macedonian politician, Hyperides. Like *On the Crown*, this speech presents a defense of Demosthenes' policies that led to conflict with Macedonia and to the defeat at Chaeronea. Not only the general tenor of the speech but even some specific arguments parallel those of Demosthenes.[56] Although these similarities between these two anti-Macedonian politicians are not surprising, they do reassure us that Demosthenes' attitudes and

---

[55] See p. 226 for a possible exception.
[56] The close parallels suggest that Hyperides and Demosthenes were at least familiar with each other's speeches and may well have collaborated on them (Carey *et al.* 2008: 3).

arguments were not idiosyncratic. In addition, every orator had to appeal to the same basic audience, the Athenian citizenry.[57] We would expect different orators to express different views about interstate relations – and some were certainly opposed to the policies of Demosthenes and Hyperides – but all would have needed to stay within the limits dictated by the expectations and shared values of their common audience.

All of our surviving assembly speeches come from Athens, and thus inferences from these speeches are directly applicable only to Athens.[58] Did the other Greeks share the same attitudes? Since we have much less evidence about attitudes outside Athens, a fair degree of agnosticism is appropriate.

On the one hand, some arguments – for example, that states should reciprocate the treatment they receive – are likely to have been as convincing in Corinth, for example, as in Athens. In *On the Peace*, delivered at Athens, Demosthenes reports a speech he made in the Messenian assembly.[59] The arguments that he claimed to make there are all familiar ones and would have been in place at Athens. In addition, that speakers at Athens invoked Athens' reputation among the other Greeks implies shared values: the other Greeks are represented as the Athenians' peers, their values are similar, and their good opinion matters to the Athenians.[60] Indeed, this interplay between Greek communal opinion and the thinking and behavior of Athenians will be a frequent concern of this book.

On the other hand, it seems *a priori* unlikely that Sparta, for example, a land power with a radically different social and political structure, simply mirrored Athenian attitudes and policies. Scholars such as G. E. M. de Ste. Croix and Paul Cartledge have made strong arguments that Sparta conducted a distinctive foreign policy.[61] In the absence of evidence comparable to the assembly speeches from outside Athens, one cannot rule out fundamental differences – in the case both of Sparta and of other non-Athenian states such as Macedonia – but I still suspect that what varied between Greek city-states was primarily the weight given to different types of arguments.

Even this compromise would be hard to prove. Such an argument is anyway not this book's concern. Rather, my focus is on understanding Athenian thinking. It might therefore be safest to talk exclusively of "Athenian" thinking, alliances, wars, and policy – and I will usually follow this practice. In some cases, however, to use "Athenian" might imply a false

---

[57] I discuss below the extent to which values were shared: pp. 39–48 and 256–64.

[58] See below, Chapter 5.   [59] Dem. 5.20–5.   [60] See pp. 208–9.

[61] Ste. Croix 1972: 89–166; Cartledge 1987: esp. 34–54, 77–98, 116–38, 242–73. Compare Xen. *Hell.* 5.2.32 with Dem. 23.100.

contrast with the rest of Greece. Accordingly, I occasionally use "Greek" to describe more general values and commonly accepted standards and switch to "Athenian" when discussing more detailed inferences from Athenian speeches.

We encounter a similar problem when it comes to the chronological scope of this project. Insofar as Athenian attitudes and values changed over time, the assembly speeches are valid evidence only for their own time period. Eighteen of our nineteen speeches fall within the twenty-four years from 354 to 330. Athenian options and policies in this period were limited by its previous loss in the Social War. Athens was still the most populous city in Greece, but it stood at the head not of an extensive league but of a reduced number of mainly smaller cities, whose protection often turned out to be beyond Athens' capability. And starting in the late 350s, Athenian foreign policy came to be dominated by a defensive struggle against the rising power of Macedonia.

This historical context affects our evidence in at least three ways. Most directly Athens' circumstances determined the types of issues discussed in the assembly. Although the speeches deal with a wide variety of issues, the struggle against Philip is disproportionately represented. Second, Athens' conception of its interests changed with its decline in power; as we shall see, the calculations of a weakened and vulnerable Athens were motivated more by a fear of power than by a taste for it. Athenian values too may have reflected its new perspective: we might expect to find, in a weaker Athens, a greater sympathy for the right to independence, a less conditional stand against aggression, and an attenuated view of what leadership of the Greek world entailed. How Athenian thinking reflected its new situation is a subject for subsequent chapters. The point here is that we cannot automatically generalize about Athenian attitudes in all periods based on evidence concentrated in one period.

As in the case of the Athenocentric nature of our evidence, a compromise position is most appealing. Many of the ways of thinking I detail were long-standing and deeply ingrained; their main lines did not vary with Athens' fortunes. In these cases, I will not hesitate to supplement the oratorical evidence with material from earlier historical accounts.[62] In contrast, to demonstrate an alteration in Athenian thinking is a more difficult proposition and often impossible. In particular, it is hard to distinguish change in Athenian attitudes from changes in the existence or nature of our evidence. Does a difference between Thucydides' speakers and Demosthenes

---

[62] See pp. 22–3.

indicate a shift in mainstream attitudes or the Thucydidean outlook of the former? We will find that the basic picture of Athenian thinking drawn from our extant assembly speeches holds true for much of the classical period. The nuances, detail, and emphases may be specific to the period of our evidence, but only occasionally will we be able to say with much certainty what has changed and when.

These nineteen speeches provide our best evidence. Several other sources are also valuable: funeral orations, works of rhetorical theory, actual treaties between states, the pamphlets of Isocrates, the views of ancient historians such as Thucydides, and the speeches presented within their works, and finally the philosophical works of Plato and Aristotle.

As public pronouncements, funeral orations provide valuable evidence. They present an idealizing picture of Athenian wars and their motivations. Because they aim to appeal to a mass audience, they allow us to discern the guiding ideals of Athenian policy. In particular, Hyperides' *Funeral Oration* (322 BC) was unusually focused on contemporary events and gives us a picture of the various justifications of the Lamian War only slightly later than the period of our other speeches.

Ancient works of rhetorical theory can be useful for understanding ancient literature in a variety of genres. The usefulness to our project of Aristotle's *Rhetoric* and the pseudo-Aristotelian *Rhetoric to Alexander* is more limited for two main reasons.[63] First, rhetorical theory developed by generalizations from effective speeches. Its application to other genres such as history may allow new insights, but its reapplication by scholars to effective speeches is essentially a circular process. Conversely, the development of rhetorical theory independent of oratorical practice may result in prescriptions that were not adhered to in practice and thus do not inform us about the views admissible in the Athenian assembly.[64] Second, the writers of rhetorical treatises seem to have better access to forensic than to deliberative speeches. Most assembly speeches were not written down and circulated: of the few assembly speeches that were available to readers in antiquity, surprisingly enough, almost all have survived.[65] Aristotle and the

---

[63] Although difficult questions surround the time of composition and unity of Aristotle's *Rhetoric*, it was essentially contemporaneous with our speeches: Kennedy 1996: 417 gives the outside limits for its period of composition as 360–334.

    The *Rhetoric to Alexander* mentions no event later than 341 (Rackham 1937: 258 n. a) and a version of it is attested on papyrus by 300 (Chiron 2007: 102). It may have been put into its final form in the early third century but seems to represent and draw its examples from the oratory of earlier periods including our own. Most scholars believe that Anaximenes was the author, but this judgment is not certain (Chiron 2007: 102–4).

[64] Carey 1994: esp. 43–4.

[65] Hansen 1984: 60, 68. Trevett 1996a argues that Aristotle consulted the texts of neither forensic nor assembly speeches.

author of the *Rhetoric to Alexander* may have attended or been informed about speeches in the Athenian assembly.[66] We should not, however, picture either author as carefully reading many now lost works, a process that adds weight to, for example, Aristotle's insights about Greek drama in the *Poetics*. Although several generalizations and examples from these works are nevertheless valuable – the *Rhetoric to Alexander*, in particular, is less theoretical and seems a better guide to typical practices[67] – our own consideration of the surviving speeches will prove to be of greater importance.

Treaties between states codify interstate agreements. When preserved on the original stone steles – rather than in a historian's account – classical Greek treaties possess an unparalleled authenticity: they reveal the actual words of a decree passed by the assembly. And indeed, the wording of treaties of alliance will prove helpful to our investigation of reciprocity, legalism, and the egalitarian ethos between states. Unfortunately, although there are exceptions – such as the programmatic statements and promises of autonomy in the decree of Aristoteles – treaties usually present us with the result of deliberations, not the deliberations themselves. Only occasionally do they allow us to discern much about the chain of reasoning that led to it. For this, again, the speeches are superior.

Two works of Isocrates, *On the Peace* and *Archidamus*, recreate speeches, at Athens and Sparta respectively, on issues of war and peace. We know from his *Panathenaicus* that Isocrates never addressed even the Athenian assembly – and the *Archidamus* purports to represent the speech of a Spartan king to the Spartans.[68] These were pamphlets and were not constrained by the need to appeal to the values of the Athenian common people.[69] It shows. The *Archidamus* presents many typical arguments for intransigence and is useful for establishing that a certain argument was indeed a staple of war oratory. But it also places special emphasis on the slavishness of Sparta's opponents, an attitude perhaps appropriate to Sparta's attempts to reconquer Messenia, but rare in Athenian assembly speeches. Isocrates' *On the Peace*, written in the aftermath of the disastrous Social War, attacks popular and emotionally charged ceremonies of Athenian militarism and patriotism. It also advocates an anti-imperialist theory of foreign policy

---

[66] Metics, such as Aristotle, could watch the proceedings of the assembly from a special section in the back (Hansen 1987: 89).

[67] Chiron 2007: 97.   [68] Isoc. 12.9–11.

[69] The *Archidamus* was probably a rhetorical exercise without political conviction (Baynes 1955: 161; Harding 1974), but I follow the arguments of Moysey 1982 (followed by Davidson 1990: 21 n. 3) against Harding 1974 that *On the Peace* advocated a policy for Athens and was not just a rhetorical display: the parallels between the two works are not so close as Harding argues, and Isoc. 15.62–6 explicitly claims a serious political purpose for *On the Peace*.

according to which advantage always follows morality. Although scholars
have connected the arguments of *On the Peace* with a moderate strain of
Athenian foreign policy thinking,[70] the starkness of his attacks on militarism, atypical even for Isocrates, and the moralistic tenor of his advice
are unparalleled among the active statesmen who had to appeal to the
assembly. Isocrates' *On the Peace* will usually serve as a foil for mainstream
opinions.

The relationship of the classical historians, especially Thucydides and
Xenophon, to the extant assembly speeches – and thus to this project – is
a complex one.[71] Their own attitudes towards issues of war and peace have
been subject to the most intense study.[72] This scholarship is fundamental to
our basic understanding of the standards applied to the conduct of Greek
city-states – and will, of course, inform this work. The speeches presented
within the historians are comparable to our core deliberative speeches.
Although they are shorter than actual assembly speeches, they encapsulate
foreign policy arguments and are more numerous than our extant orations.
Unfortunately, two problems diminish their value for this project. First,
the history of Thucydides and to a lesser extent that of Xenophon were
written in and about different periods than those of our assembly speeches.
Second, a speech composed by a historian for inclusion in his work need not
contain only arguments that would actually have appealed to the assembled
people. A historical speech, when read in conjunction with the surrounding
narrative, may aim to provide a lesson for the elite reader rather than to
depict an actual meeting of the assembly.[73] It may reflect nothing more
than the idiosyncratic ideas of the individual historian.

The speeches in Thucydides and Xenophon do not provide dependable
evidence for popular views and cannot be lumped indiscriminately with the
deliberative speeches of a later period. Nevertheless, I shall frequently note
parallels between historiographical speeches and actual assembly speeches.
These suggest, first, a certain degree of continuity in Athenian thinking over
time. Second, this rough congruence between the two bodies of evidence

---

[70] Romilly 1954.

[71] Herodotus does not report speeches at Athens and his evidence concerns an even earlier period than
that of Thucydides. Speeches preserved in Diodorus' much later history are too likely to contain
anachronistic notions to provide useful evidence.

[72] Sealey 1957, Momigliano 1966, and Cobet 1986, for example, treat the subject explicitly, but a
large fraction of the scholarship on Herodotus, Thucydides, and Xenophon covers or touches on
their understanding of war and peace, often under the heading of imperialism. See Crane 1998 and
Dillery 1995 for recent treatments – with bibliography – of Thucydides' and Xenophon's outlooks
respectively.

[73] For bibliography see Morrison 2006.

suggests that most historical speeches present arguments well within the mainstream of Athenian thinking.

Plato's and Aristotle's comments on the legitimate grounds for and root cause of war are brief; the subject was not of central interest to them.[74] Their overriding political concern was the internal organization of the state and society. War was of interest mainly in that it affected this.[75] These philosophers do briefly treat issues of war and peace. Aristotle sketches out the grounds that would justify a good state in going to war; Plato distinguishes between natural and sick wars; he also indicates what he considers to be the root cause of actual Greek wars. Together they seem to present us with a convenient *précis* of Greek thinking about war, whose weight as evidence is increased by their intellectual stature. These specious advantages have, unfortunately, contributed to several distortions in modern scholarship, for these philosophers were neither themselves typical Athenians nor did they represent more common views fairly. Just as their views of how a state should be governed were patently atypical and their depiction of democracy tendentious, so too their views about foreign policy did not reflect popular thinking and practices; their ideas were developed in opposition to mainstream conceptions and as criticisms of democratic foreign policy. Two contrasts are striking.

First, Plato and Aristotle put more emphasis on ethnocentrism and hierarchy respectively in their own justifications for wars than was common at Athens. As we shall see, Athenian thinking about states contained an ethnocentric and a hierarchical strain.[76] But it also contained a strongly egalitarian tendency and, as is well known, the Panhellenic ideal was honored almost exclusively in the breach. Most important, Athenians typically argued for or against wars on the grounds of their prospective enemy's conduct, not his status.

Second, Plato argues – and Aristotle may imply – that the root cause of actual Greek wars was the greed engendered by the desires of the body. This theory not only implies a crass and bloody materialism, but also hypocrisy. All Athenian talk of honor, justice, and freedom can be reduced not merely to calculations of interest and security – the Realist critique to be explored in Chapter 7 – but to the crudest avarice in the service of a deplorable

---

[74] See Appendix 2: Plato and Aristotle on the causes of war.

[75] E.g. Garlan 1989: 32. Most famously, the need to fight wars motivated the origins of the guardian class in Pl. *Resp.* 2.373d–374e. Cf. Pl. *Leg.* 4.706a–707d with Vidal-Naquet 1986b: 95–7. Aristotle's *Politics*, too, is intensely concerned with the effects of warfare and the military on internal politics, e.g. Arist. *Pol.* 2.1268a15–40, 2.1274a12–15, 3.1279a39–b4, 3.1288a12–15, 4.1289b33–40, 4.1297b1–28, 5.1302b27–31, 5.1304a20–9, 6.1319a20–4, 6.1321a5–26, 7.1327a40–b15, 7.1329 a2–17.

[76] See pp. 77–84, 97–107.

sensuality. This makes Plato's critique one of the most uncompromising of
the unmasking attacks on Athenian foreign policy thinking. It is also one
of the least persuasive: in our period in particular, warfare was viewed as an
expensive rather than a lucrative activity: orators had to present compelling
arguments to justify war's cost.[77]

Plato and Aristotle disapproved of Athenian foreign policy both in itself
and as part of their generally hostile attitude towards democracy; those
modern scholars who place too much credence in their testimony tend also
to take an excessively cynical approach both to Athenian foreign policy
and to the thinking behind it. Indeed, they have often combined into
one dreary composite Plato's and Aristotle's caricature of Athenian thought
together with the theories these philosophers erected in opposition to it.
Since the latter – natural hierarchies and slavery as well as ethnocentrism –
are now also objectionable, we end up with a distorted and remarkably
unattractive picture of the Athenians: they not only were motivated by
a greed that belies all their professions of morality or patriotism but also
fought their wars to acquire slaves or out of enmity to non-Greeks. This
was not the case.

Our final category of evidence, a subset of speeches in the historians
and subject to the same caveats, are those purported to have been given by
generals before battles.[78] The circumstances of these speeches mean that
they aimed to inspire and enrage, but not to deliberate about war or peace;
that had already been done. Thus these speeches tend to distill the purely
emotional appeals of assembly speeches – and add to them military advice
and encouragement. On a few key issues, the speeches of generals provide
an illuminating contrast with the assembly speeches.

My inclusion of any evidence that can help understand Greek thinking
is surely unobjectionable. But the focus of this book on deliberative oratory
is not merely a neutral one on the most useful of a number of sources. It is
also a reaction against an excessive reliance on atypical evidence addressed
to elite audiences, for example, the pamphlets of Isocrates and a few short
passages in Aristotle and Plato.[79] These sources have the appeal of being
more explicitly systematic in their approach than actual assembly speeches.
But warning lights and sirens should go off in the heads of historians whenever they find themselves reduced to using Plato or Isocrates to illustrate
Greek popular thinking. In addition to the *a priori* consideration that these

[77] See pp. 29–35.
[78] Hansen 1993 argues that generals did not actually address their troops at length, but see Pritchett
2002 and the plausible middle position of Ehrhard 1995.
[79] See pp. 73–7, 259–64, 276–8.

authors' opinions are manifestly and blatantly atypical in a host of other areas, the very fact of recourse is a bad sign: why do none of the nineteen speeches on foreign affairs not mention this argument or illustrate this way of thinking? We do not possess as many speeches as we would like, but we do have enough to give this argument from silence some weight. If Isocrates alone is obsessed with the desirability of an offensive Panhellenic crusade or if he alone claims that moral conduct is always in a state's interest, this may not be a fluke of survival. Such isolation suggests that these arguments were unusual.

SYNOPSIS

After the present introduction, I begin by treating ways of thinking that derived from the internal structure of Athenian society. Chapter 2 considers the role of economic motivations in Athenian deliberations: war had become and was known to be a losing proposition financially, but we do find a distinction between the effect of this on the rich and on the poor, with the latter more likely to favor risky or aggressive policies. Chapter 3 considers whether Athens' militaristic culture was a decisive factor in Athens' recourse to war. Athens was not unusual either in its militarism or its propensity to make war, but aspects of its culture such as a distorted and triumphalist version of Athenian history tended to make Athens too optimistic about the possible outcome of a war and thus more likely to go to war. In Chapter 4, "The unequal treatment of states," I turn to the extent to which the Athenians made decisions based on the type of state with which they were dealing rather than just the state's actions; considerations of ethnicity, religion, and politics played a demonstrable but limited role in Athenian decisions. Although states were – and are – manifestly different in power, hierarchies among states were generally censured and concealed rather than celebrated or valorized.

The next two chapters analyze analogies between the domestic and interstate sphere. Chapter 5, "Household metaphors," explores the way that orators evoked relationships within the household in their arguments about Athenian foreign policy. In their relations with other states the Athenians were not supposed to act like slaves or women, but should rather act like real men and live up to the example of their forefathers. Chapter 6, "Defense and attack," examines the way that the individual right of self-defense was applied to the relations of states. Orators attempt to rouse the emotions associated with an attack on a man, his house, or family and bring them to bear on the relation of Athens with a supposedly threatening state. A further extension of the base idea of personal self-defense was the argument that even aggressive action might be justified to prevent a putative future attack.

The next three chapters explore types of arguments more familiar to modern conceptions of international relations. Chapter 7, "Calculations of interest," examines the amoral, calculating approach to foreign relations in classical Athens. Although considerations of interest were always important, attacks on morality among states seem to have aimed mainly at countering overly emotional policies rather than to have stemmed from an overarching Realist philosophy. One particular type of calculation well attested in fourth-century Athens was the notion of a balance of power: Athens needed to prevent any other city from growing too powerful. This policy had profound practical and ideological consequences. Chapter 8 on "Reciprocity" considers the idea that states, like people, needed to pay back in kind the benefactions or the wrongs they have received. This way of thinking implied a certain morality but was also relatively advantageous as a long-term strategy in an arena lacking central authority, the world of states. Chapter 9 argues that the conception of states as bound by laws played a major role in Athenian judgments. The universal agreement that treaties should be obeyed and the various attempts to solve disputes through arbitration suggest that many Athenians hoped to duplicate in the Greek world the success of law in curbing violence within Athens.

Finally, in Chapter 10, I consider general attitudes towards war and peace. Although it was widely accepted that peace was preferable to war, this predilection was far from an absolute. Different groups found the advantages and moral superiority of peace compelling to different extents. The most fundamental criticisms of war came from elite, intellectual circles; active politicians plainly differed in their willingness to resort to war but within a more narrow range.

CHAPTER 2

Economics

General explanations of war tend to stress either internal or external factors. They locate the source of war in something within the state – for example an economy requiring imperialism or a militaristic culture – or find it in the external relationships of a state with other states – for example, one state may desire to check the growing power of another. Neorealists, in the discipline of International Relations, aim for a parsimonious theory of state behavior and argue that external factors have predominant explanatory force.[1] The primary evidence for this view – which may initially be shocking to most historians – is the similarity of the basic foreign policy decisions made by a wide variety of states: "all sorts of states with every imaginable variation of economic and social institution and of political ideology have fought wars"; "events repeat themselves endlessly."[2] Crucial to this argument's plausibility is the fact that it only tries to explain *basic* foreign policy decisions. Neorealists candidly admit that "Structures never tell us all that we want to know. Instead they tell us a small number of big and important things."[3] Historians typically aim for a more complete explanation of a particular war: they pay careful attention to the nature of the states involved and how this shaped the course of events.[4] Some theories of imperialism or militarism reverse the Neorealist position and attempt exhaustive internal explanations.[5] They argue, for example, that a militaristic culture or society accounts for decisions to go to war more often or more completely than any external threat or goal.

On the one hand, this book does not have theoretical parsimony as one of its aims but seeks a thorough understanding; there is no reason to

---

[1] Waltz 1979 is the foundational text for this approach.
[2] Waltz 1979: 37 and 66; Gaubatz 1999: 5. Cf. Hall 2007: 86.
[3] Waltz 1986: 329. See also Mearsheimer 2001: 11, 395.
[4] Among Greek historians see, e.g., Kagan 1961: 322; Wolpert 2001: 79; van Wees 2004: 43.
[5] E.g. Hobson 1938 (orig. 1902): e.g. 12; Lenin 1939 (orig. 1916, 1920): e.g. 9; Schumpeter 1951: e.g. 7, 37–8, 49, 83–4.

focus on the external relations of states to the exclusion of other causes. Internal factors did play a role. On the other hand, assembly speeches focus far more on the relations of states than they make explicit reference to or even play upon internal reasons for foreign policy decisions. Accordingly I consider internal factors that shaped Athenian foreign policy but will not give them primacy at the expense of the stated arguments based on which the assembly seems to have made its decisions. I will be arguing against the Neorealist and the militarist/imperialist theories for a middle and inclusive approach – a position hardly surprising for a historian.

This chapter and the next will consider the role of Athens' social structure in the genesis of wars. I will evaluate the actual role that (1) economic considerations and (2) a militaristic culture played in Athenian foreign policy decisions. Although these factors did predispose the Athenians – or subsets of the Athenians – to be more or less likely to go to war, there was still plenty of latitude for discretion: the Athenians considered each war, peace treaty, or alliance largely on its own merits rather than with a strong prejudice in favor of going to war or for avoiding war.

Scholars have implicated three economic factors in Athens' putative readiness to go to war. The first theory does not just apply to Athens but claims a wide scope. It holds that the concentration of wealth within a state is a cause of social stress and hence belligerence.[6] Since there is little or no evidence for such a concentration in Athens until the Hellenistic period, we do not need to consider this possibility further.[7] Second, given the slow pace – or, as some hold, the lack of technological advance – the Athenian economy could not grow internally.[8] If Athens was to become richer overall, it could do so only through war or imperialism, which usually involved war. Third, Athens depended on trade. In particular, although Attica provided some of its own food, it required large amounts of imported grain. Some scholars have posited that Athenian aggressiveness in foreign policy was due to its need to ensure the supply of corn – an object of concern amply attested in contemporary sources. These two possibilities will be considered in the next two sections.

---

[6] E.g. Hobson 1938: 85; also 58, 93, 127, 196.

[7] French 1991: 30 contra Fuks 1972: 26; H. Miller 1984: 154; Chaniotis 2005: 14–15. Even Ste. Croix, who argues that there was a growing concentration of wealth and displacement of peasants in the classical period, sees less of this trend in Athens because of its democracy (1983: 294–5).

[8] War results from socioeconomic problems: Fuks 1972; Pecirka 1982: 122–3; Soesberger 1982–3; Cartledge 1990: 465 on Garlan; Dillery 1993: 9 (implicitly); Chaniotis 2005: 14. See Saller 2002 for the extent to which internal growth was possible in the ancient world. Cf. van Wees 2004: 36.

PROFITABLE WARS?

There were a number of ways in which warfare could materially benefit the Athenians. Occasionally warfare led to the capture of valuable booty.[9] Kendrick Pritchett has collected an extensive list of cases where the acquisition of booty was given as the reason for war.[10] None of these refer to Athens in our period, but they do make it clear that the hope for plunder could, in some circumstances, stand among the motivations for war. The desire to acquire land was another possible motivation. Borderlands were always in play, and towns such as Oropus were sometimes subject to Athens and sometimes to Thebes. In the main, however, Athens was more successful in acquiring land from maritime states in the Aegean, usually by the establishment of cleruchies, settlements of Athenians sent overseas into the territory of a less powerful state. In the fifth century cleruchies were one of the most important perquisites of the Athenian empire. In the fourth century these usually originated in an allied state's request for assistance and protection from Athens against a threatening neighbor – as in the case of Potidaea.[11] These settlements, an outgrowth of Athenian power, if not always aggression, must have provided land for some poor citizens.[12] The desire for more cleruchies might have given Athens an incentive to play an active role especially on the north coast of the Aegean, where Athens had established cleruchies in both the fifth and the fourth centuries and where its interests would first collide with those of Philip of Macedon.

The tribute that Athens had collected in the fifth century, to its great benefit, was not an option by the time of Demosthenes. The funds of the Second Athenian League, now called contributions rather than tribute, were never diverted to Athenian use.[13] Only during the Social War did Athens extort extra money from its allies, which it used to pay part – and only part – of the expenses of that war. But even if we eliminate regular tribute from league members as a "perk" of empire, there were still all the other material benefits of war – not to mention that non-league members were not exempt from Athenian exactions. So, at first blush, it seems that a hope for profit may have influenced the Athenians as they cast their votes in the assembly, especially if we allow that the Athenians

---

[9] Dem. 20.77 (Chabrias: 3,000 captives and 110 talents); Dem. 24.11 (9 talents); Isae. 11.48–9 (privateering). Cf. Sealey 1966: 241 and Rawlings 1977 on the purpose of the Delian League; Chaniotis 2005: 130 on plunder as a goal of Hellenistic wars.

[10] Pritchett 1971–91: v.439–44.   [11] *IG* ii² 114, lines 9–11; Cargill 1981: 148–50.

[12] Griffith 1978: 139; Isoc. 8.24.   [13] Cargill 1981: 124–7.

remembered, and keenly missed, the wealth made possible by the fifth-century empire.[14]

Xenophon's *Poroi* and Isocrates' *On the Peace* present counter-arguments against the notion that Athens could become wealthy through war.[15] This would seem to indicate that at least some other Athenians did in fact have this hope. How much weight we should place on these claims is less clear. To begin with, these are not assembly speeches and both works are quite atypical in several respects.[16] More important, Xenophon and Isocrates may be constructing a straw man – similar to Plato's and Aristotle's negative portrayals of democratic foreign policy – by portraying Athenian activism as motivated only by greed.

The evidence of assembly speeches is more straightforward. In these we hear little about material gain and a great deal about the high cost of war. One could, of course, explain this by saying that there was a certain reticence about admitting going to war for profit, especially in the assembly, whose proceedings were considered to be broadcast to Greece. Going to war for the sake of material gain might have been something to be ashamed of and perhaps would not be mentioned.[17] This line of argument runs into problems when we consider Athenian oratorical appraisals of the motivation of other states. In these cases Athenian speakers had no vested interest or concern for the reputation of the state involved. For example, Demosthenes argues that Thebes fought against Philip despite the lure of the cattle, slaves, and other loot they would have taken from Attica, if they had helped Philip.[18] Demosthenes portrays profit as a possible motivation of foreign policy, but obviously not a decisive one in this case. In *Against Aristocrates*, Demosthenes counters the argument of a certain Aristomachus. Aristomachus claimed that Cersobleptes, a Thracian king, would never provoke a war with Athens by seizing the Chersonese, because war would be contrary to his economic interests.[19] Although Demosthenes concedes the premise that Cersobleptes would lose considerable revenues and gain little by such a move, he counters that such considerations do not always determine actions. Among the many counter-examples he claims to know, Demosthenes cites the case of Philip of Macedon, who could be enjoying the revenues of his own country without risk

---

[14] Badian 1995.
[15] Isoc. 8.7–8, 19–20, 122, 125, 128, 140, *passim*; Xen. *Vect.* 3.6–8; 5.11–12.   [16] See pp. 21–2, 259–64.
[17] Finley's position is particularly vulnerable here. He argues that the ancients had no moral objections to successful imperialism, which makes it hard to explain their need to provide specious rationales for such conduct (M. Finley 1978a: 5).
[18] Dem. 18.213.   [19] Dem. 23.110.

had he not seized Amphipolis – because of overconfidence attendant on success.[20]

Two inferences from these passages are significant: profits were considered an important, but not always decisive, determinant of war or peace; economic considerations could just as easily keep a city from war as drive it to it. Philip, and prospectively Cersobleptes, are condemned not for seeking profit in their policies, but for making or planning economically foolish gambles in their arrogance.

For Athens itself in the mid fourth century, the main conception of the economic results of war is clear: money was a prerequisite for waging war, not a result of it.[21] One long passage in Isocrates is telling: he praises at length the campaigns of Timotheus, emphasizing how great was his success – "He made you masters of twenty-four cities."[22] But rather than detailing the profits of these outstanding endeavors, Isocrates emphasizes five times how little money Timotheus required from Athens for the conduct of these wars.[23] Demosthenes, too, again and again assumes that warfare entails monetary costs and urges the Athenians to impose these costs fairly and then to be willing to make sacrifices on behalf of their state.[24] He exhorts the poorer citizens to serve in person and the rich to support the war monetarily. Conversely, he often deplores how the Athenians' security and honor have suffered owing to their unwillingness to incur the necessary costs.[25]

In many of these cases Demosthenes is arguing for distant expeditions with a small fraction of the Athenians' full strength. A complete mobilization for a war in Attica would be far more costly:

[I]f you were obliged to take the field yourselves for a bare month, drawing from Attica the necessary supplies – I am assuming that there is no enemy in this country – I suppose your farmers would lose more than the sum spent upon the whole of the previous war. But if war comes within our borders, at what figure must we assess our losses? And you must add the insolence of the enemy and ignominy of our position, greater than any loss in a wise man's estimation.[26]

Here Demosthenes argues first in materialist terms that the cost of war close at hand would be greater than one in the north. Neither type of war would result in profits and, thus, both are exceptions to a materialist explanation of warfare – at least on Athens' side.

[20] Dem. 23.111–13. See also Dem. 4.34 and 2.15–17 on the profits and discontents of war for the Macedonians.
[21] Dem. 14.9. See also Gillis 1970: 201.   [22] Isoc. 15.113.
[23] Isoc. 15.108, 109, 111, 113 *bis*.   [24] Dem. 1.19–20; 3.19; 4.7, 28–9; 10.36–45.
[25] Dem. 3.3–5; 4.36–7; *Exordia* 21.2.   [26] Dem. 1.27.

On other occasions Demosthenes concedes that peace ensures what passes for prosperity. But mere material wealth is unworthy of Athens' traditions: he sneers that Athens is famous for its teeming markets, but a laughingstock when it comes to the military preparations it ought to have.[27] Or he argues that this affluence will not last if Philip's depredations continue.[28] Rather than playing upon an economic motivation for war, Demosthenes found it necessary to attack Athenian materialism in order to argue for war. Demosthenes can be as psychological and moralistic as Plato, but for him it is Athenian lack of discipline, decadence, and luxury that make Athens unwilling to fight. Rather than Plato's conception of luxury as a spur to unnecessary wars, Demosthenes sees it as a hindrance to necessary ones.

This conception of peace, not war, as bringing prosperity seems to have been widespread. Aristotle assumed the connection between peace and prosperity in his discussion of one way that an oligarchy or a *politeia* based on a property qualification can become democratic:

But after a time of prosperity, whether arising from peace or some other good fortune, the same property becomes many times as valuable, and then everybody participates in every office; this happens sometimes gradually and insensibly, and sometimes quickly.[29]

That peace, not war, brought prosperity was common knowledge, not only a philosopher's insight. Already Thucydides attributed the wealth of Argos to its neutrality in the first part of the Peloponnesian War.[30] In their inaccurate histories of Athens, both Andocides and Aeschines connected its prosperity with peace.[31] Isocrates linked the Megarians' enjoyment of peace and their material prosperity as results of their self-control.[32] In the late 350s Xenophon argued that now, in the mid fourth century, war was costly rather than profitable; he even contrasted the highly uncertain monetary return on waging war with the superior returns of his scheme to buy mine slaves.[33] Eubulus reportedly quashed opposition to the Peace of Philocrates by pointing out the cost of continuing the war.[34] We can see the connection of peace and prosperity in material culture too: Cephisodotus' famous statue of the goddess Peace represented her holding her child,

---

[27] Dem. 3.29; 8.67.   [28] Dem. 8.52–5; 10.46–7, 49–50, 55–7. Cf. Dem. 20.10; 22.76.
[29] Arist. *Pol.* 5.1306b9–16. Schütrumpf 1991–2005: III.505–6 ad loc. collects other passages which make a similar connection between peace and prosperity.
[30] Thuc. 5.28.2; see also Ar. *Pax* 475–7.
[31] Aeschin. 2.173–7 seems to have been copying Andoc. 3.5–9, as Edwards 1995: 108 n. 88 shows.
[32] Isoc. 8.117–19.   [33] Xen. *Vect.* 5.11–12.   [34] Dem. 19.291.

Wealth.[35] The main associations are clear: peace and prosperity, war and hardship.

This picture of war as costly rather than materially beneficial corresponds to the reality of fourth-century warfare: war was a huge drain on Athenian wealth rather than a source of it. This is the case in general. Wars are in sum costly rather than productive: they involve not merely the transfer of wealth but also widespread destruction and great expense – to say nothing of injury and death. If we use a gambling analogy, this cost constitutes an extremely high "house percentage." War is not a zero-sum game, but a negative-sum game. The thesis that the Greeks needed to fight wars because of the technological limits of their economy seems to miss the main issue of any calculating theory of warfare: why do states gamble at a table with a large house percentage?[36]

This difficulty is to some extent addressed by theories that link a state's poverty with its propensity to go to war: the poor may have no choice but to throw the dice. Thus, some modern theorists claim that the root causes of many wars lie in poverty. Strong arguments, however, have been made to the opposite effect: wealth is an aspect of strength that makes states more confident and thus more prone to war.[37] Classical Greek authors also disagreed on this issue. Isocrates believed that it was the poverty of Greece that led to its wars.[38] But Demosthenes argued that the arrogance of wealth leads states into unnecessary wars.[39] In Thucydides we see both arguments, sometimes combined: "either poverty, which brings about boldness through compulsion; [or] abundance, which brings about ambition through insolence and pride . . . will lead men into danger."[40] That war is a gamble, dangerous but potentially lucrative, and should not be undertaken by those who have a lot to lose is a common motif. Thus, Isocrates argues that the best policy is for a state to go to war when poor, but to seek peace when prosperous.[41] On the other hand, wealth not only engenders an arrogant state of mind but also makes a state more able to wage war. Already by the Peloponnesian War the Athenians had grown to conceive of money as a source of military strength; hence, Pericles could strengthen their resolve to go to war by reading a list of Athens' monetary

---

[35] Peace has the epithet "deeply wealthy" in Aristophanes fr. 109 (Kock) and Euripides fr. 453 (Nauck). On the cult of peace see pp. 241–3.

[36] Kinder and Weiss 1978; Fearon 1995; R. Powell 2002 and see pp. 62–71.

[37] See Blainey 1973: 87–96 for a concise treatment.

[38] Isoc. 4.173–4 with Fuks (1972) and Shinozaki (1980).

[39] Dem. 23.113; see also Thuc. 3.39.4; Dem. *Exordia* 43. Cf. van Wees 2004: 34.

[40] Thuc. 3.45.4; see also 1.38.5.

[41] Isoc. 6.49–51. Isocrates also emphasizes the risks and variability of war and empire (Isoc. 8.90).

resources.[42] The real problem is that those Greek states whose plight might encourage risks were least able to do well in war, given its financial demands.

The weaknesses of a calculating, economic explanation of war is particularly acute when it comes to Athens in the fourth century BC. The most Demosthenes hopes to gain out of booty from Macedonia is a fraction of the pay for the soldiers involved – and he has to defend this hope.[43] On the other hand, he claims that the successful expedition to stop Philip at Thermopylae in 353 cost the Athenians "more than two hundred talents, if you include the private expenses of your troops."[44] Other estimates of the costs of some unsuccessful fourth-century campaigns run to numbers such as 1000 and 1500 talents.[45] Margaret Cook's excellent investigation of the costs of Athens' military shows that these numbers are completely plausible.[46] For example, in rough terms, it cost a talent to build a trireme, a talent to fit it for service, and a talent per month to man it.[47] To field a typical Athenian fourth-century navy of sixty ships for a five-month sailing season would require 300 talents – and this figure does not include any land troops or mercenaries. Two figures show what a huge expense this was: Athens' annual revenues were only 45 talents per year after the Social War, which meant that naval warfare was virtually impossible; even when Athens' revenue bounced back to 450 talents per year, a full-scale war would barely have been affordable; finally, Chabrias' great victory at Naxos yielded 110 talents and 3000 captives.[48] If we value the captives at 200 drachmas, a typical hoplite ransom, his takings would have been 210 talents including both loot and captives.[49] His famous victory did not yield even enough profit to pay for a year of campaigning. By the time Demosthenes entered politics, the Athenian state did not profit from war and had not done so for sixty years.[50]

The type of war Athens had to fight in the fourth century was a crucial factor. Plato aims his criticism of Athenian foreign policy mainly at the fifth-century empire, among whose motivations must be counted profit. Finley is also mainly concerned with the economic basis of imperialism and thus fifth-century Athens – and Rome. Their theories seem less applicable

---

[42] Kallet-Marx 1994: 238 on Thuc. 2.13. Cf. Dem. 14.9.   [43] Dem. 4.29.   [44] Dem. 19.84.

[45] Isoc. 7.9; Dem. 3.28; 13.27–31. The scale of expenditure was much greater in the fifth-century empire: the Archidamian War cost Athens over 12,000 talents (Cook 1990: 89).

[46] See Cook 1990: esp. 87–95.   [47] Cook 1990: 89.   [48] Dem. 20.77.

[49] I use the highest possible figure. Arist. *Eth. Nic.* 5.7.1134b21 gives 100 drachma as a conventional ransom; cf. Pritchett 1971–91: v.247–53. Since Timotheus' captives were sold *en masse* as slaves, their prices would be even less (Pritchett 1971–91: v.242).

[50] In the context of Athenian attitudes in 415, Thuc. 6.26 refers to the accumulation of wealth during the Peace of Nicias; I doubt that any single year after that yielded a net profit for Athens. So, too, Badian 1995: 81; Christ 1990: 151.

to our period. Many of Athens' fourth-century wars were fought against formidable opponents: the Spartans, the Thebans, and finally Macedonia. This was no coincidence: Athens' security was thought to demand the maintenance of a balance of power in the Greek world.[51] The resulting policies entailed wars against Athens' most threatening rivals, whereas an economic explanation for war would suggest a pattern of wars to subjugate the weakest states, the easiest pickings.

When Finley argues for placing more weight on the profits of war, he specifies "of successful war." There are situations when a predominant state – such as Rome after the Punic Wars – is relatively sure of victory and consequently of material gain.[52] In the fourth century, however, Athens' military endeavors were far from uniformly successful. Rather, they were risky gambles. Wars against other large cities were costly and their outcome uncertain; those against small cities yielded small profits at best, and, since even small walled cities usually needed to be besieged, could be expensive as well. To fight such wars was like "fishing with a golden hook" – the policy later deprecated by Augustus.[53] Given the propensity of other large states to ally with their rivals' enemies, almost any attack that the Athenians contemplated risked conflict with powerful opponents. For every Sestus that the Athenians were able to take – with profit we assume – there was an Amphipolis on which the Athenians were said to have wasted 1,000 talents without anything to show for it.[54] Or a Corinthian War, which ended up placing Athens' food supply in jeopardy. Or a Chaeronea, after which the Athenians had to reckon with the possibility of an attack on the city itself, and which led to a final loss of control over their grain supply.

There is thus a simple explanation for why Athenian orators almost never mentioned, alluded to, or implied profits as a reason to go to war. Warfare was not a profitable business for the Athenian state or for the community as a whole.[55] If the Athenians pursued wars that we judge unnecessary, we must look elsewhere to find the reasons.

GRAIN AND TRADE

If gain through war does not by itself explain Athenian wars, then perhaps more complex economic factors do. Sea-borne trade, in particular, was of great importance to Athens and potentially to its foreign policy. The

---

[51] See pp. 168–80.   [52] See the remarks of van Wees 2004: 27.   [53] Suet. *Aug.* 25.4.

[54] Sestos: Diod. 16.34.3 (taken by Chares in 353/2). Amphipolis: Isoc. 7.9.

[55] Modern scholars, even those who argue for economic motivations, are often aware of the cost of war or its economic futility, e.g. Romilly 1954: 343; Gillis 1970: 201; Ober 1978: 120; Dillery 1993: 10–11; Badian 1995: 99; Chaniotis 2005: 30, 115–16.

thesis that Athenian foreign policy was determined by rivalry over trade has fallen from favor as unattested and excessively modern.[56] Although silver was Athens' most important export, theories ascribing great importance to a silver lobby or to competition between Athenian and Macedonian mines fail to explain either Athenian policies or the positions of individual politicians.[57] The import of grain is a different story: its importance to Athens and thus to its foreign policies was pivotal. Some scholars have argued that the need to import grain required a "naval imperialism," but trade's effect on Athenian policies was more complex than this formulation implies.

The volume of trade in and out of Athens was high for a pre-industrial state. A calculation based on a tax-farming contract of 400 BC suggests a gross volume of trade of 2,000 talents.[58] This works out to an astonishing 400 drachmas, a year's salary for a semi-skilled worker, for each of 30,000 citizen households or 40 drachmas per person in Attica – if we assume 300,000 inhabitants to keep this rough math simple. Even more important than the high volume of trade was Athens' dependence on imported grain. Although Peter Garnsey has shown that Attica remained agricultural and produced its own crops, its dependence on imported grain is undeniable.[59] Whether we estimate that Athens imported one-third or two-thirds, or even three-fourths of the grain it consumed, the Athenians had plenty of reason to pay attention to their grain supply.[60]

Athens' vulnerability to wartime interruptions of trade was exacerbated by the fact that Aigina was often hostile to Athens and, unless contained – not an easy task – might wreak havoc on Athenian shipping.[61] Euboea was also of strategic importance since it could serve as a base to threaten ships coming to or from the Piraeus.[62] Most crucial, however, were the bottlenecks in the route from the Black Sea to the Aegean. In fact, grain shortages, during which the price of grain might increase to six times its usual price, were not uncommon during the fourth century.[63] Attested

---

[56] Ste. Croix 1972: 214–20.   [57] Strauss 1984; contra Rankin 1988.

[58] French 1991: 31; Millett 2000: 41–2 comes up with 1,800 talents of trade and 350 drachmas per adult male citizen. See also Isager and Hansen 1975: 19–52, who calculate at least 2,300 talents of trade (52).

[59] Hansen 2006: 89–90 on Garnsey 1988 and 1998. Millett 2000: 40 believes that Athens supported a population of 50,000–100,000 greater than the agricultural carrying capacity of Attica. Moreno has recently estimated that only around 30 percent of Athens' grain demand could be met by domestic production (2007: 3–32, esp. 10 (table 1)).

[60] Ste. Croix 1972: 46; French 1991: 33; E. Cohen 2000: 16.

[61] Figueira 1990: 45–9.   [62] Burke 1984: 119.

[63] See Dem. 42.20 for the high price. Isager and Hansen 1975: 200–8 and Garnsey 1988: 134–64 for grain crises.

shortages occurred in 386, 357, and 335 and plagued the whole decade from 330 to 320.[64] Public and state concern with the grain supply is easy to discern: the grain supply was a mandatory topic at one assembly meeting each month; at least forty-five officials played a role in monitoring and controlling the grain markets at Athens.[65] A striking example of the state's active role is the grain law of 374/3, which required a grain tax on Lemnos, Imbros, and Scyros to be paid in kind and mandated that the grain acquired in this way be sold to the people at whatever time and price the assembly decided.[66] After Chaeronea, Demosthenes himself held the position of grain buyer and was given money to buy grain for Athens.[67]

G. E. M. de Ste. Croix has collected the numerous passages that attest to Athens' interest in the grain trade and the supply line from the Black Sea. The fact that Athens wanted and succeeded throughout our period in holding onto Lemnos, Imbros, and Scyros in the first place was not only because they were on the route to the Black Sea, but also because they were grain producers themselves.[68] The Athenians' longstanding interest in the Chersonese also derived largely from its strategic location on the route to the Black Sea. From the activities of Miltiades the Elder in the sixth century to the capture of Sestos and the enslavement of its inhabitants in 353/2, the Chersonese was a focus of Athenian activity abroad.[69] Athens' assiduous cultivation of good relations and eventual treaties with the Bosporan kingdom of the Black Sea also derives from its need to import grain, especially in the fourth century; again Demosthenes himself was responsible for a decree honoring the Spartocid kings of that region.[70] So, too, Athens founded a colony and stationed a squadron of ships on the Adriatic coast of Italy in 325/4 for the sake of its grain trade there.[71]

Concern with the grain trade was two-sided in its effects. It could motivate either the making of peace or the recourse to war. The Spartan navy's position in the Hellespont forced Athens to agree to the King's Peace in 387.[72] The grain supply was also at risk before the battle of Naxos in

---

[64] Isager and Hansen 1975: 201 n. 8.   [65] [Arist.] *Ath. Pol.* 43.4; 51.3.

[66] Stroud 1998. Stroud 1998: 25 also cites two other decrees whose stated purpose is to assure the people a good supply of grain: *IG* ii² 1629, lines 217–20; *IG* ii² 416, lines 10–11.

[67] Stroud 1998: 116.

[68] Burke 1990: 8; Stroud 1998: 32. In the fifth century Euboea was also a major source of grain for Athens (Moreno 2007: 77–102).

[69] Ste. Croix 1972: 48; Arist. *Rh.* 3.10.1411a14 calls Sestos the "meal-table" of the Piraeus; Hdt. 6.36 on Miltiades; Diod. 16.34.3 on Chares' extirpation of Sestos in 353; see also Isoc. 15.112.

[70] Din. 1.43; see Burstein 1978 and Moreno 2007: 144–208 on Athens' relations with the Bosporan kings.

[71] Isager and Hansen 1975: 208 on *IG* ii/iii² 1629 = RO no. 100.

[72] E. Harris 1995: 62, 73–4; Sinclair 1978: 49 on Xen. *Hell.* 5.1.28–9.

376, but that time Athens decided to risk a battle and won.[73] One of the main reasons why Athens agreed to the Peace of Philocrates was that Philip assured them that he would advance no closer to the Hellespont and, thus, would not threaten their grain route.[74] Nevertheless, conflicts between Athenian cleruchs in the Chersonese and Philip's ally Cardia led to the heightening of tension between Philip and Athens in the late 340s. Demosthenes insisted on several occasions that Athens needed to fight to prevent Philip from threatening states such as Byzantium and the Chersonese, which lay along the grain route from the Black Sea.[75] And, indeed, Philip's attacks on Perinthus and Byzantium and his seizure of a fleet of grain ships provoked the open war that ended with the battle of Chaeronea.[76]

Although the strategic importance of the grain route is obvious, Ste. Croix tried to make a stronger point. He argued that Athens' "natural" foreign policy was a "naval imperialism" required by its need to protect its supply lines.[77] In the fourth century Athens required ships for this purpose beyond what it could afford on its own; it was faced with a constant need for funds, which made the expropriation of these from smaller states tempting if not absolutely necessary.[78] Further, Ste. Croix argues that it was not enough for Athens to have a powerful navy: given that triremes needed to put in to shore at night, Athens also needed naval bases or friendly or neutral shores along the whole of the grain route and especially in the passage between the Black Sea and the Mediterranean.[79] This argument serves in part to exculpate the imperialism of fifth-century Athens. But, in fact, Athens' concern with its grain supply is better attested in the fourth century, because it was no longer so easily able to secure it.[80] By the mid fourth century, however, imperialism of any sort was usually beyond Athens' capacity. Dependence on imported grain cannot, in any absolute sense, have required imperialism.[81]

Nevertheless, a cluster of Athens' most heavy-handed actions – the acquisition of Lemnos, Imbros, Scyros, and, most violently, Sestos – did involve the grain route; Ste. Croix's insight should not be entirely dismissed. It

---

[73] Xen. *Hell.* 5.4.60–1; discussion in Stroud 1998: 119.   [74] E. Harris 1995: 73–4.

[75] Dem 8.14–16; 9.34–35; 10.68; 18.241; cf. 18.71, 87.

[76] Theompompus and Philochorus in Didymus, *On Demosthenes* col. 10.49–62 (Harding 2006).

[77] Ste. Croix 1983: 293; Ste. Croix 1972: 45–9. See also Pecirka 1982 and Hahn 1983.

[78] Ste. Croix 1983: 607 n. 37 collects the evidence for Athens' financial straits.

[79] Ste. Croix 1972: 47–8. Stroud 1998: 49 n. 100 collects cases where triremes escort grain ships to Athens; cf. Ober 1978: 121.

[80] Ste. Croix 1972: 49. See also Harding 1988: 66–8.

[81] See also Bloedow 1975 and Garnsey 1988: 120–33.

is perhaps best to think of Athens' dependence on grain as a vulnerability with predictable though varied effects on its policies. Athens was vigilant and proactive when it came to the grain supply and, according to Demosthenes, it was one of the strategic goals to which any statesman concerned with Athens' interests had to pay attention: the first priority was the defense of Attica, but the second was "to make provision for the passage of our corn-supply along friendly coasts all the way to Piraeus."[82] When an opportunity came to seize greater control of the supply route, Athens did not hesitate to use force. When diplomatic measures appeared more effective, as with the Thracian masters of the Chersonese or the Bosporan kingdom of the Spartocids, Athens was willing to bestow honors and make alliances to serve its interest.[83] As we have seen, this vulnerability could make Athens willing to make peace, as with Philip in 346 and Sparta in 386. And, as Edmund Burke suggests the "one hard, simple lesson of the Social War – the incompatibility of sustained naval warfare and a sustained maritime trade – may have moved Eubulus to a greater caution in matters of foreign policy."[84]

RICH AND POOR

It was the poor who had the most urgent stake in trade and particularly in cheap grain. Many of them were urban dwellers and needed to buy their grain. Hence it was the popular politician Agyrrhius who proposed the grain tax law of 374/3.[85] Anna Missiou goes so far as to argue that their interest in the price of grain helps to explain why the poor favored a more aggressive and intransigent foreign policy.[86] But since war was as likely to jeopardize the grain supply as to ensure it, this consideration does not by itself settle the question. Was there in general a class division among the citizens on issues of foreign policy?

One passage of Demosthenes suggests such a differentiated perspective on the balance sheet of war. Demosthenes argued that if the Athenians took a more active approach to the war with Philip, they would be able to work for the city for full pay, rather than merely surviving on the paltry distributions of the theoric fund.[87] Success in war would yield profits to fill Athens' treasuries and pay for employment, mainly, one assumes, in the army or navy, but also on construction of arsenals, ship-sheds, or ships. This

---

[82] Dem. 18.301. See also Dem. 19.180: "Yet no man could point out two places in the whole world of more importance to the commonwealth than Thermopylae by land and the Hellespont by sea."
[83] Burstein 1978: 434.   [84] Burke 2002: 174.   [85] Stroud 1998: 16–25.
[86] Missiou 1992: 76–8.   [87] Dem. 3.33–5 with Sandys 1897: 220.

passage's appeal to the poorer citizens provides a parallel to the earlier and more famous statement in Thucydides about the various motives for the Sicilian Expedition: the masses hoped to be "earning money in the military for now and acquiring dominion that would provide unending service for pay."[88] Though war was costly for the state overall – in the fourth century that is – it provided a livelihood for the people hired for navy service. War also provided other sorts of employment. Although Aristophanes' *Peace* 447–51 lists both a shield maker and an aspirant general as potential opponents of peace, it was the workers at the shipyards of the Piraeus, whose numbers may have run into the thousands and whose livelihood was closely connected with military spending, who were probably the most politically important group with a vested interest in war – or at least the preparation for war. It was mainly the rich, who were likely to foot the bill, who objected most vociferously. So warfare might have been a losing proposition as a whole but may have involved a redistribution of wealth that was welcome to the poorer majority of the citizens.

This inference from Demosthenes is not only closely parallel to Thucydides' earlier statement but is confirmed by a series of generalizations about the attitudes of the rich and poor to war. In these the rich are sometimes grouped with farmers in terms of their attitudes towards war. Although some modern scholars try to argue them away, these generalizations make sense, are numerous, and all point in the same direction. As Claude Mossé points out, this difference between rich and poor is "stressed by all contemporary writers of the first years of the fourth century"[89] – and one can extend the general picture from the fifth century down through the outbreak of the Lamian War.

Three separate passages in three different genres – history, oratory, and comedy – depict a division between rich and poor on foreign policy before and during the Corinthian War. The *Hellenica Oxyrhynchia* relates that, in the Demaenetus affair, the wealthy wanted to placate Sparta by condemning Demaenetus and disowning his actions. The poor had to be intimidated and persuaded to go along with this policy.[90] Athens eventually did go to war against Sparta. In the middle of this war Andocides gave a speech in favor of making peace with Sparta. In it he represents the slogans on both sides of the issue: the supporters of peace would be content if Athens could keep its "walls and ships," while those who want to continue the fight argue that "they are not recovering their own private property from abroad;

---

[88] Thuc. 6.24.3–4.   [89] Mossé 1973: 16, 30–1, 32, 54, 57. Cf. Strauss 1986: 109.
[90] *Hell. Oxy.* Lond. Pap. 1–3 (FA 9.2–3).

and walls cannot feed them."[91] It may be that some of these intransigent and imperialistic Athenians were once rich, but their concern with getting enough to eat makes it clear that by the time of Andocides' speech they were no longer rich.[92] A passage from Aristophanes' *Ecclesiazusae*, which was produced around 393–392, has a similar content: "Someone proposes new ships for the navy: the poor say yes, the rich men and the farmers say no."[93] Again, the poor are portrayed as more prone to favor war – or to be precise, military preparations – than the rich.

In this passage the rich are also described as farmers. Indeed, Anna Missiou argues that Aristophanes' phrase is best translated as "the rich farmers."[94] Farmers were economically vulnerable in times of war, since their farms could be overrun and their crops ravaged.[95] Pseudo-Xenophon's *Constitution of the Athenians*, usually dated to the mid or late fifth century, makes a similar point about the rich, the farmers, and the poor:

> As it is, of the Athenians the farmers and the wealthy curry favour with the enemy, whereas the common people, knowing that nothing of theirs will be burnt or cut down, live without fear and refuse to fawn upon the enemy.[96]

Here we see that the farmers are again lumped together with the wealthy – and again presented as less belligerent – whereas the common people are conceived of as all living within the walls and thus immune to the threat of invasion. This scheme cannot be accurate in detail: there must have been some poor farmers and there were certainly many affluent city dwellers. Nevertheless, some recent studies that consider the limited amount of arable land in Attica support this general picture. There was not enough land in Attica for many thete farmers in addition to the well-attested farms of the upper three census classes. Literary evidence seems to confirm that the farmers of Attica were primarily well-to-do.[97]

In the mid fourth century Xenophon prefaces his *Ways and Means* with an admission that "owing to the poverty of the masses, we [the Athenians] are forced to be somewhat unjust in our treatment of the cities."[98] This is apparently a reference to some aspect of Athenian imperialism, a topical

---

[91] Andoc. 3.36–9.   [92] Missiou 1992: 85.

[93] Ar. *Eccl.* 197–8 with Ussher 1973: 102. Ussher 1973: xxv for the date.   [94] Missiou 1992: 165.

[95] Cf. Arist. *Pol.* 7.1330a18–23. Even if we concede that permanent damage was hard to inflict – as in Hanson 1998 – the loss of even a year's crop would be a damaging blow.

[96] [Xen.] *Ath. Pol.* 2.14. This would be our earliest case of this distinction based on wealth, unless Hornblower 2000: 173 is correct in dating Pseudo-Xenophon to the early fourth century, in which case it would provide additional support to our three passages from the Corinthian War period. On farmers see also Thuc. 1.141.5 and Arist. *Pol.* 7.1330a18–23.

[97] Jameson 1992: 144–5.   [98] Xen. *Vect.* 1.1.

issue in the period of the Social War. Xenophon lays the blame for this abuse on the poverty of the common people and hopes that his economic proposals will relieve them of their poverty, so they will not have to oppress the other Greek cities. Diodorus, whose text is probably based on that of a contemporary historian, depicts the outbreak of the Lamian War in 323 in terms similar to those used by the Oxyrhynchus historian of the preludes to the Corinthian War:

> while the men of property were advising that no action be taken and the dema-
> gogues were rousing the people and urging them to prosecute the war vigorously,
> those who preferred war and were accustomed to make their living from paid
> military service were far superior in numbers.[99]

And again we come back to the motive of the common people: to make money by serving in the military.

The motivations of the rich – as of farmers – can also be fleshed out from other sources. We have copious evidence of tax evasion by the wealthy – and the lion's share of taxes were due to war expenditures.[100] Other sources voice the complaints of the rich about taxation. One striking example appears in Xenophon's *Oeconomicus*. Socrates addresses Critoboulos as follows:

> Moreover, I observe that already the state is exacting heavy contributions from
> you: you must needs keep horses, pay for choruses and gymnastic competitions,
> and accept presidencies; and if war breaks out, I know they will require you to
> maintain a ship and pay taxes that will nearly crush you.[101]

Given that the rich often concealed their wealth and complained about war taxes, it is not far-fetched that Critoboulos, for example, would take the likely effects on his finances into account when he cast his vote in the assembly on an issue of war and peace.

Despite this logic and this unanimity of evidence, many historians are skeptical of the ancient generalizations about class and proclivity for war. Before considering their arguments, we need to be precise about what sort of a claim we understand our ancient sources to be making and in what context. To begin with, none of these passages says that the poor are always in favor of any war whatsoever or that the rich are always opposed. Rather

---

[99] Diod. 18.10.1. Atkinson 1981: 46 points out the parallel with Plutarch's account of popular intransigence in the aftermath of Chaeronea (*Phoc.* 16.4).

[100] See especially Christ 1990 and 2006: 143–204; E. Cohen 1992: 190–201; Gabrielsen 1994: 9, 223–4; but Bruce 1967: 52; Trevett 1994: 191; Badian 2000: 30; and Burke 2002: 173 also mention the issue and provide evidence.

[101] Xen. *Oec.* 2.6; Gabrielsen 1994: 221 cites this passage as well as Isoc. 8.128. See also Demosthenes' hostile and likely slanted report of Meidias' complaints about taxation (Dem. 21.203) and Theophrastus' characterization of the "oligarchic man" (Theophr. *Char.* 26.6).

their statements are generally made in the context of one particular period or one particular war. Indeed, they typically discuss wars about which opinion was divided. They do not rule out the possibility of previous wars or prospective wars about which the poor and rich agreed. These sources merely discuss one factor that affected rich and poor differently. To take an obvious example, despite Thucydides' mention of the common people's desire for wages contributing to enthusiasm for the Sicilian Expedition, there is no reason to think that he thought that the outbreak of the Peloponnesian War was reducible to this same factor. Far from it: although Thucydides does take an unmasking approach to the claims and counter-claims at the beginning of that war, he finds a "truest explanation" in Spartan insecurity and not in the economic desires of the common people of Athens.

When Aristophanes describes the reactions of the poor man and the rich farmer to a proposal to build more ships, he identifies a tendency attested in other authors. But what makes it funny? Decisions on armaments or war were supposed to be determined by external threats or ambitions of the city; no funeral oration would mention fear of taxes at all or would represent the desire for jobs as motivating one of Athens' glorious wars of yore. For Aristophanes to focus on the least reputable motivation for a policy is entirely in line with his comic technique.[102] Its humor depends on and thus implies multiple motivations for decisions on war and peace. Neither do our other sources suggest a one-dimensional explanation of the decisions they treat, but they focus on one factor that became pivotal when other considerations were roughly equal.

The contingent nature of elite opposition to war emerges from a passage from *On the Navy-Boards*. Demosthenes argues that the rich will resist taxation if they do not think that a war is necessary, but will make their resources available if they believe that Athens is under attack. The rich do not normally wish to give up their wealth; but they will when other considerations predominate.[103] His claim that the rich can either make their wealth available or retain it seems to reflect economic reality. Land could not be concealed, but other forms of wealth could be and often were hidden from the state and thus were not available for taxation.[104] Thus, although the poor could always out-vote the rich in the assembly, to prosecute a war

---

[102] Aristophanes' explanation of the origins of the Peloponnesian War in *Acharnians* 515–56 is the most obvious parallel. Cf. Plato's attitude towards the common people in *Leg.* 8.831c.
[103] Christ 1990: 159 on Dem. 14.25–8; cf. Isoc. 7.35.
[104] E. Cohen 1992: 191–201. Gabrielsen 1994: 224–5 explains the leniency of Athens towards delinquent trierarchs in these terms.

successfully required some degree of concord between rich and poor despite the divergent tendencies we are exploring here. Demosthenes sometimes treats rich and poor separately as having different motives and making different contributions. Nevertheless, he does not feel that just because he is arguing for war he cannot not win over the rich. In retrospect he is proud that he did – in part through his reforms of naval financing.[105]

But do our sources really mean that every rich person was opposed to these specific wars, as their simple statements seem to imply? This is improbable and I would not expect an intelligent ancient observer to commit to such a position. I imagine that if we pressed one of these authors he would add something like "in general." In fact, given that "leaders of the people" seem always to have been men of some wealth, Diodorus' account, with its reference to demagogues inciting the masses to war, depicts a situation in which not all the rich were opposed to war. Nor is Pseudo-Xenophon likely to have thought that Pericles, for example, was either poor or likely to curry favor with the enemy. Finally, we cannot say that each of these authors believed that every single Athenian was either rich or poor. If their claims do not imply unanimity among the rich, even less will they explain the tendencies of however large a group of Athenians each particular author believed were somewhere between rich and poor. Thus, when scholars argue that there is only some correlation between wealth and attitude towards war, they are not really disproving these ancient generalizations as much as they think.

When modern political scientists want to be more precise about the political tendencies of different groups, they turn to polls on the subject. The presidential election of 2000 in the United States was close – notoriously so. About 50 percent of the voters chose Gore and about 50 percent chose Bush, but exit polls revealed strong tendencies among different groups: 91 percent of black voters, 56 percent of women, but only 36 percent of the people who attended church once or more each week voted for Gore.[106] These statistics confirm impressions that someone might have reached on their own about the political leanings of women, blacks, and regular churchgoers, especially evangelical Christians. But in the ancient world there were no polls that might inform or confirm the judgments of historians. How much should we trust their generalizations?

First, I doubt that an effect as slight as the tendency of women to vote Democratic (56 percent in 2000) would be noticeable even to an

---

[105] Dem. 4.7; 10.36–45; 18.107–8. See Gabrielsen 1994: 207–13 on Demosthenes' reform of 340.
[106] Pew 2003.

astute observer. Pseudo-Xenophon, for example, would hardly even have noticed that eleven out of twenty of his rich friends favored peace in a case when people in general were evenly divided. When an ancient source generalizes about "the rich" or "the poor" they are probably making a stronger claim, since they would not have noticed a weak tendency. We are probably in the range of either the modern black or churchgoing tendencies, either of which might be noticeable to an intelligent observer: if we stay with Pseudo-Xenophon's twenty hypothetical friends, a ratio of thirteen to seven (parallel the churchgoing 36 percent) on an issue would mean that almost twice as many rich men opposed war as favored it in a case when assembly sentiment seemed evenly divided. Such a ratio might easily be apparent to somebody, like our authors, whose social circle consisted of the rich men: "Boy, the talk at the gym sure isn't the same as what you hear among the contemptible vegetable-sellers shuffling into the assembly." The question of context brings us to the other side of this issue; a majority may intimidate.[107] If most rich people thought that going to war against Macedonia was a stupid idea in 323, the talk at *symposia* might have been even more skewed in that direction: the rich men who were in favor of the war for any number of reasons would have bitten their tongues.[108]

With these distinctions in mind we can now treat a few of the scholarly objections to the existence of a rich versus poor divide on the topic of war. The existence of some men who were rich and tended to favor taking a hard line against Macedonia, for example, does not invalidate claims about the rich in general. One cannot cite Demosthenes' wealth to disprove these claims; the existence of a black Republican leader such as Colin Powell does not disprove the strong tendency of blacks to vote Democratic. The fact that rich Athenians joined the war effort against Philip does not mean that their opinions were the same as those of the poor; they just did not take their opposition to the war to the point of treason. And many were probably eventually convinced that other considerations outweighed their monetary interest in peace.

A second argument requires more detailed treatment. Several scholars argue that the depiction of a rich versus poor divide is politically or ideologically motivated. In particular, Ernst Badian attributes such generalization

---

[107] See Thuc. 6.24.4.
[108] A false generalization can often be the result of someone's extrapolating to the public in general from the opinions of his or her friends. Thus, Thucydides claims that everybody was in favor of the Spartans at the beginning of the Peloponnesian war, he is really only reporting the sentiment of his class (Thuc. 2.8.4 with *HCT* ii.9–10 and Hornblower 1991–2009: 1.246). The generalizations we are treating explicitly include both rich and poor, both pro-and anti-war, and would not seem to be subject to this particular distortion.

to "anti-democratic historians."[109] He portrays the contrast between rich and poor attitudes in the *Hellenica Oxyrhynchia* as "merely a mark of his [the author's] political attitude."[110] In particular, the leaders of the pro-war group are described as being in favor of war so that "it might be possible for them to enrich themselves from the public treasury..." – hardly a favorable presentation of their motives.[111] Diodorus, too, is critical of the faction favoring war against Macedonia: he calls them "the men of whom Philip once said that war was peace and peace war for them" and concludes that the Athenians decided to fight against Macedonia "more promptly than was wise."[112] The thesis of an ideological slant finds support also in Isocrates: he links the decline in responsible government – of the Areopagus in particular – with war taxes, poverty, and wars, among other evils.[113] Mass democracy was certainly subject to the criticism of foolish belligerence.

At first sight, Badian's argument seems convincing: our sources are biased. But we need to consider not just the likelihood of ideological distortion, but precisely what role it plays in these descriptions. Badian's underlying assumption seems to be that a desire to go to war was considered bad and that this could be attributed to any political opponent or group regardless of its true attitude – to the common people and their leaders in this case. But war was not by itself regarded as a bad thing in classical Athens; it all depended on the particular war and the motives behind it. The desire for peace was also susceptible of different judgments: it could be a sign of self-control and reasonableness or, often indeed, a mark of shameless and effeminate cowardice.[114] Either proclivity could be portrayed in a positive or negative way depending on the goals of the speaker.

There is an obvious asymmetry in our case: it is the poor and not the rich who are accused of a culpable desire for reckless war. If the whole picture was an ideological invention for the sake of attacking the common people and their spokesmen, anti-democratic authors could just as easily have portrayed them as exhibiting a cowardly desire for peace. In fact, these authors did not take this tack. The simplest explanation is that it was well known that the Athenian poor tended to favor a more aggressive foreign policy; they could be attacked on this basis, but not as spineless pacifists. This picture is confirmed by Pseudo-Xenophon's description of this divide: instead of condemning the poor as belligerent, as do our other

[109] Badian 1995: 101. See also Sealey 1956: esp. 179–80, 185, 202; Perlman 1968: 258–9; Tritle 1988: 125; Burckhardt 1996: 132.
[110] Badian 1995: 82. See also Bruce 1967: 9–10.
[111] *Hell. Oxy.* Lond. Pap. col. 2, line 13–14 (Behrwald 2005; trans. Ha no. 11a).
[112] Diod. 18.10.1–4.   [113] Isoc. 7.51.   [114] E.g. Thuc. 1.120.3–4.

texts, Pseudo-Xenophon takes aim at the rich. He pictures the "farmers and rich" as "fawning on the enemy," a description that is plainly derogatory.[115] Pseudo-Xenophon is here, as in other respects, a curious text. But his argument fits within the framework of a world in which the rich are less likely to want to go to war, and this unwillingness – just like the relative eagerness of the poor – admits of a negative interpretation. In a nutshell, I believe that our texts put an ideological and negative slant on political tendencies that did in fact characterize rich and poor Athenians; they did not invent these tendencies out of whole cloth.

Athenian culture, most definitely including its elite culture, put a high value on military service. Many rich men aspired to excel at war and expected approbation for this ambition. J. E. Lendon has shown how important the model of the Iliad, the elitist text *par excellence*, was to Greek military culture.[116] There was plenty of martial enthusiasm among the upper class: to take just one example, Theophrastus uses a cavalryman who walks around in his spurs and riding cloak after a cavalry review as an example of petty ambition.[117] This aspect of elite culture seems, however, to have been outweighed, in general and on most occasions, by rich citizens' financial interest in peace. In the same way, the rich gained public prestige by their benefactions including their contributions during war, but the extent of liturgy avoidance suggests that in most cases economic forces won out there too.

War could, on the other hand, also provide opportunities for the rich: equipping and sending out a large fleet was the most costly project the Athenian state ever undertook. There must have been money to be made, for example, in the import of raw materials such as wood for ship hulls, linen for sails, or flax for ropes, in the construction of ships, and for merchants providing provisions for expeditions. To become rich during war was, however, considered a bad thing. It was acceptable for the poor to collect their three obols or a drachma per day for personal and risky service, but in several passages war-profiteering is used as an accusation to besmirch the reputation of an opponent in the law courts – or is vehemently denied.[118] In war the rich were supposed to gain prestige by making sacrifices for the good of the state; they were not supposed to make money.

The interests of the poor were also ambivalent. Service in the military meant certain hardship and possible death. Despite the generalizations about the poor wanting war, we have plenty of evidence for desertion and

---

[115] [Xen.] *Ath. Pol.* 2.14.   [116] Lendon 2005: e.g. 37–8, 85, 97, 118.   [117] Theophr. *Char.* 21.8.
[118] Burckhardt 1996: 173 cites Lysias 28.3 and 29.3, to which one might add Lys. 26.22, 24; 27.9–10; 29.3–4; and Aeschin. 2.161.

conscription, both of which suggest that military service was far from an unmitigated boon. A second problem could come up when the Athenian treasury was entirely exhausted because of war – as seems to have occurred as a result of the Social War. At that time, the state was not only impelled to enforce the financial obligations of the rich with vigor but probably forced to suspend the government functions that provided jobs, or at least extra money: building projects, jury service, and attendance at the assembly.[119] Even the wages for military service might never be paid. These were blows felt most acutely by the poor.

CHANGE OVER TIME

Our picture so far suggests that attitudes towards war were not entirely determined by wealth but varied with all sorts of factors, mainly external ones having to do with each war. I have drawn attention to one continuity in rich and poor attitudes towards war over a period of over a century, but there were probably all sorts of short-term variations in what exactly a particular war or even a particular campaigning season would entail. People might anticipate a profitable and safe war – as the mercenary rowers in the Athenian navy expected the Sicilian Expedition to be[120] – or a hard war, in which death or injury might be more prominent in the mind of the potential soldier than would the attractions of regular pay. For example, in Lysias' speech on behalf of Mantitheus, we hear that everybody thought that the campaign to fight against the Spartans at Haliartus would be dangerous for the hoplites, but safe for cavalrymen.[121] There were probably many occasions when such expectations influenced how attractive or not military service seemed and how expensive the war appeared likely to be.[122] Longer-term trends may also have come into play. The glory associated with being a trierarch declined as it became less a solitary and heroic enterprise and more and more a mandatory tax shared among a board none of whom would necessarily captain the trireme himself.[123] Most important for our

---

[119] During much of our period the theoric fund played a large role in the non-military uses of Athenian revenue. See Demosthenes' *Against Leptines* and *Against Androtion* for severe measures to exact taxes, with Burke 2002: 170. The significance of Athenian jury pay is a tricky issue; see Todd 2007 for a thorough treatment.

[120] Thuc. 7.13.2.

[121] Lys. 16.13. Ober 1978: 130 n. 72 suggests that the poor found naval service more attractive in the early than in the later fourth century as shown by the need for conscription in the latter period.

[122] E.g. Christ 1990: 151 argues that rich resentment peaked in the Corinthian and Social Wars.

[123] Gabrielsen 1994: 220. See also Christ 1990: 148, 153; Missiou 1992: 39–40.

period, the institution of the theoric fund affected the class politics of war and peace and introduced another dimension of change over time.

In the aftermath of the Social War the board of the theoric fund, under the leadership of Eubulus, was given all surplus funds for each year.[124] Laws protected the theoric fund from tampering and this meant that its moneys could not be used for war.[125] Indeed, it was not until 339/8, in preparation for the campaign that ended at Chaeronea, that the Athenians voted to devote the theoric fund to military purposes.[126] The theoric board seems to have spent its money in two ways: it funded direct distributions to all citizens to enable them to celebrate festivals – originally just for the price of tickets to the theater – and it was used to pay for a number of important public works: arsenals, dockyards, and streets.[127]

The theoric fund in part served as a make-work system that kept the poor from becoming discontent and potentially revolutionary; hence Demades called the theoric fund the "glue of the democracy."[128] More important for our topic, state subsidies and employment were available to the poor even when Athens was not at war: as Badian put it "they now had a common interest in peace."[129] Indeed, none of our passages contrasting rich and poor come from the period when the theoric board was powerful: 352–331.[130] There are too few such passages in any period for an argument from silence to carry too much weight, but this gap is consistent with the thesis that the theoric fund changed the poor's attitude by giving them less of an incentive to vote for war.

A number of passages – whatever other obscurities they contain – make it clear that the theoric board's use of Athenian revenues was sometimes in competition with direct military use of the funds.[131] The threat that the theoric distributions would be cut in the event of war became a possible argument for peace. One story recorded in Plutarch is that the Athenians were on the point of supporting the war of Agis against Macedonia when Demades convinced them not to: he claimed that the theoric board had been prepared to give every citizen a 50 drachma grant for the Festival of the Pitchers, but that they would have to devote the money to the war

---

[124] Buchanan 1962: 58.
[125] Dem. 1.19–20; 3.10–11, 19, 20; 19.291; [Dem.] 59.4–5. Discussions of the problems in understanding these passages include Sandys 1897: 144–6; Buchanan 1962: 60–74; Hansen 1976; Carey 1992: 152–7; E. Harris 1996.
[126] Buchanan 1962: 70–1 on Philochorus (*FGrH* 53–6) in Dion. Hal. *ad Ammaeum* I.11.
[127] Buchanan 1962: 58. On the amount of the subsidies see Buchanan 1962: 84–6; contra Ste. Croix 1964.
[128] Plut. *Quaest. Plat.* 1011b. See E. Harris 1996: esp. 74; cf. Buchanan 1962: 70.
[129] Badian 1995: 101.   [130] Buchanan 1962: 58, 82 for the dates.   [131] See note 125 in this chapter.

effort instead; the Athenians decided to enjoy a rich festival rather than join Sparta's war against Macedon.[132] Contemporary speeches suggest that similar considerations could influence Athenian decisions – if not as profitably and shamefully as Demades' supposed intercession. Demosthenes, in his speech *On the False Embassy*, claims that Eubulus scared the Athenians into accepting the Peace of Philocrates by a triple threat:

They must go down to the Piraeus at once, pay the war-tax and turn the theoric fund into a war-chest, or else vote for the resolution that was supported by Aeschines and moved by that abominable Philocrates . . . [133]

One is hesitant to believe Demosthenes' account of anything having to do with the Peace of Philocrates, but his own speeches reveal a concern to counter these same incentives for peace. For example, in *On the Chersonese* Demosthenes argues for a provocative policy vis-à-vis Philip's allies in the Chersonese; he inveighs against the shame of the situation in which the Athenians will not pay *eisphora*, nor campaign themselves, nor keep away from the public funds – this last a likely reference to the theoric fund.[134] In both the argument attributed to Eubulus and the passage from his own speech, a desire to use the public funds for something else is seen as an obstacle to war. Eubulus took advantage of the obstacle, while Demosthenes deplored it.

In conclusion, in the mid fourth century, war required sacrifice and promised little gain. The rich would have to pay; the poor would have to serve; and the people at large would be unable to use the state revenue for other purposes. If we are to seek internal reasons for war in Athens, we must look somewhere other than the economy. Perhaps the culture of Athens made it prone to go to war.

---

[132] Plut. *Prae. ger. reip.* 818e–f with Buchanan 1962: 80 n. 2.
[133] Dem. 19.291.   [134] Dem. 8.21.

CHAPTER 3

Militarism

Various scholars have proposed cultural rather than economic explanations for Athenian and Greek warfare. Such theories have, in fact, been more popular in recent years than the economic theories discussed in the previous chapter. They can be divided into two types. Some scholars, Kurt Raaflaub for example, emphasize the high value that Athenian culture placed on waging war.[1] The resulting militaristic culture made warfare important to the advancement of ambitious individuals and to the political clout of those groups whose military participation could be invoked to justify their prerogatives. According to this type of explanation, such individuals and groups were predisposed to favor war because it was the arena in which prestige could be gained or rights ensured. Other historians argue that the Athenians thought about and judged the action of states in terms of analogies with individuals and that these analogies tended to encourage competitiveness and intransigence among states and thus warfare. The application of individual analogies to the actions of states will be an ongoing concern of this book, but this chapter will focus on the first of these two types of cultural explanation. Two crucial points will emerge. First, Athenian militarism had mainly external causes and thus had the potential to contribute to a vicious cycle: war and the threat of war made Athens militaristic; this militarism made Athens more likely to go to war. Second, the most direct path that led from militarism to war was the Athenians' systematic miscalculation of their own power due to a distorted, glorified understanding of Athenian history, which was in turn an outgrowth of militarism.

One line of argument supporting the thesis that militarism led to warfare appears simple and direct, but it is flawed. A brief treatment here will

---

[1] Raaflaub 1994, 2001; Dawson 1996: 14; Runciman 1998: 745. See the criticisms of this approach in Eckstein 2000: 866–8.

suffice. A direct effect of warfare on a society is that it requires some men at least to become soldiers. If the society is a militaristic one that values soldiers highly, these men are likely to play an important role in the leadership and decision-making process of that society. One might think that "martial values," in the narrow sense of the values fostered by being a soldier and taking part in warfare, would encourage the recourse to war: "Men conditioned to violence are potentially dangerous."[2] This seems not to be the case. To begin with, we have no empirical evidence to support it.[3] Indeed, ancient sources regarded those experienced in war as being cautious; it was the young, unacquainted with the realities of war, who tended to favor war.[4] The actual experience of war seems not to have encouraged belligerence, but to have acted as a brake. Second, although aggressive bravery and fierceness are virtues in a soldier, other virtues such as cooperativeness and self-sacrifice play an arguably larger role in military effectiveness.[5] The prowess of Achilles on the battlefield contributes to the proud and uncompromising attitude he shows in his quarrel with Agamemnon, but in classical Athens good order and obedience are more prominent among the military virtues.[6] So, far from being an arena in which self-assertion and touchy pride had free rein, the Athenian military – including the navy, famous for its discipline – was a sphere in which cooperation and even subordination was highly valued. Third, individual Athenians often displayed a touchy sense of honor. This character trait, when applied to the interactions of states, probably made the recourse to war more frequent – as J. E. Lendon and Hans van Wees have asserted.[7] The roots of this ethos, however, do not lie in the experiences of soldiers, but rather in values of the feuding society from which Athens had recently evolved.[8] For all these reasons I shall set aside this argument, that military service itself encouraged Athenian belligerence.

---

[2] Konstan 2007: 193. Konstan, however, is concerned with the individual violence of soldiers, not with whether they would be more or less likely to vote for a war.

[3] Studies of the impact of modern war on soldiers (e.g. Grossman 1995) and comparative works on ancient and modern impacts (Shay 1994; Tritle 2000) focus on the psychological damage wrought on the individual rather than on the effects on soldiers' political beliefs and attitudes towards further wars. Those effects are likely to be complex and difficult to generalize; on the one hand, we find cases such as the fascist, militaristic veterans in the German *Freikorps*, on the other hand, we find veterans active in opposing wars (e.g. Lembcke 1998 on Vietnam veterans).

[4] See pp. 131–2.

[5] Adkins 1997: 712–13 discusses ways that, even in Homer, the competitive virtues can be counterproductive.

[6] Cf. Lendon 2005: 39–77.   [7] Van Wees 2004: 34–40; Lendon 2000 and 2006.

[8] See pp. 197–214.

ROOTS OF MILITARISM

Militarism is a word, like ideology, that has not only a pejorative popular meaning but also a host of competing scholarly meanings. In common usage it means something like "the propensity of people to favor war or a state to go to war without good reason."[9] Scholars variously define militarism as "the organization of a society based on the model of an army," "the dominance of the military in a society" or, more broadly, "every system of thinking . . . which ranks military institutions and ways above the ways of civilian life."[10] Here I will be using a strictly limited version of this last definition: militarism is "the tendency for a society and culture to place a high value on military prowess and service."[11] In addition, rather than striving to define a "militaristic society," I have aimed for a militarism that societies display to greater or lesser extents: classical Athens, I shall argue, was somewhere in the middle of the spectrum of militarism, not close to either extreme.

There are two kinds of factors, internal and external, that contribute to militarism in this sense. A state may value military prowess and service for internal reasons, because its dominant class has a stake in such a value system: for example medieval knights justified their position in society by their military role; they would not readily concede that good merchants contributed more than they to the state or that skill in accounting was more important than skill with the lance. External forces may also make a state more militaristic. States often place a high value on military prowess and service because they need to reward such abilities in order to prosper or even to survive in a world of hostile states.

The external sources of militarism are dramatically illustrated in the title story from Andrew Schmookler's book *The Parable of the Tribes: The Problem of Power in Social Evolution*. He posits a thought experiment involving a number of tribes in contact with each other, only one of which is not committed to "the way of peace" but is rather "ambitious for expansion and conquest." The other, originally peaceful, tribes would be

---

[9] The *OED* has the following definition: "1. Military attitudes or ideals, esp. the belief or policy that a country should maintain a strong military capability and be prepared to use it aggressively to defend or promote national interests. Also: a political condition characterized by the predominance of the military in government or administration or a reliance on military force in political or diplomatic matters." To connect such a militarism with the recourse to war would be a tautology.

[10] Silverthorne 1973 has this first definition of militarism in mind. The last is from Vagts 1959: 17.

[11] Dawson's "civic militarism" is similar in that it focuses on the political rewards derived from the high esteem in which military prowess and service was held (Dawson 1996: 5).

destroyed, conquered, or forced to flee, unless they took steps to counter the threatening tribe:

> But the irony is that successful defense against a power-maximizing aggressor requires a society to become more like the society that threatens it. Power can be stopped only by power, and if the threatening society has discovered ways to magnify its power through innovations in organization and technology (or whatever), the defensive society will have to transform itself into something more like its foe in order to resist the external force.[12]

Schmookler emphasizes the role of constraint: the choices that people and states do and can reasonably make are drastically limited by considerations of security.[13] This turns out to produce a one-dimensional and distinctly gloomy account of human history, but it does provide insight into how war and the threat of war foster militarism.[14]

Schmookler locates his initial thought experiment in prehistory, hence the "tribes" of his parable. If we consider ancient Greece, we are not speaking about a hypothetical initial decision to foster militarism. Rather we are speaking about an ongoing process driven by continuous pressure on states; for the Greek city-states were patently not all interested "in the way of peace." Already in the archaic period Messenia had been reduced to abject subjugation. Only occasionally was a city destroyed, its inhabitants either killed or enslaved, but such things did happen and no doubt caught the attention of other Greek cities.[15]

Although Schmookler is most interested in the human costs of centralized authority and larger political units, militarism in my sense fits into his theory of power-maximization. Scholars have recently emphasized the innovations in its military forces that Athens undertook to contend more successfully with other city-states.[16] A longer-term and less obvious adaptation that states make is militarism.[17] States need to reward their soldiers, especially those who sacrifice their lives and those who fight with great success. The rewards can be material. They often also consist of public praise and honors. Conversely, the condemnation of those who fail to fight

---

[12] Schmookler 1995: 21. Although he is not interested in the domestic structure of states, Alexander Wendt, in a classic article, argues that "predator states" can be responsible for making interstate anarchy a compelling rather than a permissive cause of self-help and conflict (1992: 407–9).

[13] See pp. 156–7, 159–61 on Realism.

[14] Gellner 1991 for a more positive view and R. Ferguson 1997: 339 for criticisms of Schmookler's pessimism.

[15] Hansen and Nielsen 2004: 120–3. Eckstein argues that the militaristic culture of classical Greece was largely due to external factors (2006: 76).

[16] E.g. Hunt 2007 esp. 110, 118, 120–1, 122, 135; Pritchard 2007: 332–6.

[17] Compare Balot (forthcoming).

bravely for the community can be equally motivating. Praise and condemnation are cheap, but they lead to a city's acquiring a militaristic set of values. A state that did not praise and reward military valor or sacrifice would be at a disadvantage in a war against one that did, but praising valor means that this virtue eventually takes a high place in a culture's constellation of values.

In some ways, militarism is both fair to soldiers and advantageous for a state at war. We must admit that soldiers do make great sacrifices, often their lives, for the good of the community. The notion that people who make sacrifices or provide benefits ought to be paid back is probably natural and ahistorical. In any case, there is abundant evidence for this feeling in classical Athens. Orators and philosophers applied the notion of fair payback specifically to the state's treatment of soldiers and especially of those who had died in war.[18] Indeed, such a feeling was the premise of every funeral oration: by this ceremony the community attempted to pay back in public honors what it owed to those who died for it.[19]

So militarism made sense and seemed utterly natural within a moral system, such as that of classical Athens, in which reciprocity played a large part. It was also advantageous and recognized as such. I am not sure what would have happened to a Greek city-state that did not reward military service, prowess, and sacrifice. I do not think it would have won many battles. In fact, the Greeks were quite aware that those states that rewarded military prowess and best harnessed their citizens' ambitions would prosper not only materially but also in prestige and in power; those that did not would not. For example, Xenophon describes the policies of Cyrus the Younger in the following terms:

[Cyrus] honored greatly those who fought well . . . by making them governors of conquered territories and then with other gifts. And he made it obvious that the brave deserved to be very prosperous while cowards deserved to be their slaves. As a result, many people were willing to take risks when they thought Cyrus would find out about it.[20]

As a deliberate policy or an unconscious reaction in recompense of services rendered or the display of bravery, Greek culture reserved some of its highest praise for those who served or excelled in warfare.

---

[18] See, for example, the articles collected in Gill, Postlethwaite, and Seaford 1998. Conversely, Arist. *Rh.* 1.13.1373b18–24 identifies not serving in the army as a crime against the community rather than against an individual.

[19] Lycurg. *Leoc.* 46 states this explicitly.

[20] Xen. *An.* 1.9.15. See also Lys. 16.21; Xen. *Cyr.* 3.3.51–2, *Lac.* 8.5; Pl. *Leg.* 11.921d–922a, 12.942d; Aeschin. 3.179–88; Dem. 20, e.g. 5–14, 141; 22.12–16; 24.216–17 (cf. Isoc. 5.135); Lycurg. *Leoc.* 130.

Compared with these direct and strong causal factors contributing to Athenian militarism, internal forces seem to have played a subsidiary role. The warriors depicted in Homer and, in the classical period, the hoplite or cavalry class in various oligarchies may have justified their rule by their military role – most conspicuously at Sparta. Such groups would have had some stake in maintaining military prowess and service as a determinant of worth and thus of social status – although property requirements for citizenship paralleled the military ones. At Athens we hear of politically motivated redefinitions of what constituted military service: for example, oligarchs in the late fifth century affected to believe that serving the state "with body or with money" did not include the paid rowers in the fleet, who therefore should be disenfranchised.[21] But, except for two short and disastrous interludes, Athens was not an oligarchy. In fifth-century Athens the poor may have justified their new-found rights on their contributions to the navy and thus the Athenian empire. One might posit that the poor were thus committed to militarism as fundamental to their position in society – we shall encounter a similar argument below. But by the mid fourth century the rights of the poor were well established and did not depend on their military role or the primacy of military virtues. In addition, all the classes among the citizenry had their own opportunities for military service, from the thetes in the proud Athenian navy to the well-to-do farmers in the hoplites to the elite young men in the cavalry or the rich defraying the expense of a trireme.[22] No one group among the citizens benefited disproportionately from the prestige accorded to war; no group had a preferential stake in the military virtues. Finally, Athenians were not professional soldiers, but amateurs with other occupations. War was an interruption of their usual lives – as farmers, traders, retailers, mine owners, absentee landlords, or whatever – and not their *raison d'être*. Whereas a warrior elite is inevitably committed to the valorization of war, neither the Athenians as a whole nor any subset of them needed to be.[23]

Although relations between groups within the citizenry did not play a major role in promoting Athenian militarism, another internal factor probably did play a role – how great a role is hard to judge. As we shall see, free men justified their rule over women and over slaves by reference to their role as protectors in the one case and as victors in the other – slavery was sometimes the result of defeat in war and the notion of slaves

---

[21] Thuc. 8.65.3; cf. [Arist.] *Ath. Pol.* 29.5.
[22] On the prestige accorded to different types of military service see van Wees 1995; Hunt 1998: 185–94; Pritchard 1998; Strauss 2000; Hunt 2007: 125–7.
[23] Lynn 2003: 109.

as deserving their status due to cowardly surrender was a reassuring one. Regardless of the frequency of war or their likely role in it, Athenian men did have a stake in the high value placed on the military: each citizen was at least a potential warrior and thus free and a man.

THE EXTENT OF ATHENIAN MILITARISM

External and internal factors ensured that military service and prowess were highly valued, both in Athens and in Greek society and culture in general.[24] Service in the armed forces also gave claims – albeit not always respected – to political and social rights as well as to general good treatment. For example, all prospective officeholders were asked among other questions whether they had served the state in war.[25] Men could suffer loss of political rights for throwing away their shields in battle; false accusations of such behavior were common enough that they were a recognized category of slander and penalized with a 500 drachma fine.[26] Rituals such as the public presentation of armor to the sons of the war dead at their coming of age – after they had been supported in their childhood by the state – celebrated the continuity of Athenian might and dramatized the prestige that sacrifice in war brought.[27] Soldiers earned praise or material rewards for their families by mere service or the passive act of self-sacrifice, but they could also fight well, successfully defend their city, or vanquish the enemy. Encouraging this led to a more active flavor of praise and militarism. In Athens rewards both material and honorific were bestowed upon successful warriors in recompense for their services. In his paper, "Father of All, Destroyer of All: Warfare in Late Fifth-century Athenian Discourse and Ideology," Kurt Raaflaub imagines a walk through classical Athens and shows vividly how conspicuous and ubiquitous were the inducements to military glory: artistic depictions of wars, inscriptions honoring successful armies, temples hung with spoils and other reminders of Athenian military glory were all over the city. Even drama was permeated with military concerns.[28] Success in battle brought glory that no other accomplishments could easily match.

The extent to which Athens had become less militaristic in the fourth century than in the fifth will concern us later.[29] Regardless of this limited

[24] E.g. Adkins 1960 and 1972; Havelock 1972; Müller 1989; Raaflaub 1994 and 2001; Burckhardt 1996; Dawson 1996; Pritchard 1998; Hunt 1998. Van Wees 1995 shows how malleable such claims could be, but not that they lacked persuasive power.
[25] Rhodes 1992: 617–18 ad [Arist.] *Ath. Pol.* 55.3 provides a discussion of these questions with references to other sources including Din. 2.17; Dem. 57.66–70; Aeschin. 1.28–9.
[26] Aeschin. 1.29; Lys. 10.12. [27] Aeschin. 3.152–4. [28] Raaflaub 2001. [29] See pp. 253–6.

shift, even in the fourth century Athenians continued to place a high value on the military virtues. The litigants in our surviving law-court speeches, for example, often felt it worth their while to mention their military service or to impugn that of their opponents. Indeed they did this about as often as they mentioned their financial contributions to the city.[30] Two related considerations seem to motivate these references to military service.

On the one hand, these passages show the importance of the martial virtues. Litigants deployed accounts of their military service and, if possible, their military leadership and prowess as part of their presentation of themselves as citizens of good character. They tried to portray their opponents as the opposite. Even the military success or failure of family members could be brought to bear as in the following passage from Lysias:

[My father] was general many times, and shared your peril besides in many a conflict . . . Even now, gentlemen, the memorials of his valour are hanging in your temples, while those of this man's and his father's baseness are seen in the temples of the enemy, so ingrained is cowardice in their nature.[31]

On the other hand, the mention of military service could be the basis, explicitly or implicitly, for a claim to rights or consideration. According to the ethics of reciprocity – which we shall be revisiting in more detail – litigants who had served the community could expect some recompense. A striking example is when Mantitheus spells out why he was particularly steadfast and even sought out dangerous posts:

I acted in this way, not because I did not think it a serious thing to do battle with the Lacedaemonians, but in order that, if ever I should be involved in an unjust prosecution, the better opinion that you would form of me on this account might avail to secure me the full measure of my rights.[32]

The notion of reciprocity is even more explicit earlier in the paragraph, where Mantitheus mentions the resentment against those who claim prerogatives without holding up their side of the bargain by serving in the military.[33]

Only about 40 percent of our extant speeches make any mention of service to the state. Even if we eliminate some speeches, such as deliberative ones, from consideration, the proportion of speeches that include claims of service will still not rise above 50 percent.[34] In some cases, a speech-writer

---

[30] See Appendix 3: Claims of service.   [31] Lys. 10.28.

[32] Lys. 16.17. On this speech and passage see Balot (forthcoming).

[33] Lys. 16.17: "So if any of you are incensed against those who claim the management of the city's affairs and yet evade its dangers, you can have no right to regard me with any such feeling."

[34] See Appendix 3: Claims of service.

may have thought that it was more advantageous to focus on the facts of the case in question – especially if his client's case was the stronger and his opponent's service to the state more impressive. Some litigants may simply have done little for the state. Demosthenes' father seems to have been one of these.[35] Nevertheless, Demosthenes won judgments against his guardians even before he had services of his own to which he could point.[36] Regardless of the exact explanation of every case, to have done a liturgy or to have served in war was not necessary for one to obtain his rights in court. Athens was not an extremely militaristic state, in which, for example, entrance into manhood depended upon making one's first kill.[37] Nevertheless, the fact that military service so often played a part marks a contrast with a modern legal system and illustrates the high value and regularity of military service.

Not only individuals but also groups made claims derived from militarism: if a group contributed to the defense or military success of the state, it deserved some reward or recognition in return. As a result, the issue of military service played a significant role in a variety of political debates.[38] The argument from military service was a particularly important one for the political rights of the poor in the fifth century.[39] These rights were an innovation, not accepted throughout the Greek world, and had few other persuasive justifications. The evidence from law-court speeches and Raaflaub's findings thus confirm what Schmookler would have predicted: external threats led to the development of a militaristic culture that placed a high value on the military prowess and service of individuals and groups.

The pressure to reward soldiers and its effect on a state's system of values is a constant that acts on any state with enemies or potential enemies. Nothing so far suggests that Athens was exceptional in its militarism; nor have scholars undertaken or even considered the comparisons that might determine this. Indeed, several lines of reasoning suggest that Athens was not particularly militaristic by the standards of its time – and probably by the standard of most times and places. Rather it may be the case that modern democracies, whence come most ancient historians, are

---

[35] Burke 2002: 172 n. 33.
[36] Demosthenes won the case presented in the *Against Aphobus I* (Dem. 27).
[37] Ehrenreich 1997: 127–8 gives examples of such societies; others were known to the Greeks – see pp. 60–1.
[38] E.g. [Xen.] *Ath. Pol.* 1.2; Thuc. 5.39.2; 8.65.3 (cf. [Arist.] *Ath. Pol.* 29.5; 33.1); Ar. *Ran.* 701–2, *Eq.* 576–80 (cf. Lys. 16.18); Isoc. 16.15; Xen. *Hell.* 2.3.48; Arist. *Pol.* 3.1279b1.
[39] Raaflaub 1994: 144; Raaflaub 2001: 340; contra Ceccarelli 1993.

exceptionally unmilitaristic.[40] Let us then consider critically the common claim that Athens was a particularly militaristic society.

To begin with, military values are never the only values in a society and are always in competition with other claims to merit: for example, ambitious young Athenians probably spent as much time in activities designed to make themselves good public speakers as they did in activities to gain or display military prowess.[41] The groups possessed of other claims to prestige and political power, most conspicuously the wealthy and well-born along with the well-spoken, are not likely to have wholeheartedly endorsed a system of values based entirely on military virtues. The lack of congruence between militarism and other sources of prestige and political power limited the impact of militarism on Athenian society. In contrast, societies ruled by warrior elites do not suffer this limitation on the value that they place on the martial virtues.[42]

Second, Athenians themselves did not feel that their militarism was anything special; on the contrary, a number of passages attribute militarism to other states and several evince the belief that other states placed a higher value on military prowess than did Athens. Already Herodotus depicts military prowess as crucially important to Lydian and Persian culture and society – and scholars of Achaemenid Persia agree.[43] The militaristic customs Herodotus attributes to the Scythians make the Athenians look like a bunch of peaceniks.[44] In Thucydides, Nicias explains to the assembly that the Spartans placed the greatest emphasis on military prowess.[45] Isocrates takes it for granted that the Spartans focus their attention on military matters, but he adds the claim that they took this idea from the Egyptians.[46] And when Xenophon wants to propound a more militaristic state to the Greeks, he has the legendary Persian ruler, Cyrus the Great, as his model or expounds on the Spartan constitution.[47] Most striking is a passage in Aristotle's *Politics*: the laws of Crete and Sparta aim mainly at success in war, and laws or customs among the Scythians, Persians, Thracians, Macedonians, Celts, Iberians, and Carthaginians also confer conspicuous rewards

---

[40] E.g. Woodrow Wilson: "We shall not ask our young men to spend the best years of their lives making soldiers of themselves" (Knock 1992: 59).

[41] Cf. van Wees 1998a.   [42] Ehrenreich 1997: 144–58; Hanson 2000.

[43] E.g. Hdt. 1.37, 136: 7.238.2; Briant 2002.   [44] Hdt. 4.64–6.

[45] Thuc. 6.11.6–7 (cf. Thuc. 2.39). The word used is *aretē*, and the context makes a military sense unambiguous. This portrayal of Sparta is typical.

[46] Isoc. 11.18–19.

[47] See Hunt 1998: 146–58 on Xenophon's *Cyropaedia* for the militarism of this work.

on military prowess or service.[48] The accuracy of some of these claims is unknown, but they clearly imply that the Athenians did not believe that they focused more on military prowess than did other states around them – and we possess no good evidence that would allow us to contradict them.[49]

A third problem for the picture of an extremely militaristic Athens is the existence of and responses to the draft. Not only was conscription necessary – Athens' army was not a volunteer army – but there were also draft dodgers and deserters.[50] Nobody seems to have complained that he was not allowed to serve and thus was deprived of a chance to show his prowess, demonstrate his manly courage, become a real man, and rise in society; on the contrary, we find a host of indignant complaints about having to fight on endless campaigns while others, the rich, the powerful, the dishonest, and malingerers avoid military service. This atmosphere seems quite distant from the picture of Athens as driven into wars by its militaristic values, by its culture.

Nevertheless, I do not want entirely to reverse that appraisal; there are still the monuments, the funeral orations, the undeniable prestige derived from military service in the law courts and in politics. Individuals were sometimes eager to serve in the army and even sought out dangerous assignments with their attendant glory.[51] But we are dealing with a mixed and complex picture. After all, leaders could and often did lose battles and get killed; they could be disgraced or condemned to exile, a crushing fine, or even execution.[52] Soldiers and sailors were taken away from their families and occupations and could be killed – that is why they had to be conscripted into the military. Leaders and, to a lesser extent, the poor had other claims to rights available besides military service and prowess. We are in an area of trade-offs, risks, and rewards and not just of simple and general advancement through war.

---

[48] Arist. *Pol.* 7.1324b8–23. See also Pl. *Leg.* 1.626a–b, 628e, 633b–c. Macedonian men reportedly were not recognized as real men – with the right to wear a belt – until they had killed an enemy in battle (Hammond and Griffith 1979: 11.23). Cf. Dawson 1996: 17–18 and Eckstein 2000: 870 for the ubiquity of militarism.

[49] Lycurgus, in *Against Leocrates* 51, does make a limited claim of this type, but then at 130–1 holds up Spartan militarism as a model.

[50] Christ 2001, and 2006: 46–65 on e.g. Thuc. 6.26.2, 31.3; Ar. *Pax* 1180–1, *Eq.* 1269–72; Plut. *Nic.* 13.5, *Alc.* 17.5; Lys. 9.4–6; 14.6–7; Aeschin. 3.175. Cf. Theophr. *Char.* 25.3–6.

[51] See esp. Lys. 16.13–17.

[52] On Athenian generals, see Pritchett 1971–91: 11.4–132; Wheeler 1991; Tritle 1992a and 1992b; Hamel 1998. For the varied motives of leaders see Thuc. 5.16.1–5.17.1.

OPTIMISM AND THE RECOURSE TO WAR

Even if Athenian militarism was neither unlimited nor exceptional for its time and place, it still seems *a priori* likely that it made the recourse to war appear more attractive to the Athenians.[53] Raaflaub makes an explicit case for such a causal relationship. Combining the arguments from individual and group status deriving from war, he concludes that what I am calling militarism made the late-fifth-century Athenian assembly more likely to vote for war. He paints a picture of leaders who knew that glory, power, and probably wealth could come from success in war and of a demos whose main claim to political power was its role in the Athenian navy and thus the Athenian empire. This combination produced an "atmosphere where appeals to patriotism and exaggerated expectations were cheap."[54] As a result, the assembly tended to make aggressive decisions and to reject peace offers. I find Raaflaub's arguments generally persuasive – and will flesh out below the argument for "exaggerated expectations" – but one issue should be acknowledged at the outset: the types of arguments that seem to have been most common in Athenian assembly speeches.

We find all sorts of appeals in these speeches, but only rarely the direct argument or even the implication that the Athenians needed to fight a war because war was the context in which individuals or groups could display virtues and earn praise; nor did speakers arguing against a war attack this position. The high value placed upon military success does provide the moral context within which a variety of arguments work. For example, the argument that the Athenians should try to match the prowess and bravery of their ancestors only carries conviction if prowess and bravery are judged important qualities. But, in line with Neorealist theory, the speeches overwhelmingly emphasize external reasons for war: if Corcyra falls into the power of Corinth, Athens' naval superiority would be at risk; Philip has attacked our allies; Philip wants to subjugate all Greece; if we don't fight him in the north, we'll have to fight him in Attica. Is there a way to connect some of these external arguments, which seem to be the most prevalent ones, with Athenian militarism? I believe there is.

This line of reasoning is a simple one in outline: praise of soldiers, a result of militarism, often requires praise of their exploits and leads to a

---

[53] McCauley 1990: 9; Lynn 2003: 109 for this general observation.

[54] Raaflaub 2001: 319–20. Cf. Chaniotis 2005: 45 on bellicose youths in the Hellenistic period: "Making war and excelling in battle were the ultimate ideals of their education." McCauley 1990: 9 argues of less complex societies that "a warrior class in chiefdom or village is likely to press for continuing conflict to the extent that their material interests and self definition depend on war and the threat of war."

brand of history distorted by patriotism. Such a history may lead a state to war, because it distorts its calculation of how the war is likely to turn out. It makes the state optimistic. But, before we can investigate this connection between militarism and the recourse to war, we need to examine the surprising idea that optimism plays a major role in the outbreak of wars.

Geoffrey Blainey first proposed this theory in his insightful and amusing *The Causes of War* in 1973. Blainey makes his argument within a Realist tradition: indeed, he is even more dismissive of interstate morality than the average Realist.[55] At first glance, his theory appears to be based on a view of states as rational calculators: war is the result of at least two opposing states deciding that they will gain more from a recourse to arms than from negotiation.[56] Such an approach at first appears far from hospitable to a role for militarism. Frequently, however, at least one side and often both are disappointed in this expectation. States typically miscalculate the outcomes of wars and their costs and they miscalculate systematically. They are too optimistic: "the optimism on the eve of the First World War belonged to a long but unnoticed tradition." As Blainey generalizes, "[t]his recurring optimism is a vital prelude to war. Anything which dampens that optimism is a cause of peace."[57]

Blainey puts this tendency in the context of an alternation between war and peace. Before a war, states tend to overestimate their power with respect to their enemy – this mutual optimism impedes the ability of states to come to an agreement short of war. As the war progresses, states' estimates of their relative power become more and more realistic. When both sides agree on their respective power, they may make peace. The concrete experience of war eventually banishes the overestimation of power by both sides and their consequent optimism. This alternation will be familiar to readers of Thucydides: on the one hand, Pericles' prediction of an Athenian victory has puzzled generations of scholars but seems to have convinced the Athenians to vote for war; on the other hand, most people at the time – including the Spartans themselves – expected Sparta to win within a couple of years.[58] It was the mutual disappointments of the Archidamian War that Thucydides considers most responsible for turning people's thoughts towards peace.[59] By 421 both sides understood that their chances of winning outright were slight, they assessed the losses they had

---

[55] Blainey 1973: 164: "the façade of international morality."   [56] Blainey 1973: 159.
[57] Blainey 1973: 47, 53. D. Johnson 2004 develops at length a version of this basic argument, albeit with a Darwinian twist.
[58] Thuc. 7.28.3. Cf. 4.108 and 8.2 on the sentiments of Athens' subjects.
[59] Thuc. 5.14–15. The deaths of Cleon and Brasidas also contributed.

suffered, and they more accurately calculated the risks they were taking. So, they made peace.

Now Blainey's theory explains only the failure of negotiation to settle differences; it is not relevant if one side aims to exterminate or enslave the other. It does not say anything about the original dispute that needed to be settled and cannot be taken as a complete explanation of war and peace.[60] The very different relations between the United States and Canada and between the United States and Iran today are hardly explicable by the extent to which these states agree on their relative power. Nevertheless, the decision to fight rather than bargain is an important step on the road to war and the attitudes that lead to it an important cause of war. Blainey's theory does possess explanatory force there. I will first show that optimism was an important feature of the oratory that led to war and will then show how that optimism grew out of the militarism of Athenian society.

Let us begin with the advice of the pseudo-Aristotelian *Rhetoric to Alexander*. In a section about the arguments to be used in recommending war, Pseudo-Aristotle advises that the orator should show that the war will have a successful outcome by "belittling the points of superiority possessed by the enemy and exaggerating those which we ourselves enjoy."[61] This unsurprising passage advises the war orator to encourage optimism in his audience; hence we have a striking parallel between what orators are to say and Blainey's analysis of the true cause of war. But is this theoretical prescription representative of how people actually spoke in the assembly?

I think it is. Many of Demosthenes' speeches urged Athens to undertake wars against Macedonia. The *First Philippic* and *The Olynthiacs* advocated a more active prosecution of the war with Philip. This first conflict with Philip ended with the humiliating Peace of Philocrates, which required the abandonment of Athens' ally Phocis and the acknowledgment of Philip's conquests in the north – including several Athenian allies. The *Second Philippic*, *Third Philippic*, *Fourth Philippic* and *On the Chersonese* advocated the renewal of war that led to the defeat at Chaeronea. It may even be that Demosthenes did not foresee Athens' alliance with Thebes in 339, which occurred after the last of these speeches.[62] An expectation that Athens could beat Philip without Theban help would have been even more optimistic than the disappointed hope that the two city-states together could defeat Philip.

---

[60] See the criticisms in Steele 1981, a strongly positive review overall: "If, after a punch-up between two individuals, we asked: 'What caused the fight?' we might be disappointed to be told: 'they disagreed about their comparative strengths'" (7).

[61] [Arist.] *Rh. Al.* 2.1425a27–8.   [62] See Cawkwell 1963b: 207–8.

Demosthenes often attempted to raise the hopes of his audience. He plainly connected Athenian self-confidence with their willingness to go to war or to prosecute a war vigorously. In the *First Philippic* he argues that the Athenians should not despair at Philip's advantages; if Philip had been discouraged by Athens' great advantages at the beginning of his reign, he would never have succeeded in turning the tables on Athens and "would have achieved none of his recent successes, nor acquired this great power."[63] In the *Second Olynthiac* Demosthenes says that he will tell the story of Philip's rise in such a way that "Philip shall appear as worthless as he really is, and those who stand aghast at his apparent invincibility shall see that he has exhausted all the arts of chicanery on which his greatness was founded at the first, and that his career has now reached its extreme limit."[64] Demosthenes' speeches are peppered with a wide variety of arguments to justify optimism in the face of Philip's apparent superiority.[65] His statement that "His present prospects are not so bright or satisfactory as they seem and as a superficial observer might pronounce them" is typical.[66]

As usual the situation is not a simple or straightforward one: the opposite tendency, to exaggerate the strength of the enemy, is also important in war oratory.[67] Demosthenes must portray vividly the threat that Philip presents, for Demosthenes can only invoke the necessity of self-defense to goad Athens into action by showing that Philip is a grave threat to Athens. This argument presents a dilemma: the more Demosthenes claims that Philip is a grave menace, the more difficult is his job of convincing the Athenians that they can defeat him. Demosthenes usually breaks this impasse with one of two related arguments. First, Philip's power is growing, so he can be beaten now (optimism), but not later (threat).[68] Second, optimism is amply justified, but only if every Athenian citizen does his duty for the state, something that they have failed to do in the past. Thus, Philip is now a threat; he can be beaten if the Athenians act as they ought.[69]

We can never tell which of Demosthenes' many arguments were decisive, but the frequent emphasis he places on encouraging optimism supports

---

[63] Dem. 4.4–5.   [64] Dem. 2.5.   [65] E.g. Dem. 1.22–3; 2.3–4, 15–16, 17–20; 4.8.
[66] Dem. 1.21. See Dem. 15.12–13 and [Dem.] 17.25 for more improbable optimism.
[67] Yunis 1996: 257–68 discusses this dilemma. Cf. Usher 1999: 240. This may explain an observation of Connor 1966: 57: Demosthenes' picture of Philip and Macedonian power is hopelessly contradictory since "[h]e is simultaneously obsessed with the menace of Philip . . . and convinced of his weakness."
[68] For example, in the *First Olynthiac* Demosthenes first concedes that Philip currently risks seeming insane with his threats against Athens (optimism), but then argues that, if Athens does not defeat Philip in the north, it risks fighting for Attica itself (threat) (Dem. 1.25–6).
[69] Dem. 2.3–4, 13; 3.16; 4.2, 7, 10; 9.4–5, 52; 10.59.

the generalization of the *Rhetoric to Alexander* and suggests optimism's importance in the genesis of Athens' wars.

As we have seen, Blainey's model of states as rational calculators, albeit systematically inaccurate ones, neglects many motivations for war, for example anger. But other cultural factors enter into Blainey's theory as sources of optimism and make for a more inclusive and descriptive theory than its foundation on a rational-choice model might suggest:

"Optimism may come from economic conditions [prosperity], the seasons [Spring in particular], ideologies and patriotism. It may come from a failure to imagine what war is like; for time muffles the pain and sharpens the glories of past wars, and national mythology explains away defeats and enshrines victories."[70]

We do not have enough economic information to judge the effect that economic prosperity might have in fostering "a sense of mastery of the environment" and consequent optimism and military adventurism – though one might recall that some ancient explanations of aggression focused on the arrogance bred of wealth.[71] Since campaigning in ancient times was rigorously determined by the seasons, we cannot control for the seasonality of campaigning, as Blainey attempts to do, and check his suggestion that it is the blooming spring that turns a state's thoughts to war.

On the issue of "national mythology" as a cause of optimism, scholars of classical Athens are in better shape. Popular understandings of Athenian history – represented in public oratory rather than in the written histories aimed at an elite readership – focused on its past glories with little regard for accuracy; this is precisely the brand of history likely to foster optimism and thus the recourse to war.[72] Three particular cases exemplify the way that a distorted view of the past made Athens more belligerent than it would otherwise have been: the oratorical use of the Persian Wars and the Corinthian War, and the tendency to discount the Peace of Philocrates.[73]

Athens' role in the Persian Wars served in the fifth century to justify the Athenian empire. In the fourth century the example of the Persian Wars was often deployed in support of Athens' policy of opposing other Greek cities that threatened to become predominant. The connection of optimism and intransigence is particularly clear in the use of the oaths of Marathon and Salamis in oratorical appeals against Philip.[74] Demosthenes

---

[70] Blainey 1973: 54.   [71] See p. 33.

[72] For more detailed considerations of oratorical uses of history see Pearson 1941; Hamilton 1979; Worthington 1994; and Milns 1995.

[73] See Badian 1995 for the similar argument that the "ghost of empire" repeatedly led Athens to overconfident mistakes in its fourth-century foreign policy; cf. Chambers 1975.

[74] See MacDowell 2000: 337–8 on these oaths.

recounts Aeschines' reading of these oaths in the assembly as part of his "fine long speeches" advocating resistance to Philip – a stance Aeschines abandoned after his supposed corruption by Philip.[75] Hearing these oaths not only stirred the ambitions of Athenian men to match their forefathers but also encouraged them to associate intransigence with glorious victory.

The question "what have we done lately?" seems sometimes to have occurred to Athenian speakers and to have suggested a search for more recent grounds for optimism. Oratorical references to the Corinthian War, more recent than the Persian Wars though barely in living memory, illustrate well Blainey's general observation that national memory is selective and that indecisive wars often slip surreptitiously into the list of victorious wars. Since every nation tends to believe that each of its past wars was fought in self-defense, any result that did not change the *status quo ante* for the worse is likely to be remembered as a victory.[76] Despite the condemnation of the King's Peace with which the Corinthian War ended – a condemnation which Demosthenes himself represents as universal[77] – and despite the continuation of the Spartan dominance which that treaty ensured, campaigns from the Corinthian War contained grounds for optimism according to Demosthenes. He invokes Athenian participation in the battle of Haliartus as one of a number of examples likely to scare Philip with an indication of what the Athenians can do. Considering Spartan dominance, it was a brave act for the Athenians to march out in support of the Thebans at Haliartus. But, in fact, the Athenians arrived too late to take part in that battle, though Demosthenes' inspirational history has little use for such details.[78] In another case, the Athenians serving together with their mercenaries around Corinth did inflict a defeat on Sparta, but it was manifestly inconclusive – indeed, immediately after the defeat, Sparta ravaged the territory of Athens' allies – and, to repeat the key point, the Athenians did not win the war.[79]

I have mentioned already Blainey's theory that states become overconfident in peacetime and acquire a realistic self-assessment during wars. An accurate view of Philip's and Athens' respective power led Athens to agree to the Peace of Philocrates. So too, the cautious tone of Demosthenes' *On the Peace*, given shortly after the Peace of Philocrates, suggests a keen awareness of Athens' vulnerability.[80] By 343 Demosthenes presents an entirely different picture of the Peace of Philocrates: Athens was doing fine in the war,

---

[75] Dem. 19.303. [76] Blainey 1973: 58. [77] Dem. 15.29. [78] Dem. 4.17.
[79] Dem. 4.24. Cf. Xen. *Hell.* 4.5.11–18 for the defeat and Xen. *Hell.* 4.5.10 for the subsequent ravaging by which Agesilaus "showed that no one wanted to come out against him."
[80] See especially Dem. 5.13–14, 24–5.

in command of the sea, threatening Philip's supply lines, and assisted by powerful allies; something like a "stab in the back" – treachery among the Athenian ambassadors in this case – brought it down.[81] This representation of the recent past stems in part from Demosthenes' enmity with Aeschines, but it also plays a role in his campaign to recommence the struggle against Philip, a course of action that the outcome of the first war would not naturally recommend. As a result, much of his attack on Aeschines in *On the False Embassy* consists of a revisionist account of Athens' motives for the Peace of Philocrates.[82] Not surprisingly, the intransigent author of *On Halonnesus* also affects to believe that that peace treaty was the result of Philip's duplicity rather than the respective power of the opponents.[83]

The incidents and wars that Demosthenes does not mention are perhaps as telling as those he does. In *For the Liberty of the Rhodians* Demosthenes argues in favor of risking a conflict with Persia in order to assist the Rhodians. He had every reason not to mention how Persia imposed the "King's Peace" on Greece to end the Corinthian War – the first of many King's Peaces. The Social War, which ended disastrously in 355, only five years before the *First Philippic*, is also conspicuous by its absence from the historical cases Demosthenes uses in that speech to bolster his case for war against Philip. Since we do not possess the speeches that opposed Demosthenes' policies – and which in both of these cases carried the day – we cannot say whether Demosthenes' omissions really reflect a collective forgetting of past failures or whether the opponents of aggressive policies deployed these counter-examples to good effect in their speeches.

This complexity raises the issue of what sort of historical tradition made it possible for such distortions and omissions to influence Athenian policy and leads us back to the connection with militarism. First, history was not a subject taught in school, so the average Athenian citizen's knowledge of it would depend on oral tradition more than on formal instruction. Few would have read a text such as Thucydides' history.[84] If there was something like an official version of Athens' past, it would have to be that retold in the annual funeral orations, which in most years were expected to recount the city's past achievements as a part of the praise of that year's war dead.[85] And it is in the funeral oration that we see most vividly the

---

[81] See for example Dem. 19.33–6, 96–7, 123, 141, 147, 149, 153, 328, 336. He repeats these claims in Dem. 18.25–7, 30–7. Demosthenes also attacks Eubulus for scaring the Athenians into accepting this peace (19.291–2).

[82] MacDowell 2000: 21–2. Demosthenes was also trying to distance himself from the increasingly unpopular Peace of Philocrates, which he helped to negotiate (MacDowell 2000: 14).

[83] [Dem.] 7.22–3, 33–4.   [84] R. Thomas 1989: 200–2.   [85] R. Thomas 1989: 211.

flaws of a strident patriotic history. Rosalind Thomas has shown that the version of history in the funeral oration served to illustrate the ancestral and intrinsic *aretē* of the Athenian people[86]:

There is a tendency for defeats to be remembered as victories . . . [in a version of history] excruciatingly smug and self-congratulatory . . . Athens' past is transformed by selection and alteration so that it consists of a series of victories – moral victories if necessary.[87]

To some extent, this bending of history was to be expected in a society whose self-image was largely unconstrained by written history – and recall that even written history has not curbed the "national mythologies" of Blainey's modern examples. The context of the funeral oration probably contributed too. Its account of history was shaped to conform to an occasion whose chief aim was to celebrate the military virtues of soldiers who had died for Athens. Two aspects of this occasion were crucial.

First, the military virtues were raised above all others in order to honor the men who sacrificed their lives:

Even for those who were worse in other ways it is right that first place be given to valor against enemies on behalf of country; by effacing evil with good, they became public benefactors rather than individual malefactors.[88]

Second, Lycurgus in his speech *Against Leocrates* brings up the funeral oration and describes its content as "the praise which is to them the only reward for danger."[89] Lycurgus himself is far from questioning the funeral oration, but I suspect that only the most extravagant praise – if even that – would compensate the families of the war dead for their losses. Athenian orators seem to have done their best to provide such praise both for the dead soldiers and for the cause – usually taken simply to be Athens – for which they died. In this context one can easily imagine that any hesitation to glorify and embellish the past might be resented as casting aspersion on the public honors of those who had recently died for Athens. No surviving oration takes any such liberty.[90]

Thomas points out that the "epitaphic tradition of Athens' past recurs wherever defence, praise or emulation of the ancestors was called for, and it gives the impression of being an automatic and conventional response."[91]

---

[86] R. Thomas 1989: 231.   [87] R. Thomas 1989: 203, 206, 231; see also Pritchard 1999: 21–2.

[88] Thuc. 2.42.3.   [89] Lycurg. *Leoc.* 46.

[90] The beginning of Plato's *Menexenus* pokes fun at the Athenian funeral oration; the families of recent war dead were not an important part of his intended audience. Although this work is difficult to classify and interpret, its account of Athenian history (239d–246a) contains in an extraordinary concentration all the flaws that plague patriotic history.

[91] R. Thomas 1989: 211.

The patriotic history of the funeral oration was not isolated from the Athenian sense of history that informed their decisions in the assembly. Thus militarism, by means of the funeral oration, tended to encourage the optimistic miscalculations that can lead to war.

Another factor also played a part. Given Athenian militarism, each generation's desire to live up to its ancestors – a topic we shall revisit in Chapter 5 – required success in war above all. Indeed, the pro-war appeal to live up to the monuments of past glories became so standard that orators opposing wars launched pre-emptive attacks on it. For example, Aeschines described the assembly leading up to the acceptance of the Peace of Philocrates:

but the popular speakers arose and with one consent ignored the question of the safety of the state, but called on you to gaze at the Propylaea of the Acropolis, and remember the battle of Salamis, and the tombs and trophies of our forefathers. I replied that we must indeed remember all these, but must imitate the wisdom of our forefathers, and beware of their mistakes and their unseasonable jealousies . . . but I urged that we should take warning from the Sicilian expedition . . . [92]

We do not possess Aeschines' actual words, but we see a second description of their basic import in Demosthenes' claim that Aeschines had changed from patriotic intransigence to shameless Philippizer after he had been bribed. After Aeschines' supposed subversion,

[he] stood up and made a speech and spoke in support of him [Philocrates], words for which (Zeus and all gods) he deserves to die many times over. He said you should not remember your ancestors or put up with people talking about trophies and naval battles . . . "[93]

It seems that Aeschines went too far by questioning the pro-war argument, "let us live up to our ancestors"; Demosthenes certainly believed that Aeschines was vulnerable here and took full advantage of his opponent's slip. Apart from this, it is only in Isocrates' *On the Peace* that the appeal to the military success of the ancestors is questioned – and this was a pamphlet for an elite readership, not an assembly speech.[94] Thus, Aeschines' misstep and Isocrates' pamphlet are the exceptions that prove the rule: the invocation

---

[92] Aeschin. 2.74–5, cf. 2.63.

[93] Dem. 19.15–16. See also Dem. 19.307, 311. I find it more probable that Aeschines was carried away in his attacks on continuing the war with Philip and succumbed to the temptation of wit and paradox rather than that Demosthenes invented this apothegm in its entirety; contra Milns 1995: 2.

[94] Isoc. 8.36–8, 79–85 (cf. 8.30, 54–5, 87–8, 90, 91–2). See pp. 262–4 on *On the Peace*.

of the Athens' military tradition was a commonly used but still powerful weapon in the arsenal of pro-war orators.[95]

This deployment of a distorted, patriotic history with roots in militarism does not, of course, tell the whole story. Athens would not have done as well as it did and might not have survived at all, if unrestrained self-flattery and grandiosity reigned supreme in the assembly.[96] To begin with, some speakers affected the pose of a stern and honest advisor not interested in flattering the demos but in benefiting it. Aeschines' argument for the Peace of Philocrates – castigated by Demosthenes but on the side that carried the day – may have fitted in that category.[97] Thucydides presents Nicias as advising strongly, though without success, against the Sicilian expedition – and on good grounds to judge by the outcome and the specific military problems the Athenians were to face.[98] Demosthenes' *On the Peace* (24–5) admonishes the Athenians, advising them to know the limits of their power.[99] In other places, although he takes a pro-war stance vis-à-vis Philip, he condemns orators who please their audience while neglecting their long-term interests.[100] A number of sayings attributed by Plutarch to Phocion, a prominent politician and general, and probably derived from contemporary sources also provide counter-examples to a one-sided picture of over-optimistic Athenian belligerence. For example, in a case involving a border dispute Phocion urged the Athenians to fight the Thebans with words, in which they were superior, rather than to fight with weapons, where the Thebans had the edge.[101] The funeral oration was manifestly not the whole of Athenian culture.

---

[95] Some examples are as follows: Arist. *Rh.* 3.10.1411a1–20; Dem. 2.24; 3.21–6; 4.17, 23–5; 6.10–12; 8.42; 9.36, 40, 45, 74–6; 10.14, 24–5 (8.48–9), 46–7; 14.1–2, 41; 15.22–3, 27–8, 35; *Exordia* 33; [Dem.] 7.7, 12; 17.30. Cf. Thuc. 1.71.7, 122.3, 144.3; 2.62.3; 4.92.7.
[96] Harding 1995.   [97] E.g. Aeschin. 2.70.   [98] Thuc. 6.9–14, 19–22.
[99] Dem. 5.24–5. See also, e.g., 4.23, 40; 9.1.
[100] E.g. Dem. 3.24; 6.3–5; 9.75; 10.3–4. See Burckhardt 1996: 221.   [101] Plut. *Phoc.* 9.4.

CHAPTER 4

The unequal treatment of states

A state's attitude and conduct towards other states can depend on the actions of those states and on their perceived status, in rough terms, on what they do and on what they are. One can order foreign policies based on the extent to which they incorporate one or the other of these criteria. One end of this spectrum is the view that two states for reasons of religion, ethnicity, or political system are natural enemies or natural friends and that no other grounds for war or, conversely, peace and alliance are necessary. An extreme example of this way of judging a state on its status rather than its actions is reported from Tsin China when the Tartars asked for a peace treaty: " 'Amity,' the prince exclaimed, 'what do they know of amity? The barbarous savages! Give them war as the portion due to our natural enemies.' "[1] This story, whether accurate or typical or not, illustrates the *status-based* extreme of our spectrum: a case where no particular action was required to provoke war and where even the request for a peace treaty could not avert "the portion due to our natural enemies." In contrast, a foreign policy that considered other states' *actions* only and took no account of political differences or similarities, putative superiority or inferiority, ethnicity or religion would occupy the opposite, *action-based* end of the spectrum.

Two major theories of international relations place a great deal of weight on this issue; both assert the superiority of the *action-based* rather than the *status-based* end of the spectrum. The notion of a rule of law among states typically encompasses an ideal of judging states on equal terms: according to international law, aggression is aggression whether the state perpetrating it is democratic or communist, Slavic or Arabian, Islamic or Christian. Paradoxically, this legalistic ideal coincides to a large extent with the prescriptions of Realism: prudent calculations about how to act towards other states take into account their power – and hence are at

[1] Phillipson 1911: 41.

odds with the egalitarian ideal of international law – but they do not take into account other status-based considerations: to worry about whether an advantageous alliance was with a communist, Chinese, or Hindu state would merely distract a statesman from determining and following his state's interest.[2] This logic lay behind Winston Churchill's famous quip about his attitude towards the Soviet Union during World War II: "if Hitler invaded Hell, I should at least make a favorable reference to the Devil in the House of Commons."[3] In part as a result of the influence of legalistic and Realist thought, the *action-based* end of the spectrum is generally considered the more modern.

In general the Athenians tended to place more weight on actions than on status: ethnic and religious judgments are attested but were of limited applicability and force. On the other hand, attitudes about the intersection of internal politics and foreign relations were complex in ways similar to modern views. Related to the question of state type in this sense is the issue of hierarchy among states. Did Athenians judge states differently on account of their power or prestige? Could a lack of deference by a less powerful state to a more powerful one be considered a *casus belli*? This issue of hierarchy is theoretically tricky and our evidence sometimes points in different directions, but recent treatments exaggerate the extent to which hierarchy among states was approved.

Although it will be useful to treat these categories – ethnicity, religion, politics, and hierarchy – separately, we should not forget that they overlapped and influenced each other. Ethnic differences or similarities were often linked to religion.[4] Isocrates' Panhellenic crusade against Persia required hierarchy in the form of a leading state to unite the Greeks.[5] Such a war would be justified not only because the Greeks considered the Persians foreign, but also because they viewed them as slavish and thus inferiors.[6] Their inferiority was linked to their monarchic system of government in which all but the king were considered slaves – according to some Greeks at least.[7]

PHILOSOPHICAL DISTORTIONS

Before we turn to the different categories of *status-based* arguments, an issue concerning our sources requires discussion: Plato and Aristotle provide

---

[2] Walt 1987: 33.   [3] Walt 1987: 38.
[4] Hornblower 1992: 174; Hall 1997: 100; van Wees 2004: 9–10.   [5] Low 2007: 64–6.
[6] Long 1986: 108; Rosivach 1999.   [7] See Missiou 1993.

brief synopses of reasons for states to go to war. These are predominantly status-based and have contributed to distorted modern views of Greek thinking about the relations of states. We have already encountered the general reasons why assembly speeches provide more trustworthy evidence for mainstream ideas than do the philosophers; one particular case will flesh out this contrast and provide an entrée to our investigations of popular Athenian views.

In the *Politics* Aristotle argues that states should not try to conquer and dominate their neighbors. Rather, military practices should aim at the following three goals:

[F]irst of all they should provide against their own enslavement, and in the second place obtain empire for the good of the governed, and not for the sake of exercising a general despotism, and in the third place they should seek to be masters only over those who deserve to be slaves.[8]

This short passage is possibly Aristotle's only comprehensive statement about legitimate war.

Plato never describes the grounds of legitimate war, but, in a long and vehement passage, he argues that Greeks and *barbaroi* are naturally enemies and that it would be a good thing to direct Hellenic aggression against the *barbaroi*.[9] When it comes to wars between Greeks, Plato is less permissive than Aristotle – perhaps because he did not distinguish different types of rule, one of which might be appropriate over Greek cities. Whereas Aristotle seems willing to countenance wars to establish benevolent rule even over Greek cities, Plato deprecates all conflict among Greeks as "sick" and "civil war," and he insists that such wars, if they were to be fought at all, should be conducted within strict limits.[10]

There are some parallels between the views of these two philosophers and popular conceptions, but neither is typical. Indeed, both philosophers seem to be arguing against more widespread views. Plato condemns most Greek wars as "sick." Aristotle's second and third reasons for war are couched in terms of limits placed on wider conceptions of what justifies war. He presents his own views as moral and restrained in contrast to popular, permissive attitudes towards war.[11] Indeed, there was a substantial difference in emphasis between Aristotle's thinking and that of the Athenian assembly.

---

[8] Arist. *Pol.* 7.1333b39–1334a3l; cf. Arist. *Pol.* 7.1324a11–12. On this passage see Garlan 1989: 28–30 and Ostwald 1996: 111–16. Cf. Laurenti 1987 on Aristotle's thinking about warfare.

[9] Pl. *Resp.* 5.469b–471b. On turning against "the barbarian" see in particular 469c, 470c. Cf. Pl. *Menex.* 245c–d.

[10] Pl. *Resp.* 5.470c–d, 471a–b. He uses *nosein . . . kai stasiazein*.

[11] See also Arist. *Rh.* 1.3.1358b25–1359a8 and Arist. *Pol.* 7.1324b5–9.

The difference does not lie, however, in Aristotle's superior morality; it lies in Aristotle's emphasis on the status of the combatants rather than their actions. A strong emphasis on the ubiquity and naturalness of hierarchy permeates Aristotle's thinking in general.[12] Here in particular his three grounds for war are expressed in terms of legitimate or illegitimate rule. Self-defense is warranted on the grounds that it would prevent unnatural enslavement – for Aristotle's ideal city is not populated by natural slaves. Rule over other cities must be like a legitimate government, which benefits both parties, and not be despotic; enslavement should be practiced only against those who deserve it. Aristotle seems almost to imply that if a state aims at legitimate rule or if another people consist of natural slaves, no further justification for an attack is necessary.[13] Plato, too, focuses on the status of the combatants: whether they are Greek or non-Greek is the crucial issue for him.

Plato and Aristotle may have possessed another, perhaps complementary, set of criteria for legitimate war based on the actions of the states involved. Even in his discussion of the "civil wars" among Greeks, Plato implies a distinction between the guilty and innocent: wars between Greek cities should be limited and "they will say that only a few at any time are their foes, those, namely, who are to blame for the quarrel . . . " and "will carry the conflict only to the point of compelling the guilty to do justice."[14] Thus the status of combatants does not exhaust Plato's criterion for judgment. So, too, Aristotle's explicit arguments for the equivalence of individual and state morality may imply that his whole ethical theory can be applied to states.[15] The likelihood that Plato's and Aristotle's full views were more complex than their few brief discussions would suggest makes it even more important not to place too much weight on their apparent emphasis on ethnicity and hierarchy.[16]

Herodotus, Thucydides, and Xenophon do not portray such issues as important to the way the Greeks justified their wars. Nor, as we shall see, were such arguments prominent in the assembly speeches of our

---

[12] Arist. *Pol.* 1.1254a20–33.

[13] So Newman 1887–1902: 1.328: "This enumeration of wars omits wars waged in defence of allies, but it is wide enough to be accepted by any conqueror, however ambitious, who might be willing to adjust his methods of rule to the claims of the states subjugated by him."

[14] Plato, *Resp.* 5.471a–b.

[15] See especially Arist. *Pol.* 7.1323b40–1324a13 with Low 2007: 160–73.

[16] I suspect that their full views might well have resembled that of Isocrates, still on one end of the spectrum of Athenian opinion. He believed that the legitimate use of military force was against "the barbarians . . . those doing wrong . . . those who invade their territory" (Isoc. 12.219–20). This conception shares Plato's and Aristotle's emphasis on considerations of status and, with its reference to "those doing wrong," is consonant with criteria of proper and improper conduct.

period. Orators typically advocated or deprecated wars on the grounds of other states' actions rather than their status.[17] A summarizing passage of Demosthenes provides a concise contrast to Aristotle's précis. Like Aristotle, Demosthenes reveals his conceptions of what justifies war by listing the legitimate reasons for military preparedness. He sums up as follows:

> [W]hen all preparation for war is on the same lines and the main objects of an armed force are the same – to be strong enough to repel the enemy, to assist one's allies, and to preserve one's own possessions – why, having open enemies enough, must we be looking out for another?[18]

Like Aristotle, Demosthenes gives us a list of three reasons for war. These reasons come out of a very different conception of what constitutes a just war.

Demosthenes' first object of military preparedness, "to repel the enemy," is an unobjectionable statement of the right of self-defense. Demosthenes' second reason for possessing an armed force is to "assist one's allies," a common enough reason for war, but one that does not imply any hierarchy between the states involved.[19] Demosthenes' third grounds for war, to protect one's possessions, cannot just be repeating the right of self-defense. He must be referring, however vaguely, either to Athens' right to defend its rule outside its own borders or to its rights to prior conquests and cleruchies.[20] Thus, we seem to have something like Aristotle's argument that, in some circumstances, imperialism can justify war. But, unlike Aristotle, Demosthenes does not try to justify the initial acquisition of rule over another state: he makes no mention of how the "possessions" had been acquired. He bases his argument on the maintenance of the *status quo* rather than on the nature of Athenian rule.

A passage in *For the Liberty of the Rhodians* provides a close parallel. There, Demosthenes relates a rule of conduct equally applicable to Athens and to Persia – an equality in itself contrary to Plato's and Aristotle's ethnic distinctions:

---

[17] Garlan 1989: 34.

[18] Dem. 14.11. We find two similar lists of grounds for war:
  (1) Euripides, *Heraclidae* 162–5: "Of what lands will you allege you have been robbed, of what booty despoiled, that you go to war with Argos? In defense of what allies, on whose behalf will you bury the fallen?"
  (2) Andoc. 3.13: "For I think that all men would agree that it is necessary to make war for these reasons, either when they are being wronged or to help those who are being wronged."

[19] See also [Arist.] *Rh. Al.* 2.1425a13–15. Pl. *Leg.* 5.737d; Arist. *Pol.* 7.1327a41–b3 mention in passing aid to neighbors as a reason for war.

[20] E.g. Dem. 4.4–6 seems to regard Potidaea, Pydna, and Methone as belonging to Athens.

For indeed, if the King admitted me to his presence and asked me for my advice, I should give him the same that I gave you – to defend his own subjects, if any of the Greeks attacked them, but to claim no sovereignty over those who did not belong to him.[21]

As in the case of "possessions," one is again left wondering how "sovereignty" is ever acquired in the first place. The elision of this issue in these two passages is not accidental. In popular thinking, the establishment of hierarchy among states was a controversial and awkward topic. It is one that Demosthenes skips when he can and never invokes as the grounds for war. In contrast, Aristotle is not ambivalent about the desirability of hierarchy in general as long as it is a natural and thus a mutually beneficial one.

In Demosthenes' summary of reasons for military preparations, war would be justified by an attack against Athens, against an ally of Athens, or against a possession of Athens. Whether the attacker was Greek or barbarian, a natural slave or ruler, mattered not a bit. Although this passage provides a prophylactic against putting too much weight on the status-dominated views of Plato and Aristotle, this completely action-based set of rules is not the complete picture. Rather, popular views were ambivalent and mixed. Let us turn now in more detail to the different categories of status-based arguments found in assembly speeches.

ETHNICITY

Athenians judged, and perhaps treated, states differently on account of their ethnicity.[22] Some states were culturally similar to Athens and could point to a fictive kinship; others were dissimilar and could not. The distinction between Ionian and Dorian Greeks played a role in interstate politics in the fifth century but had faded almost to nothing in our period. On the other hand, the contrast between Greeks and non-Greeks, or "barbarians," crystallized during the Persian Wars and, in the fourth century, provided the basis for Panhellenism, the notion that the Greek city-states should give up their mutual animosities and together attack the Persian empire. Demosthenes gave Panhellenism a new twist when he cast the Macedonians under Philip as the new barbarian threat against which the Greeks

---

[21] Dem. 15.7 (trans. modified).
[22] I will be using ethnicity in a general sense encompassing not only fictive kinship but also the "linguistic, religious, and cultural criteria" that had become more important by the fourth century (Hall 2001: 166). See also Hall 2002: 172–228 with the criticisms of Konstan 1997b.

should unite – and even recommended an alliance with Persia against the Macedonians.

Treating states in ethnic terms must have had persuasive force or orators would not have based arguments on it. Nevertheless, ethnic thinking had a limited impact on Athenian decisions: ethnic classifications and judgments were malleable and tended to be shaped by other factors rather than to determine decisions. Indeed, this section risks giving too much attention to such arguments: we will necessarily be focusing on cases where an ethnic argument could be and was made, concerning Ionians, Dorians, Persians, or Macedonians. But, in a great number of cases – for example the Peloponnesian alliances considered in *For the Megalopolitans* – no such arguments were or could be attempted.

Appeals to the division of much of the Greek world into Ionians and Dorians were common in the fifth century.[23] Though Thucydides may deny the importance of this ethnic feeling, his text reveals that arguments based on the natural affinity of these groups and their hostility towards each other were staples of political rhetoric of the Peloponnesian War period and must have carried some weight.[24] But strikingly the distinction between Ionians and Dorians seems to have disappeared from the political discourse of the fourth century.[25] This way of categorizing states was incompatible with the realities of interstate politics after the Peloponnesian War. The century began with Dorian Sparta controlling Ionia and at war with an Athens allied with the Dorian Argos and Corinth. Nor did this ethnic scheme fit subsequent alignments any better. The division into Ionians and Dorians was the tail that could not wag the dog of power politics that determined these alliances and enmities. Thucydides' earlier skepticism about the role of ethnicity was, in part, justified.

Attitudes towards Persia and especially Persian culture were more complex than contempt and hostility and could even include admiration.[26] Nevertheless, the contrast between the Greeks in general and non-Greeks remained strong and provided the basis for Panhellenism, which found its most vehement expression in the fourth century.[27] The full Panhellenic

---

[23] Aeolic solidarity is mentioned in Thuc. 8.100.3.
[24] Skepticism: Thuc. 3.86.4; 6.76.2 (Hermocrates); 7.57. Ethnic appeals: Thuc. 1.95.1, 124.1; 3.86.3; 5.9.1; 6.77.1, 80.2, 82.2; 7.5.4; 8.25.3; countered at 4.61.2–3. Cf. 5.104. On these passages see Roberts 1982: 3, also 5–6, 14.
[25] Hall 2002: 226–7; Saïd 2001: 277–8.
[26] See Hirsch 1985; M. Miller 1997; cf. Long 1986: 161: "In dealing with the foreign, the other, hardly any minds are so small as to be consistent."
[27] On Panhellenism see, e.g., Perlman 1976; Cawkwell 1982; Laforse 1998; Green 1996; Saïd 2001; Hall 2002: 205–20, and Mitchell 2007.

program, as repeatedly propounded by Isocrates, involved peace among Greek cities and a coalition to campaign against the Persian empire, the richest, most conspicuous, and most powerful non-Greek state.[28] Such a program represented the expression of Greek solidarity, on the one hand, and hostility to and superiority over non-Greeks on the other. Some statements to this effect are explicit: "Victories over barbarians require trophies, while those over Greeks demand funeral lamentation."[29] We have seen that Plato condemned wars among Greeks and approved of those against non-Greeks. Oblique evidence confirms the ubiquity of this way of thinking. For example, Alastar Jackson argues that "unease at what was coming to seem brutal and out of place in Panhellenic shrines, namely the commemoration of victories over fellow Greeks by means of armour and weapons stripped from the corpses of the slain" led to a ban of this practice – though such spoils were still dedicated within Greek cities.[30] More sinister, a few passages, concerning towns whose inhabitants were killed, enslaved, or expelled, seem to be trying to palliate this brutal practice by referring to the inhabitants as a mixed population, rather than Greeks.[31]

Most scholars agree on two points in the interpretation of Panhellenism. First, it must have appealed to popular sentiment, or speakers and writers would not have deployed the argument so frequently.[32] Second, it tended to be outweighed or distorted by more concrete considerations, conspicuous among them the mutual enmity of the Greek city-states.[33] As a result Panhellenic appeals could even be twisted to justify the quarrels of Greek states with each other.[34] For example, the Spartans put forward a specious Panhellenic justification of their installation of a puppet government in Thebes.[35] Overall, it is hard to imagine foreign policies more at odds with the ideals of Panhellenism than those actually practiced by Greek city-states through most of the fourth century: they fought each other often and not only never attacked Persia but even vied for Persian acknowledgment of their claims and Persian support of their wars against each other.

---

[28] E.g. Isoc. 4.131–6; 5.119–20, 126; 12.44, 83; *Ep.* 3.3. See also Saïd 2001: 281 on Isoc. 12.163: "he even assimilates this 'most just and necessary war' to 'the war we carry on together with all mankind against the savagery of the wild beasts.'"

[29] Gorgias fr. 84 5b (Diels–Kranz).   [30] Jackson 1991: 228, 247. See also Xen. *Hell.* 3.2.22.

[31] Van Wees 2004: 7 on Xen. *Hell.* 2.1.15; see also Thuc. 3.61.2.

[32] E.g. Perlman 1976: 5; Green 1996: 7; Laforse 1998: 57; note the caveats of Hall 2002: 219. See the survey of the scholarship in Mitchell 2007: xv–xxvi.

[33] E.g. Dunkel 1938: 305; Walbank 1951: 54–6; Saïd 2001: 286; Hall 2002: 207–8. Cf. Dem. 14.12: "But as yet their fear of Persia is subordinate to their feuds with you and, in some cases, with one another."

[34] E.g. Laforse 1998 on Xen. *Hell.* 1.6.12.   [35] Hamilton 1980: 91.

Demosthenes displays contradictory attitudes towards Panhellenism.[36] In *For the Liberty of the Rhodians* he advocates an intervention that might risk a war with the Persians, who had installed an oligarchy in Rhodes. He needs to present the Persians as less formidable than other Athenians feared.[37] He does this mainly with calculations based on power politics and with inferences from probability.[38] He also bases one argument on the inferiority of the Persians: "So, too, the Rhodians are guilty of spurning an equal alliance with Athens, Greeks and their betters, and now are slaves of slaves and barbarians."[39] He also scoffs at the Athenians for fearing Artemisia, who was not only a barbarian, but a woman.[40]

The political context of *On the Navy-Boards* was a furor roused by an action of the Persian king which suggested hostile intention.[41] Although the main aim of Demosthenes' speech is to counsel moderation, he does concede several points to Panhellenistic sentiment. He assumes the superiority of Greek soldiers.[42] He calls the Persian king the "common enemy of all the Greeks."[43] Most apropos of our topic, he argues that, were Greece united, he "should not count it wrong in us to do him [the Persian king] wrong."[44] But Greece was not united and Demosthenes is more inclined to admit this state of affairs than to rail against it as Isocrates did. Rather than peace and unity among the Greeks, Demosthenes seems to think in terms of two types of war, a milder brand within the Greek community and another against the barbarians. For the Athenians in particular, "even when wronged by them [fellow Greeks], it would not be honourable to exact such a penalty from the wrong-doers as to leave them under the heel of the barbarians."[45] There should be limits, it seems, to the enmity among Greek states; subjection of any Greek state to the barbarians is too harsh a fate for the Athenians, the defenders of liberty, to inflict.

Before we investigate the reasons to doubt whether even this limited Panhellenism commanded Demosthenes' full assent, let us consider the predominant ethnic argument in Demosthenes' oratory; for Demosthenes is famous for his opposition to Macedonia and not on account of his sundry statements about Persia. For example, in the *Third Philippic* Demosthenes invokes Hellenic prejudice against Philip and Macedonia:

---

[36] Dunkel 1938.   [37] Dem. 15.5–13.   [38] Dem. 15.10.

[39] Dem. 15.15. The Rhodians are "slaves of a slave" in that Demosthenes considers the Persian satraps slaves; see Missiou 1993.

[40] Dem. 15.23.

[41] Dem. 14.8–9 with Schäfer 1885–7: 1.455–61; Sealey 1993: 128; and Fox 1997: 177–81 for different reconstructions of the historical circumstances of the speech.

[42] Dem. 14.9.   [43] Dem. 14.3, 36.   [44] Dem. 14.37.   [45] Dem. 14.6–7. Cf. Dunkel 1938: 295.

[T]he wrongs which the Greeks suffered from the Lacedaemonians or from us, they suffered at all events at the hands of true-born sons of Greece, and they might have been regarded as the acts of a legitimate son, born to great possessions, who should be guilty of some fault or error in the management of his estate: so far he would deserve blame and reproach, yet it could not be said that it was an unrelated person or not the lawful heir who was acting thus. But if some slave or supposititious child had wasted and squandered what he had no right to, heavens! how much more monstrous and exasperating all would have called it! Yet they have no such qualms about Philip and his present conduct, though he is not only no Greek, nor related to the Greeks, but not even a barbarian from any place that can be named with honor, but a pestilent knave from Macedonia, from which it was never before possible to buy even a decent slave.[46]

Despite a long history of Macedonian claims of heroic descent – from Heracles[47] – Demosthenes here denies Philip any fictive kinship with the Greeks. The comparison of Philip with a slave is a household metaphor, but one that denies rather than affirms connections and thus rules out the possibility of mutual obligation or even accommodation.[48] It enhances the argument based on ethnicity and invokes the full weight of familial stability and hierarchy against him. For a Macedonian to defeat and rule Greek cities was a reversal of the natural and proper order of things, similar to a slave, the lowest person in the household, taking over the patrimony.[49]

Demosthenes often represents Macedonia as the new Persia, an intrinsically hostile, barbarian state threatening Greece. He argues that, in the good old days, Athens distrusted both barbarians and tyrants and thus "Greek power was dreaded by the barbarians, not the barbarian by the Greeks. But that is no longer so."[50] In a similar vein, he claims that during the period of the Athenian empire, the king of Macedonia was subject to Athens, "as a barbarian ought to be subject to Greeks" – not only an ethnocentric statement but a historical distortion.[51] Indeed, any reference to Philip as a *barbaros* served the purpose of arousing feelings of antipathy and outrage against the outsider.[52]

This type of appeal was widespread: both Eubulus and Aeschines reportedly employed it.[53] The *On Halonnesus*, Hyperides' *Funeral Oration*, and

---

[46] Dem. 9.30–1 (trans. modified) with Badian 1982: 42.   [47] Badian 1982; Borza 1995.

[48] See Chapter 5 on household metaphors. See C. Jones 1999 for the force of fictive kinship in ancient diplomacy.

[49] Aristotle, *Rhetoric* (2.9.9–10), describes the resentment aroused by those who have recently prospered.

[50] Dem. 9.45; see also 38–9.   [51] Dem. 3.24.

[52] Hajdú 2002: 275 cites Dem. 3.16; 9.31; 19.305 (quoting Aeschines), 19.308 (others so describe Philip), and 19.327. See also Dem. 3.20, 4.10.

[53] Dem. 19.303–4.

the speech *Against Diondas* also take the tack of representing the Macedonians as the new barbarian menace to Greece.[54] Even after Philip's ascendancy and Alexander's conquest of Persia in the name of Greece, the "Lamian War" against Macedonia was known at the time as the Hellenic War and thus assimilated to other wars by the Greeks against foreign invaders.[55]

Demosthenes claims that Aeschines changed his attitude to Philip as the result of bribery. His account shows the significance of the definition of Philip as barbarian or as a Greek – and that opinions could differ.[56] Before this putative, sinister transformation Aeschines described Philip as "the enemy of all the Greeks," which also was the stereotypical way of condemning the Persian king.[57] In contrast, after his conversion Aeschines supposedly described Philip in glowing terms including the compliment that he was "superlatively Greek" and, perhaps as a consequence, "a great lover of Athens."[58] The reverse of the application of ethnic arguments against Philip was the eventual popularity, even in Athens, that Philip garnered by his announcement that he was going to lead a Panhellenic crusade against Persia.[59]

To a large extent, Demosthenes was playing upon, rather than creating, antipathy against Macedonia as outsiders in the Greek world. In the late fifth century, the Macedonian king Archelaus, a patron of Greek culture, could be mocked in similar terms: Thrasymachus asked "Shall we, being Greeks, be slaves to Archelaus, a barbarian?"[60] This was not just a matter of Athenian prejudice but exemplifies a widespread feeling. Despite attempts by Alexander I, "the Philhellene," and later by Archelaus – with the help of Euripides – to construct a heroic Greek ancestry and Argive connections for the Macedonian ruling house, Greeks remained unpersuaded and Archelaus was not allowed to compete at the Olympic festival.[61] It seems that no Macedonian king before Philip II participated in Panhellenic games. That Philip was able to do so is testimony more to his overwhelming political skills backed by formidable

---

[54] [Dem.] 7.7; Hyp. 6.12; Hyp. *Against Diondas* 4.12–23 and 6.11–18 in Carey *et al.* (2008).

[55] Ashton 1984: 153–4. See also Herrman (forthcoming) on Hyperides 6.5, 12, 20, 37.

[56] Hall 2001: 160–1. [57] See pp. 78–9. [58] Dem. 19.308.

[59] Cawkwell 1978a: 120. On Athenian ambivalence see also Markle 1976 and Hall 2001. One might compare the honors bestowed on Evagoras of Cyprus for his crucial support of Athens early in the fourth century; a fragmentary honorific Athenian decree stresses his services to the Greeks and probably emphasized his own Greekness (RO no. 11 = *IG* ii² 20, lines 12, 17).

[60] Fr. II.85.2 (Diels–Kranz). See Borza 1995 on Archelaus' cultural policies.

[61] Eugene Borza has offered compelling reasons to doubt the story in Herodotus 5.22 that Alexander I competed at the Olympics (1990: 111–12).

military power than to acceptance by the Greeks of his Hellenic ancestry.[62]

Demosthenes went further than merely depicting a new barbarian threat coming from Macedon; he advocated an alliance with Persia. In his later speeches against Philip, Demosthenes not only omits any derogatory references to the Persians, of the type he made in *On the Navy-Boards*, but he explicitly reverses that opinion and condemns the exact phrase he himself had used.[63] He advises the Athenians to " drop the foolish prejudice against the Persians that has so often brought about your discomfiture – "the barbarian," "the common foe of us all," and all such phrases."[64] Demosthenes' definition and condemnation of the barbarian seems to have followed in attendance on two more important considerations in Athenian foreign policy.

First, as we shall see, the amoral pursuit of advantage, Realism, played a large part in Athenian foreign policy. In the *Third Philippic* Demosthenes argues that the Athenians need to appeal to the Persian king "for even his interests are not unaffected if we prevent Philip from subduing the whole country" and he might be "somebody to share your danger and your expenses when the time comes."[65] In the *Fourth Philippic* he repeats the argument: "There is nothing the state needs so much for the upcoming struggle as money."[66] Amoral calculations of interest, albeit defensive rather than imperial, go a long way towards explaining Demosthenes' reversal on Persia – which did open him up to criticism.[67]

Second, action-based criteria also play a role. Demosthenes sums up his position in terms of the ethic of reciprocity: "the man who is wronging both parties should be punished by both in common."[68] Earlier, in *On the Navy-Boards*, Demosthenes emphasized repeatedly that Athens should not start a war with Persia unless and until the king's hostile intentions became clear.[69] In *For the Liberty of the Rhodians* Demosthenes implied that Athens and Persia ought to live by the same rules of interstate conduct.[70] Although wars with non-Greeks sometimes required less justification than those with Greeks, they still required some. Even Alexander and Philip justified their invasion of Persia not just based on a natural enmity between Greeks and Persians, but on grounds of revenge for the Persian invasion of a century

---

[62] Borza 1995: 129.   [63] Dem. 10.31–4 with Hajdú 2002: 254–84.
[64] Dem. 10.33. Hajdú 2002: 275–6; cf. Dem. 14.3, 36.
[65] Dem. 9.71. This passage appears only in the longer version of the *Third Philippic*; see Appendix 1: Speeches and texts.
[66] Dem. 10.31.   [67] Aeschin. 3.257–9.   [68] Dem. 10.33.
[69] Dem. 14.3–5, 10, 35, 38, 41.   [70] Dem. 15.7.

and a half before, for the sake of the gods whose temples the Persians had destroyed, and in retaliation for Persia's recent support of Byzantium and Perinthus against Philip.[71] In India Alexander tried to justify his attacks even against non-Greek people.[72] Panhellenism notwithstanding, Brian Bosworth generalizes:

It seems a coherent stream of thought, transmitted from Herodotus to the early Hellenistic period: invasion and conquest, even of a barbarian people were unjustified, unless there was prior grievance to avenge.[73]

Most historians of ancient international law believe that the "laws of the Greeks" were considered equally binding when it came to relations with non-Greek states.[74] Thus, the killing of Persian ambassadors by the Spartans and Athenians before the Persian Wars was contrary to law; it incurred divine wrath and required recompense.[75] These attitudes were reflected in diplomatic practice. The Second Athenian League was open to non-Greeks – some of whom actually joined it – and treaties on equal terms between Greeks and non-Greeks are known.[76]

Ethnicity could play a part in Athenian foreign policy decisions, but its application was malleable, tended to follow upon calculations of interest, and was often subordinated to action-based considerations.

RELIGION

Greek polytheism did not require persecution of those who believed in other gods; if another state worshipped gods different than those of Athens, that was its business and no affront to Athens' gods. Greeks tended to assimilate foreign gods to their own: thus, for example, Herodotus says "Amun is the Egyptian word for Zeus."[77] Among the Greeks, even if certain gods were patrons of certain cities – as Athena was for Athens – most cities worshipped basically the same pantheon. These characteristics of Greek religion largely ruled out the possibility of religious wars, in the sense of a war whose purpose is to fight people and states who follow another religion. It does not follow, however, that the gods were of no importance in Greek thinking. In recent decades historians have explored the central role of religion in

---

[71] Bosworth 1996: 145.   [72] Bosworth 1996: 147.   [73] Bosworth 1996: 151.
[74] Phillipson 1911: 1.31; Adcock and Mosley 1975: 146.   [75] Hdt. 7.133–7.
[76] See *IG* ii² 43, lines 16–19 = RO no. 22. Alcetas, king of the Molossi, was a signatory. See also Cargill 1981: 36.
[77] E.g. Hdt. 2.42.

the life of the classical period and, accordingly, to war and the relations of states.[78]

First of all, the support of the gods was particularly important to a city contemplating or engaged in war: the *Rhetoric to Alexander* advises pro-war speakers to stress the favor of the gods for their side.[79] And, indeed, they do appear in our assembly speeches. Demosthenes and Aeschines pepper their speeches with pious interjections: "May the Gods of the city punish Philip" and "May all the Gods forbid that my warning should ever be brought to the sternest test."[80] On a number of occasions, Demosthenes takes it as given that the gods have a particular concern for Athens and take its side in war – if only the Athenians do their part.[81] This sense of divine favor did not of course prevent the Athenians from doing whatever they could to ensure divine support and to avoid alienating any gods. Such precautions might involve vows and the consultation of oracles.[82] It was also important to follow traditional ritual practices: Aeschines accuses Demosthenes of holding an assembly about the proposed Peace of Philocrates on a festival day, an unprecedented action.[83] In *Against Ctesiphon*, after depicting Demosthenes as immorally and insanely suppressing the last attempts to settle matters peacefully, Aeschines claims that Demosthenes ignored unfavorable omens before the campaign that led to the defeat at Chaeronea.[84] Aeschines hoped that the bad omens would be taken by the jury to reveal divine disapproval of Demosthenes' belligerence and that his refusal to take heed of them would be considered impious as well as catastrophic.

The unity of Greek religion was an important aspect of that ethnic identity that added impetus to the condemnation of wars among Greek states.[85] Common reverence for the gods was usually strong enough to ensure that the sacred truces for the Panhellenic games were respected even in times of war.[86] In contrast, the destruction of temples during the Persian invasion was long remembered and provided Alexander with an excuse for his invasion of the Persian empire. Similar claims also figured in anti-Macedonian rhetoric designed to justify the Lamian War: Hyperides in his *Funeral Oration* twice describes Macedonian crimes against the gods

---

[78] On religion in war see Pritchett 1971–91: 1.93–126, IV.94–260; Goodman and Holladay 1986; Jackson 1991; Jameson 1991; Parker 2000.

[79] [Arist.] *Rh. Al.* 2.1425a18–28.   [80] E.g. Dem. 3.26; 10.11; 16.2.

[81] E.g. Dem. 1.10–11; 2.22–3; 3.18; 4.45.   [82] Goodman and Holladay 1986: 152; Jackson 1991: 238–9.

[83] Aeschin. 3.67; there was a festival to Asclepius and the *proagōn* for the Great Dionysia (Richardson 1889: 90).

[84] Aeschin. 3.152.   [85] Hdt. 8.144.2; Ar. *Lys.* 1129–32; Thuc. 3.59.2. See also pp. 79, 246–7.

[86] E.g. Isoc. 4.43; Hornblower 1992: 170–1, 192–4 on Olympia and Delphi. For Isthmian games, see Thucydides 8.9.1, 10.1.

including the deification of Alexander.[87] He presents the prevention of such sacrilege as an accomplishment of the army whose dead he is honoring.

The number of "Sacred Wars" over control of the sanctuary of Apollo at Delphi is only the most conspicuous sign of the intersection of religion and interstate politics within the Greek world.[88] States possessed long-standing relations with certain gods or with certain festivals and sanctuaries. Part of how a state was or ought to be treated derived from such religious claims or lack thereof. Simon Hornblower summarizes Athens' three main assets in this religious politics: Theseus, an Athenian hero with a wide reputation, control of Eleusis, its mysteries and mythical connection with the origin of agriculture, and Athens' role as the mother city of the Ionians.[89] The cult of Theseus played a role in justifying Athens' seizure of Scyros around 475, since Theseus had been murdered there and his body needed to be brought back to Athens – among other justifications.[90] Stories about Theseus also contributed to Athenian self-conceptions and especially their view of themselves as defenders of the weak and wronged.[91] The Eleusinian mysteries enjoyed participation from throughout the Greek world and thus required the pronouncement of a sacred truce.[92] Nevertheless, the mysteries could not compete with the great festivals at Delphi and Olympia. Ionian ethnicity was connected with different cult practices and thus was also involved in palliating Athenian imperialism in the fifth century – since Athens claimed to be the mother-city of all the Ionian cities.[93] Ionian cult practices must have continued, but the implications for Athenian foreign relations had largely disappeared along with the empire and the concern for Ionian or Dorian descent in general. All in all, Hornblower is correct that "the religious cards Athens had to play . . . were not very good ones."[94] Unlike other important cities Athens had no Panhellenic sanctuary nearby; more detrimental, Athens had an ambivalent relationship with the Delphic oracle.

The Delphic oracle, through which Apollo's foreknowledge and will were ascertained, was of great importance in the relations of Greek states for two reasons. First the oracle gave responses to the questions asked of it, some of which concerned the proper behavior of states and even whether they should go to war. Although any city could convince itself of divine favor – as Athens did – the verdict of the god that commanded the most

[87] Hyp. 6.21–2, 43.   [88] Bowden 2005: 134–51.   [89] Hornblower 1992: 184–6.
[90] Plut. *Cim.* 8.5–6 (cf. Thuc. 1.98.2) with Podlecki 1971.   [91] See pp. 177–80.
[92] *IG* i³ 6 = Fornara 1983: no. 75b; *IG* i³ 78, lines 30–5, 44–7 = Fornara 1983: no. 140; Ha no. 54 = RO no. 35; [Dem.] 59.21.
[93] Barron 1964; Hornblower 1992: 182.   [94] Hornblower 1992: 184.

respect among the society of Greek cities was that of Delphi. Second, disputes about control of the sanctuary sometimes embroiled Greece in warfare.[95] These might impinge on the content of oracular responses and thus their political impact, since the God seem to regard with favor the parties in control of its sanctuary.

In many matters and at many times, Athenians, both individually and collectively, turned to Delphi without hesitation as the best conduit to the gods. As a state, Athens enjoyed a long-standing bond and position of influence at Delphi.[96] Hugh Bowden's recent treatment of the subject focuses on the positive aspects of Athens' relationship with Delphi.[97] But Athens had an ambivalent relationship with the Delphic oracle both earlier during the period of the Peloponnesian War and during its conflicts with Philip. It was other states, Athens' enemies, who could invoke Delphic oracles as evidence of the god's approbation of their foreign policies. This may have contributed to a muting of religious concerns in two of our most important sources for Athenian foreign policy: Thucydides and Demosthenes.

On the eve of the Peloponnesian War the Delphic oracle strongly supported Sparta and endorsed Sparta's decision to go to war with Athens. Apollo promised to take Sparta's side himself, a promise that some thought was redeemed when the plague struck Athens.[98] This oracle evoked hostility and suspicion at Athens.[99] This context may explain in part Thucydides' relative neglect of religion, something usually attributed to his intellectual background or interpreted as an idiosyncrasy.[100]

Bad feelings between Athens and the Amphictyonic Council, which governed Delphi, were also prominent during the career of Demosthenes. Largely out of enmity with Thebes, Athens took the side of the Phocians against the Thebans and most of the Amphictyons in the Third Sacred War of 356–346.[101] The Phocians were only able to maintain their struggle by melting down some of the treasures at Delphi and hiring mercenaries.[102] As a result, they were widely regarded as guilty of sacrilege. Thus, in the war against Phocis, Philip was able to pose as the defender of the god: for example, he had his soldiers put on wreaths of laurel, Apollo's tree, before

---

[95] See Bowden 2005: 109–33 on the wide variety of questions that might be put to the oracle.

[96] Parker 2005: 80.

[97] Bowden 2005: his index of passages does not include Plut. *Nic.* 13.5–6; Dem. 5.25; Aeschin. 3.130; and Plut. *Dem.* 20.1, the most important passages showing Athenian ambivalence towards Delphi.

[98] Thuc. 1.118.3 (cf. 1.123.1–2); 2.54.4–5. On the historical background to this partiality see Hornblower 1991–2009: 1.181–3 on Thuc. 1.112.5.

[99] For Athenian reactions see Jordan 1986: 126; Thuc. 5.32.1 with C. Powell 1979: 28; Plut. *Nic.* 13.4. On the evidence from Tragedy see B. Knox 1957: 169, 181 and Mikalson 1991: 114.

[100] E.g. Hornblower 1992. [101] Buckler 1989: 27. [102] Buckler 1989: 38.

one battle and had the prisoners he took thrown off a cliff and drowned as temple-robbers.[103] But Phocis had been Athens' ally and Athens did not accept the Macedonian and Delphian account of a "Sacred War" on behalf of Apollo against a sacrilegious Phocis – with Philip cast as the leading crusader. Rather the contemporary Athenian name for the war was the Phocian War.[104] Demosthenes regarded with horror the defeat of Athens' ally.[105] Aeschines, in contrast, described the Phocians as ruled by tyrants who were guilty of seizing the sacred treasures. He believed that Phocis' policy was wrong but even he made a distinction in favor of the innocent common people.[106]

Even before the defeat of Phocis, Philip controlled Thessaly, which traditionally had dominated the Amphictyonic Council. One result of the Sacred War was that Philip himself was given a seat with two votes on the Amphictyonic Council in the place of Phocis.[107] An Amphictyonic Council and Delphic oracle dominated by Philip II and his allies was anathema to Athenians such as Demosthenes, who were convinced that Philip was their mortal enemy. Philip also presided over the Pythian games in 346, an honor confirming his self-representation as the oracle's savior.[108] In protest, Athens declined, for the first time ever, to send a delegation to the Pythian games in 346.[109] Demosthenes adds that the Athenians "refused participation in the doings of the Amphictyonic Council" and regarded Philip as acting impiously.[110]

It is not certain what mechanisms would have allowed Philip to influence the responses of the Pythia, but earlier reports of corruption of the oracle made suspicions plausible, especially at Athens.[111] We possess three references to Demosthenes casting aspersions at Delphi during this period. First, in *On the Peace* he argues that Athens should not go to war "over the shadow in Delphi," a puzzling but certainly disrespectful reference to Apollo's ancient and true oracle and the venerable council overseeing it.[112] Second, Aeschines claims that Demosthenes accused the Pythia of going over to Philip and that he used the term *Philippizein* of the oracle. This was a derogatory word constructed on the model of *Medizein*, the term applied to Greek states who aided the "Medes" during the Persian invasion.[113] Third, Plutarch repeats this story and seems to know additional details:

In consequence he [Demosthenes] would not allow his countrymen to pay attention to the oracles or listen to the prophecies. Indeed he even suspected that the

[103] Buckler 1989: 75; Buckler 1996: 81–2; Pownall 1998: 45–6. See also Aeschin. 2.142.
[104] Pownall 1998: 39.   [105] See pp. 191–2.   [106] Aeschin. 2.117, 131, 142. See also Dem. 18.18.
[107] Diod. 16.60.   [108] Diod. 16.60.2; cf. Dem. 5.22.   [109] Dem. 19.128.   [110] Dem. 19.132.
[111] E.g. Hdt. 5.90; 6.123.   [112] Dem. 5.25 with Sandys 1900: 107–8.   [113] Aeschin. 3.130.

Pythian priestess was on the side of Philip, and he reminded the Thebans of the example of Epaminondas and the Athenians of Pericles, both of whom acted only on the promptings of reason and regarded prophecies of this kind as mere pretexts for faint-heartedness.[114]

In the Sacred or Phocion War, Demosthenes' Athens was on the side of a tyrannical regime generally regarded as guilty of sacrilege; in the second war, it was contending with a Delphi and an Amphictyonic Council firmly under Philip's thumb – which was to invite him into southern Greece in 339.[115] It is no wonder that Demosthenes did not want the Athenians listening to prophecies from Delphi.

But Athens was ambivalent and not simply hostile. We know about Demosthenes' claim that the Pythia was Philippizing from Aeschines, who must have thought that the jury would hold Demosthenes' impious slurs against him. For his part, Demosthenes only bothered to rail against oracles in the first place because these favored reconciliation with Philip *and* carried some clout in Athens. These caveats notwithstanding, in two crucial periods, the Peloponnesian War and the struggle with Philip, the oracle of Apollo at Delphi seemed to be aligned with Athens' enemies. This may explain in part why Thucydides and Demosthenes, neither of whom wanted to regard Athens as engaging in impious warfare, tended not to emphasize religious justifications for war. In their time, this type of religious argument – the gods of all the Greeks favor our cause – was not a persuasive one and thus not a congenial area of emphasis.

The present discussion of the relationship of Athens and Delphi has strayed from status-based arguments. That is because religious politics were not simply a matter of static alignments and connections such as Hornblower describes for Athens. The gods not only had relatives and favorites; they also judged actions and held political opinions: in the eyes of the Greek world Philip had no particular claims on the Olympians until he and his army became Apollo's benefactors.

POLITICAL SYSTEMS

Athens was a democracy. We occasionally find statements to the effect that its natural friends were other democracies and that oligarchies and monarchies were its natural enemies. But Athens' actual foreign policy

---

[114] Plut. *Dem.* 20.1.
[115] The Amphictyonic invitation was obviously a pretext for Philip to march on Athens – and, as it turned out, Thebes – so the resulting war was never referred to as a Sacred War in antiquity (Pownall 1998: 54).

often took little account of other states' political systems. Intervention in another state's internal politics, a possible consequence of a status-based worldview in which democracies, oligarchies, and monarchies are naturally opposed to one other, occurred occasionally. But such interference was often condemned and always required special justification.[116] These justifications included the desirability of overthrowing tyrannies and the need to counter previous interference or injustice within a state. Both the need to justify intervention and these two types of justification find close parallels in modern thinking.

The fifth-century Athenian empire tended to support democracies and its Spartan enemies favored oligarchies.[117] Sparta's behavior after its victory in the Peloponnesian War and after the King's Peace of 387/6 made its interventionist tendencies conspicuous and unpopular. The situation in the mid fourth century was much less clear. When Aristotle wants to give examples of states that impose their own form of government on other states, he hearkens back to the fifth-century rivalry between the Athenians and the Lacedaemonians rather than mentioning the Thebans or the Athenians of his own time.[118] These seem not to have provided as many or as clear-cut examples. Indeed the Decree of Aristoteles guaranteed that the allies in the Second Athenian League would enjoy constitutional arrangements of their choosing, likely an assurance that the imperialistic practices of Athens and Sparta would not be repeated. Athens generally abided by this promise.[119]

The notion that Athens should favor democracies or that democracies and oligarchies were intrinsically opposed did not disappear altogether.[120] In a couple of passages Isocrates mentions or praises the fifth-century empire's policy of supporting democracy.[121] More important, Demosthenes' speech *On the Liberty of the Rhodians* revolves around this very issue. Several points about this speech deserve emphasis.[122]

First, Demosthenes depicts a world in which democracies may fight each other, but their enmity is never as essential or bitter as that between

---

[116] Walzer 1977: 86–108.

[117] For an entrée into the bibliography on this complex and controversial subject see Rhodes 2007: esp. 27 n. 22, 33 and Hornblower 1991–2009: I.437–8 on Thuc. 3.47.1.

[118] Arist. *Pol.* 5.1307b20–4 with Newman 1887–1902: IV.378–9; Schütrumpf 1991–2005: III.519; *pace* Cawkwell 1981: 48; cf. Arist. *Pol.* 4.1296a32–6.

[119] Cargill 1981: 141–2 on lines 20–1 of the decree of Aristoteles; an Athenian force under Chares did intervene in civil strife in Corcyra (Diod. 15.95.3), which may or may not have been a league member.

[120] MacMullen 1963: 121; Cawkwell 1981: 48.   [121] Isoc. 4.16, 105; 12.54.

[122] See Fox 1997: 177–81 on the historical background of the speech.

oligarchies and democracies.[123] He also argues that Athenian activity in favor of democracy in Rhodes will gain it the favor of democracies everywhere.[124] This worldview provides the justification for Demosthenes' exhortation that the Athenians should assist some Rhodian exiles to re-establish a democracy there.

Second, his proposed intervention was not unprovoked; the Persian satrap Mausolus had already intervened in Rhodes to establish an oligarchy. Thus Demosthenes aims to save the Rhodians from their enslavement to Persia as well as from oligarchy.[125] So, too, Demosthenes holds up for emulation the example of Argos' support of Athens when the democracy had been abolished and the Thirty were ruling with Sparta's support.[126] In both cases Demosthenes approves counter-intervention, to use the modern term, to restore democracy after another power has already interfered in a state's political system. As in modern just-war theory, this seems to have been one of the circumstances in which intervention in another state's politics could be justified.[127]

Finally, Demosthenes repeatedly evokes a threat to Athens' own democracy:

I am surprised that none of you conceives that our constitution too is in danger, nor draws the conclusion that if all other states are organized on oligarchic principles, it is impossible that they should leave your democracy alone.[128]

In its emphasis on self-defense against oligarchy this passage seems less aggressive than his earlier argument for the intrinsic and irreconcilable hostility of democracies and oligarchies. Instead of George Kennan's analysis of Soviet motivation – "the innate antagonism between capitalism and socialism . . . has become imbedded in foundations of Soviet power" – we see something more like Woodrow Wilson's goal of making the "world safe for democracy."[129] Just as important is Demosthenes' rhetorical purpose: this last appeal makes an issue that might have seemed distant and unimportant to most Athenians – how Rhodes was governed – vital to Athens' own system of government and freedom. In this respect, his argument is similar to the various expansions of the argument of self-defense that

[123] Dem. 15.17. See also [Dem.] 13.8–9.   [124] Dem. 15.4.
[125] Dem. 15.3, 4, 14, 15, 16. See also Dem. *Exordia* 37.2.
[126] Dem. 15.22–3.   [127] Walzer 1977: 96–101.
[128] Dem. 15.19; see also 15.21, a reference to the possibility of the Athenian democracy requiring succor in turn.
[129] Kennan 1947: 572; cf. Mao Zedong: "All counter-revolutionary wars are unjust, all revolutionary wars are just"; Knock 1992: 121 (Wilson).

will concern us below.[130] Demosthenes' appeal seems to have failed; the Athenians did not try to intervene in Rhodes.

Demosthenes deployed similar arguments in several of his speeches against Philip. In these passages he posits an intractable enmity between tyranny – as he describes Philip's rule – and democracy.[131] Again, he emphasizes the threat to Athens' democracy that Philip poses.[132] Indeed, he repeatedly accuses Philip of forcible intervention in the internal politics of other Greek states. These are often described as the imposition of tyrannies, making Philip's crime a double one: he intervenes in other states' internal affairs and he sets up tyrannies.[133] Philip's interventions became a central pillar of Demosthenes' case against him especially in the *Third Philippic*.[134] This strand of Demosthenes' rhetoric was probably successful or, more precisely, was hardly necessary given Philip's actions. Philip's interventions seem to have alienated Greek opinion against him; at least two scholars attribute the diplomatic successes of Athens in the late 340s – alliances with Corinth, Corcyra, Messenia, and Megalopolis – to the increasing suspicion with which Philip was regarded.[135] The author of *On the Treaty with Alexander* makes similar accusations about Alexander's overthrow of democracies and support of tyrannies in a less successful bid to convince the Athenians to make war against Macedonia.[136]

These condemnations of Macedonia were in line with Greek thinking in general. Passages that condemn states for intervening in another state's affairs are common. Praise for refraining from doing this can also be found. The imposition or support of tyranny was regarded as particularly bad and intervention in favor of democracy might receive a special dispensation at Athens, but the concern about intervention as an infringement of state sovereignty was general.

Already Thucydides represents Brasidas aiming to win over Acanthus by promising not to intervene in their internal affairs:

> I have not come to side with factions, nor is it my practice to bring a dubious freedom, as I would if I disregarded ancestral institutions and enslaved the majority to the few or the minority to everyone. That would be harsher than alien rule, and for us Lacedaemonians it would not bring about thanks in return for toil, but blame instead of honor and glory . . . [137]

This policy helped Brasidas win over other cities. Xenophon portrays Timotheus as taking a similar line in Corcyra and with similar results: "he

---

[130] Pp. 150–3.   [131] Dem. 1.5–6; 9.38–9. See Leopold 1981.
[132] Dem. 6.24–5; 8.40–3; 10.11, 13.   [133] Dem. 6.22; 8.36; 9.26–7, 33, 57–8; 10.4, 10; 18.65, 71.
[134] Leopold 1981: 240–1.   [135] Brunt 1969: 260; Markle 1981: 72–6.
[136] [Dem.] 17.3–5, 10–11, 14, 15–16.   [137] Thuc. 4.86.4–5.

did not, however, enslave the inhabitants or banish individuals or change the government. As a result of this he made all the states in that region more favourably inclined to him."[138] When Agesilaus attacked Phlius in order to assert the rights of some exiles, he needed to defend his action – "he was not taking the field to do wrong, but to aid those who were suffering wrong." Nevertheless, he was criticized by Lacedaemonians themselves for alienating a significant city for the sake of a few men.[139]

Demosthenes reports a specious justification of Philip's establishment of a tyranny at Oreus:

he informed those poor wretches, the people of Oreus, that he had sent his soldiers to pay them a visit of sympathy in all goodwill, for he understood that they were suffering from acute internal trouble and it was the duty of true friends and allies to be at their side on such occasions.[140]

Demosthenes assumes that Philip's action, to send soldiers to a state in stasis, was intrinsically hostile and thus his hypocrisy manifest. The point of the passage was that Athens could not afford to wait until such a liar as Philip declared his hostile intentions towards it.

Treaties between large and small states often specified non-intervention. They guaranteed that existing constitutions would be preserved or that states could choose their own political system: "Interference of some sort in the domestic politics of the allied city was undoubtedly a widely feared consequence of an alliance with a leading state . . . "[141] So the Decree of Aristoteles assured each ally joining the league that it may continue "governing itself, according to the constitution which it prefers."[142] Although this was probably already implicit in the treaty's guarantee of *autonomia*, the decree's drafters wanted to assure prospective allies with a more concrete and less malleable assurance that their domestic arrangements were to be free from interference.[143] Parallels can be found in bilateral Athenian treaties.[144] So too the treaty regulating Philip's relations with the Greek cities after Chaeronea is quoted verbatim in Pseudo-Demosthenes, *On the Treaty with Alexander*:

---

[138] Xen. *Hell.* 5.4.64.   [139] Xen. *Hell.* 5.3.14, 3.16.

[140] Dem. 9.12; cf. Dem. 9.33. Elsewhere Demosthenes represents this as an attack against Oreos (8.59).

[141] Ryder 1965: 24.

[142] Cargill 1981: 19 translation (modified) of lines 20–1 of *IG* ii² 43 = RO no. 22.

[143] For brief recent surveys with bibliography on the meaning and political uses of *autonomia* see Sealey 1993: 241–4 and Low 2007: 187–99. Interference in a city's politics was contrary to virtually any conception of *autonomia* (e.g. Xen. *Hell.* 6.3.8; Karavites 1982b: 158; contra Low 2007: 198–9).

[144] *IG* i³ 118, lines 10–12: "[and the Selym]brians [shall establish] their constitution [autonomously in] whatever [fashion they] may know [(to be best) . . . " (Treaty between Athens and Selymbria, 407 BC; trans. Fornara 1983: no. 162). The restorations, bracketed, are uncontroversial.

If any of the parties shall overthrow the constitution established in the several states at the date when they took the oaths to observe the peace, they shall be treated as enemies by all the parties to the peace[145]

Although Athens had a preference for democracy in its foreign policy, other Greek states possessed a variety of forms of government. What they generally wanted and were assured of in many treaties was that no outside party would intervene in their internal affairs. Although not formalized and defined as state sovereignty – as in modern international law – the general desire for self-determination had the same roots and consequences.

The parties to one Athenian treaty promised a more active version of this, to assist in restoring the *status quo ante* in the event of the overthrow of the constitution. The terms of this treaty do not favor any particular type of constitution, but rather call for counter-intervention whether an oligarchy is set up in Athens, or somebody attacks the sovereign demos of Phlius, or destroys the constitution of Elis, Arcadia, or Achaea.[146] These latter constitutions seem not to have been democracies, since the treaty does not use the term demos as it does of the Athenians and Phlians.[147] Unlike our evidence from oratory and history, which often conflates the condemnation of intervention and of tyranny – or less frequently, oligarchy – treaties are more careful in excluding intervention in any existing constitution whatsoever.

Polly Low has recently treated Greek attitudes towards intervention at length.[148] Low holds that several intersecting norms dominated Greek thinking about intervention: Greeks approved of aid to those suffering injustice; they believed that "political ideology is the crucial factor in determining the legitimacy of any act of intervention"; they possessed a "fluid ideal of *autonomia*."[149]

First, intervention could certainly be justified on the basis of aiding those suffering injustice, as we have seen, in Demosthenes' proposal to "save the Rhodians" and Agesilaus' claim that he was on campaign "to aid those who were suffering wrong."

Second, in terms of political ideology, intervention to free a city from an oppressive government was generally approved. Tyranny was almost

---

[145] [Dem.] 17.10. The earlier mention of this clause (6) adds that all parties should campaign against the wrong-doer, but it is unclear whether that is an additional treaty clause or merely the speaker's elaboration of the requirement to "treat as enemies."

[146] *IG* ii² 112, lines 24–34 = RO no. 41; cf. *IG* ii² 116, lines 14–30 = RO no. 44.

[147] See Rhodes and Osborne 2003: 213.

[148] Low 2007: 175–211. Although I shall be highlighting our disagreements, I have benefited greatly from her research and we have reached similar conclusions on several main tendencies.

[149] Low 2007: 210.

everywhere so regarded.[150] Indeed, any monarchy was liable to be described as a tyranny by its enemies. Whether this carried conviction depended on the particular case and audience. At Athens oligarchies could also be considered oppressive. Political ideology was certainly important.

Third, Low emphasizes how malleable the term *autonomia* could be, which is true enough. But – and here we begin to diverge – the desire of most Greek states to decide on their own form of government is crystal clear nonetheless. The consequent general disapproval of states that interfere in another state's political system and the attractiveness of promises not to do this follow from this basic preference. Widespread judgments about the relative legitimacy of different forms of government were in conflict with a vivid awareness of the mischief that powerful states could do if they were granted the right to intervene whenever a few exiles cried tyranny. Low summarizes modern thinking about intervention in a similar way: "How can the preservation of the sovereignty of the nation-state be made consistent with the responsibility of the international community to defend human rights within those states?"[151] But Low claims that "Modern international law . . . operates with a norm of non-intervention" but "almost the exact opposite was the case in the Greek world."[152] How can what seems to me to be identity look like opposition to Low?

We differ both in our evaluation of ancient thinking and in our comparison with modern thinking. When it comes to the ancient world, Low places more emphasis on the rhetoric of fighting tyranny and oligarchy and suggests that this concern outweighs the disapproval of intervention, of which she is certainly aware.[153] I believe that the prohibition of intervention in treaties of alliance and widespread condemnation of interference in other states' internal affairs show that the two values, the overthrow of bad governments and the right of self-determination, were in conflict in ancient Greece as today.

To turn to the contrast between ancient and modern thinking, Low's argument for a "strong tradition of positive representation of intervention in classical sources" depends on a broad definition of intervention: "the interference by one state . . . in the quarrels of one or more other states (whether in an internal stasis, or in a bi- or multilateral conflict)"[154] This

---

[150] On tyrannies see Low 2007: 183 and, e.g., Xen. *Hell.* 6.5.33–4; Isoc. 4.125; [Dem.] 17.7. Tyrannies often depended on mercenaries or foreign troops, the use of whom would have made their unpopularity clear.

[151] Low 2007: 187.   [152] Low 2007:177–8.

[153] Awareness: Low 2007: 195–6, 205, 206–7.   [154] Low 2007: 178, 175.

definition, which I shall denote *intervention (general)*, includes any participation in a war between other states. This definition is much broader than the definition of intervention used in international relations theory, international law, or secular just war theory, all of which specify interference in another state's internal politics, that is *intervention (internal)*.[155] Low's broad definition allows her to cite all references to when Athenians enter a war to correct injustice as evidence for the "positive representation of intervention."[156] But such cases of intervention (general) cannot tell us anything about the type of intervention (internal) that is problematic to modern and, as I believe, ancient observers: interference in another state's internal politics. She ends up with a false contrast between ancient norms which often favor intervention (general) and modern norms which regard intervention (internal) as problematic and requiring justification.

In fact, modern just war theory and international law permit and even valorize assistance to states suffering aggression at the hands of other states – just as in Low's example from Lysias' *Funeral Oration*. For example, in *Just and Unjust Wars*, Michael Walzer argues as follows:

Aggression justifies two kinds of violent response: a war of self-defense by the victim and a war of law enforcement by the victim and any other member of international society ... As in domestic society, the obligations of bystanders are not easy to make out, but it is the tendency of the theory to undermine the right of neutrality and to require widespread participation in the business of law enforcement.[157]

Many modern nations are often quite openly and unambiguously proud of wars they fought for the sake of a state suffering external attack – for Belgium (WWI) or Poland (WWII) or Kuwait (The Gulf War) to take some British examples. Many expressions of this pride – for example, in the United States' self-representation of its mission in the world – would seem perfectly at home in an Athenian funeral oration. On the other hand, intervention in another state's internal affairs always requires special justification.

---

[155] Low 2007: 175 n. 1 cites, but does not adopt, a standard modern definition involving "the conscious aim of changing or preserving the structure of political authority in the target state." She also slips (187) into the standard definition when she argues that a major difficulty in modern views of intervention is "the perceived incompatibility between acts of intervention and a commitment to the inviolable sovereignty of the autonomous nation-state" – a difficulty that only has relevance to internal interference, i.e. the normal definition of intervention.

[156] For example, not a single one of her examples from the funeral oration of Lysias involves intervention in a state's internal affairs (Low 2007: 179–81).

[157] Walzer 1977: 62.

The real distinction between ancient and modern thinking is the systematization and elaboration of the latter. We have a technical term, intervention, to describe the problematic case when aiding the unjustly treated that may conflict with respecting a state's internal arrangements. The Greeks did not, but they shared with us the same basic conflicting sentiments – that aiding the unjustly treated and respecting a state's internal arrangements are both desirable.

HIERARCHY

The most basic and irremediable reason for a hierarchical conception of states is that states are not equal. Robert Tucker sums up:

In their physical extent, population, natural resources, and geographical position, states are, as it were, born unequal; so much so, indeed, that by comparison the natural inequalities among individuals appear almost marginal.[158]

Although Greek city-states may all appear small by modern standards, their size and power spanned a huge range: for example, the population of the largest state, Athens, was well over a hundred times that of a small city state.[159] Since the interstate realm does not enjoy a system of enforceable law, states treat others and they themselves are treated in ways that reflect their differences in power.[160] Although many systems of law grant equal rights to rich and poor, the only equality in the interstate realm is that all sovereign states have recourse to self-help – little consolation to the weak, who cannot help themselves.

Balancing behavior offers the possibility of reducing the consequences of inequality among states. As we shall see, larger Greek states were always worried that another state might gain too much power and threaten them. They tended to *balance* by making alliances against their most threatening rivals.[161] As a result, a small Greek state, threatened by a large and aggressive neighbor, could call for assistance from a rival of that neighbor. There are plenty of cases where this tactic allowed a weaker state to hold its own against a strong and aggressive neighbor: for example, during several long periods the cities of Boeotia asserted their independence from Thebes. The tendency, especially in the fourth century, for Greek states to balance was

---

[158] Tucker 1977: 3.
[159] Compare the average population of Category I (small) city-states as per Hansen 2006: 24 and his estimate of an Athenian population of 100,000 plus metics and slaves in Hansen 1991: 93.
[160] Carr 1946: 166. Tucker 1977: e.g. 3, 14 makes the same observation.
[161] See pp. 168–80.

one of the main reasons why the Greek world was not as hierarchical as the considerations cited above might suggest. Indeed, balancing helps to explain the continued coexistence of so many different states, large and small.

Three considerations limited the effectiveness of balancing in this regard.[162] First and most obvious, a threatened small state might or might not obtain powerful assistance. The possibility might give pause to a coercive and powerful state. From the point of view of the weak, this hope was not nearly as good as actually being powerful and not needing assistance. Second, rival states might make a deal among themselves to allow "equal aggrandizement," to use the modern term, against the weak. Aggression by one large state would then be balanced by aggression by another, rather than by defense of the weak.[163] Something like this seems to have been behind the notorious deal with Philip, by which Athens hoped to gain control of Amphipolis in return for allowing Philip to capture Pydna.[164] Third, the encroachments and demands of a more powerful ally could be as contrary to equality as simple aggression. Such impositions were not inevitable or irremediable, as we shall see. But, again, even assurances from a powerful ally were not the same as not needing the ally.

Thus, the egalitarian effect of balancing notwithstanding, Greek states must be regarded as intrinsically unequal. The next question is whether different norms applied to states depending on whether they were powerful and prestigious or weak and humble. If some sort of code existed that allowed more leeway to the powerful and required deference of the weak, then we could say that norms valorized and justified differences in power among states. I will be calling such a way of thinking hierarchical. If no such code existed and contrary ways of thinking were dominant, then we would need to set Greek interstate morality in opposition to the inherent inequality of states and consider the question of whether it acted as an effective check on the expression of differential power among states. It turns out that there are aspects of Greek thinking that valorize and others that denigrate hierarchy among states. In my view, recent works by scholars such as J. E. Lendon and Hans van Wees tend to exaggerate the hierarchical aspect of Greek interstate norms and to play down the egalitarian ethos that I regard as the dominant strain in Greek thinking. But, before confronting their arguments directly, it will be useful to preview how the different ways of thinking we shall consider in detail in later chapters, depending

---

[162] Tucker 1977: 6–7, 10 and *passim*.   [163] See Tucker 1977: 7 for modern cases.
[164] Dem. 2.6 with Theopompus (*FGrH* 115 F 30a, 30b). Compare the suspicions of other cities when Sparta and Athens allied during the Peace of Nicias (Thuc. 5.27).

on different domestic analogies, impacted on the issue of hierarchy versus egalitarianism. Three of these were most important: legalistic thinking, the code of reciprocity, and the use of the slave metaphor.

First, in his seminal work on international law Emeric de Vattel famously argued that "Power or weakness does not . . . produce any difference. A dwarf is as much a man as a giant; a small republic is no less a sovereign state than the most powerful kingdom."[165] Vattel's argument for the equality of states in international law has the consequence that "what is permitted to one nation is permitted to all; and what is not permitted to one is not permitted to any other."[166] The Athenian application of legalistic thinking to states had in the main the same consequences. In Athens the rich, educated, and high-born, just like the poor tradesman, were judged by large juries based on the same written laws on an equal basis. Wealth provided advantages in court – as it did in Vattel's day – not least the opportunity to hire a professional speech-writer; but the wealthy complained that juries were hostile to them, and we can occasionally detect forensic arguments based on class resentment directed at the rich.[167] Regardless of the extent to which such considerations complicated Athenian legal practice, the ideal of Athenian law was egalitarian – though one must add the proviso, among male citizens.[168] Pericles' funeral oration in Thucydides puts this succinctly: "there are equal rights for all in private disputes in accordance with the laws . . . "[169] Parallels to this statement abound.[170] The laws governing the democratic government of Athens were also egalitarian. In *For the Liberty of the Rhodians* Demosthenes castigates oligarchs for their desire to rule rather than choosing to live on equal terms as democrats do.[171] Even Isocrates, hardly a populist, takes this democratic position. He connects the egalitarian ideal within Athens with the proper conduct of states: "it is not just for the stronger to rule over the weaker [among states], even as we recognize it in the nature of the polity which has been established amongst

---

[165] Vattel 1793: liv, section 18; see also Dickinson 1920: 29–31: "the analogy between natural persons and the state."

[166] Vattel 1793: liv, section 19. This is assumed in modern international law (Phillipson 1911: 60; Tucker 1977: 8).

[167] See Ober 1989: 192–247, esp. 205–14.

[168] Slaves and women had almost no legal personality; legal procedures were different for metics, who, for example, were liable to be tortured and needed to be represented by a citizen in most courts – but not the maritime courts (E. Cohen 2005: 300).

[169] Thuc. 2.37.1.

[170] E.g. Eur. *Supp.* 433–4; Solon 36.18–19 (West 1989). Compare the parody of this in "Gnathaena's Rules" for a brothel in Davidson 1997: 104.

[171] Dem. 15.18.

ourselves."[172] Thus, it was this idealized notion of an equal law that was applied to the conduct of states.[173]

One complication and partial exception requires mention. The terms of treaties were an important part of the interstate law of ancient Greece, but there was no guarantee that their terms were equal. The rule that all states should obey their sworn treaty obligations reflects the conception of law as egalitarian. But the terms of treaties, especially those that ended a war, often reflected the relative power of the parties and could be dictated at spear point, as it were.[174] Hence we shall see that Demosthenes criticizes law among states as determined by power.[175] Ancient treaties encapsulate the tensions, emphasized in international relations theory, between equality before the law and unequal power.[176]

The code of reciprocity was also ambivalent in its relation to hierarchy. In one sense it operated on the basis of equality. States owed revenge or benefits to each other depending on injuries or benefits received, not on the power or rank of the doer. But a more powerful state might justify an unequal relationship with another state in terms of having it in its debt.[177] The origins of the moral code of reciprocity in the relationships of aristocrats, whose claims to equal honor were acknowledged, tended to work against inequality. No gift or benefit could make a Homeric aristocrat into an inferior; no benefit could justify the subordination of a state. To turn to classical Athens, David Konstan has shown that it was primarily equal friendship that was valorized there. He adds that "democracy thus tended to repress discourses involving hierarchical relations of friendship between leaders and followers or wealthy men and their dependents."[178] Thus the Athenians tended to project onto the relations between states a template that placed a positive value on equal personal relationships.[179]

Frank Steward contrasts the right to "the respect due to an equal," which he calls "horizontal honor" with "the right to special respect enjoyed by

[172] Isoc. 8.69. Cf. Dem. 10.4; 19.295.
[173] Cf. Ager 1996: 1 "The institution of arbitration might be the only protection smaller states could have in their dealings with greater powers." Cf. Suganami 1978: 112 on the function of the law within states to protect the weaker members.
[174] See Missiou-Ladi 1987.   [175] Dem. 15.28–9. See p. 227.
[176] Tucker 1977: 14.   [177] See pp. 192–7.
[178] Konstan 1998: 279, 280. See also Konstan 1997a and Schofield 1998: 49–50 on Aristotle's conception of friendship and Millett 1989 on the avoidance of patronage in Athens; *pace* Zelnick-Abramovitz 2000.
[179] Lendon's model, with its emphasis on hierarchy and the expectation of deference, may be more appropriate for the foreign policy thinking within oligarchic states such as Sparta. Compare Mitchell 1997: 132 on Persian social relations and foreign policy.

those who are superior," which he calls vertical honor.[180] J. E. Lendon stresses the importance of "vertical honor" within the state and its application to the interstate world.[181] I would put more stress on the "horizontal honor" of the democratic citizen. In classical Athens we find, both within the state and among states, that horizontal honor was the dominant conception. Ill-treatment occasioned indignation, and even legal action, by the humblest of the citizens even against the rich, successful, and well born; insults and injuries were resented by the weakest of states – and such states could often call in more powerful allies on this basis. The concept of *hybris* was important in the genesis of Greek wars, as Lendon insists.[182] But it was part of a strongly egalitarian strain in Greek thinking, aimed primarily against the abuse of power and not at justifying power.

Third, slavery was the opposite of egalitarian friendship in several respects. It was not only an extremely unequal relationship but also often conceived of as a hostile one.[183] As we shall see, the metaphor of slavery was often and vividly applied to the relationship of states, almost always to exaggerate and condemn an unequal relationship.[184] This use of the metaphor of slavery complemented the metaphor of equal friendship: both rendered the justification of hierarchy difficult. So Isocrates claims that it was the word "freedom" that destroyed the empires of Athens and Sparta.[185] The Thebans, who played a vital part in the overthrow of both of these empires, presented their role in the same light: they fought for the freedom of others but did not themselves aim to rule.[186]

Legalistic thinking was clearly egalitarian. The use of the model of positive reciprocity was two-edged: obligations could justify subordination, but the idealized relationship was one between equals. The application of the slave metaphor was overwhelmingly one-sided: states should be neither like slaves nor like masters.

The scope of this egalitarian tendency requires precise delineation. Within Athenian society, the equality of citizens did not efface competition for status, nor economic and social distinctions. It did ensure certain equal legal and political rights to all Athenian men: no citizen could be struck or dishonored; each hand raised in the assembly counted equally.[187] In a similar way, among states there were spheres in which inequality and competition reigned and others, including their diplomatic relations and the moral codes according to which they were judged, in which states

---

[180] See Stewart 1994: 54–62.   [181] Lendon 2000, 2006 and most systematically in 2007: 261–2.
[182] Lendon 2007: 276; see also van Wees 2004: 25.   [183] See Hunt 1998: 115–20, 160–4.
[184] Pp. 112–17.   [185] Isoc. 5.104.   [186] Thuc. 4.92.7; Paus. 9.15.6.
[187] See also Dem. 15.29; and Isoc. 8.69 on equality for weak and strong within the state.

asserted and were accorded equal rights. States could compete for superior status, for example, in their dedications at Olympia or in the order in which they were allowed to consult the oracle at Delphi. They could argue over which state possessed more honor when allies were deciding on their order of battle – for there were more or less honorable positions in the line.[188] Demosthenes could argue that Athens' reputation and traditions demanded of it a higher standard; Athens in particular could not have stepped aside and allowed other states to fight Philip for the freedom of Greece.[189] Greek states were not always equal and they were manifestly competitive about their relative status.

In addition, hegemonic powers bound their subject allies by bilateral treaties or more commonly through a treaty organization such as the Delian League. They tended to emphasize their benefactions to justify their rule over their subject allies. They may even have expected deference from their subjects. But when Sparta or Athens punished a subject ally, their justification was always substantial: an insult, a refusal to pay tribute or to go on expedition. On the other hand, there were various ways that even these obvious superiors tried to obscure their own power.[190] The reason for this obfuscation was the unacceptability of subordinating relationships among states.[191] In our period the Peloponnesian League was defunct; only the rump of the Second Athenian League remained after the Social War, and Thebes' sphere of influence, never institutionalized, diminished.[192] Fewer states than ever were members of hegemonic leagues.[193] And states which were not in a hegemonic relationship treated each other as equals regardless of differences in their size and power – which could be vast.

This egalitarian ethos can be seen in Athenian diplomatic practice – which seems to reflect the practices of the Greeks in general. On the reliefs above treaties or honorary decrees, states are represented by their patron gods or goddesses, heroes or personifications. When they are represented shaking hands in *dexiōsis* to confirm their friendship – as they often are – the images suggest not only a bond similar to individual reciprocal friendship, but also terms of equality between them.[194] So, too, do states honor each other with commendations and crowns: Athens both bestowed crowns on helpful states and potentates and received them in turn when it had done

---

[188] Hdt. 9.26–8. [189] Dem. 18.200–1. [190] E.g. Thuc. 1.77.
[191] Runciman 1990: 355; contra Dawson 1996: 66–9.
[192] See Munn 1997: esp. 87, 94–5. [193] *Pace* Hall 2007: 105.
[194] Low 2007: 45–6; Knippschild 2002: 17–54. Even when *dexiōsis* is not portrayed, the common depiction of states as Olympian gods – Zeus seems to have been avoided – is congenial to the ideal of equality between them. See Lawton 1995: no. 24 (Athens and Arcadia, Achaia, Elis, Phlius), no. 96 (Athens and Corcyra).

other states good turns.[195] It was not considered demeaning, but noble to acknowledge gratitude to other states.[196]

Treaties between cities of manifestly different strengths were symmetrical, often precisely so: both cities had the same obligation to "give assistance with all their strength, in whatever way is requested by [their allies] . . . to the best of their ability."[197] Athens made many treaties containing precisely equal obligations with smaller states.[198] Some of these equal terms could have concrete and important consequences.[199] In the late fifth century Athens, with its empire of over a hundred cities, made an alliance with Argos, Mantinea, and Elis. Despite the disparity in the cities' power, leadership of joint expeditions was to be shared equally: so Elis would supply a general with equal power to Athens' commander. Each party was to have sole command in its own territory; hence the Mantineans not only took the place of honor on the right but were also in command at the battle of Mantinea that occurred shortly thereafter.[200] This division of military authority seems to have been conventional and is attested also in a treaty between Athens, Arcadia, Elis, and Phlius of 362/1.[201] So, if Athens had sent a force to aid Phlius – something entirely possible given Athenian participation in the battle of Mantinea in 362 – the troops and generals of most populous state in Greece would have been subject to the orders of a Phlian general. This makes perfect sense in terms of state sovereignty since the army would be in Phlius, but it would certainly have been an affront to hierarchy.[202]

Lendon has attempted to dismiss this body of evidence with the argument that "The shaming quality of deep debt . . . explains the rhetoric of equal exchange that is so often used in diplomatic speeches . . . This is

---

[195] E.g. *IG* ii² 1 = RO no. 2; *IG* ii² 28 = RO no. 18; *IG* i² 1388 = Ha no. 10, lines 32–7; *IG* xii (7) 5 = Ha no. 68, lines 19–21 = RO no. 51; *IG* ii² 212+ = Ha no. 82, lines 24–39 = RO no. 64; *IG* ii² 233 = Ha no. 97, lines 36–9 = RO no. 72; *IG* ii² 237+ = Ha no. 100, lines 14–15 = RO no. 77; *IG* ii² 448 = Ha no. 123a, lines 22–6 Dem. 18.89, 92, 94 with Yunis 2001: 161. Cf. Aeschin. 3.230–1.

[196] See the public acknowledgments of gratitude in the above note and also Dem. 20.36, 51–8 and esp. 64.

[197] E.g. *IG* ii² 14 = RO no. 6; *IG* ii² 34, lines 26–30 = RO no. 20; *IG* ii² 97; *IG* ii² 116 = RO no. 44. So also in literary references to treaties: Aeschin. 3.100; Xen. *An.* 2.5.39; Thuc. 1.44.1; 3.70.6; 5.47.

[198] E.g. *IG* ii² 14 = Ha no. 14 = RO no. 6 (Alliance of Athens and Boeotians); *IG* ii² 34 = Ha no. 31 = RO no. 20 (Athens and Chios); *IG* ii² 97 = Ha no. 42 (Alliance of Athens and Corcyra in); *IG* ii² 116 = Ha no. 59 = RO no. 44 (Alliance of Athens and Thessaly); *IG* ii² 157 = Ha no. 70 = RO no. 53 (Alliance of Athens and Thracian Kings).

[199] Contra Lendon 2006: 93–4.   [200] Thuc. 5.47.7, 67.2.

[201] *IG* ii² 112 = Ha no. 56 = RO no. 41. Among other complaints about the terms of Athens' alliance with Thebes, Aeschines accused Demosthenes of handing the command on land over to Thebes (3.143); but this was only to be expected since the war took place and was expected to take place in Boeotia. Cf. Dem. 18.238–41.

[202] Contrast Hdt. 7.157–63.

politeness; real power inheres not in equal exchange, but in getting the other party as deeply as possible in one's debt."[203] Two considerations incline me to a different view. First, even deep debt was compatible with equal status. Indeed, powerful states openly acknowledged their debts to the weak: for example, Athens did not make itself inferior to any of the many cities, Samos, Neapolis, and Mytilene, that it publicly thanked for their assistance in various contexts. Second, Lendon's distinction between "real power" and "politeness" is a false contrast. The force of reputation sometimes pressured states into dutiful reciprocity, but many states ignored claims upon them when their interests demanded – and there was no authority to require them to pay back debts. No "real power" here: indeed, it would only be a slight exaggeration to say that Greek cities were a bunch of incorrigible ingrates: Athens did not repay Corinth for its interventions on Athens' behalf in the past when the dispute over Corcyra arose; Athens did not act grateful to Sparta for preventing its destruction at the end of the Peloponnesian War but rather allied itself with Thebes, which had been pressing for this punishment; Olynthus turned against Philip, who had given them Potidaea. The list goes on and on. States benefited from a reputation for paying back their debts, so sometimes they did.[204] This long-term consideration is on precisely the same level as the politeness of diplomatic equality.

Diplomatic practice, of course, did not make Neapolis as powerful as Athens. It did convey tangible benefits for Athens.[205] Interstate politics is not a zero-sum game in all respects.[206] In particular, one cannot overstate how advantageous it is to have allies in a war: they fight on your side. When Demosthenes defends his record in the diplomacy leading up to Chaeronea, he places special emphasis on his success in winning allies over to Athens, a task he presents as an obvious one confronting any statesman.[207] The establishment – or not – of some sort of superiority over small cities in Euboea or Megara or Byzantium – much less Thebes – was a matter of supreme indifference to Athenian interests. Having hoplites on their side of the battlefield was what mattered, and diplomatic equality between the largest state in Greece and whoever would join the fight against Philip was the best way to obtain these. Given an atmosphere in which hierarchy was

---

[203] Lendon 2006: 93–4.   [204] See pp. 186–92.

[205] Compare the argument of Viola 2008, who locates the modern genesis of the notion of sovereign equality in the advantages of diplomacy in the context of a balance of power among the Italian city-states.

[206] Cf. Hall 2007: 96.   [207] Dem. 18.237, 301–2; cf. 10.51.

something to conceal or to be ashamed of, egalitarian diplomacy was the most advantageous kind.

This egalitarian ideology goes some way towards explaining why the world of Greek city-states was not a world of deferential and grateful small states with their powerful patrons.[208] On the contrary, it was a world in which the weak decided, astonishingly often, to thumb their noses at the strong. Melos would not pay tribute to Athens; it had been free, albeit tiny, for three hundred years and its citizens insisted on and died for a horizontal view of honor. Melos may also have hoped for assistance from Sparta, but consider the resistance of Phlius to Sparta, to whom it not only was inferior in power but also owed specific duties as a member of the Peloponnesian League. No notion of deference or rank can have played any part in this state's decision to resist Sparta, which at that point was backed by the Persian king and the Peloponnesian League and which had just cowed Argos, Corinth, Thebes, and Athens itself into submission. Here we have the epitome of horizontal honor. Phlius was a state, albeit small, and just like the poorest citizen it had its honor; no Spartan interference in its internal affairs would be tolerated by Phlius.[209] By Phlius!

Even in unequal alliances the independence of the weaker partners was more and more explicitly protected as the fourth century wore on. The concept of *autonomia* developed in the fifth century to define more precisely the independence of small cities from hegemonic states.[210] The King's Peace enshrined *autonomia* as an ideal for all Greek states: the Greek cities, both small and great, should be left independent.[211] The Decree of Aristoteles, which created the Second Athenian League, set out its terms within the framework of the King's Peace.[212] This limited the extent to which Athens' superior power could affect its relations with its allies: Athens promised not to exact tribute, impose garrisons or a governor, interfere in the allies' political systems, or settle cleruchies. These were abuses that large states such as Athens and Sparta had imposed before on those they had "liberated" and were "protecting."[213] Cities of any size – outside the domain of the Persian king – were allowed to join the Athenian League "remaining free and autonomous . . . on the same terms (as those) on which (the) Chians and the Thebans and the other allies (did)."[214] The

[208] Runciman 1990: 355.   [209] Xen. *Hell.* 5.3.16, 3.21–5.
[210] Ostwald 1982; Karavites 1982b: 152–3; *Pace* Sealey 1993: 241–4.
[211] Xen. *Hell.* 5.1.31.   [212] Cargill 1981: 9–11, 30–2 against Cawkwell 1973: esp. 52–4.
[213] *IG* ii² 43 = RO no. 22. See Griffith 1978: 131–60 and Cargill 1981 on Athenian adherence to these clauses.
[214] *IG* ii² 43, lines 23–5; trans. Ha no. 35 = RO no. 22.

inscription recording the alliance of Athens with Chios, a powerful and rich island, which survives, is one of the treaties with the symmetrical promises of assistance mentioned above.[215] As G. T. Griffith concludes, the King's Peace and the Decree of Aristoteles provided "an excellent rule of thumb" for determining what is empire and what is alliance.[216] Overall, standards of what constituted a proper bond between states in the fourth century tended more and more to resemble the equal friendship valorized within a city.

The rights of smaller states vis-à-vis their "benefactors" grew in strength in the mid fourth century for a number of reasons. Competition for allies among the main hegemonic cities was an important factor. In 378 Athens desperately needed help against Sparta; imperial hopes took a back seat to this exigency, so Athens made the commitments of the Decree of Aristoteles. After the Social War, only states that wanted to belonged to the Athenian League. By the time Thebes began to extend its influence after Leuctra, the precedent of the Decree of Aristoteles had already been set: Thebes never formalized its leadership, which rested mainly on its role in organizing resistance to Sparta. Thebes also had to contract ties with distant Peloponnesian states, some of which soon became powerful enough to defend themselves and thus to take an independent line in foreign policy.[217]

It is hard to judge the extent to which the egalitarian ethos influenced a main tendency in Greek diplomatic history, the continued independence of hundreds of small Greek city states. This may be fully explained by more concrete factors. In addition to the deliberate cultivation of a "balance-of-power," one might point to the rudimentary techniques of siege warfare; Aristotle noticed that city walls allow weaker cities to avoid disaster or humiliation.[218] The lack of external threats due to the military superiority of hoplites, the relative geographic isolation by land of many individual cities, the lasting effects of their early history, or the particular policy failures of a succession of would-be ruling cities probably contributed. Yet I suspect that the structure of Greek thinking was crucial too.

Whether we decide that this insubordinate tendency led Greece to failure is another question. Isocrates and Panhellenism notwithstanding, the teleological view of the fourth-century city-states as a failed Greek

---

[215] *IG* ii² 34, lines 26–30 = RO no. 20. The existence of this clause is not affected by the controversies discussed by Cargill 1981: 52–4.

[216] Griffith 1978: 133.

[217] Buckler 1980: 221–2. Admittedly, nearer to home, the small Boeotian cities in Thebes' backyard fared much worse.

[218] Arist. *Pol.* 7.1330b–1331a7.

nation, a perspective that dominates modern discussions, was not shared by the city-states themselves. They had not the slightest desire to be subordinated to a national government – much less to a neighboring city. T. T. B. Ryder has made an intriguing and persuasive contrary argument: thanks to the ideals of a succession of Common Peace treaties, after 362/1 small states were able to protect themselves and were less dominated by leading states than at any time in the previous two hundred years.[219] So, a period which is sometimes described as the "Collapse of the Leading Powers"[220] – and which, indeed, was marked by a lack of the power that centralization brings – was a golden age of independence and local rule for the hundreds of smaller cities of Greece.[221]

CONCLUSION

Athenian decisions sometimes took notice of the ethnicity, relationship to the gods, rank, and political system of other states. On occasion speakers found it useful to invoke each of these qualities, which therefore must have carried some weight with the assembled citizens. Several considerations preclude putting too much emphasis on these types of arguments compared with calculations of interests and the various evaluative systems by which actions, rather than status, were judged. First, none of these factors are mentioned nearly as regularly or stressed to as great an extent as interest and the normative judgment of conduct. Second, the evaluation of a state's status was particularly uncertain: ethnicity was malleable, the will of the gods was not well known, differences in power were disguised by dominant egalitarian ways of thinking, and a preference for democracies was balanced by the odium attached to intervention in another state's internal affairs. Finally and most decisive is the realist observation that none of these supposed preferences seem to have any effect on Athenian policy – or on the policies of Greek states in general. The Greeks did not stop fighting each other and unite against Persia; oligarchic, democratic, and monarchic states were allies of each other as often as enemies. Even the Sacred War, which seems a clear case of religious motivation, is liable to this type of unmasking: Thebes, Thessaly, and Macedonia were already arrayed against Phocis, Athens, and Sparta before the control of the sanctuary of Delphi came into play.

---

[219] Ryder 1965: 120–1.   [220] A chapter of Hammond 1986 has this title.
[221] The human costs of the need for centralization in the face of threats is well treated in Schmookler 1995: esp. 74–121.

CHAPTER 5

Household metaphors

One of the main themes of this book is the way that relationships between states were conceived of in terms of those within a society. Four aspects of this tendency deserve emphasis. First, it was quite natural: the abstract realm of relations between states – which only developed in the archaic period – was mapped onto the more concrete and long-established realm of relationships between individuals or families. Second, these analogies or metaphors allowed speakers on foreign policy to evoke the emotions and values associated with the internal relationships. Third, they seem to have been effective, to judge from their frequent use by expert orators. Finally, the ubiquitous application of internal metaphors to interstate conduct – like the influence of the economy and militarism – represents a path by which internal factors affected how Athens thought about and conducted itself in the world of states.

The most direct, simple, and emotional appeals of Athenian war rhetoric, the topic of this chapter, were based on the intimate and emotionally laden relationships within the house. Aristotle lists three relationships as constituting the Greek household: those between master and slave, between husband and wife, and between parents and children.[1] The relationship of master and slave was metaphorically applied to the relationship of states in a class of arguments that encouraged intransigence in foreign policy: "fight for your freedom" or "to give in, even a little, would be slavish." The relationship of husbands and wives provided the source for another type of goading metaphor: an aggressive foreign policy was often considered manly whereas a desire for peace or accommodation could be deplored as effeminate. I will make several arguments about the third relationship, that of different generations: the forefathers were invoked as models in all aspects of life; their deployment in arguments about war was common, presumably

---

[1] Arist. *Pol.* 1.1253b7–8. In addition, states could claim a kinship, a sort of brotherhood, on the basis of a common ancestor, which was an important part of the bonds of ethnicity, especially in the archaic period; see pp. 77 n. 22, 81–3.

effective, and mainly served to encourage belligerence; in contrast, ancient generalizations represented young men as bellicose and the old as cautious.

SLAVERY

The extent of slave ownership within Athenian society was crucial to the rhetorical use of slavery. Although the proportion of slaves in the population was about the same in fifth-century Athens as, for example, in the pre-Civil War South, the distribution of slaves among the citizens was more even: ownership of slaves in Athens was not concentrated in a small proportion of the citizens as it was in the South.[2] Perhaps as many as a half of the citizen households would include at least one slave. So, when an orator alluded to slavery, liberty, or enslavement, he was referring to something concrete and quotidian in the experience of most Athenians, even those who did not own a slave themselves.

In one speech Lysias even affects to assume that all the members of his audience are slave owners.[3] This was not the case, but he was unlikely to have offended: Athenian citizens often thought of themselves as a unity distinct from slaves. This way of thinking was conducive to civic harmony: divisions and tensions among the citizens could be submerged in the light of the divide that separated free and slave.[4] So even those Athenians who did not own slaves themselves had a stake in maintaining the dichotomy between free and slave and in their position above the dividing line.

Another more general cultural effect of slavery deserves notice here. In his wide-ranging comparative study *Slavery and Social Death*, Orlando Patterson argues that the presence of slavery contributed to a society's emphasis on personal honor.[5] It is easy to flesh out how this might have worked. Slave masters needed always to maintain their position of superiority to their slaves, even to those slaves in daily and intimate contact with them. They could never stop being masters. And, insofar as the common people at Athens adopted the habits and ideals of the elite, they might also affect the haughty demeanor of slaveholders, men accustomed to command. More important perhaps, Athenian slave masters were used to commanding their inferiors in the household. Why not their inferiors in the city? The richest and most powerful Athenians were invariably slave owners and only grudgingly accepted the rough political equality of the democracy. So, in a dynamic well explored by Kurt Raaflaub, elite Athenians occasionally

---

[2] Degler 1959; Fisher 1993: 34–47.   [3] Lys. 5.5.
[4] Mactoux 1980: 215; Hunt 1998: 126–38.   [5] O. Patterson 1982: 77–101.

revealed the attitude that poor Athenians were scarcely better than slaves.[6] Given the existence of such attitudes, even citizens who did not own slaves were imbued with a strong sense of personal honor and resentful of slights: to accept insult from another citizen was to risk being assimilated to a slave. The institution of slavery was one that raised the stakes in relationships between individual Athenians. It thus contributed to the aristocratic sensitivity to slight that marked Athens' persona in the Greek world, a topic to which we shall return.[7]

Athenians did not want to behave in a slavish manner for other, fairly obvious, reasons: slaves were seen as outsiders and as deservedly in subjection because of their cowardice. Most slaves were imported and usually from non-Greek peoples whom the Athenians affected to despise; slaves were thus considered inferior foreigners and likely to be hostile.[8] For example, Apollodorus expected to turn a jury of Athenian citizens against Phormion, an ex-slave of his father, with the following attack – among many similar ones:

> You perhaps suppose, because he talks funny, that he is a barbarian and contemptible. Well, he is a barbarian who hates those he ought to honor.[9]

But slaves were not just barbarians. Many slaves owed their status to defeat in war.[10] A common militaristic justification of slavery was that slaves deserved their condition as losers in war, whose lives had been spared on condition of their servitude.[11] The state of slavery, to this way of thinking, revealed the cowardice of the slave and also the harsh and humiliating results of such cowardice. Another factor was possibly even more important to the association of slavery with cowardice. Individual slaves were stereotyped as trivial, cowardly, shiftless, and childish.[12] This image, found in a variety of other slave societies, derived in part from the actual behavior of relatively powerless slaves. More profoundly, "the worst, or most easily patronized" traits were seized upon and expanded into a general theory, because of masters' need to despise those they oppressed.[13] The ways that orators deployed slavery reflect all of these negative views of slaves.

The imputation of slavishness to an individual opponent could raise suspicions of hostility to the citizen class or of a foreigner's lack of concern for Athens. This could be employed with equal effectiveness against opponents who favored or who opposed war. For example, Demosthenes accuses

---

[6] Raaflaub 1983: 535.   [7] See pp. 201–14.   [8] E.g. Rosivach 1999.   [9] [Dem.] 45.30.
[10] See Garlan 1999 and Pritchett 1971–91: v.223–45.   [11] See Hunt 1998: 154–5, 200–1.
[12] Dover 1974: 114–16; Dover 1993: 43–9; Hunt 1998: 160–4.   [13] O. Patterson 1971: 217.

Aeschines of having a slave father and doing jobs more appropriate for a slave.[14] In this and other cases we can tell that the accusations were exaggerated if not entirely fictitious.[15] On the other hand, Aeschines denounces the example of Cleophon, a popular Athenian leader of the late Peloponnesian War. Aeschines begins this passage by describing Cleophon as a lyre-maker, "whom many remembered bound in fetters." Thus Aeschines conjures up for his audience the most humiliating, most unfree experience of Cleophon's supposed slavery. Aeschines' portrayal, however, does not imply that Cleophon was a coward; rather, he was a rabid war-monger who "threatened to take his knife and slit the throat of any man who should make mention of peace."[16] Aeschines uses the accusation of slavishness, in its harshest colors, to show that Cleophon was not really an Athenian and was perhaps hostile to the interests of Athens. This attack on a politician of the previous century served as a prelude to Aeschines' attack on Demosthenes as "a descendant through [his] mother of the nomad Scythians" and "more a slave than freeman, all but branded as a runaway."[17] In Aeschines' account, Demosthenes, like Cleophon, tried to get Athens to continue fighting when that was beyond its power and not in its interest.

In one case Demosthenes applies a similar type of slur to a whole country. In the *Third Philippic* he describes Philip as "not even a barbarian from any place that can be named with honour, but a pestilent knave from Macedonia, whence it was never yet possible to buy a decent slave."[18] Demosthenes invites his audience – a significant portion of whom were not, in fact, slave owners – to put themselves in the position of discerning purchasers of slaves; King Philip – and Macedonia as a whole – is demoted to the status of an inadequate slave in order to invoke a slave master's proud indignation at Philip's current high status and power in the Greek world, a monstrous reversal.

Greeks applied the slave metaphor to any number of stark, hierarchical dichotomies, such as that between the mind and the body or between an absolute government and its subjects.[19] Some of these uses were positive or neutral: according to Plato and Aristotle, it was good that the mind ruled

---

[14] Dem. 18.129.   [15] Yunis 2001: 185.

[16] Aeschin. 2.76. Similar contemporary slurs are attested: Ar. *Ran.* 678–85, 1532–3; the comic poet Plato's play, *Cleophon*, represented Cleophon as speaking broken Greek (Rogers 1902–16: v.101).

[17] Aeschin. 2.78, 79. Cf. Aeschin. 3.171–2. See Richardson 1889: 176 ad Aeschin. 3.171.2 on the question of whether Demosthenes' maternal grandmother was Thracian.

[18] Dem. 9.30–1. Cf. Arist. *Rh.* 2.9.1387a19–31 on indignation aroused by those who have recently had good luck.

[19] See Vlastos 1941 on the use of the slave metaphor in Plato.

the body.[20] But when the metaphor was applied to relationships between free people, it almost always had a pejorative sense; only slaves ought to be subject to slavery. Using the metaphor to condemn unequal relationships between states was particularly common in the histories of Herodotus, Thucydides, and Xenophon.[21] It was also widespread in Athenian oratory on foreign policy.[22] States that enslaved others were often condemned; those that allowed themselves to suffer metaphoric enslavement were also castigated or required exculpation.[23] Orators sometimes gave extra force to the argument against acting like slaves: the Athenians, since they were accustomed to rule or to pre-eminence, were especially debarred from any conduct that could be construed as slavish.[24]

Such condemnation of slavishness tended to be part of an incitement to war. If such wars are fought against the aggression of larger powers, we tend not to judge the exaggeration implicit in the slave metaphor harshly. We may regard the Melians, who refused to accept "slavery," as foolish, but only the most steadfast pacifist would deny their right to resist Athenian aggression.[25] Unfortunately, the slave metaphor seems to have been powerful also when it was a matter not of resisting aggression, but of compromising. It was often just a way of making more vivid the imputation of cowardice to anybody opposed to a war. According to Thucydides, Pericles made this argument in a particularly explicit form:

> For any demand, of the greatest or the smallest importance, means the same subservience if it is a command issued by an equal to an equal before there is arbitration.[26]

In our period, Demosthenes ignores the complexities of the conflict between Athens and Macedonia and argues repeatedly that the war against Philip is one for freedom. For example, in the *Third Philippic* Demosthenes argues that "even if all the other states agree to be slaves, nevertheless, we must fight for freedom."[27] In *On the Chersonese* he claims that for Athens not to fight back against Philip's aggression would be to endure

---

[20] Schütrumpf 1993.

[21] Hunt 1998: 46–51, 128, 158–60. On the ideal of freedom and its relation to chattel slavery see O. Patterson 1991 with the criticisms of Raaflaub 2004: 42.

[22] E.g. Isoc. 6.43; 14.5, 12, 17, 19, 29–30, 34, 41, 43, 61; Aeschin. 3.85; Dem. 1.23; 2.8; 8.46, 49, 60, 62, 74; 9.22, 26–7, 36, 59; 15.3, 57; 18.72, 182–3, 205, 289 (Chaeronea Epitaph), 295; 19.81, 137.

[23] E.g. Isoc. 14.12, 29–30. Dem. 18.203 condemns both sides of the relationship at once.

[24] This theme is stressed throughout one of the most brilliant passages in *On the Crown* (Dem. 18.199–205). Cf. Isoc. 6.94; Thuc. 8.68.4.

[25] See Walzer 1977: 51–73.   [26] Thuc. 1.141.1 (trans. modified). Cf. Isoc. 6.51.

[27] Dem. 9.70–1. Compare Demosthenes' praise of the Athenian defense of freedom in the Persian Wars (Dem. 9.36; 18.205).

slavery.[28] Athens was the most populous city-state and Greece's dominant naval power, but nevertheless, it is portrayed as barely warding off
metaphorical slavery.

Five of our speeches deprecate war, advocate making peace, or criticize
an excessive belligerence: Andocides' *On the Peace*, Demosthenes' *On the
Navy-Boards* and *On the Peace*, Aeschines' *On the False Embassy*, and *Against
Ctesiphon*. That these speeches either do not use or explicitly reject the
application of the slave metaphor confirms that it had a bellicose force.
Andocides is quite forthright: "for what reason should we make war? That
our city may be free? But this is what it already is?"[29] In *On the Peace*
Demosthenes, uncharacteristically, is arguing for restraint. In this oration,
alone of his assembly speeches, he avoids the explicit evocation of slavery.
Nevertheless, he needs to counter an argument that may well have been
posed in terms of slavery:

"'Must we then,' you ask, 'do as we are told for fear of the consequences? Do you
of all men advise that?' Far from it. No, I think we ought so to act as to do nothing
unworthy of Athens and yet avoid war."[30]

In his speech *On the Navy-Boards* Demosthenes deprecates the declaration
of a crusade against Persia. Accordingly, he avoids any reference to the
motif of slavery and freedom that dominated the Greeks' thinking about
their conflicts with Persia. Only once does he refer to slavery, and this
was the slavery of Persian subjects, not a slavery with which Persia might
be threatening Greece.[31] Aeschines in his legal conflicts with the more
bellicose Demosthenes generally avoids speaking of the slavery of states.[32]
The Melian dialogue in Thucydides provides a contrast that sums up our
evidence – and suggests that the deployment of the slave metaphor was not
limited to our period. The intransigent Melians repeatedly talk in terms of
slave metaphors, but the otherwise blunt Athenians, who wish to subjugate
Melos without a fight, avoid this provocative terminology.[33]

Some invocations of the threat of "slavery" for a state can seem vague and
abstract, unconnected with the actual practice of slavery. To say that a state
was "enslaved" may simply have indicated its loss of autonomy in foreign
affairs, its paying of a tribute, or the imposition upon it of an unwanted

---

[28] Dem. 8.59, see also Dem. 10.61.   [29] Andoc. 3.13–14.

[30] Dem. 5.24. Yunis 2001: 222 calls "doing what is ordered," a standard expression for slavery in
discussing Dem. 18.202; cf. Isoc 6.94.

[31] Dem. 14.32.

[32] Aeschin. 3.85 is the only exception and here Aeschines is praising an expedition to Euboea, which
the Thebans were attempting to enslave. Cf. Dem. 8.74.

[33] Thuc. 5.86, 92, 100; 112.2.

government; the practices of chattel slavery may hardly have been present to the mind of the speaker or to his audience. In modern war oratory, the imperative to fight for liberty or against slavery is often asserted. But there we can detect only the faintest connotations of the actual institution of chattel slavery. Was the metaphor of slavery already "dead" in classical Athens?

One would guess not: the metaphor of slavery could never have become so inert in the slave society of Athens as in the modern westernized world, in which what little chattel slavery exists is distant and almost invisible.[34] Everywhere around him, an Athenian citizen could see the stark difference between the freedom of a citizen or mastery and slavery. The mere mention of enslavement would evoke recollections of slaves being sold or for rent, of the public or private punishment of slaves or their abuse in comedy. It might evoke vague fears of the threat of capture in war or abduction into slavery, a frequently mentioned and capital crime.

Rather than seeing the metaphor of slavery as dead, it might be better to think of it as sleeping, exhausted by frequent use in discussions and debates on interstate relations and in the condemnation of overly hierarchical political relationships within a state. In several cases, orators deliberately wake the sleeping metaphor of slavery – an indication that the metaphor by itself had become insufficiently vivid. When Isocrates wants to highlight the tyrannical behavior of the Thebans, he claims that some of their neighbors are "no less slaves than those who have been bought with money."[35] He needs to insist that their subjection was so severe as to resemble actual slavery, something the metaphor must no longer have implied. Demosthenes excoriates the city-states that entrusted themselves to Philip's partisans: "they are slaves, doomed to the whipping-post and scaffold."[36] The mention of "whipping" evokes the specter of actual chattel slavery more vividly than the mere word "slavery" could.

A passage from Demosthenes' *Fourth Philippic* shows how potent the slave metaphor could be when brought to life with a reference to the punishment of slaves. As the culmination of his jeremiad against Athenian lethargy, Demosthenes attacks any tendency to procrastination as follows:

When, men of Athens, shall we consent to do our duty? "Whenever it is necessary," you will say. But what any free man would call necessity is not merely present now, but is long ago past, and from the necessity that constrains a slave we must surely pray to be delivered. Do you ask the difference? The strongest necessity that a free man feels is shame for his own position, and I know not if we could name a

---

[34] See Finnegan 2000 for current chattel slavery.   [35] Isoc. 14.18.   [36] Dem. 9.66.

stronger; but for a slave necessity means blows and bodily outrage, unfit to name here, may it not occur.[37]

Demosthenes places his Athenian audience in a no-man's land between being free men and being slaves: they have already failed to respond to "what any free man would call necessity." There is some doubt whether the Athenians are really free men. But they have not yet become slaves: Demosthenes prays that "the necessity that constrains a slave" be averted. Demosthenes then defines his two "necessities." He says that shame is the "strongest necessity that a free man feels." For a slave, however, "blows and bodily outrage" constitute "necessity." Demosthenes thus makes the threat of slavery vivid and compelling; for "blows and bodily outrage" refers to a key distinction between slave and free. Elsewhere, in two forensic speeches, Demosthenes insists that slave and free are distinguished most decisively in how they can be punished: slaves are answerable with their bodies, but free men are not.[38] Although scholars have noted some exceptions to the rule of citizen immunity from physical punishment, this picture of the contrast between citizen and slave for the most part reflected Athenian practice.[39] Slave liability to corporal punishment is obvious; the requirement that they give legal testimony only under torture is notorious if puzzling.[40] Demosthenes harnesses the feelings of outrage and indignation that Athenian citizens would feel at the threat of corporal punishment, being treated like a slave. Demosthenes makes the relationship between Athens and Philip's Macedonia, a relationship that may have seemed distant and abstract to many Athenians, into something concrete and emotionally charged by his evocation of this familiar but dramatic aspect of Athenian slavery.

If it could be brought to life, the metaphor of slavery was far more useful to the pro-war orator than the bare accusation of cowardice. All Athenians could remember a terrified slave, or a slave being punished – in comedy at least – and would want never to risk being in the same position or seeming to deserve to be. Within the state, to treat a free individual as a slave was considered *hybris*, as Fisher puts it, "the serious assault on the honour of another, which is likely to cause shame and lead to anger and attempts at revenge."[41] This angry and vengeful state was just what an orator arguing for a war would like to inculcate in his audience. If he could convince them that Athens as a whole had been treated as a slave or was in danger of acting in a slavish way, he was close to winning his argument.

[37] Dem. 10.27 (cf. 4.10) (trans. modified).   [38] Dem. 22.55; see also Dem. 24.166–7.
[39] E.g. Hunter 1994: 154–84.
[40] See duBois 1991: 39–45; Gagarin 1996; Mirhady 1996; Thür 1996 on the torture of slave witnesses.
[41] Fisher 1992: 1, 48–53.

The potency of the slave metaphor probably contributed to the frequency of warfare: it encouraged weaker states to fight even when obviously over-matched; it made compromise more difficult all around. If peace were the only thing of value, we might simply condemn the slave metaphor as dysfunctional. But a willingness to fight, enforced by the shame of acting "slavishly," was also a curb on the oppression of the weak by the powerful. In many situations their apparent willingness to fight would have gained small states better treatment, since war had its costs and risks even for a more powerful state. Game Theory illuminates this effect: in his classic work, *The Strategy of Conflict*, Thomas Schelling argues that in certain situations "some voluntary but irreversible sacrifice of freedom of choice" is advantageous.[42] One of Schelling's examples makes the application to our topic clear: "If national representatives can arrange to be charged with appeasement for every small concession, they place concession visibly beyond their reach."[43] This elimination of alternatives is precisely what the interpretation of interstate relations in terms of the slavery metaphor accomplished. The almost ubiquitous application of the slave metaphor increased the chance of war, but improved the bargaining position of weak states vis-à-vis the powerful.

We turn finally from the slave metaphor to slavery itself. Greek states occasionally sold the surviving population of a captured city into slavery. Although this grim fate did not befall many cities, it was always a possibility. The threat of enslavement was too pessimistic, abhorrent, and distant to be used directly in the Athenian assembly as an argument against risking war.[44] But strong popular sentiments against the enslaving of Greeks could be roused against states that did this. In particular, Macedonian expansion involved the enslavement of several Greek cities and was condemned on this basis: Demosthenes lists among Philip's crimes that he razed some cities and sold their populations into slavery.[45]

Olynthus, in particular, was a major city and an ally of Athens when it was destroyed and its people were enslaved by Philip. The fate of its people became a *cause célèbre*. Demosthenes praised an early speech of Aeschines that expressed outrage at seeing thirty Olynthian women and children brought as slaves to the Peloponnese by one of Philip's mercenaries.[46] The accusation of having taken part in the abuse of a female Olynthian slave

---

[42] Schelling 1960: 22   [43] Schelling 1960: 29.
[44] Contrast Isoc. 8.37, 75–6; 15.319. Cf. Andoc. 3.21. Generals could invoke the threat of slavery in an attempt to get their troops to fight more resolutely, e.g. Thuc. 5.9.9.
[45] Dem. 18.182. See also Hyp. 6.17.   [46] Dem. 19.305–6.

was an important one in Demosthenes' attack on Aeschines' later, supposedly corrupt attitude towards Philip.[47] Aeschines indignantly denied the charge.[48] Demosthenes himself prosecuted and had a certain Euthymachus condemned to death for putting an Olynthian female slave in a brothel.[49]

A mysterious *nomos* of Lycurgus, mentioned by Plutarch, seems to forbid the purchase of freeborn captives as slaves in Athens.[50] This law probably aimed to protect, at Athens at least, the liberty and rights of the citizens of some specific allied city that had been enslaved. Just as Demosthenes and Hyperides, leading anti-Macedonian statesmen, took advantage of the courts to keep Philip's most brutal and offensive actions in the public view, so, too, was Lycurgus active in a series of patriotic prosecutions – of a man who fled Athens after Chaeronea, for example.[51] It would not have been out of character for him to seize the moral high ground – regarding, perhaps, Theban slaves after the sack of Thebes in 335 – with a patriotic and anti-Macedonian measure, albeit one that would not provoke a war. Unfortunately, disagreement about a needed supplementation to the text of Plutarch and the fact that a *psēphisma* rather than a *nomos* would be appropriate for a single case makes this reconstruction less certain than we would wish.[52]

WOMEN

Women played a role in war oratory similar to that of slaves.[53] Although the exhortation to prove one's manliness by going to war was not as prominent or ubiquitous as the appeal to assert one's freedom, it was also a goading metaphor. Speakers could demand that the men in the assembly prove that they were real men by their willingness to go to war.

On one level, the reason why Athenian men did not want to be likened to women is obvious and derives from the subordinate position of women in society and especially in male thinking. But the impact of the accusation depended also on a certain insecurity on the part of Athenian men. John Winkler argues for an "odd belief in the reversibility of the male

---

[47] Dem. 19.196–8, 305–9. Cf. Plutarch, *Alc.* 16   [48] Aeschin. 2.4, 153–8.

[49] Din. 1.23 with Worthington 1992: 170. See also Dem. 19.309 with MacDowell 2000: 340–1 on Philocrates and Hyperides, fr. B 19.1 on Euthycrates; cf. Dem. 19.192–5.

[50] [Plut.] *Mor.* 842a.   [51] Cf. Burke 1977: 337.

[52] See Pritchett 1971–91: v.416–17; Garlan 1999: 16; Rosivach 1999: 141. Klees 1998: 334–54 provides a full discussion with bibliography and settles on a different interpretation of the law.

[53] The arguments to avoid slavish and womanish behavior were sometimes deployed in parallel (Dem. 3.31; Aeschin. 2.127. Cf. Xen. *Hell.* 3.4.19).

person, always in peril of slipping into the servile or the feminine."[54] Such uneasiness could only be heightened when men failed in the tasks and virtues by which they justified their dominance over women. These most obviously included military service and courage. Although masculinity is not the whole of courage – nor is courage the whole of masculinity – in Greece their connection was strong. Indeed, one of the most common Greek words for courage was *andreia*, which literally means "manliness."[55] Ryan Balot points out that in ancient Greece "[c]ourage had always been the defining attribute of socially approved manhood and especially of those willing to fight and die for their communities."[56]

A few pieces of evidence will highlight the masculinity of military courage and prowess, which should be anything but startling. The historian and philosopher Xenophon warns that cavalrymen who are poorly trained will perform in battle like women fighting against men.[57] In Plato, a cowardly commander would be fit only for women.[58] Kenneth Dover argues that "[i]n the Athens of Aristophanes the supreme effeminacy was cowardice on the battlefield; Eupolis' comedy *Astrateutoi* ('men who have not been on military service') had the alternative title *Androgunoi* ('women-men')."[59] In Plato's *Timaeus*, men who were unjust or cowardly might well be reincarnated as women.[60]

In fact, the threat was rather more urgent than one's fate in a possible reincarnation. A man who had disgraced himself in military service, *ipso facto* and without a trial, suffered *atimia*. He was excluded from the agora, the meeting place and political center of the city, and from temples. He could not speak in the assembly or hold any public office including membership in the boule or a jury. Owing to his inability to speak, he was barred from "all procedural protection of his rights as a citizen."[61] In several concrete ways a man who had demonstrably failed in his military duties by the revocation of his political and legal rights was demoted to the status of a women.

Aeschines repeatedly insinuates that Demosthenes deserved such a demotion, especially because of his performance at Chaeronea.[62]

---

[54] Winkler 1990: 50. See also Roisman 2005: 197–8.   [55] Roisman 2005: 188.

[56] Balot 2007: 37–8.   [57] Xen. *Eq. mag.* 8.2.   [58] Pl. *Leg.* 1.639b.

[59] Aristophanes attacks Cleonymus both for cowardice and effeminacy (Dover 1978: 144 on *Eq.* 1372, *Nub.* 353–5, 670–80, *Vesp.* 15–23, and *Pax* 446, 670–8, 1295–1301).

[60] Pl. *Ti.* 90e. See also Hdt. 2.102.5.

[61] Harrison 1971: 171. MacDowell 1978: 74 notes that other people could bring various suits on his behalf. See Ste. Croix 1972: 280–4; [Dem.] 59.26–8.

[62] Aeschin. 3.159–60, 167, 247; and 3.155: "this man, if he is a man." See also Dorjahn 1940; and Wankel 1976: 1078–9, who lists the passages in which Aeschines repeats the accusation that Demosthenes was a coward or "left the ranks" at Chaeronea: Aeschin. 3.151, 152, 155, 159, 175, 181, 187, 244, 253.

Individuals – for Demosthenes was not a general but merely a soldier at Chaeronea – needed to be brave and face the risks of battle; leaders could display manliness in their foreign policies or their aggressive use of military command. Herodotus has the Persian queen, Atossa, urge King Darius to war against the Greeks with a very Greek appeal: "to show the Persians that they have a man to rule them."[63] Generals, too, must show manliness in their strategies: Thucydides has Cleon taunt Nicias for his failure to capture the Spartans on Sphacteria: "it was easy – if the generals were men – to sail and capture the troops on the island."[64] Aeschines attacks Demosthenes for being unmanly in his motions for the defense of Athens in the immediate aftermath of the Peace of Philocrates: he had the Athenians bring Athenian property in from the fields, although Athens' position was secure.[65]

The sovereign assembly of the Athenians did not delegate much of its power to anybody. So, usually it was the citizens as a whole who made decisions and risked effeminacy if they did not assert their rights vis-à-vis other states. This is an important theme in Demosthenes' arguments for taking a strong line in foreign policy from his earliest speeches. In the *For the Liberty of the Rhodians* he argues that the Athenians should not restrain their support for the Rhodians out of fear of becoming embroiled in a war with Artemisia, ruler of Caria: would it not be disgraceful for the Athenians to "fear one who is at once a barbarian and a woman?"[66] In the same speech Demosthenes also makes a Realist argument – to which we shall return – with a gendered twist: since all other cities act unjustly, advocates of Athenian restraint are not urging justice, but rationalizing unmanliness.[67] We can discern here a contrast between advocates of intervention, who used the slogan "be manly," and more cautious Athenians, who appeal to justice. Demosthenes, an expert orator, must have thought that the specter of effeminacy would have some impact or he would not have deployed it; that Athens decided against his advice and did not intervene in Rhodes warns us not to overemphasize the force of this appeal.

In the *First Philippic* Demosthenes affects to believe that Philip's continued aggressiveness is due to divine intervention:

---

[63] Hdt. 3.134. See also Hdt. 1.37 and Xen. *Hell.* 7.1.24; cf. Xen. *An.* 7.1.21.
[64] Thuc. 4.27.5.   [65] Aeschin. 2.139.
[66] Dem. 15.23. At Salamis, the Athenians offered a special prize for the capture of another, earlier Artemisia in resentment at having a woman fighting against them (Hdt. 8.93). See also Gera 1997: 10 on *Tractatus de Mulieribus* section 13.
[67] Dem. 15.28.

For if he did nothing more, but were willing to rest satisfied . . . I believe some of you would be quite content with what must bring the deepest disgrace upon us and brand us as an unmanly nation.[68]

The manliness of Athens has been offended and Demosthenes pretends to welcome the fact that Philip is giving them another chance to redeem their reputation. As when he evoked the specter of slavishness, Demosthenes' rhetoric avoids directly insulting the Athenians. They are not yet slaves or women, but they are on a slippery slope, from which only aggressive action can save them.

In *On the False Embassy* Demosthenes puts his audience in another dilemma. The results of the Peace of Philocrates were so disgraceful that the Athenians must have been hoodwinked by Aeschines into accepting it. Otherwise, he tells the Athenians:

[You must} confess yourselves so unmanly and so cowardly that, with no enemy within your borders, no blockade of your ports, no imperilment of your capital, with corn-prices low . . . with the foreknowledge . . . that your allies would be ruined . . . you thereupon cheerfully made the peace.[69]

Demosthenes uses the specter of effeminacy to persuade the Athenians that they should find Aeschines guilty.

In addition to the references by the historians and in oratorical passages, two other types of evidence suggest that the argument from masculinity was a common pro-war appeal. First, the threat of unmanliness appears four times in Isocrates' *Archidamus*, which is teeming with pro-war *topoi*.[70] So Isocrates' exemplary, if fictional, pro-war speech repeatedly invokes the threat of unmanliness. Second, orators who argued against wars, seem to have expected the accusation of "unmanliness" to be raised against policies of accommodation in interstate relations; they sometimes tried to preclude its use. In *On the False Embassy* Aeschines lambastes the hypocrisy of those who are "pro-war and call peace unmanliness."[71] In Thucydides, Archidamus also finds it necessary to counter the accusation of unmanliness: "And let no one think it unmanliness that a multitude hesitates to attack a single city."[72] The appeal to avoid effeminacy was a typical slogan or

---

[68] Dem. 4.42.

[69] Dem. 19.218–19 (trans. modified). The words translated "unmanly and "cowardly" are *anandria* and *kakia*.

[70] Isoc. 6.7, 13, 56–7, 94.   [71] Aeschin. 2.137.

[72] Thuc. 1.83.1 (trans. modified). The word *anandria* could also be applied to individuals who were thought insufficiently aggressive (Pl. *Resp.* 8.560d; Xen. *An.* 2.6.25).

rallying cry for orators who felt Athens was not taking an aggressive enough policy.

Whenever an orator accused another of unmanliness or urged the Athenians not to act like women, the possibility of a more concrete sexual transgression was in the background: *kinaidia*, taking what the Athenians saw as the woman's role in sex by being penetrated by another man. Many passages reveal that, to Athenian thinking, being penetrated made a man into a woman.[73] Unsurprisingly, the masculine ideal was the warrior – and the hoplite in particular – and its opposite, among men, was the *kinaidos* – perhaps best translated "fairy" or "pansy."[74] So, for example, Aeschines calls Timarchus a woman on the grounds that he was penetrated.[75] In *On the False Embassy* he repeatedly attacked Demosthenes as a *kinaidos*.[76]

The imputation of *kinaidia* to an individual was a relatively straightforward insult; as a goading metaphor to encourage belligerence, the comparison of Athens itself or the Athenian assembly with a *kinaidos* was problematic. In comedy, Aristophanes could directly call his audience "wide-assed."[77] But, as we have seen, the orator was constantly faced with the dilemma of goading without insulting and alienating his audience. The imputation of being a *kinaidos* was too insulting to be applied to the people of Athens and the word itself was considered language inappropriate for the assembly.[78] Rather, orators preferred the vague word *malakos*, "soft." Although *malakos* has a range of meanings, when used of a person it evoked effeminacy. Greek male culture contrasted the hard, courageous men, active outside the house and the softer, fearful women who lived inside.[79]

Thus, though the insinuation of "softness" was less direct than calling a man or policy unmanly or womanish, it could imply something like *kinaidia*. For example, in the Aristotelian *Athenian Constitution*, Pisistratus' son Thessalus insults Harmodius by preventing his sister from marching in a sacred procession and by calling him *malakos*.[80] These insults inspired the plot against the lives of the tyrants. Significantly, Harmodius was the *erōmenos* of Aristogiton. The accusation that he was soft constituted "fighting words," since it implied that he was penetrated and thus effeminized. The imputation of *malakia* is likely to be a fourth-century addition to the

---

[73] Dover 1978: 76; Winkler 1990: 50; D. Cohen 1991: 184–7.

[74] Winkler 1990: 45, 47; Cartledge 1998a: 63; van Wees 2004: 40.   [75] Aeschin. 1.110–11.

[76] Aeschin. 2.88, 99; see also 2.151 and 1.131 with Dover 1978: 75. See also the passages linking *kinaidia* and effeminacy in Henderson 1991: 213.

[77] Ar. *Nub.* 1085–1104.

[78] Dover 1974: 33: "The sexual language of oratory is circumspect, sometimes even coy."

[79] Versnel 1987: 59. Cf. Dean-Jones 1994: 186.   [80] [Arist.] *Ath. Pol.* 18.2.

story.[81] It reveals that *malakos* was an insult and a challenge when applied to an individual and this seems to have been a common practice in the assembly and courtroom.

Malakos can denote individual cowardice in battle much as *anandros* does.[82] Generals and political leaders could also be *malakos* if they were insufficiently aggressive. In Thucydides, Archidamus was thought *malakos* for not organizing the invasion of Attica with enough vigor.[83] In *On the Chersonese* Demosthenes feels the need to defend himself from the accusation that he is "undaring and soft" in that he does not propose a motion against Philip but merely urges the support of Diopithes. He insists that he is "more manly" than the many reckless politicians whose self-interested and destructive policies he proceeds to attack.[84] In Aeschines' account in *On the False Embassy*, Demosthenes admits that he was *malakos* in that he did not want to stir up hostility with Thebes: he invokes considerations of prudence in his defense.[85] Demosthenes may have actually been willing briefly to admit *malakia* in a rhetorically daring gambit, but we should not put full faith in the verbatim fidelity of Aeschines' narration of Demosthenes' speech.

Malakos also seems to be a standard word to denote a city's unwillingness to fight. The hope of Philip's friendship, in which they were sadly disappointed, made the Phocians, previously determined to hold out to the end, soft (*malakos*) and thus unwilling to fight against Philip and the Thebans at the end of the Sacred War.[86] In Pseudo-Demosthenes' *On the Treaty with Alexander* the speaker claims that the Macedonians have "discovered that there is an indescribable slackness and softness [*malakia*] in our city"; this is why the Macedonians expect to break the terms of their peace treaty with impunity.[87]

As in the case of *anandria*, those arguing against war tried to preclude accusations of *malakia*. In the prelude to the Sicilian expedition Nicias urges the older men in the assembly not to be ashamed or fearful of being thought *malakos* for voting against the campaign.[88] The insinuation that a policy was *malakos* was another goad in the arsenal of the war orator, one that Nicias felt he needed to counter.

In his perceptive book *The Rhetoric of Manhood: Masculinity in the Attic Orators*, Joseph Roisman stresses that the ideal of masculinity was a flexible one and included the virtues of rationality and restraint, traits that could serve to discourage the recourse to war.[89] Nevertheless, he concedes, "the

---

[81] Lavelle 1986: 329–30.　　[82] Dem. 18.245.　　[83] Thuc. 2.18.3.　　[84] Dem. 8.68.
[85] Aeschin. 2.106.　　[86] Dem. 19.54.　　[87] [Dem.] 17.29 (trans. modified).
[88] Thuc. 6.13.1.　　[89] Roisman 2005: 114, 116.

prestige of war seemed to have given speakers who advocated taking a belligerent option a rhetorical advantage, since it was easy to identify peace or the reluctance to go to war with cowardice."[90]

Metaphors having as their source the relationships of fathers and sons played a large role in Athenian political discourse. These metaphors could be deployed to idealize the relationship either of the Athenians to the state – "we are sons of Athens" – or of the present to the past – "let us live up to our (fore)fathers." The first use could serve to encourage patriotism – of which military service and sacrifice were a large part: "act towards your state as you would act towards your father to whom you owe so much." The second was usually a goading metaphor: "Live up to the martial traditions of Athens' past as you wish to live up to your (fore)fathers."[91] This last use of the paternal metaphor appears paradoxical in one respect: ancient sources often emphasize a generational gap in terms of desire to go to war: it is the young who are eager for war, while the older men are the advocates of restraint.

In *Fathers and Sons in Athens: Ideology and Society in the Era of the Peloponnesian War*, Barry Strauss argues persuasively for a history of generational relationships.[92] He believes that from 440 to 413 Athenian culture displayed an increasing focus on youth, but after the failure of the Sicilian Expedition Athens experienced a reactionary turn back to the father.[93] Karl Jost earlier examined the use of the forefathers in history and oratory. He found that the exhortation to equal the feats of the ancestors was most common in the mid fourth century: Isocrates based much of his worldview on the idea of returning to the ways of an idealized past; most crucial for this book, Demosthenes portrayed the ancestors and Athens' past as placing important demands on the present.[94]

These cultural histories are as convincing as our limited and possibly unrepresentative sources allow. Nevertheless, deep continuities in such basic relationships are likely: two tendencies, devotion and competition between fathers and sons, are probably universal. Love, respect, and devotion towards a father were always expected and approved in Athens. Laws

[90] Roisman 2005: 113 citing Lys. 34.11; Aeschin. 2.137; Dem. 15.28, 19.218–19; Thuc. 6.13.1.
[91] Dem. 10.73 provides a particularly explicit example of this analogy.
[92] The following paragraphs follow Strauss' treatment. See also C. Patterson 1998 and the articles collected in Bertman 1976.
[93] Strauss 1993a: 128.
[94] Jost 1936: 249 (peak), 159–60 (Isocrates), 242 (Demosthenes). See also Yunis 2000.

required sons not to maltreat their parents, but to support them in their old age, and to arrange for their burials.[95] During the *dokimasia* before taking public office Athenians were asked several questions whose answers were to reveal if they deserved the trust of the state. Two of these are immediately relevant: do you treat your parents well? Do you have an ancestral tomb?[96] Such laws reflect strong normative expectations about how sons should feel and behave towards their fathers – and, in the case of ancestral tombs, their forefathers.[97]

Strauss explains that these expectations of filial devotion gave emotional force to the variety of words derived from *patēr*, father.[98] To some extent every reference to "fatherland" in oratory invokes a family relationship in order to confirm the feelings of patriotism. As in the case of slavishness and manliness, it may be that "fatherland" was sometimes a dead metaphor, which did not evoke the relationship of fathers and sons much more than "patriotic" does today.[99] But in some passages, the appeal to filial feeling is explicit. Demosthenes argues that every Athenian man of the Persian War period believed himself born to the state and not only to his parents: what such patriots felt for Athens is even greater and nobler than what others feel for their parents.[100] This appeal to the filial love of true Athenians for their country is embedded within an argument justifying the fight against Philip – as are many of Demosthenes' references to the fathers or forefathers.

The appeal to live up to the deeds of the ancestors was as important as the comparison of patriotism with filial devotion and belongs to the same cluster of ideas. Fathers and forefathers were closely connected in the Athenian worldview.[101] Indeed, the plural of fathers, *pateres*, could mean "forefathers" or "ancestors," and a group of adjectives denoting "traditional" or "hereditary" were also derived from "father."[102] Furthermore, in Greek culture the spokesman for ancestral ways was often an older man or father figure, a fact which makes patent the connection between the fathers and the ancestors in the Athenian worldview. Nevertheless the Athenians' sense of their past was not just a matter of filial feeling; other emotions and

---

[95] Strauss 1993a: 3, 44.

[96] Rhodes 1992: 617–18 ad [Arist.] *Ath. Pol.* 55.3 provides a discussion of these questions with references to other sources including Din. 2.17; Dem. 57.66–70; Aeschin. 1.28.

[97] Strauss 1993b: 263–4.

[98] Strauss 1993a: 27. See G. Johnson 1986 and 1987 for a Darwinian interpretation of the use of kin terms in political discourse.

[99] Cf. Strauss 1993a: 57–60.

[100] Straus 1993a: 49 on Dem. 18.205; these forefathers also rejected "servile security."

[101] Thuc. 2.36.1–2 is almost unique in stressing a distinction between the "fathers" and the "ancestors." See Hornblower 1991–2009: I.297 ad loc.

[102] Strauss 1993a: 24–5.

experiences certainly contributed to it. The militarism of Athenian public culture – the monuments, rituals, drama, and funeral orations discussed in Chapter 3 – immortalized a militant past and ensured its constant presence in the consciousness of Athenians. The relationship of fathers and sons does not provide an exhaustive explanation for the "burden of the Athenian past," as Harvey Yunis puts it; it did contribute to it.[103]

By the fourth century the ancestors were held up as models to be imitated in many spheres of life. In the realm of politics and interstate relations the example of the ancestors could recommend all sorts of actions and attitudes: not complaining in a petty way about the terms of an alliance, preferring the good of the state to personal wealth, not being flattered by orators, treating advocates of submission harshly, distrusting tyrants and barbarians, and not deserting one's post.[104] Its most common use, however, was to persuade an audience to match the martial valor of the past and not to compromise or yield to other states.[105]

We can distinguish three categories of this appeal: first, the Athenians can be portrayed as inheritors of a patrimony which they should not squander or allow to be diminished; second, the male lineage can be invoked as an audience; third, the present Athenians can be incited to rival the martial valor and deeds of their forefathers. Although it will be useful to distinguish these three types of appeals, some passages evoked more than one of these aspects of the relationship with the forefathers.

Strauss points out that Athens as a fatherland could be represented as a patrimony to be preserved and not squandered.[106] The male head of the household in particular was responsible for handing down the family property intact; indeed, there was a law against the "dissipation of patrimony, the *graphē argias*..."[107] So, too, the Athenians as a whole could be exhorted not to squander the city's good name or power, which was their inheritance.[108] Since not passing on a reduced inheritance could mean maintaining the power of one's state in the face of an outside threat – whether actual, perceived, or invented – this metaphor was applied in a

[103] Yunis 2000.
[104] Dem. 3.24, 25–6; 18.204, 238–41 (see Wankel 1976: 945–51 on this and a similar story in Hdt. 9.5); Dem. 9.38–9; Aeschin. 3.181, 253.
[105] Burckhardt 1996: 229.
[106] Strauss 1993a: 45. Strauss' examples use the verb *paradidōmi*, but *kataleipō* is often used and carries the same connotation of the passing down of a patrimony.
[107] See Davidson 1997: 206–10 on the censure incurred by those who squander their inherited wealth; 242 for the *graphē argias*.
[108] Thuc. 1.71.7 and 2.36.1–2 are cited by Strauss 1993a: 45. See also, e.g., Isoc. 6.8, 12, 57, 110; Thuc. 1.144.3–4; Xen. *Hell.* 7.1.30.

wide range of circumstances. In his speeches against Philip, Demosthenes encouraged the Athenians not to abandon the post that their ancestors bequeathed to them, a formulation which combines a military metaphor with the concept of an Athenian inheritance.[109] This metaphor of the state as a patrimony was also be implicit in the ephebes' oath, in which young Athenians as they come of age swear: "I shall not hand down (to my descendants) a lessened fatherland, but one that is increased in size and strength . . . "[110] This oath itself was sometimes quoted or alluded to by orators with various bellicose agenda.[111]

Both an estate and the greatness of Athens were timeless compared with the individual. Grandfathers and fathers may die, but the *klēros*, the family estate, lives on.[112] The preservation of the *klēros* and the continuation of the male line and its religious rituals seem to have been the main motive for adoption, a relatively common practice.[113] So, too, soldiers may die for Athens and generations come and go, but the glory of the city remains great: the deeds of the ancestors are often described as attaining immortality.[114] Thus the evocation of the Athenian tradition in war oratory displaces the specific occasion in interstate politics with a timeless, greater issue. The use of this metaphor implies that the question is not, for example, whether to help Olynthus, until recently an enemy of Athens, but rather whether Athens will maintain the reputation it has enjoyed over the centuries.[115]

Both the idea of the *klēros* and of the timeless greatness of Athens play also on the individual's hope for immortality. Private citizens seem often to have died content in the knowledge that they had done their part for the *klēros*, that their tomb would be tended, and the family and its property continue to exist. The citizen-soldiers of Athens were repeatedly assured that death in battle was not really death at all; not only would Athens go on, but the memory of its wars and their accomplishments would never fade.[116] To reject an appeal to the Athenian tradition was not only disloyalty to the ancestors and to some extent to one's father; it was also to destroy one's own chance of escaping death, of sharing in the city's immortality.

---

[109] Dem. 3.36. Cf. 10.46; 18.200. [110] Tod 1946–8: no. 204; trans. Ha no. 109 = RO no. 88.

[111] Siewert 1977: 108 on Plut. *Alc.* 15.4; Thuc. 1.144.4; Dem. 19.303; and Lycurg. *Leoc.* 76–8.

[112] LSJ *klēros* III.3: "legacy, inheritance, heritable estate."

[113] Isae. 7.30 with Wyse 1904: 576 and Just 1989: 90–5.

[114] The reputation acquired by the ancestors is praised as immortal, still alive, or inextinguishable at Dem. 20.69; 22.77; 23.208; 24.185; and 25.97 collected in Jost 1936: 221.

[115] See also the Melians' invocation of their three hundred years of independence in their final reply to the Athenians (Thuc. 5.112.2).

[116] Thuc. 2.43.2; Lys. 2.79–80; Dem. 60.32, 34, 36; Hyp. 6.27, 41–2.

A family's *klēros* resembles the ancestral greatness of Athens in another way; both are the property of an all-male lineage.[117] The requirement that property follow agnatic lines of kinship in Athens and the prohibition, through the institution of the *epiklēros*, of the alienation of an estate from the paternal family are well known.[118] So too warrior elites often represent themselves as an all male line of warriors: they understand "themselves to be part of one long, unbroken tradition linking father and son and, more generally, the fighting men of one time to those of another. In their own minds, they form a special kind of lineage – of which General Douglas MacArthur's famous image of a "long gray line" of West Point alumni is one example."[119]

I suspect that this notion was less influential in Athens than among a warrior elite. First of all, the Athenian citizens did not comprise a warrior elite. In the fourth century they were but occasional soldiers not warriors. Nevertheless, it may have flattered and puffed up, for example, a cart-driver and sometimes rower to think of himself in terms appropriate to a Homeric hero or an archaic aristocrat, groups with much more of the warrior ethos. As in other ways, the democracy adopted and made common the values and ideals belonging to earlier periods and richer classes; this allowed war orators to invoke a long lineage of men described largely in terms of military prowess and to urge upon their audiences a responsibility to this lineage. For example, Demosthenes in his *Funeral Oration* claims that the members of each of the ten tribes, which were the basis for the ten units of the Athenian army, were inspired by the feats of the mythical characters after which their tribe was named.[120] Although the tribes were established in 508 and some of the associated myths were elaborated only after that time, Demosthenes tries to show that the Athenian war dead were part of a lineage stretching back to mythical times.

A final and crucial function of the invocation of the ancestors was to expand the audience before whom the Athenians saw themselves as acting. Orators occasionally emphasized that the Athenians' actions will be known to all of Greece. The family, a less numerous but more distinct and intimate audience, could also be invoked.[121] The ancestors, sometimes in tandem with posterity, provided an audience extended across time and

---

[117] Cf. Ehrenreich 1997: 154, 157.   [118] Just 1989: 95–8.

[119] Ehrenreich 1997: 151; see also Theweleit 1989: 360–1 on the psychology of the *Freikorps* in inter-war Germany.

[120] Dem. 60.27–31. Surprisingly this was not an all-male lineage; women are prominent in the myths Demosthenes relates here.

[121] Xen. *Hell.* 7.1.30; Isoc. 6.110.

one that commanded the respect of all Athenian men, a crucial attribute of a shaming audience.[122] Barbara Ehrenreich discusses a modern example in which the lineage of a warrior elite serves as an audience:

Addressing the cadets at West Point, General MacArthur conjured up a ghostly succession of American warriors who were to serve as the superegos of the young. Were the cadets ever to fail in their duty, "a million ghosts in olive drab, in brown khaki, in blue and gray, would rise from their white crosses, thundering those magic words: Duty, honor, country."[123]

The military ancestors served a similar purpose in Athenian minds as an "internalized other."[124] Thus, they could be invoked as witnesses to an oath just as the gods could. Near the end of *Against Ctesiphon* Aeschines invokes a list of great Athenian warriors and heroes and asks whether "the very sepulchers of your fathers, will groan aloud" if Demosthenes is crowned.[125] In *On the Crown* Demosthenes strikes back with a justly famous oath: he asserts that the city could not have been wrong to take risks "on behalf of everyone and for the sake of freedom and safety." He swears by the ancestors "those who fought in front at Marathon . . . those who fought the naval battle of Salamis . . . those who fought at Artemesium and the many others buried in the public cemetery."[126]

When orators invoked the glories of the forefathers they were also evoking a feeling of competition with fathers. Hence the challenge in war oratory to live up to the ancestors plays off the sense of rivalry with an older generation; it works because sons not only love their fathers but compete with them. Strauss points out that

"Some father–son conflict indeed seems inevitable, given the universal struggle in all societies over the intergenerational transmission of power and property, and the universal alternation of dependence and independence."[127]

This tension is one reason why the appeal to match the ancestors works. Given the primacy of military virtues and that military exploits were the most important events in the cultural memory of Athens, this was a particularly important arena for competition.[128] Hence the invocation of rivalry with the fathers and forefathers typically served to recommend a proud refusal to compromise and a determination not to be beaten in war.

We have seen that a distorted national history of the ancestors' glorious victories could lead to miscalculations and excessive optimism about the

---

[122] See Dover 1974: 243–6; Williams 1993: 82–4.   [123] Ehrenreich 1997: 153.
[124] Williams 1993: 82–5; see also the formulation of Yunis 2000: 110.   [125] Aeschin. 3.257–9.
[126] Dem. 18.208 (my translation). See also Dem. 18.199–201 with Yunis 2000: esp. 107–8; Lys. 12.100; Din. 1.66 with Dover 1974: 246; and perhaps Hyp. 6.31 with Herrman (forthcoming).
[127] Strauss 1993a: 13, discussed in detail 100–29.   [128] Cf. Dem. 19.269.

outcome of wars; the invocation of the forefathers and their glories had an emotional impact which was just as potent in prodding the Athenians to fight wars. For example, in *On the Liberty of the Rhodians* Demosthenes argues that Mausolus and Artemisia seized Cos and Rhodes and other places "for which the Greek of those days face many dangers and won much honor in the field."[129] Here Demosthenes dares his audience to try not to fall below the standard of their ancestors. When Demosthenes incites the Athenians to war with Philip, he often argues in terms of the simple obligation to live up to Athens' glorious past.[130]

But skillful orators would add twists on the basic idea. For example, Demosthenes describes the Athenians as constantly hearing about their ancestors and seeing the memorials of their prowess and, in a second passage, as delighting in this. These experiences form the basis for a conclusion of the form "so how could we give up our liberty without a fight."[131] An unusual set of appeals to the ancestors occurs in Demosthenes' speech *On the Navy-Boards*. The political context of this speech was the perceived threat of Persian aggression and a call to make war against the Great King. This setting seems to have led, inevitably perhaps, to appeals to the great days of the Persian War and the forefathers who had defended Greek liberty. Demosthenes aimed to prevent the Athenians from starting a war with Persia. The other main emphasis of his speech was the reform of the financing of the Athenian navy, a crucial and useful but unheroic, topic. Despite the apparently inappropriate subject matter, Demosthenes repeatedly invokes the ancestors. But in each case he presents an alternative to the standard, patriotic, and belligerent formulation. Demosthenes begins by deflating the appeal to the ancestors by pointing out a difficulty, the impossibility of doing them justice. His emphasis will be on action not words: "I shall confine myself to how you can best prepare for war."[132] But he does not necessarily want the preparation to be used in a war against the Persians. He gives priority to the justice of the ancestors – also undeniable of course – rather than to their prowess:

you must employ those same forces in self-defense against the King and against all who venture to do you wrong, though you must not set the example of wrong, either in word or in deed; and you must see to it that our actions, rather than the speeches delivered from this platform are worthy of our fathers.[133]

---

[129] Dem. 15.27–8.
[130] Jost 1936: 242; Yunis 2000: 109. E.g. Dem. 10.74 = Dem. 8.49; Isoc. 6.12; Dem. 10.24–5, see also [Dem] 7.7. This appeal is commonly depicted in Thucydides too: 1.122.3; 2.11.2; 4.92.7; and 4.95.3.
[131] Dem. 15.35; 18.68. [132] Dem. 14.1–2. See also Dem. *Exordia* 33. See also [Dem.] 13.12.
[133] Dem. 14.41.

Demosthenes also presents the argument that Athenian preparations, when reported to the king, will intimidate him when he considers the outcome of the Persian War.[134] The force of this argument and the overall impact of his appeals to the forefathers is that they allowed Demosthenes to refer to the Persian Wars, as the warmongers were doing, and to seem to be taking an aggressive position against the Persian king, while in fact he opposes war and is merely suggesting a reorganization of military finance.

It is only in Aeschines – discussed above – and Isocrates that we see more direct objections to this use of the example of the ancestors.[135] In *On the Peace* Isocrates portrays the advocates of war as demanding that the Athenians should imitate the ancestors: he agrees that the Athenians should imitate the good ancestors of the Persian War period, but not those who exposed the city to the risk of enslavement in the Decelean War, the last phase of the Peloponnesian War.[136] Later he even condemns the folly and injustice of the Athenian empire, perpetrated by "the forefathers."[137] As in other respects, Isocrates' *On the Peace* is atypical and would probably have caused Isocrates to be jeered at and removed from the *bēma*. As with the invocation of slavishness and of effeminacy, such cases where an orator attempts to counter or pre-empt a type of argument show most decisively its ubiquity: a skilled orator would only try to preclude an argument that he thought was likely to be deployed.

Sons' feeling for the forefathers probably involved their feelings towards their fathers; thus skillful orators were making use of the rivalry between son and father when they demanded that the Athenians live up to their ancestors. But in another sense the appeal to live up to the forefathers was a profoundly unifying one. It displaced the rivalry between generations with a common challenge to match and respect the forefathers. Jost points out that in the same way as the family comes together to honor its male ancestors at festivals of the dead, so does the whole community honor its ancestors during the public burial of the war dead. This was, of course, the occasion of the funeral oration, usually laden with descriptions of the ancestors and their deeds, both historical and mythical.[138] All Athenian men could be incited to match the forefathers, the fathers common to all.

Orators could address their audience as a group of sons in relation to fathers whose prowess and accomplishments they needed to match; they could also appeal to the audience as fathers who needed to protect their

---

[134] Dem. 14.29–30.   [135] See pp. 70–1 on Aeschin. 2.74–5, cf. 2.63.
[136] Isoc. 8.36–8. See pp. 262–4.   [137] Isoc. 8.79–85.   [138] Jost 1936: 249.

families.[139] The audience would in fact comprise fathers and sons and some men would be both. But ancient sources often make a distinction: a host of passages depict the young as hot-headed and belligerent and the old as relatively restrained. To take one example, in Thucydides Nicias exhorts the old men in the audience not to be afraid of appearing soft if they vote to oppose the Sicilian expedition.[140] This implies that the older men would naturally be opposed to such an adventure but might be intimidated into going along. In several other passages where this tendency is noted, Thucydides attributes the belligerence of the young to their lack of experience. They did not know what war would be like and accordingly were overenthusiastic: "there were also many young men in the Peloponnesos and many in Athens who, in their inexperience, took on the war with no unwillingness."[141] Aristotle depicts the young as confident, passionate, and brave in contrast to the old.[142] Such characteristics are those that would conduce to favoring a riskier and more belligerent policy. Indeed, we have already seen that war orators try to stimulate these qualities: they foster confidence, they encourage a passionate touchiness about insults, they insist that war is the brave, the manly policy. The advocates of peace may attempt to encourage and emphasize the importance of self-restraint, a quality in which the old are superior. Thus, Aristotle's observation of the qualities of old and young are at one with the generalizations about the old and young's propensity to oppose or favor war.

Is this generalization merely an ancient stereotype with little basis in reality? In some sense it probably was: I need to repeat here all the caveats I attached to the claim that the rich favored peace and the poor favored war. Not every young person was more prone to vote for war than every old person; some wars must have enjoyed support throughout the citizen body, from both young and old; some were rejected by all. Yet, just as with the connection of class and warlike propensity, I believe that the generalization had a kernel of truth.

Aristotle's observations about the individual characteristics of young and old find some confirmation in studies that reveal that in all cultures there has been a greater propensity of younger men relative to women or older men to engage in potentially lethal violence.[143] But if this difference in the individual propensity towards violence between young and old is

---

[139] See below, pp. 138–50.   [140] Thuc. 6.13.1 (cf. 6.24.3–4). See also 2.20.2.

[141] Thuc. 2.8.1; See also Thuc. 1.42.1, 72.1, 80.1; 2.20.2; and 8.92.8; Xen. *Hell.* 7.4.25 and Isoc. 8.12. Cf. Chaniotis 2005: 55 on the Hellenistic period.

[142] Arist. *Rh.* 2.12.1389a25–30, 2.13.1389b29–33, 2.14.1390b5–6.

[143] Runciman 1998: 736; Daly and Wilson 1988: 146, 168–70.

ahistorical, their respective roles in warfare and thus their attitudes towards war are not. Although the army mustered by age group in our period, service was by no means confined to the young – especially in the most important campaigns when the Athenians were trying to field as large an army as they could. There is ample evidence of men being killed in battle at ages up to sixty.[144] Demosthenes was about forty-six when he took part in the battle of Chaeronea.[145] Indeed, Jason of Pherae was reported to claim that his army of mercenaries was superior in that it did not include soldiers "advanced in years and others who have not come to their prime" as did the citizen armies of most cities.[146] A few passages suggest that serving on voluntary or smaller expeditions was something that younger men would do.[147] But when the assembled Athenian citizen men voted for war, it could well turn out to be a matter of courage in a direct sense for both young and old.

The politics of young and old in the Vietnam-era United States was dramatically influenced by the fact that only young men were drafted. In 1965 Phil Ochs could sing to a generation instructed not to trust anyone over thirty: "It's always the old that lead us to the war. | It's always the young to fall."[148] Although scholars have detected an ancient generation gap, especially during the Peloponnesian War, its basis was not the greater risks of the young in war and hence their commitment to peace.[149] Its basis was the rashness and ignorance of the young men that made them eager for war.

CONCLUSION

In one passage in *For the Liberty of the Rhodians* Demosthenes mixes appeals to all the relationships I have been discussing in this chapter. He recalls Argos' refusal to cooperate with Sparta's efforts to support the Thirty:

Then would it not be discreditable, men of Athens, if when the commons of Argos feared not the authority of the Lacedaemonians in the day of their might, you, who are Athenians, should fear one who is at once a barbarian and a woman

---

[144] Hanson 1989: 89–95.

[145] Isae. 10.20 describes a father and son going on campaign together during the Corinthian War.

[146] Xen. *Hell.* 6.1.5.

[147] Isae. 2.6 cf. 12; 7.40–1. Theophr. *Char.* 27.3 has an older man learning military commands from his son, which implies that military training was a young man's business – as the ephebic reforms may have made it. See also Pierce 1998: 130.

[148] Lyrics to Phil Ochs "I ain't marching anymore" at www.azlyrics.cc/lyrics/p/phil_ochs/i_aint_marching_anymore/i_aint_marching_anymore.html. Cf. Russell 1951: 127.

[149] Forrest 1975; Strauss 1993a: esp. 130–78 on Alcibiades; Strauss 1993b: 157.

[Artemesia the Persian Satrap]? Indeed, the Argives might have pleaded that they had often been defeated by the Lacedaemonians, but you have beaten the King again and again, and have never been beaten either by his slaves or by their master himself . . . [150]

Demosthenes challenges the Athenians to live up to their noble ancestors, who defeated the Persians. He puts in question the manliness and freedom of his audience: Are you not willing to fight a woman? Are you not willing to fight a slave (of the king)?

This passage sums up how the relationships that constituted the Athenian *oikos* contributed to a prickliness that could be tapped in the assembly. In cases where Athens' decision about whether to go to war was in doubt, the nature of the Athenian family and household gave pro-war orators an advantage. Reasons to go to war existed before they were described and stimulated by these metaphors, but they were strengthened by the way they could be expressed and the persuasive power of that expression derived ultimately from the structure of Athenian society.

The relationships that served as the basis of the arguments we have been considering were intimate and emotional ones; the metaphors derived from them tend to have more emotional force than intellectual structure. Many of them can be paraphrased quite simply: "Don't be a sissy. Vote for war." This is not the whole story of Athenian decision-making. The Athenians were not simplistic, emotional warmongers, as their consistent and intelligent foreign policy in the fourth century attests, and as their influence on intellectuals and leaders in a host of cultures and times suggests. Our next subject, the right of self-defense among states, is still on the emotional and simple end of the spectrum of arguments about war. It does, however, provide criteria for discussion about certain situations among states and is thus a step closer to more complex and rational ways of thinking that derived from less intimate domestic relationships – those between friends or litigants – or claimed independence from any domestic analogy – as did some calculations of state interest. It is these that give Athenian thought its surprising modernity.

---

[150] Dem. 15.22–3. Cf. Missiou 1993.

CHAPTER 6

Defense and attack

Two beliefs were fundamental to Athenian moral thinking about war: first, starting a war without provocation was unjust and, second, states had a right to defend themselves. These judgments seem simple and familiar. When we examine the details of what counted as provocation, what it could justify, and how the argument for self-defense was deployed the picture becomes more complicated and more dependent on its specific historical and social context. We will examine condemnations of aggression in a variety of contexts, but here I will briefly preview a few of the relevant issues. I then turn to the elaborations of the argument for self-defense, the main subject of this chapter.

Despite the condemnation of unprovoked aggression, wars of self-defense were not the only type of just war: the Athenians did not believe in *defensivism*, the idea that only defensive wars were justified.[1] Indeed, Athenian morality was offended as easily by staying at peace as by going to war: wars of revenge were perfectly just; staying at peace when an ally required support was morally indefensible. So one state might invade another's territory with complete justification. Unprovoked aggression, on the other hand, was generally condemned. It would only be a slight exaggeration to say that none of the moral argumentation of deliberative oratory makes sense without reference to this basic assumption: Why would Athenian orators justify a war if war required no justification? Why would they accuse rival states of aggression if aggression were not generally condemned? So the necessity of making excuses for going to war reveals the moral code by which Greek states expected to be judged and, probably, the fear that that such judgments might have consequences.[2]

Notwithstanding this overwhelming evidence that the Greeks thought that wars required justification, two complexities, treated in detail

---

[1] Dawson 1996: 3.   [2] Karavites 1984: 192; cf. Walzer 1977: 20.

elsewhere, bear repeating here.[3] First, one strand of Greek thinking, present in oratory as well as in celebrated passages in Thucydides, denied the validity of moral norms to interstate relations. The fear of the censure that is earned by unprovoked aggression plays little part in this Realist viewpoint, as we shall see. Second, scholars vary widely in their estimation of the extent of the provocation needed for a Greek state to justify war; some argue that Greek states went to war often and with little reason – as we have seen.[4]

More immediately relevant and problematic are the references to land that is, in Aeschines' formulation, "won by the spear" and thus a legitimate possession "by the rule of war."[5] This concept may derive from the notion that victory in war resulted from superiority and that this superiority justified rule.[6] Success in war, as in other aspects of life, could also be seen as a sign of divine approval.[7] The concept of territory "won by the spear" is still perplexing: it was a diplomatic argument and not merely an assertion of the fact of possession. If this argument for just ownership were a common and compelling one, we might infer that victory in war could justify ownership, a might-makes-right notion that would seem to supersede the prohibition of aggression – in contrast, the Realist argument is that right and wrong do not matter.

In many cases the argument that land is "won by the spear" is redundant in one sense or another, so it does not need to bear full weight of conviction. For example, most references to "spear-won" territory appear in contexts where the justice of the original war is also asserted.[8] The Athenians believed that the results of a just war might include legitimate conquests, which is not the same as a blanket approval of all successful wars.

---

[3] See pp. 154–66 and 240–8 for detailed discussions.   [4] Pp. 1–6, 51–2.

[5] Aeschin. 2.33. Similar expressions or sentiments can be found in Xen. *Hell.* 3.2.23, *Cyr.* 7.5.73; Isoc. 4.177; 6.19, 32; [Dem] 12.20–3; Diod. 17.17.2. Chaniotis 2004 uses evidence from the Hellenistic era; my argument in this section, based on fourth-century evidence, generally follows his line of reasoning (187–90).

[6] Hunt 1998: 153–8.   [7] E.g. Adkins 1997: 709; Chaniotis 2005: 183.

[8] (1) Xenophon: Xen. *Hell.* 3.2.23 is a brief reference and gives no indication about the reason for the original war; in Xen. *Cyr.* 7.5.77 Cyrus insists that they hold their possessions justly since they "took revenge on those who had plotted against them."

(2) Isocrates: Isoc. 6.32 invokes crimes and an oracle of Apollo; that the Greek and Persians should possess what they had conquered would have been one possible basis for a fair peace treaty (4.177), but Isocrates then insists on an argument from the antiquity of possession (4.178).

(3) Aeschines: Aeschin. 2.32 rejects Philip's line of argument and favors one based on the recognition of Athens' right to Amphipolis by a former king of Macedonia.

(4) "Philip's Letter": Philip claims an ancestral and a treaty right to Amphipolis as well as the right of conquest ([Dem.] 12.20–3).

(5) Alexander: despite the suggestion that he claimed Asia as spear-won territory in Diod. 17.17.2, a letter, whether genuine or not, from Alexander to Darius reflects sundry Macedonian justifications for their invasion of Persia (Arr. *Anab.* 2.14.4–6; cf. Diod. 16.89.2).

Rather it is in line with their view that some offensive wars can be justified. That most wars were concluded with a sworn treaty may also help to explain "spear-won" territory, because a treaty, witnessed by the gods, gave legitimacy to the results of war, including conquests. In the passage with which we began this discussion, Aeschines concedes that Philip had won Amphipolis from its inhabitants. He then presents an argument for why this still did not give him the rights of conquest: Philip had never defeated Athens, the rightful owners of Amphipolis, and thus Philip had no rights of conquest to Amphipolis vis-à-vis Athens. Aeschines seems to think that the Amphipolitans did not gain the right of independence through their successful resistance to Athens, perhaps because Athens never conceded these in a treaty – and indeed the Peace of Nicias assigned Amphipolis to Athens. The Amphipolitans had not had their "spear-won" right to their own city confirmed and thus Philip's conquest of Amphipolis could not win him a right of conquest that Athens needed to respect. The final and decisive consideration, according to Aeschines, was that the Athenian right to Amphipolis was confirmed, as far as Macedonia was concerned, in a treaty to which a representative to the Macedonian king was a party.[9]

The passage of time, like a sworn treaty, could help to convert a violent acquisition into a legitimate possession. This is one of the arguments that Isocrates deploys to justify Sparta's rule over Messenia:

Then again you are doubtless well aware that possessions, whether private or public, when they have remained for a long time in the hands of their owner, are by all men acknowledged to be hereditary and incontestable.[10]

Indeed, most Greek states other than Athens traced their rights to their land back to an original act of conquest in the distant past.[11] But the aim of such genealogies was usually the preservation of the status quo rather than the justification of aggression. It remains today a plausible position that a few generations of possession outweigh the justice or injustice of a bygone war – although the rights and sentiments of a land's current inhabitants are more typically adduced as the basis for such a judgment.[12]

The notion of a right by conquest still strikes a discordant note that cannot be entirely explained away. We should not, however, place too much emphasis on it. References to the right of conquest are extremely rare compared with the number of passages that censure unprovoked aggression. In particular, Angelos Chaniotis has shown a pervasive distinction between mere possession and lawful ownership of land; such a generally accepted

---

[9] Aeschin. 2.32.   [10] Isoc. 6.26–7.   [11] Chaniotis 2004: 195.   [12] Walzer 1977: 55–8.

contrast implies that violent occupation by itself did not give rights.[13] The notion of a right to land "captured by the spear" is at most an eddy, well out of the mainstream of Greek thinking.

Let us turn now to the elaborations of the well-attested right to self-defense. An individual Athenian man was justified and had an obvious interest in defending himself from violence. Within his house, if he caught a thief at night – not to mention an adulterer – he had the legal right to kill him on the spot.[14] More generally, an important issue in assault cases was who attacked whom and who was merely defending himself?[15] An analogy from or multiplication of this simple situation could be used to describe the self-defense of a city-state against an invading army. Hence, a state's right to defend itself was typically assumed throughout the course of Greek history – as it is today.[16] Already in Homer, Hector says that "One bird sign is best: to fight in defense of our country," a line still quoted to inspire martial enthusiasm in the classical period.[17] And, in Thucydides, the Plataeans on trial for their lives invoked "the rule observed by all, that defense against an attacking enemy is lawful."[18]

But no oratory was necessary to convince an individual Athenian man to defend himself and his home; so too, by the time an enemy had entered Attica, speeches about whether to go to war or not were superfluous. That Athenians assumed the right of self-defense is still perfectly obvious on the state as well as on the individual level. But the fact that deliberative oratory was not appropriate or possible when simple self-defense was the issue had two important consequences both for the nature of our evidence and for the types of appeals that invoked self-defense. The references to self-defense in assembly speeches are indirect ones: orators assimilated more complex and ambiguous situations to self-defense to capitalize on this unassailable right and its associated emotions. Just as modern politicians do, Athenian orators tried to expand the right of self-defense to include pre-emptive attacks against states that were merely threatening, but who, it could be claimed, were going to attack Athens in the future. Usually, in deliberative oratory, we find ourselves at two removes from the simple case of individual self-defense: a state rather than an individual is involved and that state is not, at least in any concrete sense, being attacked.

---

[13] Chaniotis 2004: 187–90.   [14] Carey 1989: 81 on Lys. 1.36.   [15] E.g. Lys. 3.8, 12, 15; 20.1.
[16] Walzer 1977: 51–73 provides a discussion and justification of the right of self-defense for states. Pacifists, *stricto sensu*, deny the right to use violence even in self-defense: e.g. Struckmeyer 1971/2 contra Wells 1969: 825. See also Teichman 1986: 26; Collier 1991: 132.
[17] Hom. *Il.* 12.243; Arist. *Rh.* 2.21.1395a10–20. Cited also on the eve of World War II by Nestle 1938: 76.
[18] Thuc. 3.56.2.

We find direct appeals to the right of self-defense almost exclusively in the pre-battle speeches attributed to generals. When historians represent the speeches that generals made before battles, they often include the claim that the battle is being fought in self-defense.[19] By these appeals, generals aimed to rouse their troops to fight harder, since, as Demosthenes points out, "people fight most desperately to defend what they possess."[20] A passage from Aeneas Tacticus explains why this makes perfect sense:

[In contrast to the stakes in an offensive operation,] when it is in defence of the fundamentals – shrines and fatherland and parents and children and so on – that the risks are to be run, the struggle is not the same, or even similar. A successful repulse of the enemy means safety, intimidated opponents, and the unlikelihood of attack in the future, whereas a poor showing in the face of the danger leaves no hope of salvation.[21]

Aeneas takes the fundamentals to be at risk, because the topic of his work is *How to Survive under Siege*. His history gives us a view of Greek warfare from the receiving end, the "responsible passive" as David Whitehead puts it.[22] In such cases almost all the citizens of a city may jointly have been in something close to the simple situation of self-defense.

In most cases, and especially when larger cities such as Athens fought each other, the situation was considerably more complex than simple self-defense. Indeed, occasionally the generals on both sides claim to be fighting in defense. Before the battle of Delium, the general Pagondas appealed to the Thebans' national character which made them ready to ward off their enemies whether in their own territory or outside it – since they caught up with the Athenian army on its way home and already out of Boeotia.[23] Hippocrates, the opposing, Athenian general, had to be equally inventive given that the fight took place during the march home of an Athenian army of invasion which had just established a fort in Boeotia: nevertheless, he argued that defeating the Thebans would save Attica from further attacks.[24]

DEFENDENDA

Aeneas' passage does not simply speak of defense but invokes "fatherland, parents, children and so on," all items commonly invoked to make defense

---

[19] E.g. Thuc. 5.69.1 of several contingents at Mantinea; Thuc. 7.64.1 to the Athenians at Syracuse.
[20] Dem. 15.10. See also Thuc. 2.39.2.   [21] Aen. Tact. *Poliorcetica* Pref. 2. Cf. Thuc. 2.39.2.
[22] Whitehead 1990: 3.   [23] Thuc. 4.92.3, 92.7.   [24] Thuc. 4.95.2–3.

vivid and emotional.[25] For larger cities such as Athens the necessity of self-defense could be abstract on most occasions, so generals tried to make it more vivid and powerful. They did this in two basic ways: they claimed that emotionally laden symbols of the state and community were at risk; they made the attack personal by portraying it as directed against the families of every individual soldier. Both of these tactics made self-defense more vivid and concrete and were presumably calculated to rouse soldiers to fighting fury. In some cases the threat was vivid enough already, but often a defeat was likely to result in something like the loss of state autonomy, the payment of tribute, the loss of a disputed borderland – or even merely the failure of an attack, as we saw in the case of the Athenians at Delium. In the classical period defeat rarely resulted in the wholesale violation of women or the destruction of temples, both of which the generals portray as at stake.

In modern times, these emotionally charged appeals represent the nadir of war oratory. Any war, be its cause just, frivolous, insufficient, or vicious, can be portrayed as an intimate assault on the individual soldier and the things he holds most dear. The less justified the war, the more pernicious this sleight-of-hand appears. The greater the divide between the informed and calculating leaders, who made the decision for war, and the draftees, who fight, the more do these appeals seem to be deplorable propaganda: devised to enrage men whose real role, could they see it clearly, is not to defend their homes and hearths, but to fight and die for the benefit of a governing elite. In all cases, such rhetoric serves to increase fear and hatred of the enemy, who for their part often also believe that they are fighting to protect their women and children from outrage.

This condemnation must be softened when we judge a threat to be real and the state concerned to be democratic in its decision-making and egalitarian in the imposition of military service. Athenian wars varied in their justification, so no generalizations are possible there. The Athenian decision-making process excluded foreigners, slaves, and women, but it included a large proportion of the fighting men and, in particular, those fighters to whom these appeals were addressed.[26] Athens was not a society in which one group of people fought and another made the decisions.

---

[25] The final part of this list, "and so on," implies that he could go on. That he does not do so might seem dismissive, but the passage seems otherwise anything but ironic.

[26] Metics in the Athenian army might well have had homes (rented) and families in Athens that they could imagine protecting, but they did not participate in the democracy. At a naval battle a significant proportion of the combatants might be slaves or mercenaries. Whatever one might say about their motivations, they were not going to fight to defend their families, homes, tombs, and gods. Such men do not seem to be the intended audience of these appeals.

These emotional appeals may still be considered propaganda, but they were not contrived by an elite to dupe a mass audience.[27] I am not sure we should reverse entirely the modern condemnation of such appeals; in any case, their use repays investigation. In particular, these appeals reveal the most basic attachments of the Athenian soldiers. When some American soldiers said that they were fighting World War II for "mom and apple pie," they revealed a conception of that war as defensive and of "mom and apple pie" as emblematic of what they believed they were defending. So, too, when an Athenian general wanted to sum up what was most worth defending in a state, he would turn to a limited and conventional set of emblematic and emotionally charged items. The identity of these items does not reveal so much what Athenians thought about this particular war and its justice, but rather what they felt was most important, most worth defending, in their lives.

Many pre-battle speeches include appeals based on simple self-defense. Once they are on the point of a battle, soldiers are, to some extent, in a situation of self-defense: they must kill or be killed. A long tradition in ancient Greece emphasized this aspect of battle and held that the safest course is that of brave and disciplined resolution.[28] These arguments did not carry full conviction against the shrewd notion that, for example, throwing away one's shield and running looked even safer.[29] So generals also tended to sum up the communal or family life that the soldiers ought to defend even at risk to their own lives. For example, Thucydides describes Nicias' appeals just before the final naval battle of the Sicilian Expedition:

[S]aying other things as well which men in so great a time of crisis would not mention if they were guarding against appearing to speak in platitudes, especially references to women and children and ancestral gods, which are brought forward in much the same form for every occasion . . . "[30]

Thucydides thought that appeals to "women and children and ancestral gods" were hackneyed and conventional. There is no reason to doubt him: these types of appeals appear in military exhortations from Homer onwards.[31] We also find such lists when an orator wants to make vivid the bad faith of those he considered traitors: they have abandoned the

---

[27] See Carey 2005: 70 on the "horizontal or upward" direction of Athenian propaganda.

[28] Tyrtaeus 11.11–13; Thuc. 4.126.6; Pl. *Symp.* 221a–c.

[29] In contrast to the argument of Alcibiades in the *Symposium* – the official line – Socrates in the *Apology* admits that a soldier may easily save his life if he is willing to act disgracefully (Pl. *Symp.* 221a–c, *Ap.* 39a.)

[30] Thuc. 7.69.2.

[31] Hom. *Il.* 5.485–6; 8.57; 9.593–4 (quoted in Arist. *Rh.* 1.7.1365a11–15); 15.661–5; 16.265; Tyrtaeus 12.32–4 (West); Callinus of Ephesis fr. 1 (West); Aesch. *Sept.* 10–16, *Pers.* 401–5; Thuc. 6.68.3; Xen. *Hell.* 2.4.17; 7.1.30.

fatherland; they have not gone to the aid of the ancestral temples; they have abandoned the tombs of the ancestors; they have allowed the land to be subject to the enemy.[32] If we put together the items in these lists, we find that they include four interrelated groups: the temples, the land, ancestral tombs, and the family. In each case the item was valued in itself and hence worth defending; each could be represented as particularly at stake in war.[33]

The appeal to defend the temples is symptomatic of religion's continued centrality to Greek culture in the classical period.[34] The rhetorical invocation of the gods was particularly effective in this context since they possessed a power not subject to envy and some were closely connected with the state itself – for example, Athena in Athens. Soldiers in later ages would die for the king, but no mere mortal commanded such loyalty in democratic Athens; only the gods did. The gods also assisted the community in general and specifically in times of war. To lose one's temples to the enemy was to be cut off from the gods and thus from the possibility of divine assistance.[35] Finally, the defense of temples from plundering or desecration was a holy duty owed in return for divine support and this duty was taken seriously.[36] But, although vengeance for desecration is well attested, most Greek states tried not to offend an enemy's gods – who were, to a large extent, their own gods as well.[37] For example, Archidamus, the Spartan king, provides an example: before he invaded Plataean territory he took care publicly to tell the heroes and gods of the Plataeans that he was not really an aggressor.[38] Nevertheless, the possibility of the destruction of temples was one that a general could invoke to rouse a sense of outrage in his soldiers.

The gods lived in their temples, but temples, gods, and heroes were themselves located on the land, another common image used to make self-defense concrete. As Carol Thomas sums up:

[W]hat Greek citizen would not fight for the land that not only provided for his well-being but even more importantly embodied his gods, his heroes and the totality of his past?[39]

The land needed to be defended in war for two reasons: for its practical agricultural value and for its religious and symbolic value. Farms were subject to ravaging and burning during an invasion, while their inhabitants

---

[32] Lycurg. *Leoc.* 8. See also Aeschin. 3.156; Dem. 14.32.

[33] Objects in all these categories were also invoked as witnesses to good or bad actions: Thuc. 3.67.2; 7.69.2; Dem. 19.267; Aeschin. 3.259; Hyp. *Against Demosthenes*, fr. 9, col. 39). See pp. 127–8.

[34] E.g. Price 1999: 126–42.   [35] Chaniotis 2005: 157.

[36] E.g. Aeschin. 2.107–24; Arr. *Anab.* 2.14.2–5; Lycurg. *Leoc.* 81 and Diod. 11.29.3.

[37] Thuc. 4.98.1–2.   [38] Thuc. 2.74.2–3.   [39] C. Thomas 1979: 38.

might retreat behind a city's walls. The emotional impact of such devastation in an agricultural society can hardly be exaggerated: the Acharnians in Aristophanes' play of the same name will brook no peace with the Spartans, who have cut down their vineyards; Athenian ephebes swore to defend "the wheat, the barley, the vines, the olives, the figs" of their country.[40] Agricultural products were connected with gods of Athens: grain was the gift of Demeter that was celebrated at the Eleusinian Mysteries and Athena had given Athens the olive.[41] Demosthenes explicitly describes the land as the seat of the gods' worship, when he accuses Aeschines of betraying it.[42] Thus the land itself is conceived of as "sacred" and worth defending in the epitaph for the Greeks who died at Chaeronea, for example.[43]

The land was also the seat of the "ancestral" or "paternal" tombs of the Athenians. Such family tombs added another level of emotional commitment to the land and, like the temples of the gods, could also be invoked in their own right. The obligations of families to their dead were important to the Athenians.[44] Proper and regular care of tombs, both at *polis* festivals such as the Genesia and on less formal occasions, perhaps even monthly, was crucial to the souls of the departed and demonstrated familial piety: as a result, one of the questions asked of candidates for office was whether they possessed an ancestral tomb and where it was; if they did not, they were presumably barred from office.[45] In one lawsuit a childless man was said to have adopted a son and heir for the express purpose, among others, of ensuring that his grave received the customary visits and rituals.[46] Given this respect for the family's dead, the Athenians would be betraying their families were they to let their ancestral tombs fall into the enemy's hands and into neglect and possibly worse.[47] In addition, once the continuity of care of the dead was broken, what could assure an Athenian man that he himself would be remembered and that his family would perform the necessary rituals for him after he died?

---

[40] Ar. *Ach.* 183, 233. Ha no. 109 = RO no. 88.

[41] On the laws protecting Attica's sacred olives see Carey 1989: 114–15 on Lys. 7.

[42] Dem. 19.257. See also [Dem.] 7.40.   [43] *Anth. Graec.* 7.245 (Beckby 1958–65).

[44] Garland 1985: 104.

[45] [Arist.] *Ath. Pol.* 55.3; Xen. *Mem.* 2.2.13; Dem. 57.67; Din. 2.17 are cited in Rhodes 1992: 618. Aeschines lists shrines and tombs of ancestors as proofs of being native Athenians (2.23; cf. Thuc. 1.26.3). See also Isae. 2.36 and 4.19 for the importance of proper funeral arrangements and Isoc. 6.65 for visits to the tomb.

[46] Garland 1985: 104 on Isae. 2.10.

[47] For different threats to ancestral tombs see Isoc. 14.61 (neglect of customary rites at tombs) and Isoc. 8.88 (burial of foreign interlopers in the public burial grounds). According to Herodotus, their ancestral tombs were the only things for which the Scythians would fight (4.127). Despite other contrasts between Scythians and Greeks, this attitude would have been quite comprehensible to Herodotus' Greek audience.

So the temples, land, and tombs were important parts of the life of Athens. The appeal to protect them would doubtless strike a chord in the hearts of its soldiers, regardless of the particular war involved. Before we turn to direct appeals for soldiers to fight to protect their families, we should note that familial ties figure, albeit indirectly, in the appeals we have considered already: the paternal line is most conspicuously brought to bear in the exhortation to defend the ancestral or "paternal" tombs. In addition, the word for the land that is to be defended is often *patria*, the "fatherland." This wording suggests the importance of patriarchy to the world soldiers fought to defend. Mothers and women were also implicit in appeals to defend the land and crops. The goddess of the grain harvest was Demeter and the Earth itself was Gē, another female deity. In Aeschylus' *Seven against Thebes*, Gē is represented as a nurse and a nourishing mother, whom the Thebans are bound to defend against the enemy's invasion.[48] So, in defending the land, crops, tombs, and gods, soldiers were already defending their families, an obligation whose explicit invocation we shall examine next.

THE WOMEN

The emotional impact of these appeals depended on men's attachment to their objects. This attachment could be entirely communal, as in the case of the land and temples, or could become more individual, when each soldier is urged to think of the tombs of his own family members. References to the defense of the home also assimilated a war to a personal conflict. Rather than asking the soldiers as a group to defend their country, each is individually asked to defend his own home.[49] More commonly, generals asked the soldiers to fight hard and sacrifice themselves to protect the family members who lived in their homes. We find parents and children mentioned as requiring defense in battle. Both groups were regarded with affection and had strong claims on an Athenian man's protection. But the most interesting, common, and perhaps most powerful familial appeal was to protect the women and especially to protect them from sexual violation.[50]

As we have seen, Nicias used this exhortation when addressing the Athenian navy, which was not, in fact, in Sicily to protect their "wives, children, and national gods" – and Thucydides notes that this appeal was

---

[48] Aesch. *Sept.* 16–20; cf. Pl. *Resp.* 3.414d–e. Compare Parnell in Carr 1946: 151: "You would never have got young men to sacrifice themselves for so unlucky a country as Ireland, only that they pictured her as a woman."
[49] E.g. Xen. *Hell.* 2.4.17.   [50] Schaps 1982: 196–7. See also Cartledge 1998b: 183.

a cliché. Gyllipus, on the other side, is portrayed as insisting that the Syracusans fight the Athenians with rage in their hearts because

> [The Athenians] came against our land to enslave it, whereby, if they had succeeded, they would have conferred on the men the worst pain, on the children and women the greatest disgrace, and on the whole city the most shameful title.[51]

So, too, Hyperides gave his *Funeral Oration* in the context of an ongoing war with Macedonia. In it, he twice evokes the threat to all the women of Greece from Macedonian *hybris* – and affects to believe that this danger has been averted.[52]

This same theme appears in an episode from Plutarch's *Pelopidas*. Before the battle of Leuctra, the general Pelopidas told a dream about the Leuctridae, two girls whose tombs were located on that plain. Although Plutarch's fascinating narrative revolves around opposing attitudes towards human sacrifice and the gods' involvement in war, another aspect of the story is relevant here: the Leuctridae were raped by Spartans and they and then their father committed suicide – after cursing the Spartan race: "forever after prophecies and oracles continually warned the Spartans to beware of the vengeance of Leuctra."[53] Pelopidas' dream and the subsequent sacrifice of a filly, "the red-haired maiden" demanded in the dream, assured the Thebans of divine support; the connection of the ritual with a story about women outraged by Spartans would have added righteous indignation at the Spartans, whose outrageous behavior in the past was mirrored or at least threatened in their current invasion.

The appeal to protect the women was probably more common than these few examples suggest. In addition to Thucydides' claim that the appeal was conventional, two other sources suggest its ubiquity. In *Against Aristocrates* Demosthenes characterizes wives, concubines, and female relatives as those "for whose sake we fight our enemies, to save them from indignity and licentiousness."[54] The pseudo-Demosthenic *On the Treaty with Alexander* contains a passage in which the speaker asks the rhetorical question, "What would most rouse your indignation?" He answers himself that the imposition of tyranny would be worse than slavery and explains why:

> [N]o one would intentionally kill his own servant, but the victims of tyranny may be seen executed without trial, as well as outraged in the persons of their wives and children.[55]

---

[51] Thuc. 7.68.2. See also Thuc. 8.74.3; Dem. 23.55–6.   [52] Hyp. 6.20, 36.
[53] Plut. *Pel.* 20.3–4.   [54] Dem. 23.56.   [55] [Dem.] 17.3–4. Cf. Thuc. 8.74.3.

The efficacy of this common plea depended, first, on the fact that rape was a possibility in classical warfare – and featured prominently in Greek literature about war – and, second, on the importance to Greek men of defending their women and, in particular, guaranteeing their sexual inviolability. So, the threat was a real one, if unlikely in most cases, and was one Greek men desperately wanted to prevent.

Even today warfare can involve rape either incidentally or as the result of deliberate policy.[56] In classical Greece there are few specific references to wartime rape, but the general expectation that the violation of the women would be part of the sack of a city is clear enough. Herodotus tells us that some Phocian women were raped by so many Persian soldiers that they died.[57] The sack of Thebes by Alexander provides another case narrated by Plutarch.[58] Such atrocities became a stereotypical feature of literary narratives of the sack of cities. For example, in the *Seven against Thebes* the chorus of women fears this fate, should their defenders fail.[59] Until Philip, the violent capture of a classical city was an infrequent occurrence, but women could also be captured in an unexpected invasion, especially by cavalry. Thus, it was important to bring all the women and children – and slaves – in from the countryside in the event of an attack.[60]

The possibility of violent rape at the time of capture was compounded by the threat of sexual violation in the slavery that might well follow capture: a female slave was often sexually available to her master, and women captured in war were often enslaved. It may not be an absolute rule that, as Lucy Byrne claims, "Being enslaved of course includes being raped."[61] Nevertheless, we find frequent references to women – ranging from Chryseis and Briseis in Homer's *Iliad* to Alcibiades' Melian mistress – captured in war, whose enslavement involved sex with their masters.[62]

To judge from contemporary historical accounts and deliberative oratory, it does not seem that the prospect of raping the women of another city and the consequent humiliation of their men figured large as a reason for Greek cities to go to war. It must be admitted, however, that such deplorable perquisites may occasionally have provided some incentive for soldiers or added to war's attraction for young men in a vague sort of way. In the *Iliad* Nestor urges the Achaeans to battle with the plea, "Therefore

---

[56] See Walzer 1977: 133–7 on Allied mercenaries in Italy; see Gourevitch 1998: 115 on Rwanda. Unfortunately, these examples could easily be multiplied: Serbian atrocities in Bosnia and Kosovo provide infamous recent cases.

[57] Hdt. 8.33. See also the discussion in Schaps 1982: 203–4, which cites Plut. *Arat.* 31 and *Mor.* 258d–f.

[58] Plut. *Alex.* 12. See also Isoc. *Ep.* 9.10.   [59] Byrne 1997: 147 on Aesch. *Sept.* 333–5.

[60] Dem. 19.86, 125. Cf. Thuc. 2.5.4–5; Xen. *Hell.* 3.2.26; 6.2.6.   [61] Byrne 1997: 145.

[62] E.g. Andoc. 4.22–3; Plut. *Alc.* 16.4–5; Soph. *Aj.* 485–524; Xen. *An.* 4.1.12–14; 4.3.19.

let no man be urgent to take the way homeward until after he has lain in bed with the wife of a Trojan . . . "[63] Such appeals were not confined to epic. In the *Anabasis* Xenophon reports that he encouraged the Ten Thousand by saying that he was afraid, not of military defeat, but that they would not want to return to Greece after becoming acquainted with luxurious living and "the tall and beautiful women of the Medes and Persians."[64] Although such passages are rare, we cannot rule out the possibility that the association of victory in war with sexual conquest was not merely symbolic – this latter a point made by several scholars.[65] One factor limiting this tendency was the Greek ideal of self-restraint, *sōphrosynē*: "The ability to control sexuality was praiseworthy, a sign of masculine strength and endurance."[66] In *On the Crown* Demosthenes tries to paint a flattering picture of Athenian military performance despite their defeat at Chaeronea. He claims that the Thebans paid a great compliment to the Athenians' self-mastery, *sōphrosynē*, in inviting the Athenian soldiers into their houses among their children and women.[67] Athenian restraint in not taking advantage of their hosts and allies is as praiseworthy to Demosthenes as their courage and justice. This passage shows both the ideal of self-restraint and the usual expectation of trouble if a foreign army had access to women and children even of an ally.[68] When enemy soldiers invaded, the threat was even greater and could be used to make the case for self-defense more vivid and compelling.

Given this danger, the obligation and desire to defend wives and female relatives, and thus the force of this appeal, is not difficult to understand. It is nevertheless worth briefly exploring the most important bases for this appeal in classical Greece. The cry "defend your women" seems to have been triply motivated: it derived from affection and concern, it justified male domination as protectors of women, and it was crucial to a man's position of honor among other men.

Of course, the exhortation to defend your women was effective in part for the same reasons as were references to tombs, temples, and land: men's concern about their wives was genuine.[69] Despite the asymmetry of gender relations and some signs of mutual suspicion or hostility, affective ties between husbands and wives were probably strong. A wide variety of male sources, beginning with Homer's portrayal of Hector and Andromache and

---

[63] Hom. *Il.* 2.354–6; 9.128–9. See Gottschall 2008 for a Darwinian reading of Homer's world.

[64] Xen. *An.* 3.2.25. See also Hdt. 9.81.1–2; Hom. *Il.* 9.139–40.

[65] Cartledge 1998a: 56; Chaniotis 2005: 102–4; cf. Rosenberg 1993: 59.   [66] A. Cohen 1996: 119.

[67] Dem. 18.215. See also Hyp. *Against Diondas* 1.1–6 in Carey *et al.* (2008).

[68] Wankel 1976: 989 cites Plut. *Phoc.* 11 for cities refusing entry to an allied army and Aen. Tact. *Poliorcetica* 12 for precautions, if such a course should be necessary.

[69] Schaps 1982: 197.

of Odysseus and Penelope, portray an ideal of marriage based on mutual respect and affection. In the classical period, from Aristophanes' *Lysistrata* to the inscriptions on gravestones, from Euripides' *Alcestis* to Xenophon's *Oeconomicus*, husbands and wives are expected to be vitally concerned with each other's welfare.[70] Although we shall move on to other factors that made this appeal potent, we should not ignore simple affection and concern for wives, children, or female relatives, who could suffer greatly as the result of a defeat.

Greek marriages were typically contracted between older men, on average around thirty, and younger women, from fifteen to twenty.[71] This age disparity contributed to strong paternalistic feelings towards women. Men were expected to protect their wives from danger and one way they did this was by fighting for their city.[72] This strain in Greek thinking is ubiquitous, but a couple of examples will reveal its extent and depth. Aristotle felt that the masculine role of protector characterized almost all animals: his *History of Animals* states that:

the male is more courageous than the female, and more sympathetic in the way of standing by to help. Even in the case of cephalopods when the cuttlefish is struck by the trident the male stands by to help the female; but when the male is struck the female runs away."[73]

Socrates in Xenophon's *Memorabilia* tells a story about the perquisites of guard dogs vis-à-vis livestock to highlight protection as the male function that justifies patriarchy among people.[74]

Individually male citizens were supposed to guard the women of their *oikos*; together they were supposed to protect their *polis*.[75] Most revealing of the latter obligation was Agesilaus' frequent boast that no Spartan woman had ever even seen the smoke from an invading army – since no hostile army had ever invaded Laconia.[76] Agesilaus may have implied the concern the Spartans displayed for their women and that they justly ruled their households, as superlative watch-dogs, but he was mainly making a competitive statement. The Spartan men surpassed those of other states, because their women were never even threatened.

This leads us to the third reason that Greek men felt that they were bound to defend their women: failure to protect women was shameful and

[70] E.g. Dover 1972: 160–1; Leader 1997: 693–4; Pomeroy 1994: 34–7.
[71] See Xen. *Oec.* 3.13, 7.5 with Pomeroy 1994: 232, 268–9 and Solon 27.9–10 (West 1989).
[72] Cartledge 1981: 88; Gera 1997: 24; Homer *Il.* 6.490–3, *Od.* 1.356; Thuc. 3.74.2; Ar. *Lys.* 520, 626; Xen. *An.* 6.1.5–13; [Pl.] *Alc.* 1 126e–127a.
[73] Arist. *Hist. an.* 8.608b16–8. Compare Xen. *Oec.* 7.20–32.
[74] Xen. *Mem.* 2.7.10–14.   [75] Versnel 1987: 66.   [76] Plut. *Ages.* 31.

an injury to a man's honor. Thus, in Euripides' *Helen*, Menelaus argues that it would be "unmanly" of him not to try to rescue Helen.[77] In the *Rhetoric* Aristotle generalizes that men become angry with people who slight those whom they are supposed to protect, including their wives.[78] For a woman to be raped in war or enslaved and consequently sexually available to her master was considerably more than a "slight" and could be expected to enrage any Greek man. Within the city rape was seen as an outrage, *hybris*, not only against the victim but also against her male relatives.[79] B. M. Lavelle sums up the impact of this attitude: "[m]ales were required to answer at once and with violence to rehabilitate that honour [of a women whose chastity was threatened or impugned]."[80] And, indeed, husbands or male relatives could not be charged with murder for killing a rapist – or adulterer – if he were caught in the act.[81] For a general before a battle to mention a threat to the sexual integrity of their women was an attempt to put the soldiers on notice that their honor was at stake in a particularly crucial and intimate way. Whereas in civilian life few men could have had the opportunity or reason violently to avenge their honor, in war they had weapons in their hands and the enemy soldiers might be just a few hundred yards away. Generals invoked the outrage of the women in hopes that their soldiers would charge against the enemy with the same rage they would feel towards a would-be rapist or adulterer.

In the assembly, however, these appeals were limited in their usefulness. In our whole corpus we do not find a single instance of an orator's directly urging war, preparations for war, or increased effort in war on the ground that Athenian women were threatened and thus Athenian honor was at stake. The appeal to defend the women was perhaps too unrestrainedly emotional or too hackneyed for the assembly's taste. In addition, war and its possible consequences were more immediate just before a battle; in the assembly the threat to the women of Athens might have seemed too remote for a powerful state such as Athens to be a plausible consideration in deciding foreign policy. Most crucially, our pro-war speeches typically do not urge a last ditch defense but advocate a war that, if only the Athenians would do their duty, could be won – and, indeed, could usually be won far from Attica.[82] This optimism was out of harmony with the appeal to protect the women from disgrace.

---

[77] Eur. *Hel.* 808.   [78] Arist. *Rh.* 2.2.1379b28–9. Cf. Arist. *Eth. Nic.* 3.6.1115a23.

[79] Fisher 1992: 13.   [80] Lavelle 1986: 323.

[81] E. Harris 1990 and D. Cohen 1993. Cf. Pl. *Leg.* 9.874c.

[82] Our picture might be different, if we possessed any of the assembly speeches delivered in the few days between the battle of Chaeronea and Philip's offer of peace terms to Athens.

Although the direct appeal to defend the women was not possible, various indirect arguments depended on men's feelings that their honor was at stake in protecting women. In *On the False Embassy* Demosthenes takes the opportunity to promote his bellicose policy by using a contrast similar to those in his pro-war assembly speeches. He contrasts the favorable results of supporting Phocis and keeping Philip out of Greece with the disastrous results of Aeschines' machinations and the Peace of Philocrates:

[W]hen you did your duty, you made it an occasion of services of praise and thanksgiving, both at Athens and abroad; but when you had been led astray by these men, you brought your wives and children in from the country and ordered the festival of Heracles to be held within the walls, in time of peace.[83]

Aeschines' policies endangered both the Athenians' religion and their women. In part this was simply an attack on Aeschines; it is also consonant with his arguments for a stronger stance against Philip. A threat against Athens' women could be invoked in pro-war oratory – at least when the threat was safely in the past.

Ill-treatment of the women of allied cities also allowed orators to engage the emotions of their audience without undercutting the optimism essential to their project. In *On the Treaty with Alexander* the speaker details the many ways in which Alexander has broken his peace treaty with Athens. One of Alexander's infractions was to establish tyrants who sexually abuse children and women.[84] In this case righteous indignation is directed against Alexander without implying that Athenian women were not well protected.

When Philip captured the city of Olynthus, an ally of Athens, the surviving inhabitants were sold into slavery. We have already seen that the enslavement of Greeks provided Demosthenes with the material for a number of oratorical attacks. Some were sharpened by an emphasis on the violation of Olynthian women. Formerly free, they were reduced to slavery and vulnerable to sexual exploitation. In one place Demosthenes described the admirable behavior of Satyrus, a comic poet.[85] Satyrus convinced Philip to free and to entrust to him several daughters of a friend, who had been enslaved when Olynthus fell. Satyrus sought no gain from this, but even undertook to provide these women with dowries since they were of marriageable age. This story served as the foil for Demosthenes'

---

[83] Dem. 19.86. Cf. Dem. 19.65, 100, 125.
[84] [Dem.] 17.3–4. Cf. This complaint against the Macedonians is also reported in Din. 1.19 and was a typical indictment of tyrants or bad governments in general (e.g. Hdt. 3.80; Thuc. 8.74.3; Isoc. 4.114).
[85] Dem. 19.192–5.

account of a drunken party at which Aeschines was present. There an Olynthian slave woman, "good looking, yes, but free-born and modest," was ordered by the increasingly drunk company to sing and to lie down on the dining couches with them. Unused to such treatment – respectable free women did not even attend symposia – and not knowing how to sing, she refused. According to Demosthenes, Aeschines and a certain Phryno deplored her insubordination and haughtiness and the poor woman was stripped and whipped.[86] Aeschines indignantly argued that the story was fictitious and claimed that the jury refused even to listen to Demosthenes' lies.[87] Aeschines himself had earlier referred to the plight of Olynthian women in an impassioned plea to fight Philip: he was indignant at seeing one of Philip's mercenaries with thirty slaves, women and children from Olynthus in his train.[88] This speech of Aeschines, whose veracity we have no reason to doubt, raised indignation at the enslavement of Greek women and children.[89]

In sum, men's protective feelings and sense of honor could be aroused by descriptions of the treatment of allied women in the past to encourage a more vigorous war effort. When a war had already broken out, generals could invoke a threat to the women to rouse their men, to make the appeal to self-defense vivid, and firmly to engage their men's honor in the struggle. But in the assembly, orators were usually not in a situation where they could or wanted to portray a dire threat to the women of Athens. They were able to enlist protective feelings towards women and consequent anger, but only indirectly.

ANTICIPATING THREATS

The pre-emptive or anticipatory attack is an obvious extension of the right to self-defense: if a state knows of an impending attack, it need not await it but has the right to strike first. Thus a prediction of aggression in the future can become the basis for action in the present. This type of argument is

---

[86] Dem. 19.196–8. See also Dem. 19.309 with MacDowell 2000: 340–1.

[87] Aeschin. 2.4–5, 153–8 with Julien and Péréra 1902: 5. The stripping and beating may be Demosthenes' invention; nevertheless, an Athenian abroad, presumably a slave owner himself, could hardly enforce a demand that a slave woman from Olynthus not be treated as slave women usually were, that is, harshly and with no respect for the modesty central to the honor of a free woman. Good manners to a host and loyalty to a former ally – if not humane feelings – would have been in irremediable conflict in such situations.

[88] Dem. 19.305–7. Cf. Dem. 19.309.

[89] Philip was the enemy of all Greece (Dem. 19.302); Philip was plotting while Athens slept (Dem. 19.303). Aeschines read to the Athenians the ephebic oath (see Siewert 1977) and brought up the decrees of Miltiades and Themistocles and the battles of Marathon and Salamis (Dem. 19.303, 311).

so simple on the individual level and so easily transferred to states that it was probably in use even before we first see it in Herodotus.[90] Thucydides also presents us with a host of examples.[91] By our period Aristotle's *Rhetoric* shows that the argument was a standard one.[92]

The right to anticipate attack was a centerpiece of Demosthenes' case for war against Philip, one that he developed and deployed with a wide variety of embellishments and twists. In the *Third Philippic* Demosthenes lists Philip's transgressions, but seems aware that these are not really attacks on Athens. He assimilates them to direct attacks by a *reductio ad absurdum* analogy with an actual military invasion:

> I assert that when he lays hands on Megara, sets up tyrannies in Euboea, makes his way, as now, into Thrace, hatches plots in the Peloponnese, and carries out all these operations with his armed force, he is breaking the peace and making war upon you – unless you are prepared to say that the men who bring up the siege-engines are keeping the peace until they actually bring them to bear on the walls. But you will not admit that; for he who makes and devises the means by which I may be captured is at war with me, even though he has not yet hurled a javelin or shot a bolt.[93]

Philip's actions make an Athenian military response just; not to respond, like letting an enemy set up its siege engines outside one's wall at leisure, would also represent a ludicrous neglect of Athenian interests. In particular, fighting Philip sooner and further away was more advantageous than waiting until he became stronger and then having to defend the homeland: "Everybody knows that if we allow him to extend his power he will be more formidable when we have to fight him."[94] An evocation of the specter of fighting in Attica can also lend vividness to the abstract argument: "and if we refuse to fight now in Thrace, we shall perhaps be forced to fight here at home . . ."[95]

In another passage Demosthenes tries to prove the connection between the actions of Philip and his sinister intentions towards Athens. He contrasts the prizes to be won by Philip in the north and in southern Greece:

> For no man is so simple as to believe that though Philip covets these wretched objects in Thrace – for what else can one call Drongilus and Cabyle and Mastira and the other places that he is now occupying and equipping? – and though he endure toil and winter storms and deadly peril for the privilege of taking them, yet he does not covet the Athenian harbours and dockyards and war-galleys and

---

[90] E.g. Hdt. 1.46; 4.118; 7.11, 157.   [91] E.g. Thuc. 1.33.3–4, 44.2, 120.2, 124.2; 6.91.4, 92.5.
[92] Arist. *Rh.* 1.12.1373a21–5; 2.20.1393b30–1394a3.   [93] Dem. 9.17. Cf. Dem. 1.24.
[94] Dem. 8.50.   [95] Dem. 4.50. See also Dem. 1.25–6; 8.18.

silver mines and the like sources of wealth, but will allow you to retain them, while he winters in that purgatory for the sake of the rye and millet of the Thracian store-pits. It is not so, but it is to win these prizes that he devotes his activities to all those other objects.[96]

This passage flattered Athenian self-regard rather more than it accurately represented Philip's strategic thinking, but Demosthenes at least made a show of logical argumentation. In other passages Demosthenes simply asserted that all of Philip's wars had the final goal of strengthening him against Athens.[97]

In modern just-war theory, a pre-emptive attack is justified only under certain stringent conditions.[98] These limits serve precisely to prevent the types of arguments Demosthenes sometimes made: for example, that any gain for Philip was a threat to Athens. In ancient Greece there was no systematic theory to curb the abuses of this argument. Nevertheless, the claim of anticipation was eminently contestable: speakers already in Herodotus and Thucydides counter it and sometimes with success.[99] Isocrates judges that the king of Persia made war, "not entirely irrationally," on Evagoras because of the latter's growing power, but since he began hostilities while Evagoras was friendly to him, the king was not acting justly.[100]

It may even be that such an easily abused argument typically evoked suspicion. Demosthenes himself, in his earlier speech *On the Navy-Boards*, urges the Athenians not to go to war against the Persian king until it is obvious to all the Greeks that the king's intentions are aggressive; the claim that he *intended* to invade Greece would not carry conviction and the other Greeks would not side with Athens.[101] In the case of the conflict with Philip, Demosthenes mentions opponents who claim that Athens is the real aggressor. These men cannot have believed that all Philip's actions betokened his imminent hostility to Athens.[102] More telling, Aeschines makes fun of the small Thracian cities upon whose conquest by Philip Demosthenes put such weight:

It is he, fellow citizens, who first discovered Serrhium-Teichus and Doriscus and Ergisca and Myrtisca and Ganus and Ganias; for before that we did not even know the names of these places.[103]

---

[96] Dem. 8.44–5. In the parallel passage from the *Fourth Philippic* 15–16, Demosthenes adds the flattering "and the place itself and the glory of it" to the attractions of Athens. Cf. [Dem.] 7.16.

[97] Dem. 8.55.   [98] Walzer 1977: 74–80.   [99] Hdt. 4.119; Thuc. 1.42.2.

[100] Isoc. 9.58–60.   [101] Dem. 14.3–7.

[102] Dem. 9.6; 10.17; 18.70. The first passage appears only in the longer version of the *Third Philippic*; see Appendix 1: Speeches and texts.

[103] Aeschin. 3.82 (trans. modified).

Aeschines clearly rejected the arguments of Demosthenes that Philip's encroachments in Thrace had anything to do with Athens, much less that they constituted the prelude to an attack and thus justified self-defense.

CONCLUSION

Self-defense is demanded both by self-interest and by morality. Individuals do not have to be reminded to defend themselves, but an important strain of war rhetoric aims at bringing the simple and strong emotions of an individual defending himself to the more complex reality of a state's war. References to *defendenda*, especially before battles, aim to rouse anger and determination and to reduce fear in what has in fact become a situation in which one must kill or be killed. Finally, the argument for self-defense is applied to cases in which the state has not even been attacked, but an orator merely envisions that possibility. This expansion of the argument, occasionally of dubious validity, is largely driven by the strength of the simple appeal and shows just how uncontestable individual self-defense was.

CHAPTER 7

Calculations of interest

Owing to the towering influence of Thucydides, classical Athens enjoys an extraordinary reputation for the clear-sighted and openly expressed pursuit of advantage in its foreign policy. In particular, Realist scholars and students in the discipline of International Relations, preparing others or themselves eager someday to serve their own nation's interests, admire the Athenians' precise and complex calculations of expedience and envy them their frankness. Consequently, Thucydides appears on lists of canonical Realist texts alongside such twentieth-century classics as Edward Carr, *The Twenty Years' Crisis: 1919–1939* and Kenneth Waltz, *Theory of International Politics.*[1] A prudent foreign policy, free of self-serving cant and hypocrisy and immune to the emotions of anger and hatred, has an obvious appeal. And, indeed, a significant strain in Athenian thinking about the relations of states did possess these characteristics. Even as we paint a more complete, and inevitably more complex, picture of Athenian thinking and even as we explore the limitations of using interests as a guide to conduct, we should keep in mind two points: first, the attractions of a calculating policy are real and significant; second, we would not be studying Athenian thinking about foreign policy at all were it not for the Athenians' attempt, however doomed, to subject it to rational calculation; for this, as much as anything else, distinguishes their thinking.

I make four main arguments in this chapter. First, both considerations of interest and morality played independent and important roles in Athenian decision-making; nevertheless, orators sometimes affected a Realist pose in order to debunk the moral claims of their opponents and to present a hard-headed persona to a nervous assembly. Second, a shift in the Realist strain in Greek thinking between Thucydides and Demosthenes made the latter's Realist arguments more palatable to the average Athenian. Third,

---

[1] E.g. Eric Gartman, *Listmania: The Best of Realist Theory*, on Amazon.com contains Carr 1946, Waltz 1979, and Thucydides.

Athenians were used to making relatively complex calculations of interest. In particular, Athens aimed to preserve a balance of power among the Greek states. This often meant that Realist arguments were in line with the long-standing Athenian ideal of helping the weak and the wronged. Fourth, determining a state's interests is not easy. Among other difficulties, it requires knowledge of the future. Thus, we find a general tendency for orators who stress interest to claim that they can foresee the future and for orators who invoke justice to emphasize the way that chance and change make such forecasts difficult or impossible.

JUSTICE AND INTEREST

In a well-known passage in his *Rhetoric* Aristotle argues that, while forensic oratory focuses on justice, deliberative oratory is essentially about expediency:

"The deliberative orator aims at establishing the expediency [*to sympheron*] or the harmfulness of a proposed course of action; if he urges its acceptance, he does so on the ground that it will do good; if he urges its rejection, he does so on the ground that it will do harm; and all other points, such as whether the proposal is just or unjust, honourable or dishonourable, he brings in as subsidiary and relative to this main contention . . . [D]eliberative speakers often make any concession short of admitting that they are recommending their hearers to take an inexpedient course or not to take an expedient one. The question whether it is unjust for a city to enslave its innocent neighbours often does not trouble them at all."[2]

In this passage Aristotle does not merely claim that considerations of interest are important to Athenian deliberations on foreign policy – the main focus of preserved deliberative oratory – but that they are predominant and overwhelm moral considerations.[3] If Aristotle were right, Athenian orators and the assembled citizens to whom they appealed would be adherents of the theory of interstate relations known as Realism.

---

[2] Arist. *Rh.* 1.3.1358b21–37 (modified by the deletion of "not," approved by Grimaldi 1980: 84 ad b36); cf. Arist. *Pol.* 7.1324b33–7 and [Pl.] *Alc.* I 113d. On justice in forensic oratory see Arist. *Rh.* 1.3.1358b21–29.

[3] Deliberative oratory may treat a variety of topics (see Low 2007: 165) and not just foreign relations. Nevertheless, the issues of war and peace, with which we are concerned, are prominent among them and Aristotle's reference to "enslaving the neighbors" suggests that he too was thinking of interstate relations. According to Aristotle, deliberative orators must know about five subjects: state revenue, the defense of Attica, trade, legislation, and issues of war and peace (Ar. *Rh.* 1.4.1359b19–24); see also [Pl.] *Alc.* I 112b–c and 107d for an even great emphasis on foreign relations in the assembly.

Realism is a tendency rather than a particular philosophical position, but there are a few common beliefs at its core.[4] Realists emphasize how various and incompatible the interests of different states can be.[5] These conflicts of interests often lead to war, since states operate in an anarchic realm. That the interstate realm is anarchic does not imply that it is confused or violent – though it can be. Rather, Realists point to the lack of any authority above states that might enforce rules of conduct or even treaty obligations. States have to look out for themselves since there is no higher power for them to turn to. Even worse, since a state's security depends entirely on its power relative to that of potential enemies, states are necessarily competitive: the growth of a potential enemy's power is *ipso facto* a security threat.[6] In such a world, due care for their security may force states to act in ways contrary to the codes of morality accepted within their societies.

Realism is often presented as a prescriptive theory for active statesmen, a claim which implies that states do not naturally act in their interests. Although a common Realist oratorical tactic is to point out that other states do not act justly, this claim does not mean that states typically act in their interests either; they can go to war, for example, for revenge or out of pride; they can fight out of religious or ethnic hatred. Realist calculations may act as a check on such behavior. Both in the modern era and in ancient Greece much of Realism's appeal derived from the restraints it placed on such irrational hatreds and touchy pride.[7] So although Realism admits no curb on calculated aggression, adherence to its tenets could prevent the many wars fought for other reasons. It is these considerations that led Henry Kissinger to wax eloquent in praise of Richelieu's Realism: "In an age still dominated by religious zeal and ideological fanaticism, a dispassionate foreign policy free of moral imperatives stood out like a snow-covered alp in the desert."[8] Accordingly we should not fall into the trap of contrasting Realist policies exclusively with those based on an altruistic or a legalistic morality. Amorality is not necessarily belligerent. Nor is a value-driven policy necessarily pacific.

The fifth-century historian Thucydides is generally considered the father of Realism. The extent to which Thucydides consistently espoused a philosophy we could call Realist, rather than merely presenting it, is a controversial – and in all likelihood insoluble – question: there are strong

---

[4] Haslam 2002: 12, 250 identifies a core of Realism, but mainly argues that it includes a "spectrum of ideas" (249). See Doyle 1991 and Mearsheimer 2001: 18–22 for two classifications of different strains of Realist thought. We have already encountered one claim of "structural realism": pp. 27–8.
[5] E.g. Carr 1946: 41–62.   [6] E.g. Mearsheimer 2001: 36, 45–6, 52.
[7] Haslam 2002: 30, 251; Konstan 2007: 201.   [8] Kissinger 1994: 62.

arguments on both sides.[9] That several main features of modern Realism are well developed within Thucydides – especially in the speeches – is clear. For the investigation of fourth-century war oratory, Thucydides' speeches would be invaluable *comparanda*, but the historicity of these speeches is a vexed question.[10] Parallels between Thucydides and the late fifth-century intellectuals known as Sophists – and Thucydides' claim that his speeches followed the gist of what was actually said – make it likely that Realist arguments were in the air and not a unique and original creation of Thucydides.[11] Their prominence, ubiquity, and overall consistency, however, may reflect Thucydides' own thinking rather than the sorts of arguments speakers actually used. Indeed, like Sophistic ideas in general, Thucydides' outlook may have been shocking to many people.[12] Consequently, it is hard either to confirm or to deny with certainty that Realist arguments were persuasive or even acceptable in the Athenian assembly in the late fifth century.

In contrast to the Realism expounded in Thucydides, several Athenian thinkers tried to subordinate interest to justice. Plato contended that justice is always in itself advantageous. Isocrates contended that the goodwill that attends on just action always makes justice an advantageous course of action for a state.[13] In his speech *On the Navy-Boards* Demosthenes follows this line of argument: it is in Athens' interest that its grounds for war against the Persian king be manifestly just.[14] Such arguments tend to minimize the possibility of conflict between interest and justice and, indeed, integrate these two factors into one coherent system based on justice.

It is much more common in the assembly speeches to find exclusively neither Realism nor the moralism of Plato or Isocrates, but rather simple addition: both justice and interest are important whether or not they are related.[15] On the one hand, every one of our assembly speeches invokes the interests of Athens.[16] These references to expediency are often stressed by

---

[9] The following recent works focus on Thucydides' relation to modern Realism and provide an entrée to the scholarship: Doyle 1991; Crane 1998: 61–71; Ober 2001; and Lebow 2001. Eckstein 2006: 37–78 provides a modern Realist interpretation of classical Greek history.

[10] See Morrison 2006 for a recent treatment with bibliography.

[11] Thuc. 1.22.1. J. Finley 1967 and Fritz 1973–4 place Thucydides in the context of Sophistic thought.

[12] Crane 1998: 100.   [13] Romilly 1958.

[14] Dem. 14.3, 41. See also Low 2007: 160–73; Kennedy 1959: 136–7; 1963: 224.

[15] Dem. 5.10; 14.28; 15.28; 16.9, 10; 18.298; 19.132; Aeschin. 2.118; 3.8; [Dem.] 7.46; [Dem.] 17.2, 9, 18, 30. Appeals to interest and morality are considered in parallel in rhetorical theory with no hint that they are mutually exclusive or subordinated one to the other (Arist. *Rh.* 3.17.1417b34–7; [Arist.] *Rh. Al.* 1.1422b26–30 and 2.1425a17–18).

[16] Many references to expedience use a word related to the verb *sympherō*: Dem. 5.1, 10, 12, 19; 6.7, 12, 27; 8.1, 3, 16, 69; 9.4, 28, 71, 76; 10.1, 17, 32, 36, 54, 56 (cf. 8.54); 14.1, 3, 6, 28, 32, 36, 41; 15.13, 15, 18, 34;

their placement in either the opening or the closing sections of speeches. They are thus marked as pivotal arguments for the policy proposed.[17] Furthermore, a number of passages in Demosthenes, Aeschines, and Hyperides imply that it is the duty of the orator or ambassador to serve the interest of the city.[18] On the other hand, this concern with advantage is not always linked to a Realist way of thinking in which interest trumps morality. In some cases, moral standards gave little guidance to actions. For example, the choice of whether to conclude an alliance with an unaligned city was often neither required nor prohibited by moral criteria; it was decided on the basis of interest. More significant, in none of the extant speeches does an orator concede that he is recommending an unjust course of action. In fact, all five of our deliberative orators on occasion claim explicitly that their policies are both just and in the city's interest.[19]

This mixed approach to interest and justice among states is intellectually untidy and, perhaps as a result, tends to be neglected by scholars.[20] A philosophical consideration of this issue would be beyond the scope of this book, but such an approach is, in fact, a popular position in the modern world. Its attraction is largely due to the difficulties of basing a foreign policy exclusively on interest or on justice.

On the one hand – as we shall see – the demands of interest provide no hard and fast guide for conduct. There are not only profound problems involved with defining a state's interest, but also difficulties in assessing long- and short-term interests and in predicting the outcomes of different courses of action. These complexities preclude certainty in judgments about what is advantageous. Far from having a clear vision of where their interests lie, in practice states are faced with a variety of possible courses of actions, each of which carries costs, advantages, and different degrees of risk.[21] On the other hand, the moral course of action is often hard to discern. For example, when an originally small conflict grows more intense

---

16.4–5, 9, 10, 23, 27–8, 31, 32; [Dem.] 7.1, 23, 46; [Dem.] 17.2, 9, 13, 18, 24, 30. Andocides uses *agatha*, good things, to denote what is advantageous for Athens (3.39–40); cf. Arist. *Rh.* 1.5.1361b37–1362a11, 1.6.1362a13–21. Although Dem. 18 and 19 and Aeschin. 2 and 3 are forensic speeches and are thus not included in Aristotle's generalization, their focus on interstate politics ensures that *symphero* words show up often, 38, 20, 7, and 8 times respectively.

[17] Opening sections: Dem. 5.1; 8.1; 9.4; 10.1; 14.1; [Dem.] 17.2. Closing sections: Dem. 14.41; 15.34; 16.32; [Dem.] 7.46; [Dem.] 17.30.

[18] E.g. Aeschin. 2.183; 3.8; Hyp. *Against Diondas* 1.21–5; Dem. 5.12; 8.69; 10.17; 18.25, 190, 197, 278, 309; 19.5, 7–8, 183–4, 203, 302; [Dem.] 7.1; [Dem.] 17.13.

[19] Aeschin. 2.118; Dem. 5.10; 14.3, 41; 16.10; [Dem.] 7.46; [Dem.] 17.18, 30. Andocides lacks such compact statements but he emphasizes throughout *On the Peace* the issues both of justice and of Athenian interest, e.g. Andoc. 3.13–16.

[20] See the critique of Kant 1983: 135 section 380.   [21] Walzer 1977: 8.

as each side reacts to the other, it can be hard to decide which decision was the culpable one that caused the resulting war. In addition, different moral arguments often conflict: as we have seen, the argument against intervention in another state's affairs often stands in the way of protecting human rights or overthrowing a despot.[22] Such apparent contradictions can be decided on the basis of a more finely structured concept of justice, but the need to trade off one value against another blunts the edge of moral absolutism. The Athenian assembly granted some sway to both interest and morality without the implausible, if intellectually appealing, subordination of one to the other.

Realism in the assembly

Despite this overall tendency to take into account both interest and justice, orators sometimes insist on the overwhelming importance of interest, distinguish between internal and external morality, note the hypocrisy of moral claims in the light of a determining interest, or dismiss grounds for action other than expedience. Such passages evince a Realist strain in the assembly speeches. Conspicuous among these passages is Demosthenes' synopsis of interstate politics in his speech *For the Liberty of the Rhodians*. Here Demosthenes is trying to persuade the Athenians to provide military support to some democratic exiles who wanted to wrest control of Rhodes from an oligarchy backed by a garrison installed by the Persian satrap of Caria. As we have seen, his main positive argument is that Athens has an obligation to assist democrats against oligarchs – as well as an interest in doing so. He counters first the objection that supporting the democrats will involve Athens in a dangerous war with the Persian king.[23] Demosthenes then debunks the arguments of some Athenians "who are very clever at invoking justice against you on the behalf of others."[24] It apparently did not serve Demosthenes' agenda to go into the specifics of this invocation of justice. His counter-arguments, however, make it clear that his opponents' strongest points were not based on justice in general, but on the terms of treaties. The particular treaty obligations they cited could have been either guarantees of autonomy made to Rhodes at the end of the Social War or the general autonomy clauses of a Common Peace. These arguments provoke the following statement:

In my opinion it is right to restore the Rhodian Democracy; yet even if it were not right, I should feel justified in urging you to restore it, when I observe what

---

[22] See, for example, Walzer 1977: 86–108.   [23] Dem. 15.5–13, 23–4.
[24] Dem. 15.25 (my translation).

these people are doing. Why so? Because, men of Athens, if every state was bent on doing right, it would be disgraceful if we alone refused; but when the others, without exception, are preparing the means to do wrong, for us alone to make profession of right, without engaging in any enterprise seems to me not love of right but want of courage. For I notice that all men have their rights conceded to them in proportion to the power at their disposal. I can cite an instance that is familiar to you all. The Greeks have two treaties with the King, one made by our city and commended by all, and the later one made by the Lacedaemonians, which is of course condemned by all; and in these two treaties rights are diversely defined. Of private rights within a state, the laws of that state grant an equal and impartial share to all, weak and strong alike; but the international rights of Greek states are defined by the strong for the weak."[25]

This passage encompasses several central Realist themes. If anything, Demosthenes' exegesis is more comprehensive and systematic than that of most of the speakers in Thucydides. He makes a twofold attack on interstate justice and specifically on the moral force of treaties.

To begin with, Demosthenes invokes the absence of morality among other states and insists that this would excuse unjust action on Athens' part: "the others, without exception, are preparing the means to do wrong."[26] This observation summarizes the examples Demosthenes has laid out in the previous section of the speech: Byzantium and the Persian satraps have taken over states to which they had no rights contrary to "oaths and agreements."[27] This characterization of the interstate world has a practical corollary: states must act to protect their own interests and are constrained only by their power or lack thereof.

Demosthenes makes a second and more unusual attack on the moral force of treaties. He argues that these very accords are shaped by power relations: the Persians granted far more rights to the Athenians in the Peace of Callias, when the Athenian empire was powerful, than to the Spartans in the King's Peace, when the Spartans needed Persian aid.[28] Rather than stressing the impotence of treaties, he argues that these treaties themselves were products of power.[29]

A number of shorter passages echo this emphasis on how power politics overwhelms justice among states – though not his explanation of treaty rights in terms of power. In his speech *For the Megalopolitans* Demosthenes

---

[25] Dem. 15.28–9. Cf. Thuc 6.79.2–3.   [26] Dem. 16.6–7 provides a variant on the same argument.
[27] Dem. 15.26–7.   [28] See Radicke 1995: 153 on which two treaties are meant.
[29] Demosthenes' argument is parallel to that of Thrasymachus in Plato's *Republic* about laws within the state: it is not that the powerful can disobey the laws, rather that the powerful are the ones who make the laws and they make them in their own interests (Low 2007: 160–4 on Pl. *Resp.* 1.338c–339a; cf. Pl. *Grg.* 483b–c).

argues that if Sparta would be satisfied with Megalopolis, Athens should let it be taken regardless of how unjust this action would be.[30] In the *First Philippic* he endorses the view he attributes to Philip that, contrary to the usual conceptions of justice, "by natural right the property of the absent belongs to those who are on the spot, and the property of the careless to those who can face toil and danger."[31] Most interesting, Demosthenes argues for a certain policy towards Thrace by telling an anecdote about Philocrates, son of Ephialtes. Philocrates had told the Spartans, who were trying to offer him guarantees of their good intentions, that

the only possible assurance would be that they should satisfy him that, if they had a mind to injure him, they would not have the power; "for," he added, "I am quite certain that you will always have the mind, and there can be no assurance so long as you have the power."[32]

In an anarchic world, security comes from power considerations and power considerations alone.

Such views are not only found in Demosthenes. Aeschines claims that Demosthenes betrayed Athens' interest in the assemblies that led up to the Peace of Philocrates: he contrasts Demosthenes' perfidy with the behavior of Philip, who could not be blamed for acting in his own interest.[33] The author of *On the Treaty with Alexander* claims that at some times opportunity is strong and men pursue interest without justice – but he adds the claim that justice too is on Athens' side – a move typical of assembly speeches.[34]

A Realist interpretation of alliances is also well attested. Rather than viewing alliances as analogous to individual friendships or as legalistic agreements sanctioned by the gods – a topic to which we shall return[35] – some Greeks believed that the strength of an alliance depended on the interests of the parties involved. Even in pursuit of Athenian assistance against Sparta, the Megalopolitans seem to have been reluctant to destroy the steles that recorded their alliance with Thebes. Demosthenes represents them as arguing that "it is not steles but interest that makes friendship and they considered those who aid them to be allies."[36] He also represents Athens as bound to aid Messene, if it were attacked, because of treaty obligations. But he adds the Realist view that these obligations were inescapable owing

---

[30] Dem. 16.8–9; but Sparta will not be satisfied, his argument continues.
[31] Dem. 4.5. Usher 1999: 218 n. 170 cites parallels in Thuc 4.61.5 and elsewhere.
[32] Dem. 23.117.   [33] Aeschin. 3.66.   [34] [Dem.] 17.9.   [35] See pp. 186–92.
[36] Dem. 16.27 (trans. modified). Demosthenes' reaction to this claim is ambiguous: even if the Megalapolitans are right, the Athenians should demand that they destroy their treaty stones. See also Xen. *Hell.* 7.1.2.

to Athens' interest in containing the power of Sparta.[37] In *On the False Embassy* Demosthenes argues that Athens defended other Greek cities not because of their virtue – and despite their previous treatment of Athens as we shall see below – but simply because their survival benefited Athens. He even refers in disparaging terms to several such cities.[38] Such a cynical view of treaties of alliance was well adapted to fourth-century Greece, a world in which – as we shall see – balance-of-power considerations often required shifts of alignment even at the expense of treaty obligations and the friendships they often formalized.

The consciousness that moral claims actually covered up self-interested motivations, a view prevalent in Thucydides, remained common in fourth-century Athens – and remains common among ancient historians today.[39] Much of Realism's emotional appeal rides on its claim to discern the true motivations behind the public justification of a state's actions. Thucydides' Athenians put it succinctly: we were "well regarded by you also until now, when you calculate your own interests and use the argument about justice."[40] In the late-fourth-century text *The Alcibiades*, Alcibiades is asked whether he would advise the Athenians to wage war on states that were treating Athens justly. He replies that "[e]ven if someone thought it was necessary to wage war on people who were treating us justly, he wouldn't admit it."[41] At one point, Demosthenes assumes that the Greeks at large can take this unmasking attitude towards professions of justice. He argues that Athens should act before Sparta has taken Megalopolis and is threatening Messene. If Athens hesitates until Megalopolis is taken, "everyone will see clearly that you wish to preserve Messene less for the sake of justice than for fear of the Lacedaemonians."[42] To return to *On the Liberty of the Rhodians*, Demosthenes explicitly deploys a variant of this typical Realist argument: he unmasks the invocation of justice on the part of those who oppose helping the Rhodian democrats. According to Demosthenes, his opponents are not really concerned for justice. Their arguments merely put a moralizing screen on a calculation of interest, a cowardly and apathetic calculation quite different from his own. So Demosthenes claims to see through the professions of morality and to discern the actual reason behind them.

---

[37] Dem. 16.9.   [38] Dem. 19.75. See also Dem. 8.16; 18.93–5.

[39] E.g. Seager 1974: 63 and Sealey 1993: 159.

[40] Thuc. 1.76 (trans. modified). Cf. Keohane 1986: 162: "...to make the actions of states understandable (despite obfuscatory statements by their spokesmen)"; Blainey 1973: 164: "The façade of international morality..."

[41] [Pl.] *Alc.* I 109b–c. Arist. *Rh.* 2.23.1399a31–4 considers this a general human attribute.

[42] Dem. 16.9–10. Demosthenes then argues that the Athenians should act justly now to avoid this eventual Realist critique of their motives, if they only act later.

Many Athenian assembly speeches were full of specious moral claims screening – or at least congruent with – calculations of power. Realist, debunking arguments provided the needle with which to puncture such professions of high-minded morality – and could also function as a curb on anger or revenge. While one side in a debate might invoke shame, honor, glory, and ancestral traditions, our evidence suggests that Realist attacks on these appeals were also an option.[43] Such arguments gave the speaker an aura of hard-headed thinking, of perception beyond the surface, and of that cleverness in pursuit of advantage admired by Greeks since the *Odyssey*, if not before.[44] Expedience was a pervasive consideration and played a major role in Athenian thinking; but the pointed contrast between solid interest and specious moral professions, the Realist unmasking, tended to be a tactical measure, a useful rebuttal, rather than part of an overall philosophy of state relations.[45]

A DEVELOPMENT

A crucial development in Realist thinking may have made it less objectionable in the fourth century than in the fifth: the distinction between amorality between states and morality within a state became more explicit. According to most Realists it is only the international arena that is anarchic and in which power so dominates morality. In our passage Demosthenes states: "Of private rights within a state, the laws of that state grant an equal and impartial share to all, weak and strong alike; but the international rights of Greek states are defined by the strong for the weak." Demosthenes alludes to this distinction again in *On the Chersonese*:

For if Diopithes is acting outrageously in detaining the merchantmen, a note, men of Athens, a brief note, could put a stop to all this at once; and there are the laws, which direct us to impeach such offenders . . . "

He goes on to point out that Athens maintains military forces for use against its enemies who "are not amenable to the laws."[46] So within the state, laws govern behavior; outside, it is only the force of arms that can enforce justice.

Another instance of this idea, though not an endorsement, appears in Demosthenes' *Against Aristocrates*. There Demosthenes reports a *graphē*

---

[43] E.g. Thuc. 5.111.3.

[44] The persona of the speaker was thought particularly crucial in deliberative oratory (Arist. *Rhet.* 2.1.3.1377b). Grant 1965 notes a direct, even blunt, tone to Greek diplomacy that may reflect, especially in Thucydides, an effect of Realist criticisms of moralistic pretensions.

[45] Heath 1996: 393.   [46] Dem. 8.28–9. See also Dem. 8.32–3 and 10.57.

paranomōn case: although the defendant's proposal was manifestly illegal, he argued strongly that it was in the state's interest and he should be acquitted. Demosthenes says that this was a "frank, but rather shameless argument."[47] The defendant seems to have been arguing that the interstate interests of Athens superseded the laws, an argument he could not have made for an individual. Here, too, one can infer a distinction between the sphere of law and the interstate sphere in which Athens' interests take precedence.

In his book on *Greek Oratory: Tradition and Originality*, Stephen Usher argues that this distinction between the internal force and external irrelevance of justice is Demosthenes' original contribution.[48] With this distinction Demosthenes distances himself from the attitude that the domain of power is unlimited and derives from human nature, that power dominates human relations within as well as between states.[49] Peter Green has argued that such a view was pervasive in Greek culture.[50] For example, in Plato's *Gorgias*, Callicles argues that "Nature . . . shows that this is what justice has been decided to be: that the superior rule the inferior and have a greater share than they."[51] The context makes it clear that this code applies both to the rule of governments over citizens and to the rule of some states over others. Such ideas about individual morality are found in a variety of intellectual contexts.[52] But they are unlikely to have been as widespread as Green claims: for example, the attacks on Sophistic immorality in Aristophanes' *Clouds* attest to their unpopularity with the average Athenian.[53] Such ideas represented baggage Demosthenes was wise to jettison; but was this an innovation?

First of all, Demosthenes' move was adumbrated in Thucydides where Diodotus argues in the Mytilenian dialogue that, "we are not taking them to court to get justice but deliberating as to how they might be of use to us."[54] One could infer from Diodotus the distinction between an amoral interstate realm and the justice at issue within a state.[55] In Thucydides those who expect states to act according to laws tend to be disappointed, but

---

[47] Dem. 23.100. Cf. Xen. *Hell.* 5.2.32 on Spartan policy.
[48] Usher 1999: 214. Cf. Dover 1974: 311–12.   [49] Doyle 1991: 171.
[50] Green 1999: 97, 104, 106. See the similar picture of Adkins 1960: 231–40.
[51] Pl. *Grg.* 483d. Cf. Pl. *Resp.* 1.338c.
[52] Plato may distort his opponents' views, but other evidence of such critiques exists; see Gibert 2002: 36–9 for a concise discussion and bibliography on Sophistic critiques of morality in general.
[53] Ar. *Nub.* esp. 1399–1511.
[54] Thuc. 3.44.4, cf. 1.73.1. The scholia to *On the Liberty of the Rhodians* mention the Mytilenian dialogue (Radicke 1995: 155).
[55] Ste. Croix 1972: 16–28 argues that Thucydides made this distinction, but he admits that neither the speeches nor his own statements are as developed as those of Demosthenes (16–17).

only in the deplorable breakdowns of internal order – during the plague at Athens and the Corcyraean stasis – do relations of individuals within the state sink to the level of amorality common among states.[56] So, Thucydides at least adumbrates the distinction we see in Demosthenes.

In *On the Peace* Isocrates makes the following claim:

"At that time [when Athens was mobilizing Greece against Spartan rule], then, we recognized the principle that it is not just for the stronger to rule over the weaker, even as now we recognize it in the nature of the polity which has been established amongst ourselves."[57]

Isocrates argues that it is never just for the strong to rule the weak. He opposes himself to those who make a distinction between justice within and between states. His opponents seem to maintain that (a) strong states should not be hindered by justice from ruling the weak; but that (b) the strong should not rule the weak within the state. Presumably such arguments as Isocrates opposes were in the air before *On the Peace* (*c.* 355 BC) and thus before Demosthenes' *For the Liberty of the Rhodians* (351 BC).[58]

Aristotle's *Rhetoric* and *Politics* provide roughly contemporary parallels to Demosthenes' distinction.[59] I began this chapter with a quotation from Aristotle's *Rhetoric* that contrasted deliberative oratory, which turned on considerations of expedience, with law-court speeches, which aimed to convince on the basis of justice.[60] Aristotle does not approve of the amorality of deliberative oratory, as his example of "enslaving the neighbors" makes clear. In his *Politics*, too, Aristotle objects to the popular perception that a different morality obtains between states and within a state.[61] In neither of these cases does Aristotle endorse the distinction that Demosthenes was to make, but both passages do indicate that such a dichotomy was a popular one.

Though there are hints of this distinction in Thucydides, Isocrates, and Aristotle, Usher is correct in that Demosthenes' speech is the first extant work to make this distinction explicit and clear. This move, whatever its particular origin, was crucial to the continuing appeal of Realism, both in the

---

[56] Disappointed: e.g. Thuc. 3.53.1; 5.18.4; Plague: Thuc. 2.53; Corcyra: Thuc. 3.82–4. Contrast the Athenians' usual obedience to the laws (Thuc. 2.37.3).

[57] Isoc. 8.69.

[58] Scholars date *On the Peace* from 356 to 354: 356 (Laistner 1927: 17), 355 (Cawkwell 1982: 325; Weißenberger 2007), 355/4 (Harding 1974: 147). See Radicke 1995: 32–3 for the date of Dem. 15.

[59] Kennedy 1996: 417 gives the outside limits for the dates of the *Rhetoric*'s composition as 360–334. The *Politics* mentions events as late as 336, the assassination of Philip, so it too provides a roughly contemporary parallel rather than an antecedent for Demosthenes' *On the Liberty of the Rhodians*.

[60] Arist. *Rh.* 1.3.1358b21–37.   [61] Arist. *Pol.* 7.1324b30–42; 7.1333b29–39; 7.1334a11–14.

fourth century and in modern times. In the fourth century no statesman in the popular assembly could associate himself with the excesses of sophistic thought caricatured in Aristophanes' *Clouds* or attacked by Plato. To sever openly and explicitly such connections allowed Demosthenes to appear hard-headed, but not immoral and subversive. This explicit dichotomy of Demosthenes – and of modern Realists – allows for a realm of *to sympheron*, *raison d'état*, or *realpolitik* without arousing the opposition that would be provoked by an attack on morality in general. Such a limited sphere of amorality did not threaten the deep-rooted and concrete morality within a state. To put it bluntly, this brand of Realism denies only the moral claims of unknown people a long way away.

REALIST CALCULATIONS

The *Rhetoric to Alexander* sums up the interests of a state: "For a community such things as concord, strength for war, wealth, a plentiful supply of revenue, and excellence and abundance of allies are expedient."[62] These assets are essentially the same components of interest, narrowly defined, that modern Realists consider to be the proper goals of foreign policy. How such advantages are to be pursued may not be philosophically interesting but is difficult and complex in practice. This was particularly the case in Greece, where the independent machinations of a dozen or so larger cities and smaller cities numbering in the hundreds made for a bewildering kaleidoscope of alliances and enmities.[63] The civil strife that afflicted many cities further complicated this picture. Since different parties within a state sometimes pursued opposed foreign policies, changes in government often resulted in abrupt changes in foreign policy.[64] This complexity – along with the assembly's high level of interest and experience – made for oratorical arguments about power politics that are occasionally more reminiscent of the machinations of a Bismarck than of the sound-bite pronouncements of a contemporary democracy. As David Hume observed:

Whoever will read Demosthenes' oration for the Megalopolitans may see the utmost refinements on this principle [the balance of power] that ever entered the head of a Venetian or English speculatist.[65]

---

[62] [Arist.] *Rh. Al.* 1.1422a12–14. See Dem. 9.40; 10.49–50; 18.234–7 for similar conceptions of what things benefit a state.
[63] Cf. Dem. 10.53.   [64] See MacMullen 1963 on the effect of civil wars. Cf. Mosley 1974.
[65] David Hume, *Of the Balance of Power*, cited in Phillipson 1911: II.105–6.

The most extreme examples of this occur when Demosthenes and Aeschines accuse each other of complex interstate conspiracies in connection with Philip's entrance into southern Greece as the commander of the Amphictyons in 339, a topic well explored in Joseph Roisman's *The Rhetoric of Conspiracy in Ancient Athens*.[66] Demosthenes claims that Aeschines was bribed by Philip to accuse Amphissa of impiety and to set into motion a series of events that would only much later result in Philip's invitation into Greece. This scenario is, in fact, unlikely, but it shows just how calculating and duplicitous an Athenian audience thought states and leaders could be.

As the *Rhetoric to Alexander* states, the possession of good allies is one of the interests of a state. Accordingly orators emphasize that the "projection" of power can attract allies: other cities will join Athens, if the Persian king attacks, and they see Athens ready with a thousand cavalry, plentiful infantry, and three hundred ships;[67] the presence of a full Athenian levy at Eleusis emboldened the partisans of Athens at Thebes after Philip's capture of Elatea.[68] Demosthenes states the general principle: "For indeed alliance and respect are willingly offered by all men to those whom they see ready and prompt to take action."[69] The converse of this is the risk of inactivity or admitting weakness: Demosthenes argues that if Athens fails to come to the aid of a threatened city, it risks driving it into the hands of a rival power such as Thebes;[70] according to the author of *On Halonnesus*, if the Athenians cooperate with Philip in suppressing piracy, they will confess that they cannot do this on their own and Philip, set up as a naval power himself and free to cruise the seas, will be able to incite revolts among Athens' allies.[71]

The principle of strategic interests, even distant ones, was well established. In the Peloponnesian War some Athenians claimed that they were pre-empting a Syracusan attack on Athens by their interference in Sicily.[72] With more justice did Demosthenes argue that if the Athenians were ever too slow to counter Philip near the Hellespont, they would "never again be able to save the situation."[73] Such matters as the need for Phocian control of Thermopylae to keep Philip and Thebes from uniting were represented as being obvious to all Athenians.[74]

The prevalence of *realpolitik* at Athens is confirmed by the Athenian hopes for the Peace of Philocrates. Amazingly, many Athenians believed that Philip, after years of war against Phocis and Athens in league with Thebes,

---

[66] Roisman 2006: 133–45.   [67] Dem. 14.13.   [68] Dem. 18.177 reporting his earlier advice.
[69] Dem. 4.6.   [70] Dem. 16.31. See also Xen. *Hell.* 7.4.2, 5.1–2.   [71] [Dem.] 7.14–15.
[72] Thuc. 6.18.1, 87.2.   [73] Dem. 8.3.   [74] Dem. 19.83, 153.

was going to throw over his ally in their moment of victory: Phocis was
going to be saved, Thebes punished, and Athens rewarded.[75] Calculations of
interest, that the Thebans were becoming too powerful and arrogant, were
thought sufficient to motivate this startling reversal. Whether Philip ever
intended such a reversal, which of course never occurred, is controversial.[76]
I doubt that he did, but the fact that the Athenians believed that he would
suggests that such complex and amoral calculations were not considered
implausible in interstate politics – though wishful thinking also played a
part in this case.

    Some of the most difficult calculations of interest involve a conflict
between short-term false interests and long-term, true interests. Demosthenes plays upon this dichotomy constantly in his appeals to fight Philip
more aggressively: it is hard work to raise money, serve in the army, or
counter Philip in the north, but it will be worse to fight him later.[77] One
subset of such arguments depended upon a significant analogy: power is
like money. In the *First Olynthiac* Demosthenes warns that the theater of
war may be transferred from the Chalcidice to Attica:

Yet if that comes to pass, I am afraid, men of Athens, that just as men who borrow
money recklessly at high interest enjoy a temporary accommodation only to forfeit
their estates in the end, so we may find that we have paid a heavy price for our
indolence . . . [78]

Conversely, Demosthenes compares the advantages of an Olynthian
alliance with money.[79] Moral arguments about foreign affairs often
depended upon evocations of value-laden relationships within society; in
contrast, considerations of interest could be expressed in terms of money,
which the Greeks sometimes conceived of as a solvent of traditional virtues
and relationships.[80]

THE BALANCE OF POWER

Realism in the Melian dialogue, and to a lesser extent in Demosthenes'
For the Liberty of the Rhodians, was employed to defend aggressive policies.

[75] Dem. 5.9–10; 8.64; 9.11; 19.35–8, 41, 44, 62–3, 68; Aeschin. 1.169; 2.119.
[76] Markle 1974 and Ellis 1982 believe that this was in fact Philip's preferred plan, but I find the counter-
   arguments of Cawkwell 1978a: 108–13; 1978b: 101–4; and Hammond and Griffith 1979: 345 n. 1
   persuasive.
[77] Dem. 6.5, 27; 9.64; 10.24, 46–7.
[78] Dem. 1.15. Demosthenes uses the same analogy to condemn the Peace of Philocrates (Dem. 19.96).
[79] Dem. 1.11. See also Dem. 3.19. Cf. Tuplin 1998: 283–4.
[80] See Kallet 2001: 288, 291; Figueira 1995: 53; and Bakewell 2007 on the relationship of money and
   morality in Greek thinking, but note the caveats of Kroll 2000 on Kurke 1999.

But the self-interest that Realism serves can range from self-preservation to global conquest; Realism does not dictate whether more aggressive or more pacific policies best serve a state's interest.[81] For example, Diodotus in Thucydides' Mytilenian debates argues for mercy strictly on the basis of Athens' interests.[82]

When does interest tend to recommend unprovoked aggression, as the Athenians undertook against Melos?[83] When does a more moderate or even benevolent self-interest dominate interstate politics? Part of the answer lies in factors outside the world of Realist calculations: the internal structure of a state may favor or discourage a self-perpetuating cycle of war and militarism; states sharing a common culture may feel that justice is appropriate even between independent states; religious hostilities may make war the moral choice;[84] revenge may be an obligation regardless of its cost. There exists, however, a purely Realist and external model of why some international regimes foster a more aggressive and some a more pacific understanding of self-interest. This model and its application to classical Greece will be our next topic.

Aggression can be against a state's interest in a simple and immediate sense. No Realist, indeed no intelligent person, would advise a small and weak state to attack a large and powerful one. Even aggression by strong states can often be more costly than advantageous. More interesting is the coincidence or conflict of the short- and long-term consequences of aggression. In some cases, aggression brings future as well as immediate advantages: every successful attack brings additional power, which makes a state more formidable in the future. This power may simply lie in the accession of territory, manpower, or resources. In addition, unaligned states may decide to throw in their lot with the winning side. It is often the case in international politics that "nothing succeeds like success." Worse yet, nothing fails like failure: even leading states that display weakness or a lack of resolve risk their allies, their pre-eminence, and even their security. In these situations, the short-term gains of successful aggression are compounded by the longer-term momentum of power.

But some interstate regimes display a different pattern: every act of aggression and every gain in power attracts opposition. Unaligned states may view a growing power *ipso facto* as a threat. Aggressive behavior is likely

---

[81] Keohane 1986: 174.   [82] Thuc. 3.44.
[83] See Seaman 1997 against revisionist views that see Melian contributions to Sparta's war effort as the provocation of Athens expedition.
[84] Kissinger 1994: 60–2.

to sharpen this perception and lead to states forming alliances against perceived threats. This latter type of interstate regime has long been described as marked by a "balance of power."[85] Stephen Walt's classic *The Origins of Alliances*, whose terminology I shall use, contrasts such a world of "balancing" – in his view the more common situation – with that in which states "bandwagon" to join a rising power.[86]

This modern theory and terminology provides insight into the Greek world of small city-states, however distant in time, size, and culture. For the types of calculations Walt systematizes are almost ahistorical. The continuity of balance-of-power policies in different areas and times is, in fact, so striking that it provides important evidence for the Structural Realist claim that the nature of the interstate system, rather than the types of states involved, determines international politics.[87] If we compare Kissinger's description of the balance of power in seventeenth- to nineteenth-century Europe with descriptions and arguments for similar strategies in fourth-century Greece, we cannot help but grant that, for all its simplification, Structural Realism may explain "a small number of big and important things."[88] Kissinger states that "When any state threatened to become dominant, its neighbors formed a coalition – not in pursuit of a theory of international relations but out of pure self-interest to block the ambitions of the most powerful."[89] One may compare the formulation of David Hume in *Of the Balance of Power*:

But whether we ascribe the shifting of sides in all the Grecian republics to jealous emulation or cautious politics, the effects were alike, and every prevailing power was sure to meet with a confederacy against it, and that often composed of its former friends and allies.[90]

Indeed, the application of Walt's theory runs the risk, not of anachronism, but rather of merely providing a systematization of what ancient historians have long known. Throughout the classical period Athens was one of the leading states of Greece. As is typical of powerful states, Athens was rarely tempted to align itself with growing threats, that is, to "bandwagon." Athens was either a growing power itself, as in the fifth century,

---

[85] Haslam 2002: 89–127.

[86] Walt 1987: 17–33. I am indebted to the treatment of Strauss 1991a, which applies these terms to the Greek world. Strauss finds more bandwagoning than I do, in part since he is more concerned with the fifth than the fourth century (200, 201, 209 n. 37). See also Eckstein 2006: 65–7.

[87] Waltz 1986: 341; see also 13–14.   [88] Waltz 1986: 329.   [89] Kissinger 1994: 70.

[90] Cited in Phillipson 1911: ii.105. For similar judgments see Seager 1974; Strauss 1991a: 197; Bederman 2001: 35. As our examples and treatment will make clear, the skepticism of Sheehan 1996: 24–9 is untenable and consequently so is his supposed disproof of Structural Realism.

or a "balancer," as in our period. Classical cases of balancing behavior are not hard to find and the motivation behind them is often quite explicit. The Athenians reversed their alliance with Thebes to help the Spartans after the latter's defeat at Leuctra in 371: the Spartan ambassador on this occasion is represented as arguing that it was disadvantageous for Athens to have an overly strong Thebes as a neighbor.[91] In his argument for a defensive alliance with Megalopolis, Demosthenes made a similar argument: it is in Athens' interest that Thebes be weakened without Sparta becoming too strong.[92] He repeats this point in *Against Aristocrates* and adds a parallel argument about Thrace: it is to Athens' advantage that Thrace remain divided.[93] Phillip Harding sums up Athens' fourth-century foreign policy: Athens pursued a defensive strategy and "adopted a cleverly calculating balance-of-power policy" to keep any other state from becoming too strong.[94]

Athenian conduct was not only designed to curb the ambitions of other leading states; throughout the classical period Athens tried to attract and keep allies itself and to prevent its rivals from gaining allies.[95] Thus, the Athenians made foreign policy decisions based on how they expected weaker states to act. While strong states typically balance against power – and certainly did in the fourth century – the behavior of small states can vary. Walt sums up as follows:

> In general, the weaker the state, the more likely it is to bandwagon rather than balance . . . Because weak states can do little to affect the outcome [of a conflict] (and may suffer grievously in the process), they must choose the winning side.[96]

In the fourth century a number of small states aligned themselves with Athens, Thebes, or Macedonia depending on which state's power was ascendant: for example, the growth of Macedonian influence was at the cost of Theban power, whose difficulties in the Sacred War rendered it a less effective protector of its allies.[97]

---

[91] Xen. *Hell.* 6.5.39. Cf. the argument of Leptines – probably on this occasion (MacDowell 2000: 235) – reported in Arist. *Rh.* 3.10.1411a2–3 that "he would not stand by and see Greece deprived of one of her eyes."

[92] Dem. 16.4–5. He returns to this point at 23–4.

[93] Dem. 23.102 (Thebes and Sparta) and 23.103–17 (the Kingdom of Thrace).

[94] Harding 1995: 108–9; *pace* Wolpert 2001: 78. Sparta, another leading state, was amenable to the same calculations, e.g. Xen. *Hell.* 5.2.16. See Cartledge 1987: 274–313 on Sparta's successes and failures as a balancer.

[95] For example, Demosthenes fears the possibility that Megalopolis will go back to Thebes for help if Athens does not make an alliance with it (Dem. 16.30).

[96] Walt 1987: 29.   [97] Kelly 1980: 66–8, 83.

Two factors made this tendency of weaker states to bandwagon less decisive in the fourth century. First, not all small states did in fact try to bandwagon. Even relatively weak neighbors of the rising Macedonian power tried to resist it by appealing for Athenian aid: Olynthus, Byzantium, and even Perinthus and the tiny Neapolis, for example, all tried to balance against Macedonia rather than aligning themselves with it. Second, many of these alliances with rising states were designed to "balance" a threat closer to home: Messenia, for one, allied itself with Thebes and then Macedonia to protect itself from Spartan attack. Even weak states, therefore, sometimes tried to balance against power; the stronger states, whose conduct had the greatest impact on Athenian calculations, were even more pronounced in their predilection for balancing. Demosthenes, for example, argued that the allies of Athens and Thebes would help each defend itself, but they would not help either city destroy the other; for, in that case, the winner would become too powerful.[98]

States are more likely to balance against a growing power if they see it as particularly dangerous.[99] This adds a moral dimension to balancing. Unprovoked aggression, for example, may spur balancing, because an aggressive state is perceived as more threatening. According to Xenophon, the Theban general Epaminondas realized before the battle of Mantinea that "through his expedition to the Peloponnesus [he] had made himself the cause of the union of the Lacedaemonians, the Arcadians, the Achaeans, the Eleans, and the Athenians."[100] His aggressive policies – as well as Theban power – had aroused suspicion and opposition. In the *Third Philippic* Demosthenes claimed that no previous leading states had the right of unrestricted action that Philip was allowed:

On the contrary, when you, or rather the Athenians of that day, were thought to be showing a want of consideration in dealing with others, all felt it their duty, even those who had no grievance against them, to go to war in support of those who had been injured . . . [101]

Here Demosthenes may have been too pessimistic. Admittedly, Philip's growing power in the north did not by itself induce many Greek states

---

[98] Dem. 5.16–17. Cf. [Arist.] *Rh. Al.* 1.1423a5–9: "The Lacedaemonians, when they had conquered the Athenians, thought it expedient not to enslave their city; and on another occasion the Athenians and Thebans, when it was within their power to depopulate Sparta, thought it expedient to allow the Lacedaemonians to survive." In both cases, the decisions were motivated by a fear of Theban power. Cf. Xen. *Hell.* 6.5.38–9.

[99] Walt 1987: 263–6.   [100] Xen. *Hell.* 7.5.18.

[101] Dem. 9.23–4. Cf. Romilly 1958: 93 on Isocrates' theory that aggressive states lose *eunoia*, good will, and risk facing a coalition of weaker states.

to balance against him before the Peace of Philocrates. But his subsequent interventions in the internal politics of the southern Greek states brought him little additional power, while making him appear far more threatening. This may explain Athens' success in attracting allies against Philip in the late 340s.[102]

Although its role was complex, Persia too was involved in checking the ambitions of powerful Greek states. The Persian king had a vested interest in making sure that no one state in Greece became too powerful: such a power could threaten his control of the coast of Asia Minor as well as island possessions such as Rhodes and Cyprus – as had fifth-century Athens and Sparta in the 390s.[103] Although Persia did back the power of leading states in Greece – such as Sparta in the first King's Peace of 387/6 – it insisted on city-state autonomy and was willing to change sides to balance a threatening power.[104] Some Greeks felt – and many affected – outrage that Persian intervention made Greece weak. But Persia's intervention for the sake of keeping any state from dominating Greece was of a kind with the balance-of-power policies of the Greek cities themselves. Demosthenes included Persia in a couple of his balance-of-power arguments: in 354 he argued that if Persia attacked and showed itself a real threat, the Greek cities would stop fighting among themselves and unite against it.[105] They would balance against a threatening power. Later, he pictured the Persian king as likely to balance just like a typical Greek city. He would help Athens against Philip since "Philip is much more dangerous to the king if he has attacked us first."[106] Demosthenes was correct that the Persian king considered Macedonia to be a threat: the king helped to defend Perinthus and Byzantium against Philip.

Fourth-century Greece increasingly became a world without a dominant state – or even a dominant pair of states. Rather, a number of powerful city-states competed in wars with each other and as defenders and patrons of smaller states. The foreign policy decisions of the leading states, and often the weaker ones, were determined by the strategy of balancing. In such a system, aggression could easily backfire and leave the aggressor facing more and stronger enemies than before.

The scope and results of this general tendency require nice delineation lest we vaguely equate balance-of-power calculations with pacific or even

---

[102] See Markle 1981; contra Cawkwell 1978a: 131–5.
[103] Strauss 1991a: 191: "Perhaps the canniest player in the game of balancing was Persia."
[104] See Ryder 1965 and Jehne 1994 on the Common Peace and its guarantee of autonomy (cf. Baltrusch 1997).
[105] Dem. 14.12.   [106] Dem. 10.33, cf. 9.71. See also Hajdú 2002: 270 for more parallels.

just policies. First of all, balancing provides a brake and not a prophylactic against aggression. For example, after its defeat in the Social War, Athens extirpated the population of Sestos and took over the island.[107] This may have contributed to Athens' troubles in recruiting allies to fight Philip in the north – we do not know – but this calculation did not stop the Athenians.

The history of the fourth century shows clearly that balancing does not make for a more peaceful world. Indeed, balancing often requires states to enter wars they would not have otherwise entered. It does tend, however, to make wars less decisive. Such inconclusive wars raise the expectation of repeated interaction and, thus, are often fought at a lower level of ferocity than wars that are expected to be decisive.[108] Indeed, until the advent of Philip, the wars of the fourth century never reached the level of intensity and brutality that characterized the Peloponnesian War.

Balancing is intrinsically no more moral than it is peaceful. In particular, the need to balance does not allow for a moral choice of allies or for much emphasis on loyalty to friends.[109] For example, given Athens' policy of balancing against Thebes after the battle of Leuctra, its alliance with Phocis in the Sacred War was predictable. Phocis' later use of temple funds to finance a mercenary army was embarrassing to Athens, but Athens remained an ally nevertheless. More commonly, balancing required a switch of alliance. Such a switch, often without a real ground of complaint, was contrary to the strongly held ideal of loyalty to friends, which we examine in the next chapter. In all these ways, balancing behavior, while providing a brake on some would-be imperialist aggressors, was neither a particularly moral nor a pacific way to conduct foreign policy.

The most important effect of balancing by Greek states may be the simplest: for several centuries no one state was able to unite Greece. Of the many consequences of this fact, two are particularly important for this study. First, the fact that the Greek states were culturally similar, but politically distinct, led them to think about different states as peers and subject to the same moral standards and, perhaps, even laws. Second, the history of the Greek city-states leaves the impression of incessant fighting; in part, that is a consequence of the fact that no one state succeeded in conquering and thus pacifying the others, one of the most common ways that local warfare ceases in an area. This failure was, to some extent, a result of the prevalence of balancing.

---

[107] Diod. 16.34.3.   [108] Cf. Howard 2000: 23–4. See Axelrod 1984: 12–16, 20–1, 58, 77.
[109] Haslam 2002: 99.

A brief discussion of the conduct of states in Thucydides will provide a foil for the mid fourth century and will show how different calculations of interest emerge out of different interstate regimes. In general, the world of the late fifth century was more marked by bandwagoning than by balancing. Accordingly, it fostered the particularly nasty calculations of Thucydidean Realism.

The prevalence of bandwagoning is manifest in the political geography of the fifth century. Walt generalizes about the different patterns of alliances that result from balancing and bandwagoning: "When proximate threats [the most important type of threat to balance against] trigger a balancing response, alliance networks that resemble checkerboards are the likely result . . . when a threat from a proximate power leads to bandwagoning, the familiar phenomena of a sphere of influence is created."[110] In the fifth century Sparta's allies were concentrated in the Peloponnese. Athens' allies were islands and coastal cities and particularly those beyond the reach of Sparta's land army: its sphere of influence was based on its naval dominance of the Aegean. Such a pattern was the result of bandwagoning strategies, as each state allied itself with, rather than against, power.

One of the key factors that can encourage bandwagoning is the absence of allies with whom to balance.[111] In the fifth century Sparta's dominance of land warfare and Athens' naval supremacy gave smaller states few options. For an Aegean Island, the choice was accommodation with Athens or unsupported revolt. Such an island did not have the option of balancing against Athens by allying with another state with a powerful navy. As a handful of rebellious islands discovered to their cost, no other state could contest Athenian naval dominance. Even more obviously, small Peloponnesian states could hardly expect the Athenian navy to protect them from the Spartan army.

In contrast, by the age of Demosthenes, no city enjoyed uncontested land superiority. Although Athens' navy was usually stronger than that of any other state, the resurgence of piracy and the outcome of the Social War made its decline obvious. In part as a result of this, the fourth century's geography of alliance was strikingly different. The Spartans were ringed about by hostile Megalopolitans and Messenians. Athens was the ally of Phocis and enemy of Thebes in another "checkerboard" pattern. The Athenian League was still based on its naval dominance and included mainly coastal cities and islands. The protections of the Decree of Aristoteles and the outcome of the Social War drastically limited Athens' power over its allies. Rather,

---

[110] Walt 1987: 23.   [111] Walt 1987: 173, 175–6.

by the time of Demosthenes, its allies were motivated mainly by the need to balance local threats – for example, their inland neighbors – rather than being attracted or intimidated by Athens' attenuated and circumscribed power.[112]

The calculations of interest in Thucydides reflect the earlier interstate regime with which he and his speakers were familiar. His speakers often express a fear of growing power, but rarely the possibility that it may be limited by balancing. According to Thucydides, Sparta was forced into war by the fear of growing Athenian power.[113] On the other side, Athens feared that Corinthian aggression would win over Corcyra and its navy.[114] These and other key decisions came out of a belief in the momentum of power rather than an attempt to balance.

Sparta refused arbitration – and later regretted this – out of an exaggerated concern for its ally Corinth.[115] As Walt argues, "When statesmen fear bandwagoning, they fear the cascading effects that even a single defection might produce. In such circumstances, patrons are willing to invest large sums to prevent the loss of even a minor ally."[116] Corinth was hardly a minor ally, so Sparta's concern is more than understandable. Athens' attack on Melos provides a more striking example of a policy predicated on bandwagoning behavior. According to Thucydides' account, the Athenian ambassadors argued that Athens needed to subjugate Melos to make their superior power manifest to their subject allies.[117] This would keep them from revolting. Although the Melians warned that states would turn against a more threatening Athens, such reasoning was ruled out by the Athenians, who clearly believed that power, however threatening, attracts adherence rather than opposition.[118]

In the fourth century a different distribution of power led to a situation in which the short-term and long-term advantages of aggression were at odds. Adherence to a "balance of power" policy is intrinsically amoral; it can, however, be an "important corrective to the idea that unenlightened short-term interest should irrevocably hold sway."[119] Not only did the tendency to balance put the occasional brake on the ambitions of the powerful, but – as with all these ambiguities of calculated interest – by

---

[112] One would not want to rule out protection from local threats as an incentive for membership in the fifth-century empire. See Anderson and Dix 2004.

[113] Thuc. 1.23.6, 118.2–3.   [114] Thuc. 1.44.

[115] For example, Thuc. 1.86 mentions Sparta's allies four times. See Thuc. 7.18.2 for Spartan regrets.

[116] Walt 1987: 45.   [117] Thuc. 5.95–7.

[118] Thuc. 5.98–9; some cities in Sicily, where distance attenuated the power of Athens, seem to have been balancers (Thuc. 7.15.1).

[119] Haslam 2002: 15.

clouding the dictates of interest, it allowed more scope in foreign policy for moral considerations.

In the early modern period the Balance of Power came to have a moral tone: it was according to natural law that states aligned themselves to prevent another state from acquiring dominance. The metaphor of an actual physical balance added to this aura of naturalness that made the Balance of Power the subject of approbation for several centuries – in contrast the concept of *raison d'état* was controversial from its inception.[120] In Athens the interested calculations to prevent another state's dominance were not valorized in themselves. Rather, fighting against dominating powers and "bringing succor to the weak" represented important ideals in Athenian foreign policy; Athens' record of taking such stands was a source of great patriotic pride. This ideal is prominent in tragedy, in funeral orations, as well as in deliberative oratory.[121] At least four factors help us understand the origins and continued strength of this tradition. Let us begin with the more charitable explanations.

The first explanation is a historical one.[122] Athenian experience in the fifth and fourth centuries included dramatic cases of succor received and given. The Athenians themselves had been refugees during the invasion of Xerxes. Many of them were again driven from their homes, if not their city, during the Peloponnesian War. Athens had offered sanctuary to refugees such as the Messenians after the Ithome revolt as well as to the Plataeans and the Samians after the Peloponnesian League's capture of those cities. The hospitality shown at Argos and Thebes to the exiles from the Thirty was long remembered in the fourth century, during which the Athenians received Theban exiles and Plataean refugees again as well as Olynthians and Phocians. The consciousness of benefits given and received was, as it were, the sand which the oyster of a creative patriotic discourse turned into the pearl of this important ideal.

Such an explanation helps us understand the continued vitality and relevance of "aiding the weak and wronged." But the elaboration of myths about Athenian aid to suppliants seems to have preceded these historical events. Most conspicuously, the cult of Heracles' family, who were the most prominent mythic beneficiaries of Athenian succor, predates all these events

---

[120] Haslam 2002: 89–127, esp. 89, 95, 98, 119.

[121] Low 2007: 178–83. Karavites 1984: 173 argues that this was an ideal in Greece at large. The wide spread of balance-of-power considerations could contribute to this ideal even in places without Athens' historical experience or internal colonization.

[122] In this paragraph and the next I follow the arguments of Jameson 2006 and refer the reader to the bibliography there.

by a half-century. We must look earlier for a full explanation of this ideal. It may have had its origins in the internal colonization of Attica, a movement of settlers into the countryside that would have favored ideologies praising the generous treatment of newcomers to rural communities. So there may have been another older source for the tradition of helping the weak.

Two Realist explanations lead to similar results. The first will be treated in detail in the next chapter: to aid the weak was to put them under an obligation and gave an excuse for activist, if not imperialist, foreign policies. Such a motivation for aiding the weak did not disappear, but it was perhaps more important to the powerful and confident Athens of the fifth and early fourth centuries than to the Athens of the mid fourth century, whose foreign policy was driven more by a fear of than a taste for power.

Second, and most pertinent here, helping the weak against the strong was often congruent with calculations aimed at maintaining a balance of power: the strong were potential threats; the weak were their usual victims. Was "helping the weak" merely a cover for calculations of interest?[123] An examination of Demosthenes' oratory is revealing. The theme of assisting the weak against the attacks of the strong was a cornerstone of his deliberative oratory throughout his preserved speeches, from the *For the Megalopolitans* in 353/2 to *On the Crown* in 330. In the former, Demosthenes seems to be arguing not for an ideal, but strictly for a prudential policy: "I have said what I consider expedient for you; and I urge you not to abandon the Megalopolitans, and absolutely never to sacrifice the weak to the strong."[124] In *Against Aristocrates* Demosthenes again argues that it is in the interest of Athens that neither Thebes nor Sparta be too strong.[125] It is in *On the False Embassy* that Demosthenes is most explicit in his Realism: "It wasn't because of their virtue that you saved the Spartans at one time, or those damn Euboeans, or many other people; it was because their preservation was in the interest of Athens, as is the case with the Phocians now."[126]

Such a calculating approach would seem to undercut the well-attested patriotic narrative that the Athenian rescues first of Thebes and then of Sparta were motivated by disinterested nobility. Demosthenes, however, is

---

[123] Cf. Eckstein 2000: 876–7.

[124] Dem. 16.32 (trans modified). Cf. Kissinger 1994: 98: "the fixed principle of British foreign policy, whether acknowledged or not, was its role as protector of the balance of power, which in general meant supporting the weaker against the stronger."

[125] Dem. 23.102–3. Demosthenes' main argument is that such a balance of power and mutual suspicion in Thrace benefits Athenian settlers in the Chersonese.

[126] Dem. 19.75.

not consistent. In the *Second Olynthiac*, for example, Demosthenes presents the altruistic interpretation of Athenian policy. He argues that the Athenians need to live up to their state's former actions:

[you] lavished your treasure and jeopardized . . . [your] lives in the field that others might enjoy their rights . . . I am surprised that you, who have so often saved the other states, both all of them together and each separately in turn, should sit down under the loss of what is your own.[127]

Demosthenes denies Athenian imperialism in *On the Chersonese*:

For nature has not equipped you to seek aggrandizement and secure empire, but you are clever at thwarting another's designs and wresting from him his gains, and quick to confound the plots of the ambitious and to vindicate the freedom of all mankind."[128]

In *On the Crown* Demosthenes argues that this tradition also took priority over the other great motivation of Greek states, the standard of reciprocity. He claims that the Athenians help states in need if they have not benefited, and have even injured, Athens in the past:

"[Y]ou keep your resentment for proper occasions, but if ever their life or their liberty is endangered, you will not indulge your rancour or take your wrongs into account."[129]

Conversely, he excoriates Aeschines – and he repeats the argument in the clear expectation that it would carry some weight – on the grounds that Aeschines proposed that Athens should not help any state that had not helped Athens first.[130] Later, Demosthenes justified Athens' failed policy of opposition to Philip on these grounds: Demosthenes would have deserved death if he had sought to "tarnish Athens' honourable traditions" of helping those in distress.[131] He adds the words:

But if it was right that some one should intervene, on whom did the duty fall, if not on the Athenian democracy? That then was my policy. I saw a man enslaving all mankind, and I stood in his way. I never ceased warning you and admonishing you to surrender nothing.[132]

Although Athens' interests demanded a policy of seeking allies among Philip's victims, and thus a policy of helping the weak, Demosthenes sometimes argued for this policy in elevated and moral terms.

Such an inconsistent group of professed motives for the same type of conduct may seem ripe for Realist unmasking: Athens' true and interested

---

[127] Dem. 2.24.   [128] Dem. 8.42 (10.14).   [129] Dem. 18.99.
[130] Dem. 19.16, 307.   [131] Dem. 18.101.   [132] Dem. 18.72.

motives were sometimes frankly stated and on other occasions palliated with high-flown rhetoric.[133] It is hard to deny that some of Demosthenes' claims are specious, but two considerations suggest a more moderate and nuanced conclusion. First, Athenian policy was not determined by Demosthenes or by any powerful body other than the assembly. There was no powerful official or group of officials who might decide on a policy for one set of real reasons and then try to justify it to public opinion on other, more moral, grounds. Rather, whatever arguments convinced the sovereign assembly have every claim to be considered the true reason for policy. And the argument from Athens' noble traditions was apparently as potent as was that from the need to balance against power. Second, if one believes, as I do, that Philip's Macedonia was irremediably aggressive and, in reality, a threat to the independence of all Greek states and not just to Athenian interests, one might concede that Athens' interests in maintaining its power and autonomy in the Greek world and its ideal of fighting for freedom were closely aligned in this period.[134]

In some interstate systems the policy of helping the weak and those unjustly attacked can amount to suicide: Athens' allies helped it to attack Melos; nobody came to Thebes' aid when it was destroyed by Alexander. But Greece of the mid fourth century was not such a world until after Chaeronea. The ideal of helping the weak and vindicating freedom could thrive in such a world. So, Athens did not try to appease Philip but backed a succession of smaller victims of his aggression to its eventual – but not inevitable – cost.[135]

PREDICTION

The calculation of interest, then, can involve the evaluation and comparison of long-term versus immediate interests, strategic goals, and bandwagoning versus balance-of-power strategies. It begins to seem less and less a solid and simple basis for policy. In addition, knowing a state's interest involves predicting the future, a difficult task. For a speaker arguing from interest, the obscurity of the future presented an oratorical challenge: making their prognostications carry conviction. Conversely, orators trying to minimize the significance of an apparent interest or to argue a just course of action tended to emphasize the impossibility of prediction and the importance of luck. These are only general tendencies, but they are important ones.

---

[133] Compare Lendon 2000: 2 on the mix of motives for Spartan wars.
[134] Kennedy 1959; Harding's 1979 on Cawkwell 1978a; Sealey 1993 summarized at 219.
[135] Harding 1995: 124.

In his *Rhetoric* Aristotle treats the problem of predicting the future in deliberative oratory. He distinguishes the types of oratory according to the time period they address: deliberative oratory has to do with the unknown future and is accordingly the more difficult than forensic oratory.[136] We have noted already that Aristotle believed that considerations of expedience predominated in deliberative oratory. This is consonant with his concern with understanding the future; for the expedient is only known insofar as the future is predictable. In contrast, determining the just course does not necessarily require prediction: for example, a state should not make an unprovoked attack and should help friends and retaliate against enemies. Such values may conflict with each other, but moral decisions do not necessarily involve the problem of predicting the future.[137]

Orators who wanted to emphasize a state's interest as the basis for action often had to make forecasts of the future and to confirm them with appeals to their expertise or to historical precedents. Thucydides, with his focus on expedience, considered the ability to see the future to be crucial for a statesman. He praised the foresight of both Themistocles and Pericles.[138] Demosthenes occasionally needed to do the same for himself. This was particularly true when he was arguing against the moral sense of the Athenians and thus had to present considerations of interest as decisive: in *On the Peace* he details three cases where his predictions about the future were correct.[139] This long section was clearly important to his argument that the Athenians should ignore their grievances, consult their interests, and not go to war at that juncture. In other cases he contrasts, either implicitly or directly, his insight with the failure of other people to see what is going to happen – and shows that this enabled him to advise Athens well about its interests.[140]

Another way to predict the future is to consider cases from the past.[141] This strategy was ubiquitous, but a couple of examples should suffice. Andocides explicitly and at length uses Athens' past treaties with Sparta as a guide to what future treaties will bring – and thus to show that the one under consideration would be advantageous.[142] Demosthenes argues that Philip will not admit that he is at war with Athens, just as he concealed his enmity from the Pheraeans and Olynthians – and thus the Athenians would be foolish to take him at his word.[143]

---

[136] Arist. *Rh.* 1.3.1358b13–15, 3.17.1418a22–4.   [137] See Kant 1983: 127 (*Perpetual Peace* 370).
[138] Thuc. 1.138.3; 2.65.5, 65.13.   [139] Dem. 5.4–12.   [140] Dem 6.19, 32–3; 9.29; 19.31.
[141] Arist. *Rh.* 2.20.1394a6–8. See pp. 66–71.   [142] Andoc. 3.2; cf. Andoc. 3.32.
[143] Dem. 8.57–9. In the *Third Philippic* Demosthenes adds Phocis and Oreos to the list of places Philip has taken while professing peaceful intentions (9.10–12).

The opposite emphasis, that on the difficulty of predicting the future, was also a common motif in foreign policy deliberations. It appears in a number of Thucydidean speeches, typically those recommending restraint or peace.[144] An important effect of luck is to undermine calculations of interest. In the *Second Olynthiac* Demosthenes concedes the good fortune of Philip, but argues that Athens' is better, if only the Athenians do their duty.[145] In *On the Chersonese* Demosthenes explicitly admits the large part played by luck in the outcome of events.[146] This invocation of luck ends up bolstering his argument for resistance to Philip. Unpredictability was invoked to blur the superiority of Philip's power; by weakening the argument from apparent interest, Demosthenes tries to make his moral argument, that from Athens' tradition of defending freedom, decisive.[147]

In Thucydides and Demosthenes the argument from the uncertain future typically undermined Realist considerations. But it could favor either war or peace. In Thucydides, apparent interest could be invoked in favor of Sparta and Athens' recourse to war in a bipolar world, but the problem of prediction made the advisability of such policies less clear-cut. In the mid fourth century apparent interest dictated that Athens yield to the superior military strength of Philip. The unpredictability of the future again made the advisability of this policy less clear. Demosthenes took advantage of this to make room for an intransigent attitude towards Macedonian power: an unforeseeable future helped to undermine the preponderance of manifest, present power as a determinant of action.[148]

CONCLUSION

The arguments of Demosthenes' *On the Crown* will provide us with a conclusion. The perspective of this speech is different from that of deliberative war oratory: here Demosthenes was defending a failed policy rather than advocating a future course of action. Prognostication was no longer needed to determine Athens' interest, which seems manifestly to have been ill served by Demosthenes' policies. Nevertheless, Demosthenes not only maintained but elaborated on his expertise in understanding events: this was one of the points of his brilliant description of the assembly after the fall of Elatea.[149] Nor did he give up the claim that he served the

---

[144] E.g. Thuc. 1.42.2, 78.1–3; 4.17.4–5; 5.104. See, for example, Edmunds 1975.
[145] Dem. 2.22.   [146] Dem. 8.68–9.   [147] Dem. 2.24.
[148] I hope to explore elsewhere three passages that explicitly invoke the uncertainty of the future as grounds for moral behavior (Hdt. 1.86; Thuc. 5.90; Dem. 15.21–2).
[149] Dem. 18.172–3. See above pp. 11–13.

interests of Athens:[150] his reforms ensured that the funding for the navy was raised fairly and expeditiously;[151] he provided Athens with strong allies.[152] In particular, he defended the alliance with Thebes with a counterfactual argument: given Athens' defeat and its consequences, how much worse would it have been had the war been conducted in Attica and without Theban assistance.[153]

These palliatives, however, do not represent the main thrust of his argument. Rather he claimed that despite his expertise, patriotism, and what we might call due care, there are limits to the calculations of interests. The outcome of wars cannot be predicted.[154] Fortune and the will of the gods are obscure and may be against one side. In this context Demosthenes invoked the superiority of moral to interest claims with his famous paradox: even if we knew what was going to happen, we owed it to our traditions of helping the weak and fighting for freedom to oppose Philip. This claim was possible because Athens did possess such a tradition. But in Demosthenes' presentation, the nobility of this tradition and of his policy derives from the perfection of the Realism he sets them against: he argues against a Realism with the benefit of accurate knowledge of the future:

Suppose that the future had been revealed to all of us, that every one had known what would happen, and that you, Aeschines, had predicted and protested, and shouted and stormed – though in fact you never opened your mouth – even then the city could not have departed from that policy, if she had any regard for honour, or for our ancestors, or for the days that are to come.[155]

We have seen that these national traditions did not develop in opposition to calculations of interest, but mainly in harmony with them. Demosthenes' contrast between Athens' interest in not being defeated and its ideals here finds two explanations. First, a national tradition has a certain momentum, for good or for ill. After several generations, during which a politic concern for the weak and for freedom dominated Athenian interstate thinking, such a concern could make itself felt even in the most impolitic of decisions. Second, the national tradition of vindicating liberty grew in part to justify what was usually an advantageous long-term strategy, balancing against power or threat: it was not a strategy advantageous in every case, and it was certainly risky in the case of Philip's overwhelming might.

One can understand the force of some moral arguments in Athenian foreign policy by pointing out that they are often compatible with

---

[150] Dem. 18.232.   [151] Dem. 18.102–8.   [152] Dem. 18.237.

[153] Dem. 18.195; cf. 230. Hyperides presents a similar argument in *Against Diondas* 5.15–19.

[154] Dem. 18.192–3.   [155] Dem. 18.199. Yunis 2000: esp. 102, 109.

external advantage and by noting that systems of thought have inertia. These considerations do not fully explain the invocation of justice in Athenian assembly speeches. We need to examine in more detail the effect of the domestic analogy most central to how Athenians thought about interstate relations, the ideal of reciprocity between states, and about its moral entailments. It will turn out that, just as Realist calculations provide no absolute criteria for foreign policy, so, conversely, these moral rules of state conduct are entangled in the web of interest.

CHAPTER 8

Reciprocity

When Demosthenes, in *On the Liberty of the Rhodians*, distinguished between the equal justice within Athens and the anarchy and amorality among states, he distanced himself from those engaged in critiques of all morality. His argument also implied a rejection of another way of conceiving of internal and interstate relations: they might both be subject to the same moral code. This equivalence is usually due to the application of individual morality to the interaction of states. A central part of the moral code that the Athenians applied to the actions of states was the ideal of reciprocity.

Reciprocity requires that people or states requite the treatment they have received.[1] The requital can be of favors or gifts (positive reciprocity) or of injuries (negative reciprocity, retaliation). Although we shall see significant differences between the roots and consequences of the two types of reciprocity, both require requital for past actions.[2] The use of identical vocabulary for paying back favors and injuries confirms the unity of the Greek concept of reciprocity.[3]

The obligation to pay back good and bad was strong, but was not enforced by law.[4] So, the requirement of requital was on a different plane from the obligation to pay war taxes or not to murder. Its enforcement was not dependent on a central state power. Rather a person's sense of honor, closely linked to his reputation in the community, required reciprocity.[5] It was shameful rather than illegal either to abandon a friend or to allow an injury to remain unavenged.

Reciprocity was so important to Greek ethics that one common understanding of justice included no more than the injunction to give to "each

---

[1] Van Wees 1998b: 20 defines reciprocity as "exchange conceptualized as the performance and requital of gratuitous actions."

[2] Gehrke 1987: 131–2; van Wees 1998b: 20.   [3] Gehrke 1987: 133.

[4] See [Arist.] *Rh. Al.* 1.1421b37–1422a2; van Wees 1998b: 19.

[5] Gehrke 1987: 128; Lendon 2000: 5–11.

what is owed to him," that is, to return good to friends and bad to enemies.[6] The ideal of friendship in the classical period emphasized mutual assistance.[7] Vengeance, too, was often seen as an obligation. We shall see that in the fourth century classical Athens was no longer a "gift economy," in which positive reciprocity dominated market exchange. Nor was it a feuding society, in which the lack of recourse to law required a touchy sense of honor and consequent violent retaliation for injuries and insults. Nevertheless, currents in Athenian thinking that originated in such societies persisted and were still strong in the classical period. The obligation to requite good and evil was applied to states with important consequences.[8]

This chapter treats five main topics: reciprocity's role in friendship and alliance between states; the way that the obligation to repay favors could confirm hierarchies among states; the need for states to avenge their wrongs even when this was against their interests; conversely, the strategic advantages of reciprocity; finally, the mixture of calculating and emotional considerations in confirming the obligation to reciprocate.

FRIENDSHIP AND ALLIANCE

Individuals were morally obliged to help their friends and especially those in distress: a friend said of the metic Callias that since he "is not only a friend of mine but was one of my father's so long as he lived . . . I felt it would be disgraceful not to support Callias' case so far as my ability permits."[9] States were also supposed to repay favors done to them. In one passage Demosthenes complains that a law to rescind tax exemptions benefactors of Athens would require the city to insult the king of the Bosporus, whose generosity to Athens has been immense: this measure would "make the state less trustworthy than an individual."[10] More typically, positive reciprocity among states consisted of the exchange of military aid and played a large role

[6] Pl. *Resp.* 1.331e–332b, 334b. Of particular significance for deliberative oratory is the statement in [Arist.], *Rh. Al.* 1.1422a28-b1. Demosthenes uses *adikein*, to act unjustly, to describe a failure to pay back a good turn (Dem. 16.17). See Dover 1974: 180–4; Blundell 1989: 26–59; Mitchell 1996: 11; D. Cohen 1995: 66.

[7] Konstan 1998: 280.

[8] Anna Missiou 1998a: 188–9 argues that the Athenians in the classical period uniquely rejected "the demand of reciprocation" as "not in the interest of their new constitution." They conferred benefits "freely without asking for a return" (199). Reciprocal generosity was an "element of diplomatic rhetoric" used by kings and oligarchs but "was incompatible with democracy" (196). We do find disavowal of reciprocity, e.g. Dem. 18.99; 19.16, 306–7, but in the fifth century this argument seems to neglect the importance of Athens' justification of empire on the basis of having liberated the Ionian Coast and the islanders (e.g. Thuc. 1.75; 5.89). In our period we will find plenty of appeals to the ideal of reciprocity in Athenian assembly speeches.

[9] Lys. 5.1 (trans. modified) with Mitchell 1996: 13–14. See also Konstan 1998: 280. [10] Dem. 20.36.

in the system of alliances in which almost all Greek states were enmeshed.[11] Such alliances were especially crucial to smaller cities, who might otherwise have been prey to their neighbors but, in fact, usually maintained their independence: the *Rhetoric to Alexander* begins its description of possible motivations for alliance with the statement that alliances are necessary "when one party is too weak by itself . . . "[12] For stronger cities, such as Athens, one of the main purposes of maintaining a military force was to aid their allies – the possession of whom was an important source of power.[13]

The bonds of alliance between cities were complex. We have already encountered oratorical passages that evince a Realist understanding of treaties of alliance: the view that the strength of an alliance depends only on the common interests of the two states. This was not the usual understanding of alliances. More common was the notion of alliance as binding states to act even against their immediate self-interest: this is why alliances were sanctified by oaths to the gods and were imbued with the special moral obligations associated with friendship. Two important bodies of evidence portray the bonds between states in different ways: oratory and history frequently mention the gratitude expected in requital of voluntary beneficence; the texts of treaties of alliance, however, describe mandatory obligations between states. This distinction is important. Reciprocity as I have defined it – and as it was practiced, for example, by the Homeric heroes – was what Gouldner has termed "personalized" reciprocity, a type of reciprocity which can best be understood in terms of its contrast with "formalized" obligations, which are "precisely defined and inescapable."[14]

The relations of Greek states probably started off closely modeled on the personalized reciprocity of archaic aristocrats through whose foreign connections nascent city-states first communicated. Early treaties may have done nothing more than publicize a vaguely defined friendship between cities: what is probably the earliest surviving Greek treaty, the sixth-century pact between the Sybarites and their allies and the Serdaioi, merely specifies eternal and guileless friendship.[15] In contrast, the alliance between Elis and

---

[11] In Thucydides, the Corcyraeans are considered unusual, or even unique, for not having alliances – and perhaps not even commercial treaties with other Greek states (Thuc. 1.32.4, 37.2–5).

[12] [Arist.] *Rh. Al.* 2.1424b29–33.   [13] E.g. Dem. 14.11.

[14] Van Wees 1998b: 16 summarizing Gouldner, who contrasts "formalized" and "personalized" reciprocity. I accept the arguments of van Wees 1998b: 18 and have adopted his narrower definition of reciprocity above. Thus, I contrast "formalized" obligations and reciprocity – the latter equivalent to Gouldner's "personalized" reciprocity. Other taxonomies exist, e.g. a dichotomy between "generalized" and "balanced" reciprocity (Allen 2000: 62–3).

[15] Meiggs and Lewis 1988: no. 10.

Heraea – whose date within the sixth century is disputed and could be as late as 500 – already requires each city to stand by the other especially in case of war; it also imposes a fine to be paid to Zeus Olympios in the event of a failure to do so.[16]

The language of friendship could still be used in formal diplomacy in the classical period either by itself or in conjunction with specific terms.[17] But most classical treaties were quite precise in their stipulations: they suggest "formalized" obligations rather than the give-and-take of Greek friends. A treaty of 395 is typical: it asserts that "if anyone comes against the Athenians for the purpose of making war either by land or by sea, the Boeotians shall give assistance with all their strength, in whatever way is requested by the Athenians, to the best of their ability" and vice versa.[18] Some treaties even specified the details of the cities' aid to each other: the leadership of their forces, the responsibility for feeding and paying troops, and the division of plunder.[19] These terms are "formalized" obligations, specific and mandatory.

When Athens, having sworn to aid another city in the event of an attack, lived up to its obligation, can we really say that it was conferring a favor? The "personalized" ideals of individual reciprocity do not at first seem to apply to Greek allies. But to exclude aid to allies from the sphere of positive reciprocity would severely narrow its scope; for, most of the, time cities were formally allied with those they aided in war.[20]

Further reflection shows that formal alliances did not limit the realm of reciprocity quite that much. First and most obvious, negative reciprocity consists of revenge for harm done to one and was rarely, if ever, a formal obligation. Second, one may grant that a sworn alliance could be seen as binding, sanctioned by the invocation of the gods and by the imprecations that often accompanied its confirmation.[21] Nevertheless, a variety of dodges made the adherence to an alliance a voluntary undertaking: to follow even a sworn ally in injustice was morally dubious;[22] oaths might come in conflict with each other; religious scruples might prevent adherence to a

---

[16] Meiggs and Lewis 1988: no. 17 (Bengtson 1962: no. 110). See also Mitchell 1997: 22–3 on the language of friendship in Greek treaties. Cf. Karavites 1984: 189–91.

[17] Philochorus in Didymus, *On Demosthenes*, col. 8.18–20 in Harding 2006: 70–1; Ha no. 117.

[18] *IG* ii² 14, trans. Ha no. 14 = RO no. 6. Compare the almost identical formulations of *IG* ii² 34 = RO no. 20 (384/3 BC); *IG* ii² 43 = RO no. 22 (378/7 BC); *IG* ii² 97 (*c.* 375–371 BC); *IG* ii² 116 = RO no. 44 (361/0 BC).

[19] E.g. leadership (Thuc. 5.47.7; Xen. *Hell.* 7.1.1–14; Aeschin. 3.145), paying the troops (Thuc. 5.47.6; Aeschin. 3.143), and plunder (Hdt. 6.23; Bengtson 1962: no. 147 B6). On the division of plunder see also the discussion in Pritchett 1971–91: v.363–75.

[20] Athens came to the aid of Sparta before making a treaty with it (Xen. *Hell.* 6.5.49, 7.1.1–14).

[21] See pp. 222–34.   [22] Thuc. 6.79.1; Andoc. 3.24–6; Dem. 16.6–8.

treaty obligation; states might not be capable of assisting their allies. For example, with its attenuated resources after the Social War, Athens was simply not able to send out expeditions to save every ally it had solemnly promised to protect. There was enough leeway to make support of an ally a voluntary act in practice. Third, even a precise and legalistic Greek could admit gratitude for the voluntary decision to make an alliance, if not for the mandatory fulfilling of it; most would not make the distinction. Overshadowing all this was the fact that when it came to an ally's aid, a city ran great risks, even if it did not suffer casualties, in order to save the lives, families, property, and liberty of an ally. Given the gravity of the exchange and the frailty of oaths, the formality of treaty obligations still left plenty of scope for gratitude.[23]

Consequently, the two ways of viewing alliances coexisted. The bonds of alliance could be portrayed as a pseudo-legal obligation confirmed by oaths to the gods or as part of reciprocal friendship. These two perspectives were often combined when treaties of alliance were invested with the additional moral content of friendship. It can be hard to tell which conception was foremost in a speaker's or author's mind. In many cases, it is not worthwhile to try to disentangle the two, especially since they were generally aligned.

A story from Xenophon's *Hellenica*, finished in the 350s, illustrates the moral texture of Greek alliances.[24] In it Xenophon portrays the Corinthians as exemplary allies and friends to Sparta. When hard pressed by Thebes in 366, the Corinthians wanted to make peace. They first asked and received the permission of their ally, Sparta. But Thebes then insisted on Corinth's contracting an alliance with them as the price of peace. The Corinthians refused, since such an alliance "would not be peace, but just a change of war": they would have had to fight along with Thebes against their old ally Sparta, which remained at war with Thebes. In admiration of the Corinthians' loyalty, the Thebans dropped their demand. When making their request to be allowed to consult with Sparta, the Corinthians were abiding by their treaty obligations to their allies in the Peloponnesian League. Alliances often contained a clause that hostilities against a third party could only be ended jointly; that is, no one state could make a separate peace treaty.[25] Since treaties were confirmed by oaths to the gods,

---

[23] We might compare the honors for soldiers who die in combat: most states treat with honor and gratitude soldiers who die in battle, regardless of whether they were drafted or had volunteered. Cf. Winter 1995: 98.

[24] Xen. *Hell.* 7.4.6–10.

[25] E.g. Meiggs and Lewis 1988: no. 42; Tod 1946–8: no. 111; *IG* ii² 97; *IG* ii² 116 = RO no. 44. Cf. Xen. *Hell.* 7.4.7–10, 4.40. Thuc. 5.23.1–2, 47.4.

the Corinthians could even have pleaded a religious necessity to consult Sparta. When the Corinthians address the Spartans they refer to themselves as friends of the Spartans.[26] This wording stresses the mutual and long-standing bonds between the two cities and Corinthian regret at having to be relieved of their treaty obligations. The whole passage is redolent of loyalty and the Corinthians imply that their friendly feelings will continue even after their alliance is dissolved: "For if we are saved, we might perhaps make ourselves useful to you again at some future time . . ."[27] Finally, the Thebans admire the Corinthians' reluctance to fight a benefactor. They esteem their honorable conduct according to the code of reciprocity: they have received favors and recognize their obligation to repay them – or, at least, not to fight against the Spartans.[28]

These complex bonds to allies were strong and often played a pivotal role in the wars of the city-states. Examples of the obligation to help, and not to hurt, benefactors are common in the historians.[29] Passages in Demosthenes provide ample evidence confirming the prominence of this value in popular thinking.[30]

This ethic has important consequences for understanding Athens' war against Philip in the north Aegean coast. Some scholars criticize the strategy of Demosthenes' *First Philippic* and his *Olynthiacs*, that Athens should fight Philip in the north.[31] The tactical merits of Demosthenes' policy are disputed, but modern references to "Athenian interests" in the Thraceward region ignore a moral imperative. Not only had Athens sent cleruchies to cities such as Pydna and Potidaea that fell to Philip, but it had long been allied with several other victims of Philip.[32] Athens was bound by the potent combination of sworn treaties and reciprocity to defend its allies.[33] The Athenians had sworn to the gods to come to these allies' aid "both by land and by sea, with all (their) strength to the best of (their) ability."[34] Not only their adherence to oaths but also their reputation for good faith were

---

[26] Xen. *Hell.* 7.4.8: *philoi.*   [27] Xen. *Hell.* 7.4.8.

[28] Sparta seems to have been considered a benefactor, *euergetēs*, insofar as it was the senior member of a long-standing alliance, rather than on the basis of some particular benefaction (Xen. *Hell.* 7.4.10). Nevertheless, the Corinthians claim friendship with no mark of hierarchy – they come as *philoi* (Xen. *Hell.* 7.4.8).

[29] E.g. Thuc. 1.40.5–41.1, 42.1; Xen. *Hell.* 3.5.8; 4.1.32–3; 5.2.2–3; 6.2; 8.4. Cf. Ar. *Rh.* 2.23.1398a1–3.

[30] Dem. 5.5; 15.3; 16.19. In contrast, Isoc. 8.97 and Dem. 9.34 condemn making war against an ally as an act of utter depravity.

[31] E.g. Cawkwell 1978a: 82: "The great First Philippic was greatly wrong-headed." See Leopold 1987 for bibliography and a defense of Demosthenes' strategy.

[32] Cargill 1981: 179–80.

[33] Buckler 1996: 92 n. 10 cites Bengtson 1962: no. 309 (*IG* ii/iii² 127 = RO no. 53); no. 312 (*IG* ii² 128); no. 317; and no. 323 as well as *IG* ii² 114, ii² 130 for Athenian allies defeated or captured by Philip.

[34] Ha no. 35, lines 50–2 = RO no. 22.

on the line. Hence Demosthenes repeatedly condemns Athenian lethargy and insists on their obligation to save their allies from Philip.[35] Although he often adds prudential considerations, the moral imperative not to abandon allies is often clear. In one case Demosthenes invoked not only the shame of abandoning friends, but the duties implied by treaties:

> Has not your enemy already captured all our strongholds, and if he becomes master of Chalcidice, shall we not be overwhelmed with dishonour? Are not those states actually at war which we so readily engaged in that event to protect?[36]

The allies, whom Athens eventually failed to save, included the Olynthians, a recent ally, as well as a couple of small cities on the Thracian and Macedonian coast, long-standing members of the Athenian league.[37] Neapolis, for example, had probably joined the Athenian League in order to secure protection from its Thracian neighbors. It had been a friend of Athens for generations and had been publicly honored for its conspicuous loyalty during the Peloponnesian War.[38] Neapolis did not leave the Athenian League after the Social War, so Athens was formally obliged to defend its old friend against Philip.[39] To do so was apparently too great a challenge: the circumstances and precise date of Philip's capture of Neapolis are unknown.

Even after Philip took these cities – and most notoriously razed Olynthus and enslaved its surviving inhabitants – Athens tried to do its best by the refugees and the enslaved – and to punish Olynthus' betrayers.[40] Nevertheless, the conventional treaty prohibition against making a separate peace lapsed – since Olynthus no longer existed – and Athens eventually began to contemplate peace with Philip. In central Greece, Phocis was an important Athenian ally.[41] Phocis was generally considered guilty of sacrilege and regarded with implacable enmity by Philip and his allies. Athens finally agreed to make an ambiguous peace treaty with Philip that did not explicitly include the Phocians. It may be that the instability of the Phocian leadership encouraged Athens to make peace with Philip without Phocis' participation. Or the desire for peace may simply have outweighed loyalty to an ally.[42] Certainly the Phocians' use of the Delphic treasures

---

[35] Dem. 4.23–5, 45; 10.6.   [36] Dem. 3.16. Cf. Dem. 1.12; 3.2; Thuc. 1.82.1.

[37] Maroneia is the other clear-cut case (Cargill 1981: 181).

[38] *IG* i³ 101 = Fornara 1983: no. 156. Cargill 1981: 95 argues that there was no evidence that Neapolis ever defected from the league contra Bengtson 1962: 286–8 n. 312, who thinks we posses a new treaty of alliance from 355.

[39] *IG* ii² 43, lines 46–51 in Cargill 1981: 20–1.   [40] Dem. 19.267. See pp. 116–17.

[41] Aeschin. 3.118; Dem. 19.61–2.

[42] See Ryder 2000: 58–70. Buckler 2000 is inconsistent. On the one hand, he justifies Athens' decision to make peace alone: "Phalaikos' rebuff of Proxenos and Athenian military aid justified them in

to pay their mercenaries had ended up making Athens' alliance with them an embarrassing one. The upshot, however, cast an immediate pall on the resulting Peace of Philocrates and helps to explain Demosthenes' prosecution of Aeschines.[43] After Philip made peace with Athens, he was able to move south and finish off the Sacred War by subjugating and punishing Phocis. Athens had broken its faith with Phocis by making a separate peace with Philip and failing to come to its assistance. The Athenians had not given the "friendship, alliance, support," they owed to Phocis.[44]

As we have seen, legalistic obligations were often backed by a less precisely defined, but strong, bond of mutual benefit. In particular, Athens owed an important debt of gratitude to their ally Phocis. At the end of the Peloponnesian War, the Peloponnesian League was considering the destruction of Athens and the enslavement of its inhabitants; Phocis voted against this proposal. And what had they received in return?

For it's a disgrace, isn't it – or rather, whatever is worse than a disgrace – that the people who saved us then, and cast their vote for our preservation, have met with the opposite treatment because of these men [Aeschines and Philocrates].[45]

It was only their doubts about the Phocian leadership and the unremitting pressure and continuous defeat at Philip's hands that made Athens forsake its friend and ally. Indeed Demosthenes may have advocated going to the aid of Phocis even after Philip had passed Thermopylae and Phocis' position was hopeless with or without Athens' help.[46]

SUBORDINATION AND EQUALITY

The code of reciprocity was enforced mainly by concerns about reputation, but these were evidently strong. Indeed, the expectation of reciprocity comprised a system of sufficient solidity so that states could make strategic moves within it. In particular, states could acquire debts of gratitude through their benefactions. These debts could be called in at will. A speech in Xenophon provides a clear example:

allowing Phokis to seek its own solution, while they ended their own particular war with Philip" (134). On the other hand, he writes, "they [the Athenians] abandoned an ally in its hour of peril to save their own skins" (138). He is bizarrely critical of Demosthenes: "One will read the extant speeches of Demosthenes written before 346 without finding any expression of sympathy for the Phokians. After Philip's draconian treatment of them, one finds no floodgate stout enough to hold back the orator's tears" (134). But sympathy is usual after a disaster and would have been uncanny before.

[43] Dem. 19 *passim*; Dem. 6.35–6.   [44] Dem. 19.62.
[45] Dem. 19.66. Cf. Andoc. 3.21.   [46] So Cawkwell 1962a: 459.

So to you has now been offered by some god an opportunity, in case you aid the Lacedaemonians in their need, of acquiring them for all time as friends who will plead no excuses.[47]

Indeed, seventeen years later, Demosthenes still seems to think that Sparta's sense of obligation arising out of this very transaction would force them to help Athens recapture Oropus from Thebes. He optimistically argues that Sparta would do this regardless of Athens' having chosen to make a defensive alliance with Sparta's enemies, the Megalopolitans: "how can they refuse to help us at Oropus without proving themselves the basest of mankind."[48]

In the same speech Demosthenes represents the Spartans as making calculated benefactions with a specific end in mind: they were doing favors for others, so that these others would join Sparta in attacking Messene on pain of seeming to act dishonorably.[49] Demosthenes thought that Athens, in contrast, was doing very poorly in the late 350s and early 340s in terms of acquiring obligations.[50] Demosthenes contrasts the new-found money of corrupt politicians and the prosperity of Athens' markets with the true wealth of a city, which consists of "allies, credit, good will," all of which the Athenians have lost.[51] Athens was destitute of "symbolic capital" and all its material wealth could not compensate for the loss.[52]

Earlier Demosthenes foretold that, if Athens allowed Olynthus to fall, Philip would turn south against them and they would have to fight near to home. As we have seen, it was a common oratorical tactic to assimilate a more distant threat to self-defense. In this case, Demosthenes caps it by saying that Athens will then "beg for help rather than helping others."[53] Clearly being in such a position was a fall in status that Athens very much wanted to avoid. So far we have been viewing the code of reciprocity as if it operated among equals. But, as we have seen, Greek cities were, in reputation, population, and military strength, far from equal. A powerful city such as Athens expected to rescue others; a city such as Neapolis

---

[47] Xen. *Hell.* 6.5.40–1. The notion that one state could owe another is ubiquitous: e.g. Xen. *Hell.* 4.8.9; Dem. 15.11; Aeschin. 2.26–9. Debts incurred in times of need had particular force, e.g. Xen. *Hell.* 4.8.4.

[48] Dem. 16.11–13.   [49] Dem. 16.16–18.   [50] Dem. 2.23; 4.5–7.

[51] Dem. 8.66 (10.69). The same three items are used as a criterion of a city's strength in contrast to a well-stocked market in Dem. 10.50; in this latter passage Demosthenes also includes military strength. See Hajdú 2002: 351–2 ad Dem. 10.50 for parallels to Demosthenes emphasis on *eunoia*, goodwill.

[52] Bourdieu 1977: 171–83 provides a discussion of "symbolic capital." See Crane 1998: 105–24 for an application of this concept to the relations of Greek cities.

[53] Dem. 3.8–9.

hoped to get help. But how might Neapolis oblige Athens in return? Within a society, Hans van Wees generalizes that: "Often, generosity is not meant to be repaid in kind at all, but to be reciprocated with long-term subordination to the benefactor."[54] In the relation of city-states we can see the same tendency.[55] The principle is stated most explicitly in Thucydides where Alcibiades argues, "This is the way we won our empire, and this is the way all empires have been won – by coming vigorously to the help of all who ask for it, irrespective of whether they are Hellenes or not."[56] The Athenians' liberation of the Ionian coast and Aegean islands from the Persian empire was a paradigmatic case. This action provided one of the main justifications for their fifth-century empire. The Athenians in the Melian Dialogue renounced their claim of gratitude on this account as part of their Realist stance; on other occasions, they were not so reticent.[57] Later the Spartans acquired an empire of their own by "liberating" Greece. Isocrates condemned both Athens and Sparta as freeing cities only to enslave them to themselves.[58] In both cases the hegemonic powers felt justified in suppressing by force attempts by cities to renege on their obligations – specified in these cases by treaties as well as owed to their benefactors.[59]

This way of thinking may have persisted in Athens into the early fourth century. Xenophon represents the Thebans in 395 as making the following appeal:

[M]en of Athens, although we all understand that you would like to recover the dominion which you formerly possessed, we ask in what way this is more likely to come to pass than by your aiding those who are wronged by the Lacedaemonians?[60]

By the beginning of Demosthenes' career in the mid fourth century, Athens had renounced empire in the Decree of Aristoteles and had been forced to acquiesce in the revolt of its major allies in the Social War. It was in no shape for imperialist calculations.[61] The fifth-century empire attracted mistrust for arriving in Sicily with a much greater force than was necessary;

---

[54] Van Wees 1998b: 41.   [55] Cf. Low 2007: 43–8.

[56] Thuc. 6.18.2. Cf. the criticism of Andoc. 3.28.

[57] Thuc. 5.89. Cf. Thuc. 1.73–5 esp. 1.73.2: "But we must refer to the Persian Wars, to events well known to you all, even though you may be tired of constantly hearing the story . . . " See also Thuc. 6.82.3–4 and 6.76.3–4.

[58] Isoc. 12.97. Isocrates approves of leadership justified by benefits, and only condemns the abuse of that position (Isoc. 8.30).

[59] Dawson 1996: 66–9 calls this ground for war "just hegemony."

[60] Xen. *Hell.* 3.5.10. Cf. Isoc. 6.31; Pl. *Menex.* 244b–c.

[61] I favor the more benign picture of the Second Athenian League found in, e.g., Griffith 1978; Cargill 1981; and Harding 1995: 114.

fourth-century Athens was more often criticized for not matching its grand pronouncements with actions.[62]

Rather, it is Philip instead whom Demosthenes, in a series of memorable attacks, repeatedly accuses of this imperialist ploy, of sugar-coating the pill of subservience with favors. In the *Second Philippic* Demosthenes reports the arguments he made to the Messenians and Argives to dissuade them from allying with Philip:

"Can you not imagine," I said, addressing the Messenians, "how annoyed the Olynthians would have been to hear a word said against Philip in the days when he was handing over to them Anthemus . . . when he was making them a present of Potidaea . . . Do you imagine they expected to be treated as they have been, or would have believed anyone who suggested it? . . . And what of the Thessalians? Do you imagine," I said, "that when he was expelling their despots, or again when he was presenting them with Nicaea and Magnesia, they ever dreamed that a Council of Ten would be established among them, as it is today, or that the same man who restored to them the Amphictyonic meeting at Thermopylae would also appropriate their very own revenues? Impossible! But so it came to pass as all men may know . . . Beware," said I, "lest, seeking to be rid of war, you find a master."[63]

Philip eventually destroyed rather than subjugated Olynthus, but Demosthenes portrayed Thessaly – and later also Thebes and Eretria – as a state brought under Philip's sway by his favors or promises.[64]

How did Athens stand in terms of Philip's beneficence? At the time of the Peace of Philocrates, Philip seems to have allayed Athenian misgivings by hinting that he would provide great benefits to Athens: many Athenians expected him to favor Phocis, humble Thebes, and return contested towns such as Oropus to Athens.[65] These benefits did not materialize. According to Demosthenes, Athens was unique among Greek states in that it had not received benefits before having been deceived by Philip.[66] That the Athenians had ever expected favors from Philip was probably a galling memory. Athens was a powerful state. Its national tradition was one of giving aid, not accepting it; Demosthenes had represented Athens' last extremity as begging for aid rather than giving it. Being cheated of advantages rankled for some; even to have expected favors was repugnant to other, prouder Athenians.

---

[62] E.g. Dem. 4.45.
[63] Dem. 6.20–5 (trans. modified). Cf. Dem. 2.7; 5.9; 8.40; 10.64–5. Demosthenes' arguments failed to sway Messene and Argos (Dem. 6.15, 26–7).
[64] Dem. 9.57–8; 10.64–5.
[65] Dem. 5.9–10; 8.64; 9.11; 19.35–8, 41, 44, 68; Aeschin. 1.169; 2.119. See pp. 167–8.
[66] Dem. 8.63–6.

This motive for resentment lies behind much of the belligerent rhetoric of the speech *On Halonnesus*. It first complains of the supposed bad faith of the Peace of Philocrates. Although Philip promised all sorts of great favors, he was shameless and "[p]eace has been concluded, but all the good things that we were to enjoy are still to seek."[67] Later, the speech attacks Philip for promising benefits to Athens and thus showing or confirming his strength and Athenian weakness:

Philip's insolence is carried so far that he says that if the Cardians decline arbitration, he will be responsible for coercing them; as if you could not compel Cardians to do anything you wanted! He will make them do it, he says, since you cannot. Are not his favours to you great and manifest?[68]

Most notoriously, the speech defends the Athenian refusal to take back the island Halonnesus from Philip, if he described the action as "giving" it to them: the Athenians insisted that he "restore" or "return" the island. The speaker asks,

Then what does he gain by using the wrong term and making a present of it to you, instead of using the right term and restoring it? It is not that he wants to debit you with a benefaction received, for such a benefaction would be a farce; but that he wants all Greece to take notice that the Athenians are content to receive maritime strongholds from the man of Macedon.[69]

Here we have an explicit counter to the claim that it was the contraction of a moral debt that was at issue. Rather, the author argues in terms of power politics that the advertisement of Athenian weakness is Philip's goal. But, perhaps, the author of the speech "doth protest too much." He repeatedly denies that Philip has conferred, or wants to confer, a favor. At the very least, the possibility that Athens might be debited "with a benefaction received" was strong enough to be worth denunciation.

In the code of reciprocity, ingratitude was a mortal sin. The consequences of this notion could impinge on a weak state's independence, if it allowed a stronger state to bestow greater favors than the smaller state could return. Small states might often have ended up dependent on the powerful in any case; but the code of reciprocity could palliate the impositions of the strong and disarm the suspicion and hostility that naked aggression aroused. After the Peace of Philocrates, Athens was not as powerful as Philip. Not all Athenians, however, were ready to sink into subordination; they resented the benefits nearly as strongly as the injuries of Philip's growing sway.

---

[67] [Dem.] 7.34.   [68] [Dem.] 7.44.   [69] [Dem.] 7.6.

This pattern of reciprocity leading to subordination played a role in the final decay of Greek independence at the hands of Macedonian monarchs. But, as we have explored, reciprocity also had a strong egalitarian tendency, which was perhaps just as influential on the usual tone, if not the final outcome, of fourth-century interstate politics. In the late Dark Ages and Archaic period, states first communicated with each other through the "ritualised friendships" established between their aristocrats: these were reciprocal relationships between peers.[70] This origin stamped the relationships between states not only with a personal, but also with an egalitarian feel.

VENGEANCE

The author of *On the Treaty with Alexander*, convinced that Alexander has transgressed his treaty with the Greeks, considered Athens' alternatives:

[Y]ou may either voluntarily submit to wrong, making the wrongdoer a free gift of your submission, or, having definitely resolved to put justice before all other claims, pursue your own interests.[71]

This formulation with its invocation of justice and interest contains a typically mixed bag of motives for war. Here we may note that reciprocity is seen as a whole comprising the fungible requital of both good and harm. The expression translated "voluntarily submit to wrong" contains the passive form of the verb "to treat unjustly" which often signals the justification for a war of revenge. The expression "making the wrongdoer a free gift of your submission" contains the verb "to give freely, to oblige." This verb, important in the calculation of positive reciprocity, is here used to refer to the favor of not seeking vengeance.[72] In the speaker's conception, Alexander will owe the Athenians if they overlook his infringement of the treaty, in the same way as a city that Athens aided militarily might owe Athens. It was rare for the two sides of reciprocity to be brought together so tightly. It was also rare – and a bit disingenuous given Macedonia's power under Alexander – to view a state's restraint from vengeance as anything other than a dishonorable sign of weakness. The speaker, who does not, in fact, think the Athenians should be doing Philip any favors, may have tongue in cheek in suggesting that as an alternative.

---

[70] Herman 1987: 34.   [71] [Dem.] 17.1–2 (trans. modified).
[72] Lendon 2000: 6–7 points out that Homeric revenge was conceived of as a gift given to the dead person whose death was avenged.

This anomalous passage provides a bridge to the other side of reciprocity: revenge. The first thing to emphasize is that we are still in the realm of normative rules whose disregard might stain a person's or a state's honor. As J. E. Lendon argues, "[R]eciprocity has its dark side too; for just as it was obligatory for a Greek to give when given to, so too was it long obligatory to strike back when struck."[73] Revenge was not just the indulgence of anger, but a positive obligation. For example, Aristotle's *Rhetoric* insists:

It is noble to avenge oneself on one's enemies and not to come to terms with them; for requital is just, and the just is noble, and not to surrender is a sign of courage.[74]

David Cohen expands on this, arguing that

vengeance is positively valued and triply motivated. Men take vengeance because they fear shame and desire to preserve and enhance their honor as well as because of the pleasure which its contemplation and exaction bring. They also take vengeance because in such societies it is the only way to deter others from harming them.[75]

For individuals in Athens the ethos of revenge had long been losing ground to the growing power of the state and its system of justice. But in the world of city states, there was no authority to put a stop or limit to vengeance.[76] Wars often broke out when Greek notions of honor were applied to states.[77]

Many Greek wars, from those of Homer's legends through the classical period, were justified, at least in part, on the grounds of retaliating for injuries suffered or of aiding an ally who was suffering injury.[78] Revenge is hardly dead today in popular feeling about what justifies a war, but policy makers in the West rarely admit revenge as a motive for war.[79] Consequently, revenge tends to be underrated by unconsciously modernizing historians. Especially when revenge appears in a list of motives for war, as it often does, historians tend to focus on more congenial and familiar reasons and justifications for war.[80] Nevertheless, a variety of modern scholars have emphasized retaliation as a common ground of war in ancient Greece.[81]

Such an emphasis on revenge as a *casus belli* is amply confirmed in our ancient historical accounts. Herodotus' history is marked by long chains of retaliation. In particular, he portrays revenge for the Athenian burning of Sardis during the Ionian revolt as one of the main motives for the Persian invasions of Greece.[82] Even in Thucydides reciprocity plays a prominent

---

[73] Lendon 2000: 3.   [74] Arist. *Rh.* 1.9.1367a20–2. See also Gehrke 1987: esp. 128.

[75] D. Cohen 1995: 67.   [76] Gehrke 1987: 130, 140–1.   [77] Hall 2007 88–9.

[78] Gehrke 1987: 130.   [79] See Gehrke 1987: 145–9.   [80] Lendon 2000: 2.

[81] E.g. Adcock and Mosley 1975: 181 and Jackson 1993: 74 on Homeric warfare; Lendon 2000: 1–2; Austin 1993: 201; Dawson 1996: 74–5.

[82] Lendon 2000: 1–2 cites Hdt. 5.105; 6.94.

role. For though Thucydides claims that Spartan insecurity over increasing Athenian power was the root cause of the Peloponnesian War, the events that led to the war involved reciprocity in both its aspects: stasis within a small state, Epidamnus, escalated into a war between the Spartan and Athenian alliances as retaliation followed retaliation and ally called in ally. In addition, several speakers in Thucydides invoke vengeance to justify acts of war.[83] In the fourth century Xenophon was clearly more sympathetic to the demands of requital than to cold calculations of interest. He gives the reasons for Spartan wars against Elis, Thebes, and Mantinea, all former allies. In each case, Xenophon lists a broad spectrum of types of causes but focuses on the wrongs, insults or disloyalty that the Spartans were determined to avenge.[84] So, the historical sources suggest that revenge for wrongs was a common justification of war.

Oratorical sources confirm this impression. Demosthenes is full of references to the injuries that Philip has inflicted on Athens, on his perfidy, on his insulting behavior. As a result of this Athens ought to injure Philip in return but cannot:

I observe that the speeches are all about punishing Philip, while our affairs have reached a stage at which it must be our first concern to avoid disaster ourselves . . . [and to save] our allies.[85]

It is sometimes hard to distinguish cases where Demosthenes calls for revenge from cases when he advocates mere self-defense, the disinterested assertion of justice, or a crusade for freedom. Often these categories overlap.[86] So our clearest evidence of popular sentiment in favor of taking vengeance comes from cases where Demosthenes is forced to argue explicitly against indulging it. For example, when Demosthenes argues in favor of Athenian support for the democratic faction at Rhodes, he needs to placate Athenian resentment of Rhodes' successful revolt from the Athenian League in the Social War. Demosthenes treats this difficulty as follows:

I share in your satisfaction at the fate of the Rhodians . . . for they grudged you the recovery of your rights, and now have lost their own liberty; they spurned an equal alliance with you who are Greek and their superiors, and now they are slaves of barbarians . . . I say that it is your duty to try to save them and to let bygones be bygones, remembering that you too have in many cases been led by schemers

---

[83] Thuc. 1.120.3–4, 121.5; 7.68.1 (see Gehrke 1987: 137); 8.3.1.
[84] Xen. *Hell.* 3.2.21–3 (Elis); 3.5.4–5 (Thebes); 5.2.1–2 (Mantinea).
[85] Dem. 3.1–2. See also Dem. 4.43. Dem. 16.22 implies that avenging an injury would be a just cause for war, but aggrandizement was not.
[86] E.g. Dem. 1.7, 24.

into errors, for none of which you would yourselves admit that you ought to pay the penalty.[87]

The potency of the impulse towards revenge is seen in the care that Demosthenes takes to convince the Athenians that they should not take vengeance on the Rhodians by abandoning them to an oligarchy backed by a Persian garrison.

In other passages too one can see evidence that Demosthenes has to argue against the Athenians' desire for revenge. For the struggle against Philip impelled Athens to ally itself with several former enemies. Byzantium had left the Athenian league and supported the revolting states during the Social War.[88] In 346 Demosthenes complained of Byzantium's interference with Athenian shipping.[89] But he advocated going to their rescue when Philip attacked them. In *On the Chersonese* he justifies this course of action in terms of interest. If Philip attacks Byzantium, the Byzantines will ask Athens to help them:

[Y]ou say "the wretched creatures are infatuated and stupid beyond measure." Quite so, but still we are bound to preserve them in the interests of Athens.[90]

When Demosthenes looked back on Athens' decisions in *On the Crown*, policy became nobility:

But you, who might with justice have found fault with them for earlier acts of trespass, so far from being vindictive and deserting them in their distress, appeared as their deliverers, and by that conduct won renown – the goodwill of the whole world.[91]

Athens also helped Olynthus defend itself from Philip even though Olynthus had recently injured Athens by taking part in Philip's capture of Potidaea, a city inhabited in part by Athenian colonists.[92]

Most important of all was the case of Thebes. Demosthenes in *On The Crown* represents himself speaking to the Athenians after Philip's capture of Elatea:

"If," I added, "at this crisis we are determined to remember all the provocative dealings of the Thebans with us in past time, and to distrust them still on the

---

[87] Dem. 15.15–16 (trans. modified). See also Dem.15.2–4.
[88] Yunis 2001: 160 ad Dem. 18.94.   [89] Dem. 5.25.
[90] Dem. 8.16. See also his attack on Aeschines at Dem. 18.93–5.
[91] Dem. 18.94. At Dem. 18.87–9 Demosthenes claims to have moved the decrees to help Byzantium.
[92] Dem. 2.14; *IG* ii² 114. Cf. Harding 1995: 112 on Athenian aid to Olynthus: "they were prepared to commit impressive forces in aid of a state that had recently done them great harm."

score of enmity, in the first place, we shall be acting exactly as Philip would beg us to act."[93]

In these three cases and more, Athens had to forego quarrels and grievances.[94] It had to reject the demands of reciprocity for the sake of its struggle against Philip. We can well imagine that, in more speeches than have been preserved, Demosthenes and other orators had to argue against the pervasive tendency to want revenge for one or another grievance. For the popular definition of justice demanded doing injury to enemies, not making alliances with them. These cases show that interest could outweigh moral considerations, in this case the obligation to take revenge. But the arguments employed reveal that there was a contest: not everybody was ready to forsake vengeance even when the advantages of this policy were manifest.

The overall history of the mid fourth century demonstrates the extent to which negative reciprocity can blind states to their own interest. Greek city-states understood that their long-term interest lay in preventing any one state from becoming too powerful. But, although they were well aware of the advantages of maintaining a balance of power, they were not always willing to forego their ongoing feuds. Most conspicuously, Sparta did not join the coalition at Chaeronea, the Greeks' best chance against Philip. Although Sparta was hostile to Philip before the battle (because of his support of Messenia), refused to join Philip's League of Corinth afterwards, and fought without Athens or Thebes against Macedonia in 331, in the crucial campaign it apparently could not stomach an alliance with Thebes, its bitter enemy.

RECIPROCITY IN ATHENIAN SOCIETY AND AMONG THE CITY-STATES

Thus did the Athenians apply the code of reciprocity to make their own decisions and to judge the conduct of other states. The reason why reciprocity was so important is less obvious than it first appears. Current scholarship holds that reciprocity's importance in the interstate realm was an obvious extension of its use within the state. But, since reciprocity was only one of several competing systems of values within classical Athens, its application to states cannot be regarded as inevitable. There was a

---

[93] Dem. 18.176. Cf. Dem. 18.18, 63 on the reason for Athenian bitterness towards Thebes.
[94] Yunis 2001: 241 adds Megara, Corcyra, and Euboea to the list of former enemies that Athens allied with against Philip. See also Mosley 1974.

further reason for its use: reciprocity is an advantageous strategy when states or individuals interact repeatedly in the absence of a central authority to enforce justice.

In his influential book *Ritualised Friendship and the Greek City*, Gabriel Herman provides a historical explanation of the application of reciprocity to city-state relations.[95] Nascent city-states first established relations with each other through their aristocrats, who maintained hereditary *xenia*, "ritualised friendship," with their peers in other cities.[96] Their standards of conduct "provided the city with a model of its relationships with the outside world."[97] This model stressed the reciprocity so prominent in aristocratic friendships.[98] In other words, the main virtues of the friendships and alliances between states from the beginning were those of reciprocity.[99] If we turn to retaliation, a similar picture emerges. Historically, the earliest hostilities between nascent city-states may have been feuds and raids conducted on the initiative of their nobles.[100] The tit-for-tat of Homeric raiding was naturally applied to the larger-scale injuries and benefactions of the developed city-state.

Some scholars emphasize a second reason for the application of reciprocity to the relations of Greek cities. Regardless of their early history, the analogy between individual relations and those between city-states was natural enough: people typically understand the abstract and new (the relations of city-states) in terms of the concrete and familiar (the relationship of individuals).[101] In his examination of revenge, the "flip side" of "ritualised friendship," Lendon argues that, in the classical period, "[f]or vengeance to operate between cities and nations, all the men who ruled those cities had to do was to apply their everyday outlook to the international arena."[102]

These two theories largely ignore the drawbacks and advantages of the code of reciprocity. They argue that reciprocity was there among its aristocrats at a crucial point in history or within society throughout the classical period; consequently, as a matter of course, it was applied to the actions of states. But the code of reciprocity was not the only important way of thinking about individual relationships in classical Athens. We still need

---

[95] Herman 1987. See also Karavites 1982a: 106 and Adkins 1972: 1. But see the reservations of Raaflaub 1997: 21–2.

[96] Herman 1987: 139.   [97] Herman 1987: 8.   [98] Herman 1987: 6, 10.

[99] Reciprocity was not the only basis of friendship between states: campaigning in war together could also contribute to friendly feelings between states, e.g. Dem. 16.6–7.

[100] Raaflaub 1997: 23. See Jackson 1993 and van Wees 1992: 167–260 on Homeric raiding.

[101] Lakoff and Johnson 1980: 61, 112; Collins and Gentner 1987: 247. Cf. Turner 1987: 8, 16 and *passim* on familial metaphors.

[102] Lendon 2000: 13.

to explain the particular importance of this type of thinking; for reciprocity continued to be central to the relationship of Greek states, even as its strength within society was declining.[103] This will require, and I shall make, a different sort of argument, namely that the ideal of reciprocity was particularly well suited to the conduct of states.

Reciprocity is ubiquitous within societies for a number of reasons. The immediate advantage of voluntary exchange, that both sides end up with things they value more, is often not as important as the way that positive reciprocity establishes crucial relationships. For its part, negative reciprocity – revenge – can deter various degrees of aggression, intimidation, or encroachment. As a result of these basic factors, both positive and negative reciprocity are found in every human society.[104] Nevertheless, societies differ greatly in terms of the importance of reciprocity. In terms of positive reciprocity, the economies of some societies are dominated by "gifts" which are to be repaid, but not precisely and usually after some time. At the other end of the spectrum from the gift economies are free-market economies in which both sides of economic transactions take place at a single time. In such societies all exchanges are considered even and neither assume nor establish any relationship or obligations on either side – as they do in gift economies. When it comes to negative reciprocity, a similar spectrum can be imagined. On the one hand, in a perfect feuding society the only redress of injury would be retaliation and no communal codes would have any force. In a society perfectly ruled by law, every conflict would be adjudicated according to the interests or sentiments of the community as a whole without reference to the feelings of the injured party.[105] It is highly unlikely that either of these hypothetical endpoints has ever existed, but some societies lie much further to one end or the other of this spectrum.

The society depicted in Homer, which seems mainly to reflect late Dark Age or early Archaic Greece, may well have been characterized by a gift economy, in which positive reciprocity was of paramount importance.[106] Classical Athens – claims of an embedded economy notwithstanding – can

---

[103] See O'Neill 1999 on the prevalence of honor-type behavior in the interstate relations of modern nations whose societies display little emphasis on honor in their internal relations.

[104] Brown 1991 in Pinker 2002: 438.

[105] The modern West has gone far in this direction. See Daly and Wilson 1988: 239: "How have we come to such a remarkable state of 'impersonal justice'? The surviving victims of a homicide are entitled neither to revenge nor to compensation, nor even to representation in court!"

[106] On the Homeric economy see the fundamental treatment of M. Finley 1978a: 51–73 with Donlan 1997 for a recent consideration with bibliography. Tandy 1997: esp. 112–38 treats the decline of reciprocity and places it in the eighth century – but see the criticisms of Schaps 1998.

be safely located much closer to the free-market end of the spectrum.[107] In Homeric society the obligation to come to the aid of a friend or take violent revenge for his death was compelling. In addition, Homeric heroes are notoriously touchy about their own honor: insults or even a game of dice among children can lead to homicide.[108] The practice of blood feuding and pervasive violence had ceased by the classical period: one conspicuous symptom of this change is that classical Athenians no longer carried weapons.[109]

The extent to which the ethos of retaliation had also atrophied by the classical period has been the subject of recent and vigorous scholarly debate. Scholars such as David Cohen argue for continuity in the basic approval and practice of revenge, although they concede that retaliation was often achieved through the legal system rather than by personal violence.[110] Gabriel Herman counters that the involvement of the community, namely the law-court juries, marks a decisive shift away from revenge, both in practice and in thinking.[111]

Since Herman's opponents do use parallels from "the most macho, intolerant and violent societies known to anthropologists or historians" and since Herman insists that Athens placed an emphasis on restraint "unique in the annals of the Western world,"[112] an ample middle ground between the two sides would seem to be available.[113] For a society to adhere to a single, consistent set of values is anyway unlikely. Consequently, in this debate, both sides have to work hard to explain away awkward passages. For example, Herman must discount Aristotle's insistence on the nobility of revenge and the slavishness of not taking revenge as well as the common dictum "to help friends and harm enemies."[114] Evidence that the Athenians approved restraint in the face of provocation is found in forensic oratory – to which Herman rightly gives priority. These present an intractable obstacle to his critics, who insist on the primacy of Athenian masculine honor

---

[107] On the ancient economy, M. Finley again provides a starting point, 1985a. The collections of Scheidel and von Reden 2002 and Manning and Morris 2005 provide an entree to more recent controversies.

[108] Lendon 2000: 12 with Hom. *Il.* 23.86–8.   [109] Herman 1994: 99–105; van Wees 1998a.

[110] See especially D. Cohen 1995: esp. 87–142; W. Harris 1997; and Fisher 1998. Brief treatments include Dover 1974: 181–4; Gehrke 1987: 138–42; Fisher 2000: 88; and Lendon 2000: 11–13.

[111] Herman 1993, 1994, 1995, 1996, 1998a, 1998b, and 2000.

[112] Herman 2000: 9 and 26 respectively.   [113] E.g. W. Harris 1997: 366; Allen 2000: 122–8.

[114] E.g. Herman 2000: 13–14 on Arist. *Rh.* 1.11.1370b30 and *Eth. Nic.* 4.6.1126a7–8 (but see Schütrumpf 1995: 65–6); Herman 2000: 12–14 on the injunction to "help friends and harm enemies."

and the uncontested approval of revenge.[115] Although the desire for retaliation probably loomed larger in Athenian thinking than it does today – and it is far from dead today – I believe that Herman's arguments for an important shift in Athenian values are compelling.

In particular, although litigants continued to claim to be pursuing revenge through the courts, such a recourse should be sharply distinguished from a system of violent self-help.[116] In the latter case each injury or insult that remains unavenged invites more, and thus none can be safely tolerated. A sense of honor that insists on retaliation, even for slights, is almost a requirement for survival. In the former situation, each injury accepted strengthens a person's power to retaliate in the courts. Thus a driving force behind a touchy sense of honor has disappeared. The consequent decay of the sense of honor and the obligation of vengeance might take generations – and never be complete – but already, in classical Athens, litigants as often presented themselves as restrained in the face of provocation as intransigent in defense of their honor.[117]

So the code of reciprocity survived, albeit in attenuated form, within Athenian society; it flourished in interstate relations. In scale and number, market transactions dominated the Athenian economy. But alliances, the interstate equivalents of gifts, were far more important than mercenaries, the "free-market" military force – even with the fourth-century expansion of the use of mercenaries.[118] Within Athenian society, violent retaliation was only allowed in a few specific cases, such as against an adulterer caught in the act. Recourse to law was the approved response of an Athenian when injured or insulted. Retaliation for injustice suffered, however, was crucial to the conduct of states. It played a larger role than anything like the recourse to law – although we shall see that legalism was also an important ideal among states. These contrasts suggest that something more is going on than the passive use of an available system of values. To explain the persistence and even centrality of reciprocity in interstate relations in Greece, we need to explore the sources of its strength within a society and then its suitability for states.

---

[115] W. Harris 1997: 366 accepts Dem. 54.5–6 as exceptional (see also 54.19). Herman 2000: 23–4 contra W. Harris 1997 on Lys. 3. Herman 2000: 16–17 contra D. Cohen 1995: 93–101 on Dem. 21 esp. 21.29–35. Lys. 9.14 provides clear evidence against the ideal of helping friend and harming enemies.

[116] D. Cohen 1995: 83–5 on revenge as a motive for lawsuits; on the significance of the recourse to law, see Herman 1994: 108–17 and 2000: 25.

[117] Herman 1994: 107–8.

[118] See Burckhardt 1996: 76–152 on the use of mercenaries and citizen soldiers in fourth-century Athens.

Reciprocity within a society seems to vary inversely with the extent of state power. This is most conspicuous and most easily explained in the case of negative reciprocity. Rather than being a Mediterranean phenomenon, a code of honor which requires immediate and violent retaliation for insult thrives in any society with weak central authority.[119] As Arthur Eckstein points out:

> In the absence of law or the means to enforce it, a reputation for stubbornness, toughness, and even ferocity in protecting what is one's due has a pragmatic purpose: it helps ensure security, helps ensure that few will dare to interfere with your interests.[120]

The importance of acquiring and keeping allies is also greatest in such an anarchic, violent context, where a man must call on his friends and allies since he cannot turn to any central authority for protection. So, in general, as in Homeric society, reciprocity flourishes in the absence of a powerful government.[121]

The fact that individual reciprocity evolved in a context without a strong central authority makes it a code of conduct well suited to interstate affairs.[122] Like the pre-state society in which the ethic of reciprocity grew and thrived, the interstate regime lacked a sovereign power to enforce its laws. In such a context, a policy of reciprocation may be the best a state can do. Retaliation keeps a state from being taken advantage of. Perhaps more important, paying back benefactions – usually in terms of military assistance – makes it more likely that help will be available in times of need. As I shall detail below, a number of passages in the assembly speeches make it clear that the longer-term benefits of supporting allies and resisting encroachments were known.

Consequently, in an anarchic world, reciprocity and self-interest are not necessarily in opposition, but more typically harmonize. Admittedly, we have seen two cases where reciprocity and interest were in conflict: short-term Realist calculation may require states to forget grievances; a commitment to a balance of power can require changes of alliance in spite

---

[119] Herman 1995: 46, 1996: 36. See also Boehm 1984: 218–19; Stewart 1994: 76–7. O'Neill 1999: 137–8 also points out that a strong sense of honor tends to grow in pastoral societies, in which a person's whole livelihood could be stolen away overnight. The deterrence of this possibility was of the greatest importance. Since pastoral societies tend not to have developed strong states, it is hard to distinguish these two factors. Cf. Daly and Wilson 1988: 229.

[120] Eckstein 2000: 878. See also Boehm 1984: 218–19 and Daly and Wilson 1988: 231–51. Cf. Mattern 1999: xii, 23 on Roman foreign policy.

[121] Herman 1995: 47. See also Adkins 1960 and 1972 on the genesis of the "competitive" virtues in this context.

[122] O'Neill 1999: 137. Cf. Schelling 1960: 12; Dawson 1996: 18; and Eckstein 2000: 877.

of previous friendships and enmities. But, on average and over the long run, reciprocity is an expedient strategy for a state.

Indeed, in recent decades, the stock of reciprocity has risen even in the hyper-rational world of Game Theory. This trend is due largely to the results of a well-known computer tournament of different strategies in the game known as the Iterated Prisoner's Dilemma.[123] The Iterated Prisoner's Dilemma is a repeated, two-player game in which players do not communicate and have only two choices each round: they can either cooperate or defect. The best result in each round is for a player to defect while the other player cooperates, and the worst outcome is the reverse. This means that it is tempting to defect and risky to cooperate. But mutual cooperation is better than mutual defection.[124] A simple strategy of reciprocity, Tit-for-tat, won the tournament, despite competing strategies of much greater complexity and sophistication. Tit-for-tat even won a second round of the tournament, played after the results of the first round had been publicized.

Tit-for-tat is a "nice" strategy because the player is not the first to defect, but begins each interaction with another player by cooperating. It is named Tit-for-tat – and models reciprocity – because it responds to a defection by defecting in the next round and responds to cooperation by cooperating in the next round. Not only in the Iterated Prisoner's Dilemma, but also in a variety of non-zero-sum, iterated games, reciprocity turns out to be an excellent strategy:

[R]eciprocity may permit extensive cooperation without making cooperative participants inordinately vulnerable to exploitation by others. Furthermore it may deter uncooperative actions.[125]

Game theorists have claimed an extraordinary wide scope for their insights: "The framework is broad enough to encompass not only people but also nations and bacteria."[126] Scholars in the field of International Relations have tended to agree – at least about nations:

It is not surprising, therefore, that reciprocity is a popular strategy for practical negotiators as well as for analysts in the laboratory . . . [A] fundamental strategic concept . . . is that of reciprocity. Cooperation in world politics seems to be attained best not by providing benefits unilaterally to others, but by conditional cooperation.[127]

---

[123] Axelrod 1984: 27–54. Herman 1998a applies the results of the Iterated Prisoner's Dilemma to the dominance of the Athenian ideal of restraint rather than retaliation within the community.
[124] Axelrod 1984: 7–10.   [125] Axelrod and Keohane 1985: 244.
[126] Axelrod 1984: 18.   [127] Axelrod and Keohane 1985: 245, 249.

I would certainly not go so far as to insist that reciprocity's hold over Athenian interstate conduct rested solely on its utility. Its pre-existence within Greek society and, in particular, among the aristocratic city envoys of the archaic period was also a necessary condition for its use in the interstate world. But the popularity of the principle of reciprocity in the world of Game Theory and International Relations does give the lie to the argument that its use was a dysfunctional import from putative primitive values of Greek society. Rather, the advantages for states of a policy of reciprocation were pronounced and obvious.[128] It is no wonder that Greek states often followed such a policy.

Two important and difficult issues remain. First, as a strategy, reciprocity is advantageous, but only when interactions are repeated and can become the basis of a state's reputation.[129] Second, the emotional imperative to reciprocate, often enforced by a sense of honor, appears at first to be opposed to, and certainly stands in a complex relation to, the calculations that make reciprocity a strategy advantageous in the long term.

Since it is the very lack of central authority that makes the code of reciprocity appealing, nothing more forceful than the power of reputation sanctions it. It is through reputation that people who do not pay back favors find themselves receiving few, that those who do not stand by their friends may soon find themselves friendless, and that those who do not retaliate against enemies find the ranks of their enemies swelling. Reputation carries this weight in a society in which people interact repeatedly and when they communicate with each other. It is communication that ensures that a person's actions are reflected in a reputation at all. It is in the repeated interactions that a person can benefit or lose from a good or bad reputation.

The common culture and language of Greece made for lively communication at Panhellenic sanctuaries and festivals, through sightseeing, official delegations, and trade. In addition to the political discussions that must have occurred in all these contexts, Athens and other Greek cities made conscious efforts to publicize their most important interstate commitments. It seems to have been common practice to post treaties not only publicly in temples in the parties' cities but also in Panhellenic centers so they would be known in the wider Greek world.[130] The Peace of Nicias, of paramount importance to the Greek world, was posted in the territory of both Athens and Sparta and at the great three Panhellenic sanctuaries, Delphi, Isthmia, and Olympia.[131] Closer to our period and less grand, a treaty between Philip

---

[128] See below notes 151–2.   [129] Schelling 1960: 134–5.   [130] Bederman 2001: 172.
[131] Thuc. 5.18.10. See Isoc. 4.179–80; 12.106–7 on the King's Peace.

and the Chalcidians was to be posted at Dium, Olynthus, and at Delphi.[132] In addition to the evidence of treaties, a number of passages either assume or explicitly state that Athenian actions will be widely known and judged: "all Greece is watching" is a common refrain.[133]

If states do not interact repeatedly, they will not have a chance to acquire a reputation or to guide their actions by the reputations of others. In general, where one state can either destroy another or gain an irreversible advantage, short-term interest is likely to dominate over any long-term strategy such as reciprocation. To return to Game Theory, the whole model of the Iterated Prisoner's Dilemma, in which Tit-for-tat is a good strategy, depends on repeated interaction.[134] If a state can completely take over another state, this advantage may outweigh any bad reputation it engenders: we then may have a parallel to the Prisoner's Dilemma, in which defection is usually the favored strategy, but not to the Iterated Prisoner's Dilemma.

The world of the Greek city-states, however, was one in which repeated interactions could be expected most of the time. The same basic group of cities interacted for generations. Among the major states there were few new players and no city was destroyed or conquered during the entire classical period until Macedonia's destruction of Thebes in 336.

It is possible for reciprocity to operate between just two states – as in the Iterated Prisoner's Dilemma. Each gives the other "tit for tat" to influence the other's future behavior. If an international system includes a large number of states that communicate with each other, this effect is magnified. A state's actions affect its future treatment by all the states that hear about them. The Greek world included many states – and several important ones. The actions of states soon became well known – albeit in partial accounts – and other states could act accordingly. If Athens failed to aid an ally, it not only suffered the alienation of that ally but also risked the defection of old allies and the inability to attract new ones.

Notwithstanding these factors that conspired to give reputation particular force among the Greek city-states, we have seen that they did not always obey its dictates. Nor were the results of reciprocity, either negative or positive, necessarily happy ones. To say that retaliation could be an *advantageous* strategy only means that it was better than not retaliating or than unprovoked and unselective aggression. It might better reflect the grim situation to say that retaliation is a *necessary* strategy in a society of

---

[132] Ha no. 67, lines 9–10 = RO no. 50. See also Isoc. 4.179–80.
[133] E.g. Arist. *Rh*. 2.6.1384b32–5; Aeschin. 2.104.
[134] Fearon 1995: 402. Axelrod 1984: 125, 174, 182. Cf. Schelling 1960: 134–5.

individuals or of states without strong enough communal curbs on the use of violence.

This necessity on the individual level certainly did not mean that the code of reciprocity was "functional" for a society as a whole.[135] In particular, nothing ensures that the threat of retaliation will prevent aggression rather than that actual retaliation will ensure an endless cycle of violence. Feuding societies usually profess the ideal of proportionality in retaliation and keep count of the deaths they have inflicted and suffered – for these must be taken account of in any eventual reconciliation.[136] These attempts to limit violence do not always work. For example, one investigator of a feuding society found

no mechanisms for mediation or intervention to resolve conflict between lineages, and villagers commonly complained about their hopelessness in the face of the apparently never ending cycle of violence and revenge.[137]

Among states too, negative reciprocity can easily lead to increasingly bitter and unending enmity – and often did.[138] What one state considered "tit for tat," its victim might deplore as disproportionate and seek to even up the score. Lendon remarks "Anger calculates poorly" and shows how this systematic bias led to spirals of violence among Greek states.[139] Indeed, excessive retaliation was sometimes idealized – consider the paragon of vengeance, Achilles.[140] If injuries received are perceived more acutely than injuries given, or if vengeance is required in surfeit, endless and increasingly bitter enmities can arise out of reciprocity.[141]

Positive reciprocity in the form of alliances was a great equalizer between small and large states – and hence an important check on aggression against the weak. The strength of alliances was probably the most important factor that permitted the survival of so many independent cities of such different sizes in close proximity despite generations of warfare. Webs of alliance meant that the size and power of the original disputants often bore little relation to the forces involved in the resulting war. This fact allowed small states to be on the winning side of wars as often as large ones. But it also meant that small conflicts often escalated into large wars. Positive

---

[135] See D. Cohen 1995: 9–12 against functionalist views of feuding societies. Cf. the criticisms of Hallpike 1973.

[136] Boehm 1984: 218–19. Another of the attributes that made Tit-for-tat a good strategy in the Iterated Prisoner's Dilemma was that it was "forgiving." It only retaliated once for one defection (Axelrod 1984: 20, 54).

[137] D. Cohen 1995: 12.   [138] Lendon 2000: 13–18.   [139] Lendon 2000: 13–18.

[140] See Lendon 2000: 10 on the extent of Achilles' revenge. Cf. Xen. *Mem* 2.6.35.

[141] Cf. Axelrod 1984: 38, 138.

reciprocity did not make classical Greece a peaceful place. My claim here is not that reciprocity is perfect or that it leads to a peaceful world, but that it is often a reasonable and sometimes a necessary strategy for states. It was not an emotional and atavistic import that merely deflected states from a rational course of action.

STRATEGY AND HONOR

That any sort of strategy lay behind reciprocity can seem false to the experience of rage or shame that often motivates it. The relationship of the emotional and the strategic aspects of reciprocity is a complex one. The obligation to reciprocate was demanded by a person's or a state's sense of honor. This made reciprocity an emotional and uncalculating experience, marked primarily by an acute sensitivity to reputation. Nevertheless, orators appealed to the calculated benefits of reciprocity as often as they did to the audience's sense of honor. Both approaches were often needed, since adherence to the code of reciprocity usually entails costs and risks, which it is tempting to dodge – and which many states on many occasions did dodge.

In *On the Chersonese* Demosthenes makes an emotional appeal to the Athenians not to brook any more abuse from Philip: he argues that "The strongest necessity that a free man feels is shame for his own position, and I know not if we could name a stronger . . . "[142] It was typically shame that required states to retaliate for injuries and support their allies. Scholars no longer insist on a sharp dichotomy between the archaic "shame culture" in which the community approval is the arbiter of value and a more modern "guilt culture," perhaps first seen in Plato, in which the individual's conscience determines his or her morality.[143] Nevertheless, individual Greeks, even as late as the fourth century, were openly, intensely, and emotionally concerned with community approval.

The emotional force of reputation was strong not only within a society, but also in the culturally unified world of the Greek city-states. Just as a Homeric hero, and to a lesser extent an Athenian of the fourth century, valued his standing among his peers, a concern with reputation also characterized the Greek city-states. A state's standing depended on a wide variety of qualities; its loyalty to friends and hostility to enemies were

---

[142] Dem. 8.51. Cf. Dem. 3.16 on the shame attendant on abandoning an ally.

[143] E. R. Dodds 1951 claimed that Greece was a "shame society." Snell 1953, Adkins 1960, and Gouldner 1965: 41 argue for a profoundly primitive Greek morality. See Williams 1993 for a persuasive critique of such overly sharp dichotomies between archaic and modern ethics.

prominent among them. Most explicitly, in a speech in Xenophon, the Spartans are depicted as most likely to remember and requite Athenian aid since they "strive especially for praise and avoid disgrace."[144] Other passages connect a state's public honor, more or less closely, to its ability to pay back the good or evil it has received. The Athenian practice of publicly honoring cities that had benefited Athens requited these benefactors with public acclamation.[145] Similarly, Demosthenes could appeal to Athenian pride about the honorific crowns that cities such as Byzantium bestowed on Athens early in the final war with Philip.[146] In his *Fourth Philippic* he makes explicit the parallel between the honor of an individual and a state: just as an individual might strive for glory and reputation so too should the city of Athens.[147]

Indeed, some of the most vivid examples of moral judgments about a city's actions depend on the analogy with an individual acting before an audience. For example, Aristotle reports a vivid appeal to a reputation in his *Rhetoric*:

Cydias represented them [the Greeks] in his speech on land assignments in Samos, when he told the Athenians to imagine the Greeks to be standing all around them, actually seeing the way they voted and not merely going to hear about it afterwards.[148]

Another case is when Demosthenes, in a high point of his brilliant *On the Crown*, pictures the public shame if Athens had not fought Philip: "How could we have returned the gaze of visitors to our city . . . "[149] Conversely, in the *First Philippic*, Demosthenes claims that when the Athenians do not go out to fight themselves but send out "a general with an empty decree and the mere aspirations of this platform . . . your enemies laugh you to scorn."[150] Although Demosthenes in other places emphasizes the advantages of an effective military, here he is attempting to shame his audience with the prospect of public contempt. These appeals do not invoke a calculation of interest, but appeal to a strong sense of shame.

But the Athenians were also quite conscious of the advantages of reciprocity within the world of city-states: they did not act out of honor alone. Demosthenes' speech *Against Leptines* concerns Athens' policy of rewarding its benefactors. In it Demosthenes argues repeatedly that when Athens rewards and publicly honors friendly cities or individuals, it encourages

---

[144] Xen. *Hell.* 6.5.42.   [145] E.g. *IG* ii² 1; *IG* ii² 28; *IG* ii² 233; *IG* ii² 237+.
[146] Dem. 18.89, 92. Cf. Aeschin. 3.230–1.   [147] Dem. 10.70–4. See also Lys. 2.14.
[148] Arist. *Rh.* 2.6.1384b32–5. This passage is contained within Aristotle's discussion of shame.
[149] Dem. 18.201. Cf. [Dem.] 7.6.   [150] Dem. 4.45.

others to do the Athenians good.[151] Assembly speeches, too, are replete with arguments about the risks attendant on failure either to retaliate for injuries suffered or to support friends.[152] That orators appealed to both the calculating and the emotional motivations for reciprocity implies that both carried some weight. An orator aiming at righteous indignation or the moral high ground would talk of the shame among all the Greeks if a slight is allowed to go unavenged or an ally is left undefended. An orator, trying to project the persona of a cool and calculating guard of the state's interest, would put more stress on the long-term benefits to Athens of a good reputation. Often both appeals would find their way into a single speech.

These redundant arguments were often necessary, because neither retaliation nor paying back benefits – especially when this means going to war for an ally – are immediately advantageous; rather they are costly and risky activities. This is why the experience of reciprocity is often not that of calculation, but rather the reverse: reciprocity can be required by one's sense of honor regardless of cost or risk. As Larry O'Neill puts it: "Preserving one's reputation for honor often requires publicly enduring some cost or risk, often by participating in violence."[153] Without the goad of honor, the strategic, long-term advantages of reciprocity may often have seemed too distant to determine behavior. This model would put the honor that enforces requital in the well-known and common category of cultural values that have developed – in complex ways – to steer people away from actions whose immediate temptations are obvious but will serve them ill in the long run.[154] In the assembly speeches, the invocation of a state's honor, and the weight this carried over from internal values, served just this purpose. It gave emotional force to the less vivid strategic consequences of a good or bad reputation.

Let us sum up with an imaginary interview. If you were to ask an Athenian on the way to the assembly why Athens would want to fight Philip and aid Olynthus, he might first say that Athens had to take revenge on Philip for his bad faith and his injuries to Athens. He would add

---

[151] Dem. 20.5, 64, 103.
[152] Dem. 15.8: the more resolute Athens is, the less will it have to fight; Dem. 4.6: assertive and active states acquire alliance and respect; Dem. 1.9: if Athens had only been more vigorous in supporting earlier victims against Philip; Dem. 3.1–2: Athens could have punished Philip earlier, but is no longer able to; [Dem.] 7.7: recourse to arbitration will advertise Athens' reluctance to fight; Dem. 8.66–7 (10.68–9): advantageous not to put up with being wronged; Dem. 8.48–9 (10.24–6): it would be disastrous in the long run to allow Philip to take advantage of Athens; Dem. 10.7–10: Athens' dire situation is due to its failure to retaliate or to support potential allies; [Dem.] 17.26–9: to allow even small infractions by the Macedonians will invite more. Cf. Xen. *Hell.* 4.8.4.
[153] O'Neill 1999: 90. [154] E.g. M. Harris 1977: 221 (see also 206–8).

that it would be shameful for Athens not to aid its friends – and he
might think to add that Athens had treaty obligations as well and that
these had been confirmed by oaths by the gods. You could point out that
he was applying individual values to the actions of states and he would
find this unremarkable. It would take some argument, but it might be
possible, to convince him that the way he actually asserted his individual
honor – through recourse to law – was rather different from how he thought
Athens should maintain its honor – through military aid or retaliation. If
you caught him on his way back home after listening to a speech of
Demosthenes, he would have been more clearly aware that a reputation
for requiting good and bad was in Athens' long-term interest, despite its
immediate costs. He would almost certainly also add that he was ashamed
of Athens' humiliations and angry with Philip. And he might emphasize
that that was why he had raised his hand to vote for the expedition to
Olynthus.

CHAPTER 9

Legalism

The two most important twentieth-century movements to limit or eliminate war have been pacifism and the "peace through law" movement that
gained strength in the early twentieth century and resulted in the League
of Nations and then the United Nations.[1] This chapter and the next do
not aim to find an International Court of Justice of Greece, much less
an Athenian Gandhi, but rather to examine two related issues: the extent
to which the Athenians thought about the relationship between states as
something that was, or should be, governed by law; what sorts of objections
to war in general were voiced in Athens and how these differed from those
common today.

Athens conceived of itself as a particularly lawful society. In the *Clouds*
Aristophanes whimsically imagines a person objecting to a map of the
world, because it does not show the jury courts in Athens; the whole play
revolves around a man's attempt to escape from his debts by learning tricky
arguments to use in court.[2] The humorous premise of his *Wasps* is that an
old man needs to be cured of his addiction to jury service. More seriously,
in the *Eumenides* Aeschylus celebrates the law court's ability to put an
end to cycles of vengeance. Evidence from the forensic speeches themselves
confirms that the Athenians were proud of their system of law and especially
of the fact that it resolved conflicts without violence.[3] Herodotus' famous
contrast between the rule of law and Persian monarchy also indicates the
high repute of the former.[4] As Edward Harris sums up: "No ideal was
more cherished in classical Athens than the rule of law."[5] Written law in
particular was held in high regard as "in itself conducive to fairness, justice,
and equality" as well as to democracy.[6]

---

[1] See, for example, Knock 1992 and Suganami 1978 on the former; Brock and Young 1999 provides a
historical overview of pacifism and Fiala 2007, a philosophical summary with bibliography.
[2] Ar. *Nub.* 207–8.   [3] Lys. 3.22–3; Dem. 54.17–19.
[4] Hdt. 7.104. See also Hyp. 6.25. Cf. Leopold 1981: 228.   [5] E. Harris 1994: 132.
[6] R. Thomas 2005: 43.

Some historians emphasize the role of honor in ancient international relations and want us to picture the Athenians as reacting to an insult or injury in the interstate realm as if they were touchy, proud, and violent heroes out of the Homeric epics.[7] There is some validity to this picture as we have seen. But there were also ways in which the Athenians in their foreign relations more closely resembled the unheroic Athenians parodied in Aristophanes. When an Aristophanic character is attacked or mistreated, he or she is more likely to call upon witnesses and threaten a lawsuit than to take personal revenge to repair their honor.[8] This type of behavior is not limited to comedy: for example, law-court speeches confirm the practice of summoning witnesses in anticipation of a future lawsuit.[9] If the Athenians applied the attitudes and approaches of their everyday life to the relation of states, they would be just as likely to think of legal redress as of violent retaliation when Athens had suffered insult or injury. They would merely be thinking about the relationships between states in one of the ways they thought about individual relationships. The legal analogy may also have seemed particularly apt and full of hope for the world of states. Historically the recourse to law had replaced the blood feud as a way of resolving individual conflicts within the city; the Athenians were aware of and celebrated this advance.[10] Since the peaceful resolution of conflicts was manifestly a desideratum among Greek states, they naturally thought in terms of laws operable among states as a substitute for – or limit upon – the violence of war.[11]

The worlds of states and of individuals were not, of course, the same. Most significant, there was no world-state or sovereign authority over states to judge competing legal claims, to make and enforce its decisions, and to reserve the use of violence to itself. Modern international law has been hobbled by the anarchy of the international regime. So too the ancient hope that states could be ruled by law was limited by the lack of authoritative sanctions against law-breakers. In addition, the implicit and unwritten laws of state behavior were few, simple, and, nevertheless,

[7] E.g. Lendon 2000: 13; van Wees 2004: 22–6.

[8] E.g. Ar. *Nub.* 1222, 1255, 1277–8, 1297, *Vesp.* 1332–4, 1406–8, 1415–19. The catalogue in Scafuro 1997: 424–67 on the threat of lawsuits (and legal self-help) in New Comedy includes many similar cases.

[9] E.g. Carey and Reid 1985: 84 on Dem. 54.9; Dem. 57.14; Isae. 3.19; Humphreys 2007: 160–1, 170.

[10] E.g. Lendon 2000: 12.

[11] Krüger 2007: 170 explains the Jewish prophecies of peace established by God as a "judge of nations" (Micah 4:1–5 and Isaiah 2:2–5) in similar terms: "The most important condition . . . for a vision of overcoming violence in the international realm through justice and peaceful settlement of conflicts, seems to have been the fact that analogous developments had already taken place successfully within individual peoples and communities – in simplified terms: the overcoming of revenge through law."

open to controversy; the explicit laws established by treaties were liable to different interpretations and there existed no authority to adjudicate such disagreements. Nevertheless, the practical difficulties of imposing a rule of law on states do not make the legal analogy unimportant or void of force. We should dismiss the notion that the application of legal concepts to the interstate sphere must bring peace and, since it did not in ancient Greece, the phenomenon was insignificant. After all, even without the additional hurdles faced by interstate law, domestic law has not eliminated crime. The application of the code of reciprocity to states did not ensure either revenge or gratitude and assistance to friends. Like interstate reciprocity, legalism was one of the important systems of thinking according to which Athenians judged other states and which influenced, but did not determine, their actions, and hence it is important to the understanding of Athenian thinking about international relations.

Most scholars of international law locate its origins in the Enlightenment.[12] Historians of the ancient world have typically come to the opposite conclusion and some scholars with legal backgrounds join them in insisting that ancient Greece had developed a system of international law.[13] This second conclusion is probably correct, but the debate is largely one of definition – what counts as international law? – and of origins – when did the modern tradition of international law begin? Neither issue is relevant to foreign policy decisions in the fourth century BC. Nevertheless, arguments in favor of the classical origins of international law typically demonstrate along the way that the Athenians thought of relations between states as based on laws analogous to those within the state. They conceived of the conduct of states as rule-bound and their conflicts as liable to external resolution.[14]

The evidence for the legal analogy fits into four categories: (1) practices better explained by the application of a domestic legal institution to states than as something newly created for states, (2) the use of legal terms to describe the actions of states, and conversely (3) explicit denials of law between states. Finally, we find (4) explicit references to the "law of the Greeks," unwritten rules of conduct governing the conduct of warfare and diplomacy.

---

[12] Bederman 2001: 1 calls the thesis of a modern origin of International Law "an article of faith" within that discipline.

[13] Phillipson 1911; Mosley 1973: 1; Sheets 1994; Bederman 2001; Chaniotis 2004; Low 2007: 77–128; Alonzo 2007.

[14] Phillipson 1911: 1.43–66; Sheets 1994: 70; Bederman 2001: 6–7, 267, 275–6; Low 2007: 85.

(1) Some interstate institutions have clear internal parallels and precedents. The notion of an assembly of citizens is attested already in Homer; it is likely that the idea of reaching a binding legal decision by majority vote – either by a council, assembly, or jury – was widespread. This procedure was transferred to organizations of states, probably beginning with Amphictyonic Councils and eventually including the Peloponnesian League, the Second Athenian League, and the League of Corinth. Again the parallel between interstate and domestic procedures suggests that people thought that a process parallel to laws and institutions within the state should govern the relations of states.

Another example is arbitration, used to resolve individual disputes in Athens as well as conflicts between states.[15] Within the city, disputants could agree to submit to binding arbitration to settle differences; by the fourth century private cases involving more than 10 drachmas were required to go first to arbitration – although in these cases either side could appeal and demand a trial.[16] From the mid fifth century onwards many treaties between states included the clause that future disputes be settled by arbitration. According to Thucydides, even twenty years after the outbreak of the Peloponnesian War, the Spartans remembered and regretted their refusal to submit their differences with Athens to arbitration.[17]

(2) Although the English translation "arbitration" is often used and best conveys the procedure, Thucydides actually uses a form of *dikē* of arbitration between states. This is the word used for a private lawsuit within Athens. Thucydides' practice is typical: when treaties between states specify that disputes are to be resolved by arbitration rather than war, they often use expressions such as "by oath and justice" or "to refer to legal judgment"; these are indistinguishable from the words used to describe the recourse to law within the state.[18] The Greeks regarded arbitration as a recourse to legal justice rather than force between states.[19] The application of legalistic expressions to the actions of states – and especially to describe adherence to treaties – is ubiquitous. Two examples are most conveniently treated here. First, several texts make a legalistic distinction between mere possession and rightful

---

[15] Ager 1996: 33; Roebuck 2001: 159.   [16] Roebuck 2001: 352–8; Thür 2005: 156–7; Thür 2007.

[17] Thuc. 7.18.2; but see Tritle 2007: 175. The offer of arbitration is mentioned repeatedly: Thuc. 1.78.4, 80.1, 85.2, 140.2, 141.1, 144.2, 145.

[18] E.g. Hdt. 6.42; Thuc. 1.78.4, 80.1, 85.2, 140.2, 141.1, 144.2, 145; 4.79.1, 118.8; 5.18.4, 41.2, 79.1; [Dem.] 7.7, 36–7, 41, 43–4. See Roebuck 2001: 156.

[19] Dover 1974: 314; Sheets 1994: 55; Low 2007: 107.

ownership by states. The author of *On Halonnesus* accuses Philip of possessing what really belongs to Athens in the case of Amphipolis.[20] This distinction between one's own and others' possessions implies a law among states beyond seizure and force.[21] A witticism attributed to Phocion by Plutarch also reveals the expectation that international disputes could be settled by legal means as an alternative to war: Phocion criticized the Athenians' decision not to resolve legally, *dikazesthai*, a quarrel with Thebes and advised that they should fight the Thebans with words, in which they had the edge, rather than with arms in which the Thebans were superior.[22]

(3) That speakers often argued that legal procedures and ways of thinking were not appropriate between states reveals that the legal paradigm required refutation. On the eve of the Peloponnesian War, Sthenolaidas is represented as arguing against arbitration: "These things should not be decided by lawsuits and speeches since we are not being injured in word alone."[23] In two other cases in Thucydides a speaker has to remind the assembly that they are deliberating on foreign policy and not in court; this seems to have been an easy mistake to fall into, given the tendency to think of interstate relations in legal terms.[24] In a similar vein, ninety years later, in 342, the author of *On Halonnesus* repeatedly denounced Philip's offer to go to arbitration. He worried that Philip would get his way by bribery and that the recourse to law would reveal to the Greek world

that there is not a single thing for the sake of which you will appeal to arms, if indeed for your possessions on the sea, where you say your strength lies, you shall appeal, not to arms, but to the law courts."[25]

All these denials of interstate law reveal that that the contrary opinion was possible and probably even common.

(4) Various classical texts refer explicitly to something like "the law of the Greeks."[26] They invoke laws binding on all Greeks – and sometimes non-Greeks are included. These laws are unwritten and generally concern the conduct of war and diplomacy. A well-known debate in Thucydides between the Thebans and Athenians after the battle of Delium provides an example. The Thebans accused the Athenians of desecrating

---

[20] [Dem.] 7.26.   [21] This implication is well explored in Chaniotis 2004.
[22] Plut. *Phoc.* 9.   [23] Thuc. 1.86.3 (trans. modified).
[24] Thuc. 1.73.1; 3.44.4. See D. Cohen 1984.
[25] [Dem.] 7.7–8. See also Dem. 8.28 and [Dem.] 7.36–7, 41, 44.
[26] Phillipson 1911: 1.57–8; Low 2007: 95–7. Examples include Hdt. 7.136; Eur. *Supp.* 311; Diod. 19.63.5.

their temple and invoked "the law of the Hellenes" and the "universal custom."[27] The Athenians defended themselves and claimed that they were doing their best to respect the temple; they argued that the Theban refusal to give back the Athenian dead from the battle marked them as the "far more impious."[28] Although these laws did not impinge on the decision to go to war – other than that the decision should be made public in some sort of declaration of war – they do show another, explicit application of legal terminology to the interactions of states.

In addition to these symptoms of legalism, private international law – agreed-upon procedures for settling disputes between individual members of two states – was well established in classical Greece.[29] It could even impinge on the overall relations between states. A passage in *On Halonnesus* suggests that some Athenians, former settlers of Potidaea, wanted to take Philip to court for his seizure of their property when he captured Potidaea, an illegal act in time of peace according to them. The argument is formulated in legal terms with frequent use of the vocabulary of the Athenian justice system.[30] The speaker claims that the law directs that the decision should be made in the jury court at Athens, but Philip, not surprisingly, thought the Athenian court's decision should require his own ratification.[31] Although the ostensible issue was the proper procedure for resolution of private disputes, the speaker argues that Philip's real motive is "to get your admission that you have no reasonable claim to Potidaea," an issue between states.[32] This was an unusual and irresolvable case because one of the individuals involved was a king, but the resolution of individual disputes was covered by interstate agreements and customary practices. These aimed at, and usually succeeded in, preventing individual disputes from involving the parties' states in war.

THE SUBSTANCE OF INTERSTATE LAW

So the legal analogy was ubiquitous in discourse about interstate relations. For the purpose of analysis, legalism in foreign relations can be divided into two categories, substance and procedure, which this chapter will treat in succession. First, the substance of legal thinking included some unwritten rules having to do with the conduct of war, which were matters of general agreement; in addition, treaties were written down, displayed publicly, and universally considered to be binding. Second, states attempted to enforce

---

[27] Thuc. 4.97.2–3. [28] Thuc. 4.98.2. [29] Todd 1993: 316–40.
[30] [Dem.] 7.9–12. [31] [Dem.] 7.9. [32] [Dem.] 7.13.

this body of law in a variety of ways, some involving explicit sanctions and hierarchy and others not. The conclusion of this chapter treats the motivations behind and the results of legalistic thinking in interstate relations.

Athenian laws were written down, but they were not detailed and, in particular, did not offer precise definitions of crimes.[33] Even though litigants often insisted on the importance of sticking to the letter of law, the recourse to a sense of what is fair or extrapolation from related laws played a larger role than in modern law courts. For example, Athenian jurors took an oath before their year in office:

I will vote in accordance with the laws and with the decrees of the people of Athens and of the council of five hundred, and on matters where there are no laws, I will vote in accordance with the most just opinion.[34]

The law also gave force to contracts between people, which thus became legally binding and extended the range of the written law to affect people in individualized ways.

In the interstate realm there was no equivalent to the law code. There was no official body of written international law. There were, however, general moral judgments, based on all sorts of models as we have seen. More significant for legalistic thinking, people attributed widespread agreement to some of these moral judgments, especially those connected in some way with sacred things and the conduct of war; they called them laws.[35] These laws were not written down: they did not represent "an accepted body of International Law to which appeal could be made or which defied disobedience or misrepresentation."[36] But they were supplemented by the specific terms of sworn treaties: roughly parallel to contracts within the state and sometimes described by the same word, *synthēkai*.[37]

The unwritten "law of the Greeks" was not invoked in just any case where one might make a moral judgment and hope that it was generally shared. The "law of the Greeks" governed truces and the treatment of heralds and embassies, sacred places and the bodies of those killed in battle.[38] It also held that a state of war required a public declaration and that soldiers who surrendered should not be killed out of hand.[39] The "law of the Greeks" generally limited the conduct of war, but was not invoked regarding the

---

[33] Todd 1993: 61–2; Sealey 1994: 51–2.   [34] Trans. Sealey 1994: 51.
[35] Cf. Chaniotis 2004: 187, 205. On the general topic of written and unwritten laws and the gods see E. Harris 2004: 21–34.
[36] Adcock and Mosley 1975: 112.   [37] Isoc. 17.20.   [38] See Adcock and Mosley 1975: 153, 202.
[39] Declaration of war: Karavites 1984: 165. The treatment of captives is the most controversial of these rules: see Ducrey 1968 for an overall treatment and Sheets 1994: 57–8 for the expectation that prisoners would be spared.

reason for war, even though we have seen that going to war was judged in moral terms. This situation is closely paralleled in the modern period. The first international agreements, beginning with the first Geneva Convention of 1863, regulated how war was to be conducted and not the recourse to war: there were agreed-upon rules of war, *ius in bello*, generations before there were serious international attempts to limit the right of states to go to war, as in the condemnation of aggression in the United Nations Charter.[40] The right to decide to go to war is perhaps too intrinsic to what it means to be a sovereign state to admit readily of external curbs.

To return to ancient Greece, the criticism that such unwritten laws were vague and thus unenforceable has some merit but is partly misplaced and partly exaggerated.[41] The issue of enforcement is a real one and we shall revisit it, but it is one that always impinges upon international law whether written or not.[42] In addition, the vagueness of these laws is more a figment of our sources than a consequence of their not being written. When we focus on the indecisive arguments after the battle of Delium – about the return of the dead and the occupation of sacred ground – we may forget about the hundreds or thousands of battles after which the winners did return the bodies of the dead to the losing side under truce. We do not even hear about all the invasions during which the invader refrained from disturbing the local temples. We only hear about the controversial cases.[43] The situation after Delium was exceptional in other ways too. The Athenians were in an ambiguous and unusual position and thus the legitimacy of the Theban retaliation – refusing to grant a truce to allow the collection of the Athenian dead – was hard to judge.[44] It is not at all clear that a set of written laws would have done any good – at least not unless they were far more detailed than Athens' domestic law code.[45]

Several scholars have suggested that the notion that treaties should be binding was so well accepted that this ought to be added to the unwritten "law of the Greeks."[46] In any case, the written and specific terms of treaties complemented the unwritten and general "law of the Greeks." Private contracts served to impose more specific requirements than the laws of a state – and were common in the commerce – but generally had the

[40] Collier 1991: 122; Greenwood 1991: 133–4; Bull 2002: 127; UN Charter Chapter 1 Article 2 Paragraph 4: www.un.org/aboutun/charter/index.html.
[41] Cf. the arguments of Sheets 1994: esp. 56.
[42] See Phillipson 1911: i.49–50 for an amusing rebuttal.   [43] Sheets 1994: 59.
[44] See the discussion with bibliography of Hornblower 1991–2009: ii.311–12; cf. HCT iii.570–1; see Jordan 1986: 128–30 for a strong condemnation of the Athenian position.
[45] Low 2007: 96.   [46] Sheets 1994: 54; Bederman 2001: 52; Low 2007: 99.

full force of the law behind their enforcement.[47] Thus they supplemented domestic law. In contrast, treaties had to make up for the complete absence of a centrally established written law. For this reason, it seems that most states at peace with one another had sworn to a treaty including the specific conditions of either a peace or an alliance. Most Greek states were thus subject to written obligations.[48] While the unwritten laws of the Greeks typically limited the conduct of war, it was by reference to the terms of treaties that they could justify or argue against the recourse to war in a legalistic way. Clearly Greeks did not only justify or deplore wars in terms of treaty obligations, but such arguments were common and important and reflective of a legalistic way of thinking.

At the outset of the Peloponnesian War, the Spartan assembly was told to divide and to vote depending on whether they thought that "the treaty has been broken and that the Athenians are acting unjustly"; an affirmative vote was a vote for war.[49] An important step in the breakdown of the peace of Nicias was taken when the Athenians decided that the Spartans had not kept their oaths and had this inscribed at the bottom of the treaty stele.[50] So, too, the war of Chaeronea began when the Athenians decided to destroy the stele of the Peace of Philocrates with Philip.[51] Otherwise a treaty was a decree of the Athenian assembly and thus had the force of law in Athens.[52] In this respect, it is too weak to speak of the "legal analogy": treaties were legally binding. Before acting contrary to a treaty the Athenians had to declare it void; they sometimes publicized this by the physical destruction of the public copy of the treaty.[53] At least one passage shows that the Athenians thought that other states had the same ideas and practices.[54]

Although treaties were laws in this sense, either party could declare them void at will, unlike domestic laws and contracts. Nevertheless, states typically justified their abrogation of treaties. No state wanted to be known to have broken a treaty and the oaths that confirmed it without a good reason. For example, the Athenian commanders at Corcyra in 433 did their

---

[47] On the legal enforceability of contracts see E. Cohen 2005: 299, who cites Dem. 47.77 and 56.2; Din. 3.4; Pl. *Symp.* 196c; Arist. *Rh.* 1.15.1375b9.

[48] See Alonzo 2007 for the range of relationships possible between Greek states; he rebuts the notion that the absence of a treaty necessarily indicates a state of war.

[49] Thuc. 1.87.2 (trans. modified).   [50] Thuc. 5.56.3; Ar. *Lys.* 513–14.

[51] Philochorus in Didymus col. 1.67–74; Dion. Hal. *Epistula ad Ammaeum* 1.11; *FGrH* 328 F 54. See Harding 2006: 114–15. See also *IG* ii² 116 in Ha no. 59, lines 39–41 = RO no. 44.

[52] Hansen 1991: 172 points out that even treaties of explicitly unlimited duration were still *psēphismata*, decrees, rather than *nomoi*, laws.

[53] Adcock and Mosley 1975: 223; Harding 2006: 115; contra Bolmarcich 2007.   [54] Dem. 16.27.

best only to fight defensively in order to keep their defensive treaty of alliance with the Corcyraeans without breaking their long-standing treaty with the Peloponnesian League by fighting with Corinth. As one book on ancient international law observes, "[s]o it was that the Athenians attempted to adhere to the letter of two contradictory treaties, one with Corcyra, and the other with Corinth and Sparta."[55]

An odd diplomatic practice, somewhat paradoxically, provides more evidence of the binding force of treaties. Everett Wheeler has brought attention to a number of treaties that included an "anti-deceit" clause. This was a phrase or just a word indicating that agreement was to be upheld without verbal trickery. Wheeler concludes that "[s]ophistic interpretation of agreements were perceived as a real and present danger."[56] That states – especially Athens it turns out – would try to come up with an excuse or verbal trick to avoid fulfilling their side of a treaty makes it clear that the alternative, simply to ignore their treaty obligations, was even less palatable. Wheeler emphasizes that fear of the gods might motivate a state to try to wriggle out of its obligations in whatever way it could rather than openly break a sworn agreement; states also wanted to avoid a reputation for bad faith among the Greeks – apparently even less desirable than one for sophistry.

That treaties were written documents did not mean that their application to a changing situation was a matter of universal agreement. The application of domestic laws to a given situation was and is often in doubt.[57] So, too, there was not always agreement among states about what exactly a treaty allowed or proscribed, whether it had been broken, and whether this breach was a serious one.[58] In the vast majority of assembly speeches we see strenuous attempts to make this argument in one way or another. These constant references reveal the force that treaty terms possessed in the foreign policy deliberations of Athens.[59]

In *On the Peace* Andocides argues that the Athenians should accept the peace treaty offered by Sparta. Throughout the speech Andocides assumes that both the Spartans and the Athenians will abide by the terms of the treaty if it is made.[60] The Athenians will have to forego any attempt to regain the overseas possessions of the fifth-century empire; the Spartans will

---

[55] Bederman 2001: 213 on Thuc. 1.49, 52–3. See also Thuc 6.88.2.

[56] Wheeler 1984: 254–5.   [57] Sheets 1994: 59.

[58] Rhodes 2008 explores this subject: parties to treaties sometimes even proposed or agreed to terms whose interpretation was certain to provoke controversy – for example, the stipulation that each side should possess what was rightfully theirs (24–7).

[59] See also Isoc. 10.12, 23.   [60] Andocides makes this explicit at 3.34.

not make further demands on Athens that might imperil its democracy. Several passages in Demosthenes' *For the Liberty of the Rhodians* also reveal an atmosphere in which treaty obligations were taken seriously. At one point Demosthenes seems to condemn Byzantium and the Persian king for breaking treaties.[61] This turns out to set up his counter-argument that Athens should not be held back by treaty obligations from restoring the Rhodian democrats, an argument that implies that opposing speakers made reference to treaty obligations.[62] Demosthenes also makes a Realist critique of treaties as reflecting power rather than rights, again an argument aimed at disarming the argument from treaties.[63] In *For the Megalopolitans* he points out that if Sparta attacks Messenia, Athens will have to come to Messenia's rescue not only on account of its interest but also because of its treaty obligations.[64]

In the *Second Olynthiac* Demosthenes attempts to show that Philip is foresworn; he has reneged on various treaty obligations and is due for a fall.[65] The *Third Olynthiac* insists on Athens' promise, in what sounds like a treaty of alliance, to protect the Olynthians if Philip attacks them – which fate they were indeed suffering.[66] In the uncharacteristic and compromising *On the Peace*, Demosthenes advises the Athenians not to make any alliances or raise any moneys contrary to the Peace of Philocrates.[67] He has a second legalistic worry, that a decree of the Amphictyonic Council against Athens would give an excuse for all Athens' enemies to unite in attacking it.[68] The *Second Philippic* begins with the statement that many speakers have condemned Philip for his acts of force contrary to the peace treaty.[69] So, too, the *Third Philippic*, *On the Chersonese*, and the *Fourth Philippic* all emphasize that Philip has broken the Peace of Philocrates.[70] In the *Third Philippic* Demosthenes even argues that Philip's seemingly small infractions of the treaty, his seizure of some small towns in Thrace, are still important: they are breaches of justice and of religion, the latter because he broke his oath.[71]

The speech *On Halonnesus*, parts of which have been discussed above, is informed throughout by a legalistic view of interstate relations. Many of its arguments rest on various treaties and amendments to them. For example, the speaker attempts to show that the Peace of Philocrates was unconstitutional, *paranomos*, at Athens and that Philip had given Athens the right to amend the treaty.[72] Otherwise, complaints against Philip would

[61] Dem. 15.26–7.   [62] Dem. 15.28.   [63] See p. 160.   [64] Dem. 16.9.
[65] Dem. 2.5–7.   [66] Dem. 3.16.   [67] Dem. 5.13.   [68] Dem. 5.14, 19.
[69] Dem. 6.1.   [70] Dem. 8.5–6, 39 (= 10.11); 9.6; 10.18.   [71] Dem. 9.16.   [72] [Dem.] 7.24–5.

have to be made on the basis of that treaty, which Philip apparently had not broken. Likewise the speech *On the Treaty with Alexander* also highlights Macedonian infringement of its treaty obligations. This is apparent from its opening section:

> Our hearty assent, men of Athens, is due to those who insist that we should abide by our oaths and treaties . . . from the very terms of the treaty and from the oaths which ratified the general peace, you may at once see who are its transgressors.[73]

The terms of the peace and their transgression by the Macedonians constitute the main arguments of the speech.[74] The speaker concludes that the Athenians should declare war on Macedon since the treaty requires states to make war on whoever transgresses it.[75]

A pattern in our assembly speeches suggests that even this catalogue may underrepresent the significance of treaties in Athenian foreign policy decisions. While Demosthenes dominates this body of evidence, it is actually the three non-Demosthenic speeches that are the most legalistic: Andocides, *On the Peace*, and the pseudo-Demosthenic *On Halonnesus* and *On the Treaty with Alexander*.[76] It may be that most orators relied heavily on legalistic arguments, while Demosthenes preferred to deal with the big picture in a more emotional and generally moral way. That even Demosthenes referred to treaty obligations in his speeches reveals their importance in Athenian decisions about war. Treaties were mutual agreements with determinate, written terms. They were public documents ratified by oaths to the gods. If a speaker could persuade the Athenian assembly that a treaty had been breached, he was more than halfway to persuading them to go to war.

PROCESS AND HIERARCHY

Law is a process as well as a set of rules. When law could be applied, it could replace violence as a way of deciding disputes; arbitration between states, in particular, is sometimes explicitly represented as a substitute for war.[77] But, as Sheila Ager points out, the same problems bedevil the use of arbitration between states in the modern and ancient world, since they are inherent in an anarchic system of independent states.[78] We can expand this observation to any application of legal models to states. Since these

---

[73] [Dem.] 17.1–2.   [74] [Dem.] 17.4, 16, 20–1, 26.   [75] [Dem.] 17.30.
[76] Cf. Sealey 1993: 178 about *On Halonnesus*: "legalistic and tiresome."
[77] E.g. Thuc. 1.78.4.   [78] Ager 1993, 1996: 30–6.

criticisms come out of the Realist tradition, we have seen them before in that context. Here a brief summary will suffice.

Demosthenes pointed out that the justice is accorded to states in proportion to their power.[79] It is clear from the context that he is not talking about justice in general, but rather about treaty rights.[80] The shaping of treaties by power relations is probably ubiquitous but can be particularly clear when a treaty ends a war. For example, after Athens had been starved into submission in 404, it agreed to "count the same people friends and enemies as the Lacedaemonians did, and follow the Lacedaemonians both by land and by sea wherever they should lead the way."[81] In Athens a contract obtained through violence or the threat of violence could be declared void.[82] Hence, Andocides and Isocrates try to distinguish between voluntary treaties and those imposed on unwilling parties.[83] But all treaties, both the consensual and the coerced, were sanctified by oath and publicly displayed. And even when we do not have as drastic a situation as that of Athens in 404, the relative power of states often enters into the terms of their pacts. Thus, as Edward Carr observed of modern diplomacy, the sanctity of treaties can be "a weapon used by the ruling nations to maintain their supremacy over weaker nations on whom the treaties have been imposed."[84]

So even were treaties obeyed, the result would not be justice in any pure sense; it might be peace. But it is here that the ideal of law among states runs into its greatest problem, the lack of a sovereign authority to enforce legalistic solutions. Although written and containing some detailed terms, the legal framework provided by a treaty cannot explicitly deal with every contingency. Whereas the Athenian juror was authorized to vote "in accordance with the most just opinion," there was no such authority to decide on what was "the most just opinion" about an issue not explicitly treated in an interstate agreement. Even when a treaty did not seem to contain a gap, the application of its terms to the concrete situation – as well as the concrete situation itself – could be a matter of disagreement.[85] And again no interstate authority existed to resolve disagreement. Finally, even

---

[79] Dem. 15.29.   [80] See above pp. 159–60.
[81] Xen. *Hell.* 2.2.20. See similar cases in Missiou-Ladi 1987.   [82] [Dem.] 59.66.
[83] Andoc. 3.11; Isoc. 4.176. Isoc. 4.176 nevertheless adds the argument that the Persians have already broken all the good terms in the treaty and thus it has been annulled.
[84] Carr 1946: 189. But Suganami 1978: 118 points out that laws within the state are also affected by power relations.
[85] Two famous cases occur in Thucydides. The Corinthians argue that the clause of the Thirty-Year Peace that allows Athens or Sparta to accept new allies cannot apply to a case where the new ally, Corcyra, is already at war with an ally of either party (1.40.2). Sthenelaidas argues curtly that the requirement of the Thirty-Year Peace that disputes be settled by arbitration cannot apply to a case when one side, Athens, is already attacking the other (Thuc. 1.86.3–4).

when one side or the other was obviously breaking a treaty, no authority could impose a sanction or punishment. Lysander is supposed to have claimed that one should fool children with dice, but men with oaths – probably a reference to treaties.[86] Such unscrupulous policies were not impossible. As Ager notes "law or legal decisions, while binding in theory, are potentially empty without force to support them."[87] This observation cannot be refuted, but the impression it leaves is excessively pessimistic.

Indeed, George Sheets and Polly Low have recently presented arguments that sanctions are not an important element of the rule of law either within a state or among states. They both argue that adherence to law is not entirely due to the fear of punishment.[88] Since laws are often in line with a society's moral sense, it is hardly surprising that legal sanctions do not exhaust the motivations for obeying them. But legal sanctions do determine the extent to which a moral system has been supplemented and strengthened by the rule of law. Indeed, the Greeks themselves constantly attempted to invoke or establish authorities to enforce their laws and treaties. Within the state, Athenian law codes notoriously devoted more attention to specifying punishments and proper authorities and procedures than to defining crimes.[89] In the interstate realm one of the earliest treaties whose inscription has been found, dated to the late sixth century, was exceedingly simple and short; but it specified a fine to be paid by whichever side defaulted.[90] Throughout our period, Greek states attempted to make the gods into authorities over their treaties and to specify the sanctions the gods were to inflict on treaty-breakers: may "their wives bear children not like those who begat them, but monsters."[91] The Greeks were painfully aware of the necessity for sanctions and of their dubious enforceability. Sheets' and Low's arguments are well taken, nevertheless, that the Greek world did possess something like a code of laws, the generally accepted "laws of the Greeks" and the web of treaties. Regardless of the enforcement of these, their interstate regime was different from one without agreed rules at all – for example the Mongols and their various victims – and thus Low and Sheets are right to insist that the Greek world possessed a system of international law.

---

[86] Plut. *Lys.* 8. Plutarch is reporting Androclides, a contemporary Theban hostile to Sparta, so perhaps the anecdote is mere slander.

[87] Ager 1996: 31.

[88] Sheets 1994: 61; Low 2007: 103. This was noticed already in the early seventeenth century by Hugo Grotius (1925: 16–17 = Prolegomena sec. 20).

[89] Todd 1993: 64–7. The law on *hybris* provides a striking example.

[90] Meiggs and Lewis 1988: no. 17, cf. no. 10.   [91] Aeschin. 3.111.

To return to types of sanctions, two distinctions are important. First, all aspects of the interstate morality of the Greek states were sanctioned by public opinion and actions consequent on that opinion – as we have explored in previous chapters. These sanctions were not compelling, but they were there and exerted some influence. But it is useful to think of the Greek city-states as subject to international law only if we are saying something more than that they shared moral values that influenced their actions and their judgments. Second, two models of this imperfect enforcement are possible: Realists insist that only a hierarchical state system, in which one state has power and authority over the others, would make possible law enforcement among states; but there is also power in numbers and a strong consensus among states allows the imposition of significant costs on rule-breakers without hierarchy. Sheets points out that the Greek interstate regime is best compared to a "horizontal" legal system in which transgressors are punished by peers or by the community at large.[92] Taking up this distinction, we will first consider the horizontal aspects of Greek interstate legalism and then the attempts to establish or invoke a superior power, a hierarchy, to enforce rules.

That Greek states insisted that treaties be publicly displayed at Pan-hellenic centers reveals the expectation that the opinions of the Greek city-states, and the actions consequent on these, provided some sanction against breaking treaties. The Greek cities, of course, formed opinions about all sorts of behavior or misbehavior by states, but their judgments about adherence to treaties possessed particular force. Since a treaty was specific and written, it was probably easier to determine which state had broken it than to judge other actions or intentions of states, for example whether Thebes was acting aggressively under the cover of protecting an ally or whether Sparta was behaving ungratefully towards Athens. Written treaties have the potential to lessen, though they certainly do not destroy, the ability of states to justify in moral terms whatever actions their self-interest dictates. In addition, diplomacy was crucial to Greek city-states: it allowed them to make alliances and to end wars. A reputation for sticking to treaties was a prerequisite for either of these extremely advantageous diplomatic procedures.

Non-hierarchical organizations of states helped to structure and thus give clout to the opinions of the Greek World at large – or significant subsets thereof. These sometimes possessed enough moral authority and power to ensure their decisions could not be disobeyed with impunity. For

---

[92] Sheets 1994: 62, 70.

example, the Amphictyonic Council possessed authority with respect to the Delphic sanctuary, festivals, and games that extended over any Greek state that took part. It had the authority to impose fines and to ban states from "the sanctuaries, festivals and council of the Amphictiony" if these were not paid.[93] In some cases, the authority of Delphi was treated as if it encompassed any religious matter in which the member states of the Amphictyonic Council were in dispute – such as Sparta's seizure of the Cadmea during a religious festival.[94] The Amphictyonic Council was also the authority behind an important written limitation of warfare: the Amphictyonic states were prohibited from razing each other's cities or cutting them off from running water.[95]

But the Greeks did not rest content with publicity and "horizontal law" to enforce treaties. They strove in various ways to establish or invoke a higher power to enforce the terms of treaties. Most obviously the gods directly enforced treaties.[96] Their intervention was expected or hoped for on three levels. First and most generally there existed the belief that the gods punished arrogant behavior, *hybris*, by individuals or by states.[97] Such a conception, however moralistic, was too vague to have much effect on state policies – or at least none that we can demonstrate. In addition to perennial problems with such a view – for example the prosperity of the wicked and misfortunes of the good – few states are likely to have judged their own behavior as hubristic. Second, there is some sign that the unwritten laws of the Greeks, the various limits on the conduct of war, were viewed as sanctioned by the gods. For example, a Theban general in Thucydides encouraged his troops before battle to go forth confidently "trusting in the support of the god whose sanctuary they impiously occupy."[98] Third and most important, all treaties were sanctioned by oaths that called on gods, not only as witnesses, but as enforcers who are asked to take action against whichever party breaks a treaty.[99] Indeed, the Greek words for treaty include not only the word for contracts, *synthēkai*, but also *spondai*, after the libations made to the gods at the ratification ceremony, or *horkoi*, after

---

[93] Buckler 1989: 7.

[94] Buckler 1989: 15; Low 2007: 117–18. See also Yunis 2001: 188 on Dem. 18.134 for a case involving Athens and Delos. See also Plut. *Cim.* 8.4–5 with Podlecki 1971: 142.

[95] Aeschin. 2.115. Whether this was an authentic archaic rule or a fourth-century retrojection is not important for my argument.

[96] Phillipson 1911: 1.45–51 followed by Bederman 2001: 86 and Low 2007: 118. Cf. Grotius 1925: 14 (Prolegomena 12, 15).

[97] Adkins 1972: 83–4; Karavites 1984: 174.   [98] Thuc. 4.92.7; see also Lys. 12.96.

[99] Lonis 1980: 267.

the oaths that are sworn.[100] The treaty between Philip and the Chalcidians again provides an excellent example:

[They shall swear the oath guilelessly] and sincerely, by Zeus, Gē, Helias, Poseidon, *if they keep the oath, they shall have* many benefits, if they break the oath (they shall have) many misfortunes. The oath shall be sworn *as they sacrifice* the victims, by both sides.[101]

The inclusion of such oaths, sacrificial rituals, and curses upon treaty-breakers seems to have been standard practice in Greek treaties – and it is attested in a variety of cultures world wide.[102] In addition, a number of passages show confidence, to a greater or lesser degree, that the gods do, in fact, punish states for disregarding the oaths they swore. For example, since the Spartans refused a recourse to arbitration before the Peloponnesian War, the Athenians threatened them with the gods who witnessed their treaty oath: "we, with the gods we have sworn by as our witnesses, will attempt to defend ourselves against any move you initiate."[103] Both sides eventually shared this perception of Sparta's culpability – at least according to Thucydides.[104] Even if the gods did not intervene, to break a treaty without excuse was to show impiety and contempt for the gods, qualities hardly approved of or conducive to high standing among the Greeks: as Plutarch notes in his condemnation of Lysander, "the man who overreaches his opponent by breaking his oath reveals that he is afraid of his enemy but despises the gods he has invoked."[105]

Public display and the invocation of the gods made a powerful combination. Speakers often emphasized the obligation to obey treaties by referring to the oaths that sanctified them.[106] Their force was so generally accepted that obedience to oaths could even be used as a shield for interest: the Corinthians, subordinate allies of Sparta, refused to acknowledge the Peace of Nicias, claiming that an oath to their allies in Thrace prevented them from doing so, a pretext according to Thucydides; the Spartans were unwilling or unable to insist that the Corinthians act contrary to what they claimed were their sworn obligations.[107]

[100] Adcock and Mosley 1975: 229.
[101] Ha no. 67 = RO no. 50. Despite the various supplements, this text is secure. Another example appears in Aeschin. 3.121.
[102] Bederman 2001: 71–3 (Rome); Yates 2007: 45 (China in the Spring and Autumn period); Beal 2007: 86 (Hittites).
[103] Thuc. 1.78.4.
[104] Thuc. 7.18.2. See p. 218 above. See also Xen. *Hell.* 5.4.1, 4.17, and 6.4.3; 3.4.11.
[105] Plut. *Lys.* 8. Cf. Isoc. 5.91.
[106] Thuc. 1.71.5; 2.74.2; 5.30.1; 6.18.1; 19.1; *IG* ii² 107, line 45 (Ha no. 53 = RO no. 31).
[107] Thuc. 5.30.2; see also Xen. *Hell.* 2.4.30.

If the gods were powerful and if they took their invocation in treaties seriously, we might have found a rule of law among Greek states, based on their treaties. It might even have been more perfect than the law within a state – for who can fool the gods? But, it does not require the thesis of a loss of faith in fourth-century Athens, an implausible proposition, to explain that the gods were not, in fact, completely trusted to enforce treaty obligations. Among other difficulties, it was unclear whether state representatives could actually swear on behalf of anybody but themselves.[108] And which side broke a treaty and thus deserved divine wrath was often a disputed issue.

But there were other aspects of hierarchy in the Greek world that kept it from total anarchy. Once a state joined a strong alliance system, such as the Second Athenian League, its sovereignty could be overruled by an authoritative and written judgment by the league council: we possess one such document in which the Second Athenian League set down terms for the resolution of civil war on Paros.[109] So, too, Sparta pronounced a fine to be imposed on its allies in the event that they defaulted on their military obligations to the Peloponnesian League.[110] Within some portions of the Greek interstate world and with respect to some issues, interpretive and sanctioning authority existed and legalistic judgments were enforceable.[111]

The Greek states sometimes tried to create a sanctioning and interpretive authority in interstate relations by holding a conference to which states would send representatives. Such conferences could make new decisions – as if they were the assembly within a democratic state – or could judge the claims and counter-claims of their members. These assemblies can be placed on a spectrum in terms of the degree of hierarchy in their organization; in general, the more hierarchical the assembly, the more likely it was that its decisions could be enforced, at least against the weaker members.

Most important, the series of fourth-century Common Peace treaties were typically instituted at such conferences. Ambassadors from the participating cities, which seem often to have comprised a large part of the Greek World, swore to the resulting treaty on behalf of their states.[112] It may even be that the treaty was held to be binding on all Greek states that did not

---

[108] Lonis 1980: esp. 278.

[109] RO: no. 29, discussed in Low 2007: 92–3. This intervention was probably at the initiative of a delegation of Parians (RO no. 29, lines 12–14). Athens notoriously infringed upon the sovereignty of the members of its fifth-century empire.

[110] Xen. *Hell.* 5.2.21 discussed in Low 2007: 116.

[111] This phenomenon is entirely in line with Realist views: it is interstate anarchy that leads to lawlessness; hierarchy allows the enforcement of rules.

[112] E.g. Xen. *Hell.* 5.1.32; 6.3.19–20, 5.1–3.

explicitly renounce it.[113] The Common Peace treaty typically proclaimed that all the cities in Greece should be at peace and autonomous. This was a significant generalization of the terms of the usual bilateral treaty. Some scholars have lauded this statement, made by an authoritative body representing much of the Greek world, as representing "some kind of definition of international law."[114]

The substance of the Common Peace treaties – the requirement of peace and autonomy throughout Greece – were generally held to be praiseworthy and law-like.[115] When it came to the enforcement of such agreements, opinions varied widely. The enforcing of interstate laws depended on hierarchy, which, as we have seen, was viewed with grave suspicion. Admittedly there seem to have been Common Peace conferences in which no particular state was predominant and also a Common Peace treaty that explicitly gave any state that wished the right to enforce the terms of the peace.[116] But the Common Peace most often involved at least two degrees of hierarchy. First, the Persian king usually stood as the backer of the peace, willing to support with money and arms its upholder. Second, the Persian king typically supported one Greek state, often a particularly powerful one at the time, in enforcing the treaty. As a result, the terms of the Common Peace had some chance of authoritative interpretation and enforcement. But, just as surely, this enforcement was likely to be biased in favor of the king and the Greek state enjoying his support. It was therefore contrary to the view of the law as ensuring equal protection for the weak and strong alike.

For example, in the aftermath of the King's Peace, the first Common Peace, Sparta interpreted the autonomy clause as requiring that the other Boeotian cities be independent of Thebes and that Corinth and Argos sever their union; it was able to enforce these decisions.[117] About forty years later the League of Corinth was instituted in a treaty based on the Common Peace model.[118] Macedonian power was such that the league's decisions could be enforced. But the league's authority was almost imperceptibly replaced by that of the Macedonian king – Alexander's exile decree provides a famous case of this usurpation of league authority. In four passages an Athenian orator refers to the judgment of the king and all the Greeks, likely in a Common Peace conference, as if to an authoritative body that had declared that Athens rather than Macedonia should possess

---

[113] Ryder 1965: 173.   [114] Mosley 1973: 1. See also Ryder 1965: 120.   [115] Ryder 1965: 120.
[116] Ryder 1965: 84–7 and Jehne 1994: 96–115 on the Common Peace of 362; Low 2007: 185 on the Common Peace of 371.
[117] Xen. *Hell.* 5.1.32–4.   [118] Perlman 1985.

the Chersonese and Amphipolis.[119] Clearly, this adjudication in Athens' favor was remembered at Athens and was something to which it was worth making reference. But if this decision was enforced at all, it was only in the case of the Chersonese and this by means of Athenian military activity.[120] The actual status of Amphipolis did not change a whit as a result of its assignment to Athens. Nor can this judgment be easily reconciled with the ideal that all cities are to be autonomous.

The Amphictyons had authority within their sphere and used it; gods had plenty of power but could not be counted on to use it anytime soon; and the enforcement of the terms of the Common Peace corresponded as much to the parties' power as to any legalistic claims or rights to autonomy. Another way of establishing a sovereign authority was to use interstate arbitration: "States that resorted to arbitration were in effect surrendering their sovereignty temporarily to the arbitrator."[121] This is because both parties typically agreed to binding arbitration.[122] This abdication of sovereignty was, of course, reversible; among states, binding is not. Nevertheless, there was enough of a cost to a state's reputation in reneging after having agreed to arbitration so that states who were unwilling to restrict their freedom of action often refused arbitration altogether.[123]

CONCLUSIONS

The legal system and thinking that the Athenians applied to the realm of states was not the same as a modern system. Some of these differences lay in ways in which Athens had not developed as separate a sphere of law as modern states have.[124] Another difference is the non-hierarchical and less centralized nature of Athenian justice. In general, these differences make Athenian domestic law unsatisfactory by modern standards; they made Athenian law more easily applicable to the relations between states; law among states is necessarily more like Athenian law than it is like the law of a modern westernized state.

The Athenian systems of law depended to a large extent on self-help in the execution of court decisions or even in lieu of a jury trial.[125] A winning plaintiff in a property suit was expected to take control of the

---

[119] Dem. 9.16; 19.137, 253; [Dem.] 7.29; Aeschin. 2.32. Ryder 1965: 128–31 and MacDowell 2000: 261.
[120] Isoc. 15.112; Diod. 16.34.3.   [121] Ager 1996: 9.
[122] Ager 1996: 8–9; this was parallel to private, but not public, arbitration within the state (Todd 1993: 123–5, 128–9).
[123] Thuc. 1.34.2, 39.1–2; 4.122.5; Xen. *Hell.* 7.4.11.   [124] See Carey 1994.
[125] Herman 1993: 411; D. Cohen 2005: 226–9; cf. Wolff 2007: 95–6. See the suggestions of Pl. *Leg.* 12.958a–c.

money awarded him on his own. It was eventually possible to have the state appropriate the award, but this process required further lawsuits. Given this context, the notion, for example, that whoever wanted to could act as an enforcer of a Common Peace would have seemed more legalistic than it does to us today; legal decisions were not as closely connected to their enforcement by a sovereign authority as they are today. Binding arbitration is still a legal process today, but in Athens it was common.[126] Hence the recourse to arbitration between states would have seemed a more familiar and legal process than it does today. It may even be the case that arbitration preceded state control of the resolution of disputes.[127] Its somewhat primitive nature might have made it particularly suitable to the relationship of states, another realm lacking a sovereign power.

The ideal that a trial should focus very narrowly on the application of the law to the facts of the case was much less strong in classical Athens than it is in a modern court.[128] Even the most charitable view admits that Athenian courts took into account the "larger picture" and the history of a dispute.[129] At any rate, a fair proportion of law-court speeches concerned the general moral character of the litigants, their past crimes or good deeds, and attempts to magnify the issues at stake. We have already noted that our deliberative speeches often make legalistic arguments and refer to treaties, but that they vary greatly in the extent to which they focus on it. That approach is paralleled in actual law-court speeches; the application of the law is just one part of the case. In both cases, the general merits and status of the two parties, the interests of the audience, and the past history of the dispute all play as large a role as specific law or treaty terms.

A final feature of Athenian law courts is also worth considering. The law courts did not have judges to direct deliberations, instruct the jury, and limit what might be said. Athenians were tried by their peers and nobody else. Thus they felt no need in the interstate realms of the equivalent of a modern judge to make decisions. A non-hierarchical conference of state representatives, such as the Delphic Amphictyons, would have seemed quite familiar and a perfectly good way to legislate, to interpret the laws, and decree sanctions, whose imposition could either be assumed or assigned to whichever state was willing to take on the task.

Scholars have emphasized one of two basic motivations for the legal system at Athens: to resolve disputes without violence or to continue

---

[126] Todd 1993: 123–5, 128–9.   [127] Paulus 2007.

[128] E. Harris 1994 has argued against this consensus, but see Yunis 2005: 197 n. 13. See Lanni 2005 for a recent summary of the issue with bibliography.

[129] Rhodes 2004.

disputes in a different setting.[130] To some extent this distinction in motivation is a matter of perspective. In the abstract or as a general rule, Athenians
believed that their legal system was a great thing in part because it allowed
the resolution of disputes without violence.[131] The motivation of a particular litigant, however, was not merely to resolve his dispute, but to resolve
it to his advantage, to defeat his opponent. This same distinction is apparent among states. In the abstract, states often put clauses in their treaties
requiring the resolution of disputes by arbitration because they thought
that arbitration was better than war.[132] When a particular dispute came up,
one state would offer arbitration with the hope of gaining its goal without
fighting; the other might refuse arbitration if it feared it would not get
its way. So, the Athenians and Spartans agreed at the beginning of the
thirty-year treaty in 446 that disputes should be resolved by arbitration.
When a particular dispute came up, the Athenians stood by the letter of
the treaty while the Spartans refused, afraid that they would end up losing
the case – and disappointing their Corinthian allies. The same observation
can be made about the Common Peace conferences: these had as their real
and stated goal the establishment of peace in the whole Greek world. But it
was always peace on the terms of one state or another; that a legal analogy
was used did not mean that the result did not involve winners or losers.

[130] See bibliography on p. 204 nn. 110, 111.
[131] Conceded even by D. Cohen 1995: 34. One could go even further: within the state arbitration was
considered superior to litigation because it was a less antagonistic way of settling disputes (Roebuck
2001: 351, 354, 358).
[132] Tod 1913: 65–9 cites Hdt. 6.42; Thuc. 4.118.8; 5.18.4, 79.1; Roebuck 2001: 157.

Peace

These attempts to resolve disputes in a legalistic way rather than through force imply that peace was generally considered preferable to war.[1] Nevertheless, those historians who have tried to evaluate the extent and depth of Greek criticisms of and objections to war have come to widely divergent conclusions. On the one hand, several scholars have searched through all the major classical authors and collected, categorized, and discussed the passages critical of war, of which there are many.[2] They have tended to come to optimistic conclusions. For example, Gerardo Zampaglione was confident that "the problem of universal peace was posed, sometimes overtly, sometime less so, at the center of classical and ancient Christian thought," and Wallace Caldwell wrote of "a strong peace movement" in ancient Greece.[3] Others have argued that this or that particular work or author was, in one sense or another, anti-war.[4] On the other hand, several prominent and influential scholars have impatiently dismissed such investigations as well as the conclusions they have reached. For example, M. I. Finley contrasted the Greek attitudes with "our" modern condemnation of violence and attacked those "who blunderingly attribute similar values to the Greeks and Romans."[5]

Disagreements about the actual content of ancient thought are not quite so stark as one would think from such polemics. To begin with, "pacifism" has a different and much broader meaning in mainland Europe than in the United States or United Kingdom. In Europe attacks against militarism or an insistence on stringent criteria for approving wars can count as

---

[1] See Tritle 2007.   [2] E.g. Caldwell 1919; Nestle 1938; Zampaglione 1973. Cf. Boegehold 1982.
[3] Zampaglione 1973: 15; Caldwell 1919: 5.
[4] For example, on Eur. *Tro.*, see Goossens 1962: 524–7; Whitman 1974: 128; Waterfield 1982: 139. Although Croally 1994 attacked critics who "reduce the play to . . . slogans" (253), he also stressed the negative depiction of war in the play, e.g. 115, 130–2, 231, 253–4.
[5] M. Finley 1985b: 70; see also Green 1999: 97.

pacifist.[6] In addition, even in Anglo-American usage the definition of "pacifism" has narrowed over time to include now only principled opposition to all wars – which is the way I shall be using it.[7] So, Caldwell, Nestle, Goossens, Bearzot, and Zampaglione may be claiming less for ancient Greece than their indignant critics believe. In other cases, one scholar asserts A but B: ancient authors viewed war as necessary and military prowess and sacrifice as praise-worthy, but they were aware of the horrors of war. Another counters with B but A – and with surprising vehemence: they were aware of the horrors of war, but they viewed war as necessary, and military prowess and sacrifice as praise-worthy.[8] Since Greek culture and politics are multifaceted and diverse, historians on both sides can stress the evidence most in line with their views.

These considerations do not fully explain the stark differences of opinion. Generally, those who claim to detect "peace movements" tend to assimilate limited criticisms, sometimes of a particular war, with a more general and principled attack or they tend to assume that the depiction of brutality implies an objection to war or even a program for ridding the world of war.[9] Such a methodology risks, at the least, an excess of interpretive charity. The other side is certainly right to deny the existence of pacifism, in the strict sense, among the ancient Greeks. Unfortunately, this observation too often serves to preclude any further investigation of the subject and the rhetoric used is often smug and dismissive. In fact, the categorization implied by this approach borders on the bizarre: Greek thinking is non-pacifist or not "anti-war" and there is nothing more to say. For example, Peter Green argues that Euripides' *Troades* is not anti-war in the sense of "presenting the view that war is by definition an unmitigated moral evil."[10] But is the distinction between pacifist and non-pacifist the only important one when it comes to attitudes towards war? The term "non-pacifist" seems

---

[6] See Ceadel 1996: 23–4 and Chatfield 1996: 37–8 on the European use of "pacifism." Nestle 1938: 76; Goossens 1962: 524; Zampaglione 1973: 13–14, 78, 85, 97; Bearzot 1985: 106–7 and Gauthier 1976: 196 use pacifism of attitudes that would not fit the Anglo-American definition. The Anglophones Sealey 1955: 77 and Dillery 1993: 7 also use "pacifism" in a loose sense.

[7] On the original meaning and narrowing see Chatfield 1996: 37 and Teichman 1986: 1.

[8] This seems particularly the case in the disagreement between Green 1999 and Croally 1994, the latter of whom is fully aware of limits on ancient criticisms of war and the prominence that war had in classical values, e.g. 50, 51, 119, 131.

[9] Most scholars view objections to war in a positive light. Zampaglione 1973 views the "pacifists" as possessed of a superior and more advanced moral sense, but Nestle 1938 – published in Nazi Germany – sometimes presents "pacifism" as a sign of corruption and decline (36), so his emphasis on it does not imply a positive evaluation.

[10] Green 1999: 97. Cf. Garlan 1989: 8.

a blunt instrument indeed in that it lumps all stripes of opinion other than pacifism in one over-stuffed category.

Other scholars have introduced a number of distinctions in order to put ancient Greece on the wrong side of some line between correct, modern pacifism and primitive belligerence. So, Ryder, whose important work on the Common Peace, I have discussed already, distinguishes between "selfish pacifism" motivated by a desire for the wealth and trade made possible by peace and growing out of "war weariness" and a more idealistic pacifism.[11] In a similar vein Sealey argues that the anti-war statements of Xenophon's *Ways and Means* are just clichés and that the desire for peace is common in defeated cities.[12] Anna Missiou, in criticism of Andocides' *On the Peace*, will only approve a progressive, leftist pacifism:

There is a difference between the humane ideal of peace advanced by progressive thinkers, for whom peace is linked, to a considerable extent, with the liberation struggle against despotism and exploitation, and pacifist phraseology in the service of a political cause.[13]

So, the few anti-militarist or anti-war passages we find in ancient authors are subject to a host of other critiques. It may be correct that, for example, ancient opposition to war was greatest in defeated cities and among elite intellectuals worried about social unrest; the problem is when scholars imply a dismissive "just" or "merely" when they make such observations. That such passages require explanation does not mean they did not really exist. A satirical analogy will clarify the silliness of this whole approach. Imagine a political scientist who decided that all political views about economics, capitalism, class, and wealth were best viewed as either communist or non-communist. Suppose our hypothetical political scientist then decided that only Pol Pot was a true communist; all other communists, such as Lenin, were merely superficial reformers who left in place many of the structures of old capitalist societies and should be placed into the same category as Ronald Reagan. One would wonder about the point of this system of categorization and what purpose it might serve; it would not be much of an aid to coming to grips with the spectrum of ancient opinion.

It should also be staggeringly obvious that this categorization is not one that will usefully distinguish the modern world from that of the Greeks. Alas, "we" are not all pacifists. Green seems to believe that "our post-nuclear age . . . regards war by definition as the greatest conceivable disaster, to be

[11] Ryder 1965: 37–8. [12] Sealey 1993: 114. [13] Missiou 1992: 170.

avoided at all costs, and its instigators as criminals or moral imbeciles" – we have already seen Finley's characterization of "our" attitude to violence.[14] But, pacifists in this strong, Anglo-American sense are far from the majority. Far more common are those who, quite aware of the horrors of war – and who is not? – do not always believe war is always the worst option, "the greatest conceivable disaster." To move to the other end of the spectrum from pacifism, the glorification of war and a militaristic conception of manhood are far from dead, and probably as common as pacifism *sensu stricto*. Within a few blocks of my home there actually exists an intersection between Gandhi and Patton Streets. I do not know whether the bureaucrats responsible for these names had an odd sense of humor or were obliviously assigning names from a list of "great men," but the juxtaposition between the Indian pacifist and the American general makes clear the complexity of modern views about war and peace. Nor do ancient views fit easily into any one category – other than the catch-all non-pacifist.

GENERAL ANTIPATHY TO WAR

As part of his denial of significant anti-war sentiment among the ancient Greeks, Finley argues that arguments against war "had to be based on concrete circumstances, not on a general objection, on a question of tactics, not of principle."[15] This formulation conflates generality and principle and requires some unpacking. What Finley seeks and does not find are objections to war that are general, compelling, and principled. Were we to find such objections, we would have found Athenian pacifism. We will not. Nevertheless, questions of generality, impact, and principle can help us understand Athenian thinking and its difference from modern pacifism. There were specific objections to this war or that, but was there a general feeling that war was worse than peace? Do we find the view expressed that war should thus be a last resort? Principles, such as the code of reciprocity, guided Athenian decisions about any particular war. Was there another such guiding principle in the notion that war was morally worse than peace?

For the general preference for peace, we turn first to religion. As we have seen, Greek gods were expected to take a role in war, for one side or the

---

[14] Green 1999: 98. Ostwald 1996: 102 is more realistic but still does not fully acknowledge the militaristic strain in modern culture.

[15] M. Finley 1985b: 70.

other, rather than to try to prevent it.[16] There was one exception: Peace was a goddess for the Athenians, whose cult seems to have been established during the classical period and appears often in vase-painting, comedy, and tragedy.[17] There are already signs of a cult of Peace in Aristophanes' play of that title – although most scholars doubt the story that Cimon established an altar to Peace.[18] Euripides describes Peace as "a child nurturing goddess" in the *Bacchae*; in a fragment he describes her as "exceeding rich and of the blessed gods most beautiful."[19] The goddess Peace is pictured among Olympian gods on an altar from Brauron, probably dating from the late fifth century.[20] Peace was later represented by a cult statue, perhaps the famous work by Cephisodotos, of a goddess holding the child, Wealth. Vase paintings reveal that Wealth is in turn holding a cornucopia.[21] Similarly, in Aristophanes Peace is associated with *opōra*, the fruit-gathering season, a connection that confirms a "link between peace and (agricultural) prosperity."[22] Inscriptions record the amount realized by the sale of the hides of the oxen sacrificed at a public festival of Peace in 333/2 and 332/1, 874 and 713 drachmas respectively.[23] Given that an oxhide seems to have sold for something like 7 drachmas, it is likely that at least a full hecatomb of a hundred animals were sacrificed at the festival.[24] This would make the sacrifice to Peace one of the largest in the religious calendar, as lavish as the festivals of Bendis or Democratia and, in terms of the sacrifice at least, rivaling the City Dionysia.

Robert Parker has published a cynical view of the cult of Peace.[25] He admits the obviously pacific connotations of the cult statue, but he connects the public institution of the cult with a short-lived peace treaty obtained by Timotheus after his victory over the Spartans and his formation of an alliance with Corcyra in 375.[26] Thus, Parker believes that the cult celebrated victory more than peace – much as the closing of the temple of Janus symbolized Roman victories as much as a state of peace.[27] It is possible that Athenian victories meant that the first few years of the official

---

[16] It may also be significant that, in a fable related by Theopompus, an idealized city of peace is named the Pious City (Theopompus *FGrH* 115 F 75C [Aelian, *VH* 3.28.4]).

[17] Raaflaub 2007b: 14. See also Stafford 2000: 173–97 for a full treatment of the cult of Peace.

[18] Simon 1986: 700 on Ar. *Pax* 974; Shapiro 1993: 45, 50.

[19] Parker 1996: 229 on Eur. *Bacch.* 419–20; Nauck 1889: fr. 462.   [20] Parker 1996: 229 n. 44.

[21] Boardman 1995: pl. 24 with caption.   [22] Shapiro 1993: 50.

[23] Rosivach 1994: 50–3.   [24] Rosivach 1994: 156–7 for price of oxhides.

[25] Parker 1996: 230; accepted by Raaflaub 2007b: 14. Contrast Parke 1977: 32.

[26] This is the consensus of most scholars and is implied both by Isocrates' description (15.109–10) and a notice in Didymus' commentary on Demosthenes' *Fourth Philippic* (col. 7, lines 65–71 in Harding 2006: 68–9). See Harding 2006: 185; cf. Munn 2006: 346–9.

[27] See DeBrohun 2007 for a recent treatment of the gates of the temple of Janus.

cult's existence were colored by joy at a "glorious peace." But as a full explanation of the cult of Peace, Parker's argument is *a priori* implausible and not supported by the evidence.

First, the Athenians had plenty of ways of celebrating victories and the generals who earned them; in this case, Parker notes that "a new Gold Victory, the first of the century, appears in the inventories of the Treasurers of Athena in 374/3."[28] Aeschines mentions that Timotheus was honored by a statue.[29] These were traditional and sufficient memorials of military success. With individual and Nike statues available, why celebrate military victory with a different goddess, Peace, holding a child, Wealth? And how is the cornucopia a military symbol?

Second, the source Parker prefers, Isocrates, is not "the most reliable one," but a biased witness when it comes to Timotheus. Isocrates says that Timotheus:

> won a naval battle over the Lacedaemonians and forced them to agree to the terms of the present peace – a peace that so changed the relative positions of Athens and of Lacedaemon that from that day to this we celebrate the peace with sacrifices every year because no other treaty has been so advantageous to the city.[30]

This passage comes within an extensive section of Isocrates' *Antidosis* (101–39), long-winded even for him, devoted to praising to the skies his friend and student Timotheus. In such a context we can expect Isocrates to exaggerate as much as he could any achievement of Timotheus.

In fact, the Persian king initiated the peace treaty of 375, perhaps since he wanted Greece to be at peace so he could recruit mercenaries there more easily.[31] This seems to have given the Panhellenist Isocrates no pause. More troubling, Xenophon's account – like that of Philochorus – stresses the difficulties of the Athenians, which led to their desire to make peace with Sparta: the Thebans were growing more powerful and not contributing money to the war effort, while the Athenians "were themselves being worn out by extraordinary taxes, by plundering expeditions from Aegina, and by guarding their territory."[32] We may, with some scholars, reject the evidence of Xenophon, and infer that the Peace of 375–373 was at the time considered glorious and not just a relief from a difficult war.[33] That occasion cannot,

---

[28] Parker 1996: 230.

[29] Aeschin. 3.243; the victory at Alyzeia may also have been commemorated by a statue group at Delphi (Jehne 1994: 64 n. 94).

[30] Isoc. 15.109–10; see also Philochorus in *FGrH* 328 F 151.   [31] Ryder 1965: 125 on Diod. 15.38.

[32] Xen. *Hell.* 6.2.1; Philochorus in Didymus, *On Demosthenes* col. 7, lines 66–70 with Harding 2006: 184.

[33] See Cawkwell 1963d.

however, provide a full explanation for the cult of a goddess, who was already well attested in the previous century. And later, when around 353 in the *Antidosis*, Isocrates attributed the large annual festival of Peace with a two-year treaty obtained by Timotheus twenty years earlier, he was probably stretching his readers' credulity for the sake of praising Timotheus. After all, the battles of Leuctra and Mantinea and the Social War – not to mention Sparta's loss of Messenia – had intervened, so Sparta's position vis-à-vis Athens could not plausibly be attributed to Timotheus' victory in 375.

Finally the recent and more positive dating of an Athenian inscription seems to reveal the lavish endowment of a state festival of Peace – either a new festival or a Lycurgan revival – in the period from 345 to 320 and probably in 335/4.[34] By this time, more than forty years had passed; it is hard to believe the cult of Peace was still about an old and short-lived treaty of 375 and not really about peace. Nor can this revival have celebrated another "glorious peace"; none of the peace treaties Athens obtained during this period were anything but humiliating: the Peace of Philocrates, the peace after defeat at Chaeronea, and that after defeat in the Lamian War. The basic idea behind the cult was a general and large-scale celebration of the blessings of peace, among which wealth played a great part.[35]

The cult of Peace strongly suggests a preference – all things being equal – for peace instead of war. All this is very far from pacifism, but it is a preference that seems to be confirmed by a fourth-century diplomatic innovation. Beginning with the King's Peace of 387/6, a series of Common Peace treaties attempted to institute peace, not only between the antagonists in a single war, but throughout the whole of Greece.[36] They typically established a state of peace without the time limits of previous peace treaties.[37] So too the use of *eirēnē*, "peace," for a treaty has been interpreted as implying a higher goal than the vocabulary used before: *horkoi, synthēkai, spondai.*[38] As T. T. B. Ryder has argued, "people were thinking more widely than before that peace was the right state of affairs."[39]

Several speakers in the works of historians argue explicitly that war should only be embarked upon when necessary. In Herodotus, Croesus blames Apollo for encouraging him to go to war with Cyrus: for otherwise, "No one is fool enough to choose war instead of peace . . . "[40] A similar

---

[34] Sosin 2004: 2 n. 3 cites Steven Tracy's identification of the cutter for the range of dates (345–320) and argues for 335/4 (7–8). This evidence rules out the peace of 375/4 (Robert 1977: 211 on Roussel).

[35] See pp. 31–3.   [36] Ryder 1965: xvi; Jehne 1994: 42.

[37] Alonzo 2007: 223 n. 37 points out that states did not automatically lapse into a state of war after the expiration of a *spondai* of limited duration.

[38] Ryder 1965: xv, 5–6 and Alonzo 2007: 209 accept this pivotal finding of Keil 1916.

[39] Ryder 1965: 6; see also Alonzo 2007: 221, 223 n. 37.   [40] Hdt. 1.87.4.

formulation occurs in Thucydides, where Pericles says that "going to war is great folly for those whose general good fortune gives them a choice."[41] So, too, Hermocrates refers to the contrast between war and peace to the latter's advantage as a familiar commonplace:

Regarding war and how terrible it is, why should anyone rehearse everything it involves in a long speech among men who know this? For no one is forced into it out of ignorance any more than he is deterred by fear if he believes he will gain an advantage.[42]

This passage comes in the context of a speech advocating a peace treaty. But Thucydidean speakers, whether for or against a particular war, admit the general superiority of peace.[43] A speaker in Xenophon adds that wise men do not undertake war over small differences, but only over important matters.[44]

To turn to the oratorical evidence, speakers in the assembly did not always confine themselves to the specific and concrete aspects of the war at hand or in prospect. In preparing his attack on Aeschines for his conduct in the negotiations leading up to the Peace of Philocrates, Demosthenes anticipates that Aeschines will invoke the blessings of peace as part of his defense.[45] He claims that Aeschines is going to try to divert attention from the real issue of his bribe-taking by speaking about the blessings of peace:

[H]e'll recount all the benefits that accrue to mankind from peace, and on the other hand the evils from war, and in general he'll sing the praises of peace; that's the sort of defence he'll make.[46]

Demosthenes does not even try to counter the praise of peace in general. He concedes this point, but denies its relevance to Aeschines' case. So too, in the *Fourth Philippic* and *On the Chersonese*, Demosthenes objects to Philip's partisans, who, he claims, stand up and praise peace:

But whenever any question arises that concerns Philip, instantly up jumps someone and says there must be no nonsense talked, no declaration of war, and he at once goes on to add how good a thing it is to preserve peace, and what a bother it is to keep up a large army, and how "certain persons want to plunder your wealth" . . .[47]

---

[41] Thuc. 2.61.1.   [42] Thuc. 4.59.2; see also Hdt. 1.87. See also Hajdú 2002: 375.

[43] Thuc. 1.120.3–4; 2.61.1; 4.20.2, 62.2.   [44] Xen. *Hell.* 6.3.5.

[45] MacDowell 2000: 246 notes that Aeschines does not actually make this argument but concedes that Aeschines' historical survey of the results for Athens of war and peace (Aeschin. 2.172–7) – largely copied from Andocides – might be construed as praise of peace. See also Isoc. 5.7.

[46] Dem. 19.88. See also Dem. 19.92, 95, 151, 328, 336.

[47] Dem. 8.52. See also Dem. 10.60.

Here Demosthenes counters the argument, "how good a thing it is to preserve peace" by connecting it with a selfish concern with money – we have seen that he often connects opposition to war with materialism.[48] He regards the non-specific praise of peace to be an argument worth rebutting and, even more telling, does not try to counter it directly. But rather he goes on to argue that peace was not possible, given Philip's aggression.

Demosthenes' concern with general arguments against war would seem to have been justified. A host of oratorical passages mention sundry bad effects of war or good effects of peace. These evils of war seem to be largely bad effects on Athens. Thus these general criticisms of war strike us as largely self-interested. For example, as we have seen, war was and was known to be expensive.[49] Andocides and Aeschines also claim that war can lead to the overthrow of the democracy.[50] Aeschines emphasizes that the losses incurred in war have allowed inferior foreigners to become citizens.[51] Thucydides already assumes that the possibilities for corruption were greater during wartime; conversely Aeschines argues that "peace does not feed laziness."[52] Most striking, Aeschines and Andocides place a great deal of weight on a paradoxical advantage of peace. It allowed Athens to gather military resources: to build more triremes, to build up its walls, and to amass money in the treasury, money whose main use was to finance wars.[53] The best one can do with this argument is to assume that Andocides and Aeschines thought that military resources could be squandered needlessly or used wisely in a necessary war – and thus they were being squandered in the war under discussion. Demosthenes provides confirmation: he decries the fact that "natural anger you would feel at any sufferings in the war" might be directed against "your wisest counselors" rather than at Philip.[54] Again, the anger aroused by the evils of war is a matter of suffering experienced, not a moral qualm. This impression that the concern with the evils of war was largely self-interested is exacerbated by a passage from the *Rhetoric to Alexander*, which lists the arguments to be advanced to dissuade the people from going to war. Among them is the tack that "we must show that it is not expedient to go to war, dwelling on the disasters that befall men in warfare . . . "[55] The evils of war in general were an important weapon for orators arguing against wars. Individual wars may

---

[48] See p. 32.   [49] See pp. 31–5.
[50] Andoc. 3.1–12, esp. 12; Aeschin. 2.177 (based on Andocides). See also Isoc. 8.51, cf. 8.104 (war destroyed the democracy); 8.88–9 (foreigners become citizens).
[51] Aeschin. 2.173, 177 connects lack of citizenship to enthusiasm for war.
[52] Thuc. 5.16.1; Aeschin. 2.161.   [53] Andoc. 3.5, 7, 8–9; Aeschin. 2.173–5.   [54] Dem. 8.56–7.
[55] [Arist.] *Rh. Al.* 1425a28–34. Even Demosthenes sometimes concedes that peace is in Athens' interest (Dem. 5.24–5).

be judged immoral for any number of reasons, as we have seen, but the general evils of war were usually subsumed in the category of expedience and did not count as moral objections.

For an orator to worry about the harm wrought by war on a prospective enemy seems to have required a broader sympathy than the Athenians were willing to entertain while deliberating about foreign policy in the assembly. If we spread our net more widely and consider the negative depictions of war throughout Greek literature, collected by scholars such as Caldwell, Nestle, and Zampaglione, we frequently find a consciousness of the harm war inflicts on both sides.[56] For example, when Herodotus has Croesus claim that only fools prefer war to peace since in war fathers bury their sons, he seems concerned with an effect of war that affects all sides.[57] Such a concern is not usefully contrasted with moral principle; rather the concern for the harm caused by war provides a basis for the moral condemnation of war.[58]

From this sort of evidence some scholars have reasonably concluded that the Greeks considered war a "painful necessity" and only resorted to it when there were "compelling circumstances."[59] The devil, of course, is in the details: just what are compelling circumstances? How strong is the sense that war is indeed "painful" and thus should be a last resort? Hans van Wees, for example, is cynical: despite a frequent insistence on the superiority of peace,

it usually did not take much to convince a Greek community that it was right and necessary to make war, however disagreeable, in order to avoid harm or wipe out shame.[60]

The Panhellenic ideal, which was explored above, came closest to providing a compelling moral argument against war.[61] Isocrates consistently decried wars among Greeks. Plato's diatribe against such wars comes closest to a moral objection that would provide a compelling argument against war rather than merely one consideration to be weighed in the balance.[62] For most people and states, the argument from Panhellenism was manifestly less than compelling. In addition, such a condemnation only applied to

---

[56] There are passages from philosophers, especially Hellenistic philosophers, that seem to preclude any recourse to war, but they typically are only preserved in fragmentary form and do not allow us to reconstruct their basis or implications. For example, Zeno of Citium condemned the state, believed in the unity of humanity, and considered weapons to be useless (Nestle 1938: 39–40).

[57] Hdt. 1.87.   [58] Walzer 1977: 21–33.   [59] Zampaglione 1973: 18; Karavites 1984: 165.

[60] Van Wees 2004: 3. Compare E. H. Carr, who cites Lenin with approval: "Absolutely everybody is in favour of peace in general" (1946: 52); see also Blainey 1973: 135.

[61] Pp. 78–80.   [62] Pl. *Resp.* 5.470c–d, 471a–b.

wars among Greeks. Isocrates, in particular, is quite enthusiastic about the prospect of a war against Persia and perfectly happy to praise the warriors of the Persian War. He can praise even the aggressive exploits of Timotheus – whose successes came against other Greeks.

Except within the limited parameters of Panhellenism, the evils of war did not provide a compelling argument for peace. Today just-war theory is subject to criticism on two sides: both Realist objections, "justice is irrelevant," and pacifist objections, "wars can never be just."[63] Ancient justifications of war were subject to Realist unmasking, but not to the argument that the moral objections or general disadvantages of war were compelling. The argument that all wars were bad and should be avoided if possible was a plausible one; the notion lacks the moral absolutism and the compelling force of modern pacifist criticisms.

Part of this difference comes from the fact that the recourse to war was often considered the more moral decision – if, for example, an ally had been attacked. Another important factor pertains to the modern category of innocents, which often carries much of the weight of the pacifist critique: so many people are innocent and will be harmed by any war that "war itself turns out to be illicit and the just war theory collapses into pacifism."[64] There are hints of a concern for innocents in ancient Greece: Thucydides reports that the Athenians felt that they were doing wrong to punish all the Mytilenians and not just the ones responsible for the revolt; the suffering of women and children is highlighted in Euripides' *Troades* – indeed already Homer could portray it with great sympathy.[65] Such compassion and concern seem mainly to have influenced feelings about the conduct of war rather than the recourse to war; to use modern terms, concern for innocents was a matter of *jus in bello* rather than *jus ad bellum*. Some modern pacifists deliberately elide the distinction between the two classes of moral judgment: as long as wars are conducted with long-range weapons – tanks, artillery, machine guns, bombs, and missiles – in inhabited countrysides, civilian deaths are an expected and inevitable result.

Ancient war could be as brutal as modern when cities were attacked. Sieges have always been particularly hard on civilians[66]; the capture of a city could lead to the execution of the adult males and the enslavement of the

---

[63] The Realist objections have been treated above, pp. 154–9. See Wells 1969: 828; Santoni 1991; Ceadel 1996: 22 for pacifist attacks on just-war theory. See Greenwood 1991 for a specific rebuttal. See Walzer 1977 for the most influential and coherent defense of modern just-war theory; cf. Walzer 2004.

[64] Teichman 1986: 63.   [65] Thuc. 3.36.4; Hom. *Il.* 6.450–65, *Od.* 8.523–31.   [66] Walzer 1977: 160.

rest of the population. Such situations were the ones that evoked ancient concerns about the suffering of the innocent. But most wars did not result in such complete destruction of one of the antagonists.[67] And it could rarely have been anticipated that the result of a classical war would be so decisive. So the most common and profound effects of many classical wars were on the combatants. And, at Athens at least, many of these combatants had actively participated in the decisions that led to the war.[68] The recourse to war, in general, presented less of a moral issue than it does today, when wars always involve civilian casualties and when soldiers are conscripted to fight wars about whose causes and justification they know little and for which they cannot be held responsible.[69]

INDIVIDUALIST, FAMILIAL, AND COMMUNAL
CRITIQUES OF WAR

Athenian criticisms of war could originate from the viewpoint of an individual, of a family, or of the whole community. But the militarism of Athenian culture made it hard for individual and family critiques to gain much footing in a public forum. Although modern critics of war tend to think of militarism mainly as the celebration of killing, it also glorifies self-sacrifice for the community.[70] The critique of warfare in terms of its effect on the individual always risks appearing selfish, materialistic, and ignoble when compared with the altruistic willingness to die for the community.

The individualist critique is best exemplified in the *Acharnians* of Aristophanes. Dikaiopolis' fervent condemnation of the Peloponnesian War seems to derive very largely from selfish and individualistic interests: he wants imported food and to enjoy rural festivals on his farm instead of having to flee to the city, live among the garbage, and be drafted.[71] These complaints are no doubt real enough and important; they also make for good comedy.[72] The vivid depiction of the horrors of war in individual

---

[67] Hansen and Nielsen 2004: 120–3.

[68] But see Hunt 1998: esp. 83–101 for the participation of slaves in the Athenian military. Metics, who lacked political rights, could also be drafted, but they were not forced to stay in Athens and, in fact, many probably left when there was a threatening war. The mercenaries who fought for Athens would at least have made a free decision to do so – except insofar as they were compelled to become mercenaries out of poverty (Ducrey 1971).

[69] Walzer 1977: 34–41.   [70] Ehrenreich 1997.

[71] In contrast, the criticisms expressed in *Lysistrata* tend more to derive from Panhellenism: Lysistrata berates the Greek for fighting each other although they are all kindred and the Persians, the real enemy, are threatening (Ar. *Lys.* 1129–36).

[72] A modern parallel would be Joseph Heller's *Catch-22*, an often comic presentation of the horrors of war from the point of view of individual airmen without any serious criticisms of the justice of World War Two (Heller 1994).

terms is a mainstay of the irenic strain in modern Western culture. For example, virtually a whole genre of movies ranging from *All's Quiet on the Western Front* to *Paths of Glory* to *Born on the Fourth of July* and *Letters from Iwo Jima* focus on the plight of individuals in war and give little attention to the justice of the wars depicted. But the community ethos at Athens was too strong for such complaints to gain much of a political footing.[73] The common good was always supposed to be paramount. Thus, Andocides, Aeschines, and Isocrates can argue that peace is advantageous since it fills the public treasury; but Demosthenes has the upper hand when he lambastes individual Athenians for caring more about their private wealth than the position of Athens in the Greek world.[74] In Pericles' funeral oration, soldiers are depicted as valuing their honor and good name and the audience is urged to fall in love with Athens. Their devotion is contrasted with selfish and materialistic reasons to keep living, for example "the poor man's hope that he might still escape poverty and grow rich."[75] Even orators arguing for peace generally accept this communitarian bias; they occasionally succeed in setting the benefit of peace for the community against the selfish interests of those who stood to gain from war.[76]

Somewhat more compelling and common was criticism from the point of view of the effect of war on families. In epic and tragedy neither heroes nor poets are much concerned with the death or suffering of combatants in war. That is what men and warriors should be able to endure. They focus on and emphasize the effects of these deaths on the families of war casualties. In comedy, to take a famous example, the women of Aristophanes' *Lysistrata* are motivated to end the war to get their husbands back. The sexual aspect of their motivation obviously serves comic purposes, but the bonds of children and parent are also emphasized in the portrayals of the goddess Peace. It is natural enough that, just as war was exclusively the prerogative of men, peace should be a woman. The typical representation of peace as a woman with a child may also present a second message.[77] In peace, families can stay together. Mothers are not threatened with rape nor their children with slavery – nor will they grow up to leave for war and not come back.

In a similar fashion, Aeschines condemns the belligerent policies of Demosthenes, which he claims were due to the bribes from the Persian king. These policies led to the sacking of Thebes by Macedon. Aeschines asks his audience to picture the scene:

---

[73] Garlan 1975: 17 argues that peace later gained a positive value, but one connected with individualism and with withdrawal from civic values.
[74] See the passages collected above, p. 32.   [75] Thuc. 2.42.4.
[76] Isoc. 5.73.   [77] E.g. *LIMC* Eirene 6 and 8.

[I]magine that you see their city taken, the razing of their walls, the burning of their homes; their women and children led into captivity; their old men, their aged matrons, late in life learning to forget what freedom means; weeping supplicating you, angry not so much at those who are taking vengeance upon them, as at the men who are responsible for it all; and calling on you by no means to crown the curse of Hellas [Demosthenes] . . . "[78]

Naturally enough, Demosthenes' disastrous intransigence is represented as the result of bribe-taking rather than of manly assertiveness.

Isocrates claims that imperialistic policies, in particular the continuation of the Social War, could only be favored by "some utterly abandoned wretch who cared not for sacred matters nor for parents nor for children nor for any other thing save for the term of his own existence."[79] According to Isocrates, fifth-century imperialism had led to cruel acts such as the tearing of children away from their parents and, for the Athenians, a siege during which children could not be properly brought up.[80] Isocrates condemns the cost to families of aggressive policies.

These arguments or advantages of peace only rarely appeared in actual assembly speeches. The values derived from gender relations served usually to encourage war, just as some historical accounts relate: "women encouraging their men to be more warlike, not less so."[81] The difficulties facing the individual and familial critiques of war help to explain what seems to us the rather impoverished descriptions of the disadvantages of war we find in Andocides and Aeschines: they were largely confined to finding communal losses: triremes and money lost, the overthrow of the democracy. The death, maiming, and grief of individuals were regarded as selfish and ignoble concerns.

THE ELIMINATION OF WAR?

Another contrast with modern thinking is the absence in antiquity of a utopian hope that war could be eliminated altogether. Arnaldo Momigliano made the case that among ancient Greeks war was considered a "natural fact like birth and death about which nothing could be done: and thus they were "interested in causes of wars not in the causes of war as such."[82]

---

[78] Aeschin. 3.157; cf. Dem. 18.41.   [79] Isoc. 8.93.

[80] Isoc. 8.93. See also pp. 130, 263 on Isoc. 8.82. Compare [Dem.] 11.9, possibly a composition by Anaximenes (Sealey 1993: 239).

[81] Schaps 1982; see also Loman 2004.

[82] Momigliano 1966: 120. Similar views are expressed in Murray 1944: 5; Dover 1974: 315; Garlan 1975: 18; M. Finley 1985b: 68; Croally 1994: 51; Ostwald 1996: 103. Momigliano's conclusion about historical treatments of war is best rebutted by Cobet 1986.

Classical Greeks seem usually to have assumed that there would always be wars and, in that sense, wars were natural. That belief is still common among observers today.[83] For example, the hopes for a "new world order" after the Cold War were criticized at the time and, unfortunately, seem to have been exaggerated.[84] Nevertheless, since the Enlightenment there has also emerged an influential belief that war can be eliminated as a way of resolving conflicts.[85] This view seems to have been lacking from the world of the Greeks. Only in their notions of the mythical past did the Greeks even imagine the elimination of all wars.[86]

On the other hand, the Greeks had a strong medical tradition and, though they did not think that they would eliminate death, their doctors tried industriously to prevent as many deaths as they could. Indeed, Nestle adduces several passages that show that war itself was considered sick and unnatural and peace the normal and healthy state of affairs.[87] Although Michael Howard argues that it was only with the Enlightenment that the view of war as unnatural became dominant, this attitude was not without precedent in classical Athens.[88]

In modern times the view that war is natural is associated with militarism and suspected of making leaders more likely to go to war. William Sumner parodied this argument: politicians claim " 'War is necessary' as if to conclude, 'so let's have a little war now.' "[89] The force of several ancient passages is the opposite. Hermocrates admits that "[W]e will go to war when it suits us, I suppose, and come to terms among ourselves again, no doubt . . . "; but he does this in the context of a speech urging the Sicilian cities to make peace to preclude the threat of Athenian interference.[90] Speakers in Xenophon also admit the likelihood of future wars and even that the gods send war to mankind, but they use this as an argument for making peace right away:

We all know that wars are forever breaking out and being concluded . . . why should we wait for the time when we shall have become exhausted by a multitude of ills and not rather conclude peace as quickly as possible"[91]

---

[83] Nestle 1938: 76; Russell 1951: 151; Ostwald 1996: 102.

[84] E.g. Kissinger 1994: 804–36; Brzezinski 2007.

[85] See the excellent treatment of Howard 2000: esp. 2, 7, 25–7.

[86] A warless world, like a slaveless society or the rule of women, was relegated to a place outside history; cf. Vidal-Naquet 1986a and Theopompus (*FGrH* 115 F 75C [Aelian, *VH* 3.18.4]).

[87] Nestle 1938: 17–18, 75 onwards, e.g., Hdt. 1.87. See also Polyb. 12.25–6.   [88] Howard 2000: 25–7.

[89] Sumner 1964: 205.   [90] Thuc. 4.64.3.

[91] Xen. *Hell.* 6.3.15–16; see the similar argument at 6.3.6.

The concession that wars are inevitable was not a council of despair and fatalism but rather seemed designed to encourage actions to minimize their deleterious effect. Modern parallels are not hard to find; the utopian hope for war's elimination may be the most inspiring, but it is not the only strain of opposition to war. Bertrand Russell, for example, made an argument similar to the ancient ones: "no peace can ensure against war in another generation, so let's make a peace now which is likely to last a while."[92] So again we find a partial distinction between ancient and modern thinking, but not one that shows the Greeks as fatalistic lovers of war.

CRITICS OF MILITARISM

Modern objections to war have tended to grow in a mutually reinforcing relationship with criticisms of the high value placed on military service and prowess.[93] As important as explicit criticism of war has been the rise of competing values in the contemporary world: for example, Joseph Schumpeter has argued for a basic opposition between the atavistic, warrior ethos driving imperialism – close to what I have been calling militarism – and the civil values fostered by capitalism.[94] In contrast, ancient criticisms of war were limited by the fact that the Athenians viewed "war as a supreme human activity and the standard by which human achievement was measured."[95] Even the authors and works most critical of war reserve their highest praise for the warrior, who preserves the community with his skill and bravery at great personal risk.[96] Ancient valorization of military service was close to unanimous. Within the realm of mainstream political debate – that is, what could be said within the assembly or before a jury – we find no critique.

A few intellectuals did criticize the prioritization of military virtues. For example, Plato criticized Sparta's emphasis on military success as a measure of their political system by bringing in the example of mercenaries: they may fight with great skill and even to the death, but almost all of them are "heedless, unjust, violent and stupid."[97] Plato argues for the priority of

---

[92] Russell 1916: 122.
[93] E.g. Russell 1916: 36, 55, 63, 65; see also 36; Woodrow Wilson quoted in Knock 1992: 59.
[94] Schumpeter 1951: 83–97; e.g. Russell 1916: 51.
[95] Croally 1994: 119; see also 50. This has long been noticed, e.g. by Havelock 1972; Dover 1974: 314; Garlan 1975: 60.
[96] See Croally 1994: 131 on Eur. *Tro.* and Nestle 1938: 20–1 on Euripides in general and Nestle 1938: 27 on Aristophanes.
[97] Pl. *Leg.* 1.630b. See also Isoc. 12.186, 198.

peaceful pursuits and that men should spend most of the time at peace.[98] Aristotle directly criticizes Sparta for its excessive and unbalanced focus on inculcating the military virtues.[99] He also argues that "war must be for the sake of peace" and classes it among the necessary things rather than the noble ones.[100] Constitutions that have as their main goal efficiency at war naturally earn his condemnation.[101] Both Plato and Aristotle also make the obvious rejoinders to the notion that military victory reveals the superiority of one state over another: what about big cities that defeat smaller ones in an unjust war?[102] Nonetheless, both of their ideal states connect military function and political rights. Most conspicuously in Plato's *Republic* the need for professional soldiers motivates the creation of the guardian class.[103]

Less controversial were judgments that, while not downplaying or under-mining the glory accorded to self-sacrifice or prowess, stressed the impor-tance of activities and values other than war and militarism. So Aeschines insists that the peace-making efforts of ambassadors deserve the same praise as the victories gained by generals – a view that finds parallels.[104] This self-serving claim is actually reflected in a larger political trend: the domination of political leadership by men who had been generals was far less marked in the fourth century than in the fifth century.[105] Leadership in war was no longer the predominant avenue to political prominence; men could advance because of their speaking ability and the success of the policies they advocated. Demosthenes provides an obvious example: his rise was due to his eloquence and his policies rather than his military career.[106]

This trend provides some evidence for a reduced emphasis on military virtues in the fourth century. And until recently most scholars believed that fourth-century Athens had become less militaristic – that many of them

---

[98] Pl. *Leg.* 7.803d. See also Zampaglione 1973: 60 on Aristotle's similar views.

[99] Arist. *Pol.* 7.1333b10–31 with Zampaglione 1973: 63.

[100] Arist. *Pol.* 7.1333a31–7. See also 7.1334a4–6. Schütrumpf 1991–2005: IV.186 ad 1333a 35 cites parallels in the *Nicomachaean Ethics* and in Plato's *Laws*.

[101] Arist. *Pol.* 7.1324a5–1325a15.

[102] Pl. *Leg.* 1.638a–b; Arist. *Pol.* 1.1255a11–28. Other passages critical of militarism in Plato and Aristotle are collected in Kraut 2002: 10 n. 13.

[103] See Vidal-Naquet 1986b on the role of the military in Plato and Aristotle.

[104] Aeschin. 2.79–80, 183; cf. 2.37. See also Lycurg. fr. A.1 in Burtt 1954; Xen. *Hell.* 6.3.4; Lys. 12.38.

[105] Plut. *Phoc.* 7.5–6, Arist. *Pol.* 5.1305a8–15, and Isoc. 8.54–5 provide the basis for the traditional view that the fifth-century unity of political and military leadership had broken down by the fourth century. Although Tritle 1992a has found exceptions to this generalization, Hamel 1995: esp. 30–1 has shown that a smaller proportion of Athens' leadership in the fourth century is also known to have served as generals and thus has confirmed the ancient generalization if not the rhetorical and exaggerated terms in which it was stated. See also R. Knox 1989: 80 for criticisms of Tritle.

[106] The role of his eloquence is obvious, but Demosthenes was proud of the content of his policy: not just the opposition to Philip, but his reform of naval funding (18.102–8).

considered this a sign of decadence and a lack of patriotism incidentally highlights a modern perspective far from pacifism.[107] Already the contemporary historian Theopompus condemned the decadence of an Athens in which the money that ought to have been used to pay soldiers was distributed to the people to celebrate their festivals lavishly; modern scholars have sometimes concurred with this judgment.[108] When it came to war, the Athenians are supposed to have preferred to remain at home and employ mercenaries to fight for them. This picture has, however, been attacked on several grounds.

First, the surviving speeches of Demosthenes dominate our evidence, but their goal, to incite Athens to war, makes them unreliable as evidence. From our earliest evidence Greek war rhetoric consistently included abuse of the audience as "lax in the face of a military threat."[109] The continuation of this motif in Demosthenes tells us little about the fourth century. The retrospective speech *On the Crown* confirms that Demosthenes' emphasis on Athenian apathy is determined by his goal of urging Athens to war. *On the Crown* does not have the goal of goading the Athenians to go to war but rather describes the period when they had come to that decision. It consequently depicts the Athenians as brave and enthusiastic warriors.[110] Furthermore, if one believes that the wars Demosthenes advocated were stupid and unnecessary ones then no conclusions can be drawn about the moral fiber of his audience – whom he represents as apathetic and unwilling to serve in person – other than that they did not want to fight stupid and unnecessary wars.[111] In other ways too our surviving evidence can present a distorted contrast between the fifth and fourth centuries. Thucydides generalizes about Athenian enthusiasm and activity, but, for the fourth century we also possess law-court speeches, which necessarily involve misbehavior. For example, Apollodorus' *Against Polycles* and Demosthenes' *On the Trierarchic Crown* highlight trierarchs quarreling over their monetary obligations and represent the crews as deserting or incompetent. The comparison of such speeches with – to take an extreme but famous example – Pericles' funeral oration in Thucydides, with its fulsome praise of Athenian

---

[107] See the references in Burckhardt 1996: 11–13 and recently Samons 2004: 143–62, esp. 154.

[108] Theopompus (*FGrH* 115 F 213) with Shrimpton 1991: 170. See also Justin's *Epit.* 6.9, probably based on Theopompus (Develin 1994: 74 n. 10) and Harpokration s.v. Eubulus and Libanius' Hypothesis to Dem. 1 in Ruschenbusch 1979: 304–5. Buchanan 1962: 56 and Samons 2004: 152–3 agree with Theopompus.

[109] Carey 2005: 77 n. 24.   [110] E.g. Dem. 18.215–16, 289, 306.

[111] Demosthenes often mentions the unwillingness of the Athenians to serve in person and their unpatriotic apathy, e.g. 3.3–5, 8–9, 16, 29; 4.19, 21, 25–7; 6.27; 8.11–12, 21–3; 9.4–5, 35–6; 10.2–3, 69; *Exordia* 21.2, 41.2.

patriotism and willingness to die for country, gives a misleading impression. It taxes credulity to think that no trierarchs misbehaved or crews deserted in the fifth century; it is simply that law-court speeches have not survived from that period.[112] If we compare like with like and look at the fourth-century funeral orations of Hyperides and Demosthenes, we see that these portray the Athenians as equally patriotic and brave as their fifth-century ancestors.[113]

Second, Leonhard Burckhardt has argued persuasively and in great detail that military service and prowess continued to play an important part in the constellation of Athenian values and that the ideal of the citizen soldier persisted throughout our period.[114] My tabulation of claims of military service in the extant law-court speeches is consistent with this finding.[115] The more often litigants mention military service and the more weight they place on it, the more can we infer that such service was an important part of being a good Athenian.[116] The frequency of claims of service in law-court speeches suggests that the military virtues remained important. Three-quarters of the speeches that make claims of service in every period mention military service – the numbers are too small to be any more precise than that.

Third, when they had to, the Athenians did march out to fight. Phillip Harding points out that the Athenian hoplites went out en masse to fight at Nemea (394), Mantinea (362), Chaeronea (338), and Crannon (322).[117] The Athenians mainly employed mercenaries for distant campaigns and garrison duty or those with special skills the Athenians lacked – or as a necessary supplement to the city's full levy as in the campaign before Chaeronea or in the Lamian War.[118] Mixed crews of citizens, metics, foreigners, and slaves manned the navy throughout the classical period, in the fifth century as well as the fourth.[119]

Despite all these counter-arguments, I find a decline in enthusiasm for war in the fourth century plausible: reducing to subjection an island in the fifth-century empire with a navy paid for by tribute was not the same as paying out of your own pocket and then fighting a defensive war against the

---

[112] For example, some sort of abuse provided the motivation for the regulations about trireme crews in *IG* i³ 153, dated 440–425.

[113] Dem. 60.1, 17–20, 26, 32–34; Hyp. 6.1–2.3, 8, 15–19, 23–34, 42–3. Demosthenes mentions cowardice and slackness among the Greeks, but his point is that the Athenians, who are not included in this condemnation, did not hold this against the other Greeks but fought bravely on their behalf (60.18).

[114] Burckhardt 1996: 154–256.   [115] See Appendix 3: Claims of service.

[116] Cf. Roisman 2005: 129.   [117] Harding 1995: 111. See also Burckhardt 1996: 77.

[118] Burckhardt 1996: 139.   [119] Hunt 1998: 83–101.

formidable Macedonian army.[120] But this seems more a matter of practical circumstances rather than a shift in basic values. Insofar as my emphasis on the interstate roots of militarism is correct, the high value placed on military service and prowess was unlikely to change until Athens felt either unthreatened or impotent – as perhaps it did in the Hellenistic period.

INTELLECTUALS AND POLITICIANS

When we consider the spectrum of views about war and peace in the ancient and contemporary world, we need to specify whose views they were and in which context they were expressed. The dichotomies of Finley and Green fail largely because they are comparing apples and oranges, the ideals of some modern intellectuals and the public statements of active politicians in Athens. To flesh out the full spectrum of possible Athenian beliefs, I have been canvassing any and all opinions on war and peace rather than sticking to the public oratory that reveals mainstream opinion. But our understanding of this spectrum will be clarified by the contrast between two groups of people, politicians and intellectuals, and thus two types of sources, written tracts and assembly speeches.

Four intellectuals, Plato, Aristotle, Xenophon, and Isocrates, expressed the most explicit and searching criticisms of war and of militarism. Although we noted that even these thinkers were not consistent and did not come close to modern pacifism, they did maintain a degree of independence from popular views. Plato, in particular, was willing to go where his argument led regardless of conventional opinion: the elimination of property and the family in the *Republic* and his insistence that it was better to suffer than to commit injustice are cases in point. Aristotle, Xenophon, and Isocrates were less eccentric in their beliefs; however, these tended not to reflect popular conceptions, but rather the opinions of the rich, educated, and respectable. All four wrote to be read. They anticipated a readership, literate and leisured, rather than an audience, the common people in the assembly or the courts. As we have seen, the rich were more likely to oppose wars. They also had less of a stake in a militaristic basis for social status, since their own positions were justified in a variety of ways: the possession of money, superior education and culture, birth into prominent families.

While both ancient and modern critics of war and militarism came disproportionately from the ranks of the intelligentsia, we find also a contrast. From the beginning of the twentieth century, pacifism has been

---

[120] Hunt 1998: 198.

overwhelmingly a left-wing idea in contemporary society: for example, Zampaglione argues that "if wars were removed, fundamental changes in social priorities would threaten the 'establishment.' "[121] But the ancient critics of war tended to be anti-democratic to a greater or lesser extent. All four made fundamental criticisms of a democratic society such as Athens, which had no property qualification for citizenship and gave an equal vote to the poorest illiterate, the richest sophisticate, and the wisest philosopher. They preached to an audience among the elite and nervously condemned rather than celebrated the prospect of social unrest. The Peace Societies of Victorian Britain might provide a better modern parallel to their concerns than do twentieth-century intellectuals. In these the prospect that warfare might lead to social unrest provided an important motivation for membership: one scholar claims about Victorian pacifism that it was "never a doctrine about war alone but a demand that particular class interests be preserved and protected."[122] At least as early as Thucydides' description of events at Corcyra, war was known to be an important factor exacerbating the class hatred that led to civil war.[123] The danger of stasis, civil war between the parties of the rich and poor, certainly worried Xenophon, Plato, and Aristotle; it may have played some part in their criticisms of Greek wars and militarism. With Isocrates the threat of social unrest was almost an obsession.[124] It motivated in part his criticisms of wars among Greek cities and his clarion call for a war against Persia.[125]

To turn to active politicians, some scholars have posited a party of "moderates" or even "pacifists" – in the European sense[126] – in fourth-century Athens. Jacqueline de Romilly in particular points out correspondences between the expressed views of Isocrates, Xenophon, and Aeschines and the policies of Eubulus – to whom we might also add Phocion. She argues that these men were at the center of a party of moderates, opposed to some extent to full democracy, imperialism, and war.[127] Recent scholars have made telling criticisms of this picture. To begin with, Raphael Sealey points out that neither Isocrates nor Xenophon was an active politician.[128]

---

[121] Zampaglione 1973: 6. Another significant strain in modern pacifist thinking is religious and is difficult to put on a political spectrum. See Brock 1991: 22.

[122] Sager 1980: 236; so too, Brock 1991: 22.   [123] Thuc. 3.82.1–3.

[124] Xen. *Hell.* 2.4.20–2 and 4.4.2–6 with 4.4.12; Plato, *Resp.* 8, *Leg.* 1.627b, 630a–d; Arist. *Politics* 5.

[125] Isocrates: Baynes 1955: 157–8; Fuks 1972; Shinozaki 1980. Isocrates at points is quite explicit: war leads to civil war (5.52).

[126] Mossé 1973: 55, 57 uses "pacifist."

[127] Romilly 1954: esp. 327, 332, 344. See also Mossé 1973: 32, 42, 54.

[128] Sealey 1955: 77. Other treatments of the spectrum of political opinion in mid-fourth-century Athens include Perlman 1963; Rhodes 1978; Moysey 1987; Harding 1995; Salmond 1996.

Although some of the opinions expressed by Xenophon and Isocrates may have found sympathetic ears among active orators and thus provided some portion of the intellectual atmosphere of the time, Sealey is right to contrast writers, such as Xenophon and Isocrates, with politicians. The latter were constrained by their constant need to persuade the common people of Athens and by the realities of maintaining security in a dangerous world.

When we look at the actual policies of the remaining "moderates," Eubulus, Aeschines, and Phocion, we find that none of them were antiwar in any strong sense. To begin with, two of them had distinguished military careers. Phocion was famous for having been elected general no less than forty times![129] Aeschines does not seem to have been a general, but his military service was distinguished and he was decorated for his service in Euboea.[130] Eubulus and Aeschines were sometimes opposed to distant campaigns, but they were entirely willing to use force to defend Athenian interests. For example, the opposition to Demosthenes' proposals to fight Philip in the north in the late 350s and early 340s was arguably based on a better understanding of Athens' limited resources than on any opposition to war in general.[131] Eubulus' attempts to unite southern Greece to fight against Philip can hardly be labeled pacifist and he seems to have moved other proposals against Macedon.[132] Phocion seems also to have favored Athenian campaigns in Euboea in 348, Megara in 343, and Byzantium in 340/39, hardly the policy of a quietist.[133] After war against Macedonia broke out in 340, Aeschines, Eubulus, and Phocion all "closed ranks" with Demosthenes to help Athens oppose Philip.[134]

All active Athenian politicians were willing to go to war if necessary to ensure Athens' interests or to protect its security. But just as politicians today tend to hold different views about how much "necessity" justifies a war, so too Athenian politicians and the Athenians in general differed about issues of war and peace. A variety of sources indicate that Eubulus, Aeschines, and Phocion sometimes opposed going to war or supported peace initiatives at junctures when this was the minority opinion.[135] In that

---

[129] Plut. *Phoc.* 8.2; Tritle 1988: 111–12.   [130] Aeschin. 2.167–70.

[131] Sealey 1955: 77; Cawkwell 1978a: 78–9, 81–2, 87; Ober 1991: 261; Badian 1995: 102. Contra Leopold 1987.

[132] Cawkwell 1963c: 53. Cf. Cawkwell 1960: 417 on Aeschines. Dem. 18.70, 75.

[133] Tritle 1996: 112.   [134] Tritle 1996: 6.

[135] Eubulus: presented economic arguments for accepting the Peace of Philocrates (Dem. 19.291). Aeschines: advocated the Peace of Philocrates (Dem. 19), criticized Demosthenes' intransigence in late 340s (Aeschin. 3.82–3), and favored the peace initiative before Chaeronea, which was blocked by Demosthenes (Aeschin. 3.148–51); Phocion: argued against going to war with Thebes (Plut. *Phoc.* 9; after loss of Oropus according to Tritle 1988: 98), and argued against the war with Philip that

sense, they can be described as "moderates." We do not, however, know the basis of their objections. Many factors might have inclined a citizen in the assembly or a politician to favor accommodation of Macedonia: a foreboding about the likely outcome of war, admiration of Philip's accomplishment, even a feeling that Thebes was more of an enemy than more distant Macedonians. One such factor was probably the feeling that wars should not be undertaken unless necessary and that conflict with Macedonia did not meet this criterion; this would explain why Demosthenes characterizes his opponents as praising peace and devotes so much energy to proving that war really was necessary. This is as far as we can go.

AFTER THE SOCIAL WAR

The most general criticisms of war seem to have been limited to intellectual circles and thus largely to the rich and oligarchic. They were also concentrated in time: Athens' defeat in the Social War and the secession of many of the most important allies from the Athenian League seem to have provoked disillusionment with Athens' aspirations to leadership in the Greek and had certainly impoverished the city. This period saw the publication of the two works most critical of warfare that have survived from the fourth century: Isocrates' *On the Peace* and Xenophon's *Ways and Means*. Both focus on Athens' desire for domination as the root cause of its wars.[136] In neither case can we claim that the author was a pacifist; rather both seem to believe that some wars are just and necessary and others not. What distinguishes these works are their attacks on militarism and the strong impression they leave that the "necessity" to go to war is to be defined in a stringent rather than a permissive way.

Xenophon's *Ways and Means* was probably finished in 355, after Xenophon had returned to Athens, after his long exile, and shortly before he died.[137] The work consists mainly of suggestions for improving the financial position of Athens through government intervention, for example the public purchase of slaves to work the silver mines. Xenophon makes

---

ended with Chaeronea (Plut. *Phoc.* 16); a long series of stories in Plutarch put him in opposition to aggressive or intransigent policies. Even Demosthenes deprecated war on at least three occasions: *On the Navy-Boards* was against going to war with Persia; in *On the Peace* Demosthenes opposed breaking the Peace of Philocrates; he did not think Athens should support the revolt of Agis (Aeschin. 3.133; Diod. 17.62.7, 63.1–3; Plut. *Dem.* 24.1 with Worthington 2000). Demosthenes is not considered a member of the "moderates" largely because of his position vis-à-vis Macedonia in the late 340s, a pro-war and contested one.

[136] Parallels between the two works have long been noted: Gauthier 1976: 5 n. 2.

[137] Gauthier 1976: 4–6.

it clear that the maintenance of peace is crucial to the success of the reforms he proposes:

[I]f it seems clear that the state cannot obtain a full revenue from all sources unless she had peace, is it not worth while to set up a board of guardians of peace?"[138]

Although the name and purpose of these guardians of peace is clear, their specific responsibilities are unknown – as are the duties of the "guardians of the peace" actually instituted when Athens joined the League of Corinth after Chaeronea.[139]

Not only is peace necessary for Xenophon's financial reforms; economic growth will allow Athens to be more peaceful. Xenophon begins his work with a criticism of Athens' aggressive foreign policy: he observes that Athens is viewed with suspicion because "owing to the poverty of the masses, we are forced to be somewhat unjust in our treatment of the cities."[140] Thus he clarifies the ultimate goal of his economic projects: it is to allow the city to act justly in its foreign affairs. Athens should renounce aggression and imperialism and gain the respect and love of the Greek world through its just conduct and efforts for peace.[141] The one concrete and contemporary case that Xenophon treats avoids all bellicosity: all Greece would be grateful if Athens would help to assure the autonomy of Delphi, "not by joining in war, but by sending embassies up and down Greece."[142] It is not clear whom Xenophon thought the Athenians might fight beside and whom against; it was Athens' allies the Phocians who were occupying Delphi and the hated Thebans who would claim to be liberating it. So we cannot be sure about what sort of a war Xenophon is deprecating. In any case, he stands against entering into the war and would rather have Athens work for its diplomatic resolution.

The outlook of the *Ways and Means* is also not a militaristic one. When he enumerates the enthusiasm of different sorts of people for a peaceful Athens, he mentions merchants of all sorts, intellectuals, poets, and those who enjoy watching spectacles either religious or secular.[143] Soldiers and generals are conspicuous by their absence, especially considering the prominence of the military role in Greek society and values. He also counters the criticism that true glory comes only from warlike exploits:

If any are inclined to think that a lasting peace for our city will involve a loss of her power and glory and fame in Greece, they too, in my opinion, are out in their

---

[138] Xen. *Vect.* 5.1.   [139] Gauthier 1976: 196–8; Aeschin. 3.159. See also Ryder 1976: 86–7.
[140] Xen. *Vect.* 1.1.   [141] Xen. *Vect.* 5.5–10.
[142] Xen. *Vect.* 5.9 with Gauthier 1976: 209–10.   [143] Xen. *Vect.* 5.3–5.

calculations. For doubtless those states are reckoned the happiest that enjoy the longest period of unbroken peace; and of all states Athens is by nature most suited to flourish in peace.[144]

This is not really an argument but a bald assertion that a militaristic set of values does not correspond with our knowledge of what makes a state happy. John Dillery has shown that Xenophon recommends that Athens, in the world of Greek states, "follow a policy of quietism borrowed from the world of the individual *apragmon*," the citizen who did not seek political prominence but was content with his private life.[145] This ideal was the opposite from the militaristic ideal of the involved citizen and the activist Athens portrayed in Pericles' funeral oration and in many of Demosthenes' speeches.

Xenophon's other works are far from showing this pacific spirit. Rather they seem imbued throughout with a profound interest in war and warfare, which sometimes verges on enthusiasm. His political philosophy is decidedly militaristic; those best suited for war are also the best rulers.[146] For example, his *Cyropaedia* and *Constitution of the Lacedaemonians* are, to a large extent, devoted to the praise of militaristic societies – as long as they remain true to their values. In the *Agesilaus* he eulogizes this Spartan king, a tireless warrior and belligerent statesman. Even his insistence on the just and pious conduct of states in the *Hellenica* hardly prepares us for the renunciation of force in the *Ways and Means*.[147] And upon close inspection, even here, Xenophon has not left militarism and warfare behind entirely: the improvement in the city's finances resulting from his reforms will allow full pay for military training and service and the Athenians "will become a people more obedient, better disciplined, and more efficient in war."[148] He has not abjured preparedness for war, but it is certainly overshadowed in the *Ways and Means* by other concerns. Finally, he explicitly denies pacifism:

But some one may ask me, Do you mean to say that, even if she is wronged, the state should remain at peace with the offender? No, certainly not; but I do say that our vengeance would follow far more swiftly on our enemies if we provoked nobody by wrong-doing; for then they would look in vain for an ally.[149]

Xenophon merely insists that Athens act justly and that such action will be to the city's advantage; that he thinks it necessary to deny pacifism at all makes it clear that his conception of what would require war would not

---

[144] Xen. *Vect.* 5.2 (trans. modified).   [145] Dillery 1993: 2, 9.
[146] Hunt 1998: 144–60.   [147] See Dillery 1995 on the *Hellenica*.
[148] Xen. *Vect.* 4.51–2. See also Gauthier 1976 ad *Vect.* 2.2–5; 4.41–8; and 5.13.   [149] Xen. *Vect.* 5.13.

be a permissive one, an impression already suggested by his reaction to the Phocian seizure of Delphi. We can soften the contrast between the *Ways and Means* and the rest of his works and, indeed, with the mainstream of Athenian militarism. It will not go away.

Isocrates' *On the Peace* is a political pamphlet in the form of a speech and also belongs to the period of the end of Social War or shortly thereafter.[150] Here Isocrates subjects Athenian militarism to a withering attack and expresses strong condemnation of war and imperialism.[151] He argues that Athens should not make peace only with its rebellious allies but should make peace "with all mankind" on the terms of the King's Peace, a Common Peace requiring that all Greeks be independent.[152] Such a peace would involve the renunciation of all imperial aims, but Isocrates argues at length that the possession of or aspiration for an empire has brought Athens nothing but grief.[153] Thus what, in Isocrates' opinion, is the goal of Athenian wars is less than worthless. War itself is contrary to Athens' interest:

[T]he orators who exhort us to cling fast to peace have never caused us to suffer any misfortune whatsoever, whereas those who lightly espouse war have already plunged us into many great disasters. However, we have no memory for these facts but are always ready, without in the least advancing our own welfare, to man triremes, to levy war-taxes, and to lend aid to the campaigns of others or wage war against them, as chance may determine, as if imperiling the interests, not of our own, but of a foreign state.[154]

In addition to these disadvantages of war, such wars have given Athens a bad name among the Greeks.[155]

Isocrates also attacks the optimism with which orators try to convince the assembly to go to war:

For some of us appear to me to be overzealously bent on war, as though having heard, not from haphazard counselors, but from the gods, that we are destined to succeed in all our campaigns and to prevail easily over our foes.[156]

At one point, Isocrates almost seems to be against war in general. He claims that Athens should rid itself of war forever and realize that "tranquility is more advantageous than meddlesomeness, justice than injustice, and attention to one's own affairs than covetousness of the possessions of others" – a quietist position similar to the one that Dillery detects in Xenophon.[157] Together these passages provide as compelling a critique of war as we find in classical Greece.

---

[150] On the date of *On the Peace* see p. 165 n. 58; on its nature and purpose see pp. 21–2.
[151] On this aspect of the speech see Gillis 1970; Davidson 1990; Bettali 1992.   [152] Isoc. 8.16.
[153] Isoc. 8.64–120.   [154] Isoc. 8.12.   [155] Isoc. 8.19.   [156] Isoc. 8.8.   [157] Isoc. 8.26.

This attack on Athenian belligerence and imperialism is linked to an attack on Athenian militarism. Isocrates attacks the fifth-century Athenian empire and its practices:

For so exactly did they gauge the actions by which human beings incur the worst odium that they passed a decree to divide the surplus of the funds derived from the tributes of the allies into talents and to bring it on the stage, when the theatre was full . . . and not only was this done but at the same time they led in upon the stage the sons of those who had lost their lives in the war, seeking thus to display to our allies, on the one hand, the value of their own property which was brought in by hirelings, and to the rest of the Hellenes, on the other, the multitudes of the fatherless and the misfortunes which result from this policy of aggression.[158]

Athenian state sponsorship of children who had lost their fathers in war was elsewhere a matter of great pride.[159] It represented the community's bestowal of glory and material resources to encourage those who had and who would risk their lives for it in war. Isocrates also paints a grim picture of the annual funeral oration, another ritual inculcating militarism by the public praise of military prowess and sacrifice and another institution of which the Athenians were proud:

In a word, it was at that time a matter of regular routine to hold public funerals every year, which many both of our neighbours and of the other Hellenes used to attend, not to grieve with us for the dead, but to rejoice together at their misfortunes.[160]

In the place of Athenian pride at the funeral oration as showing the honor paid to self-sacrifice in war, Isocrates only mentions grief. Instead of impressing visitors with the nobility of Athens, the funeral oration only publicized Athenian losses – and to a Greece so hostile as to rejoice at the death of Athenians. This was not the kind of thing that could be said in the assembly.[161]

Isocrates also claims that the superiority of Athens lies not in the art of war or government, but in the quality of the Athenians' education in thought and speech.[162] This somewhat self-serving argument for an intellectual and teacher would have irritated Athens' martial pride – and raised suspicions that Isocrates was hostile to the democracy. It implied a

---

[158] Isoc. 8.82–3.
[159] E.g. Aeschin. 3.154; Thuc. 2.46.1; Arist. *Pol.* 2.1268a; Dem. 60.32; Plato, *Menex.* 248e. See also Stroud 1971 and Herrman (forthcoming) ad Hyp. 6.27.
[160] Isoc. 8.87. We also find mockery of the funeral oration in Plato's *Menexenus* and in Demosthenes' *Exordia* 33, but these are directed more against Athenian self-flattery than with the basic problem of trying to celebrate death.
[161] See Gillis 1970: 197.   [162] Isoc. 15.293–4; cf. 15.306–8.

scale of values in which the intellectual virtues could trump the military ones.

Isocrates does not mention in *On the Peace* the Panhellenic project for which he is best known and which seems to have always been close to his heart. Elsewhere the connection between establishing peace in Greece and invading Persia make Isocrates as much of a war-monger as a pacifist despite his condemnation of wars among Greeks:

What I have to say on these points is simple and easy: It is not possible for us to cement an enduring peace unless we join together in a war against the barbarians, nor for the Hellenes to attain to concord until we wrest our material advantages from one and the same source and wage our wars against one and the same enemy.[163]

The absence of this motif in *On the Peace* can be attributed to the particularly hard times and pessimistic mood of the times; Athens was in no position to lead Greece against Persia and Philip had yet to emerge as a likely leader.[164] But even within Isocrates' *On the Peace* we find signs that Isocrates approves some wars. He hopes that the acquisition of land in Thrace will allow the settlement of the exiles, mercenaries, and impoverished Greeks, whom Isocrates found so unsettling.[165] So too, Isocrates' praise of the Persian War generation does not bespeak an opposition to war. Nevertheless, *On the Peace* was overall harshly critical of Athenian militarism and belligerence. Isocrates did not address the assembly but only wrote pamphlets for a literate and elite audience; he took the condemnation of war this far in only one speech. Nevertheless, it is possible that such sentiments may have been uttered in the assembly and approved by some Athenians; perhaps by some of those speakers whom Demosthenes castigated, those who praised peace.[166]

As long as Athens found itself in a dangerous world, in which Athens could be threatened directly or through its grain supply, it was unlikely that anti-war arguments would progress much further than those offered in the *Ways and Means* or *On the Peace*. Since this dangerous interstate environment also provided powerful incentives for militarism, Isocrates' critique on that score was also as strong as one is likely to find – and was not maintained in his other works.

---

[163] Isoc. 4. Almost any treatment of Isocrates covers his Panhellenism, e.g. Laistner 1927: 15–24; Baynes 1955; Cawkwell 1982: 318, 325–7; Romilly 1992.

[164] Laistner 1927: 18; Cawkwell 1982: 325.   [165] Isoc. 8.24.

[166] See above, pp. 244–5; cf. Pericles' denunciation of citizens who would like to abandon the empire: Thuc. 2.63.2–3.

CHAPTER II

Conclusion

This book has aimed to treat the totality of Athenian feelings and thoughts about war, peace, and alliance, based primarily on the evidence of the assembly speeches of the fourth century BC. My basic methodological assumption has been that the skilled and successful orators whose works we possess did not waste their time with arguments or emotional appeals that were not likely to be persuasive. That they made such a variety of arguments strongly suggests that Athenian decisions were complex: no single consideration or system of thought seems to have dominated Athenian decision-making to the exclusion of others. This conclusion may, in part, be due to the nature of our evidence. We possess the arguments, but we can rarely tell whether some were decisive and others not.[1] Notwithstanding this limit on our knowledge and the inclusivity it enforces, three salient attributes of Athenian thinking have emerged repeatedly.

First, the use of domestic analogies was pervasive. The different internal practices and values that were applied to the relations of states ranged from the simplest and most intimate, the household metaphors, whose application to states served mainly to evoke emotional responses, to the more complex and distant relations of reciprocity and law, which allowed for a more complex and analytical approach to issues of foreign relations. Of course, most orators wanted to win both the "hearts and minds" and deployed arguments derived from a range of domestic analogies in their speeches.

Second, the rationality of Athenian thinking was not limited to those arguments that explicitly invoked calculations of interest. In some respects, militarism, reciprocity, and a touchy sense of honor, legalism, and even the general preference for peace served well Athens' long-term interests. They should not be considered simply emotional responses that diverted Athens

---

[1] Occasionally a contemporary historian explains the actual basis for a decision, e.g. Thuc. 1.44. But, as in this case, modern historians have tended to distrust such analyses.

from the path of interest; they had their strategic roots as surely as they were based in dearly held values.

Third, Athenian thinking about interstate relations was profoundly shaped by its context within a Greek world consisting of independent states sharing a common culture and language. This context ruled out status-based arguments rooted in a sense of ethnic or religious superiority or natural enmity. Communication was relatively easy and true misunderstandings rare. Finally, the Greek world was often imagined as an audience of peers who would judge Athenian decisions and to whom these needed to be justified. The deliberate balance-of-power calculations of leading Greek states contributed to the maintenance of the political division of Greece, disastrous from the anachronistic point of view of Greek nationalism but crucial to the sophistication and the overall modernity of Greek interstate relations.

In my treatments of the various strands of Athenian thinking, the question of how these compared with modern views has surfaced occasionally and been in the background more often. I have tried to strike a balance by exploring both the ways that Athenian thinking differed from modern Western ideas and the similarities between the two. But, in conclusion, I will admit that, nuance aside, I am left with an overwhelming impression of familiarity. A summary of the main reasons for this feeling will provide a recapitulation of my main findings; it will also highlight the main way in which this study differs from much recent scholarship on Athenian foreign policy: I have emphasized the modernity of much Athenian thinking and, just as important, have invoked the broad range of attitudes and the often atavistic way that people think about war, peace, and alliance today.

Important economic considerations shaped Athenian foreign policy: the hope for direct material gain was least among them in a period in which war was, and was regarded as, costly rather than profitable. More important, Athenian dependence on trade – especially the import of grain – recommended an engaged and active foreign policy. This policy could be imperialistic or bellicose, but did not have to be: indeed, war was liable to jeopardize trade; the Athenians most needed dependable access to grain. The United States' reliance on imported oil springs to mind as an obvious parallel. For the time being at least, this dependence commands the US government's attention but all its economy needs is a steady supply of oil, which it can obtain in a variety of ways – and often has obtained – without war or imperialism.

In many respects militarism has been on the decline since the Middle Ages, but the praise and rewards accorded to prowess and wartime sacrifice for the community, conspicuous in classical Athens, are hardly alien in modern states. Such militarism serves a useful function for states – and will do so until war disappears – but it can make them more liable to go to war. War can provide a critical arena in which groups and individuals can gain in status. In addition, excessive optimism, encouraged by distorted, militaristic patriotic histories, can make the recourse to war more attractive and hence likely today and for classical Athens.

The modern aspiration to a foreign policy independent of religious and ethnic distinctions finds no parallel in Demosthenes' Athens. Athens took the nature of other states into account in its relations with them. Nevertheless, this was but one consideration among many and a limited one at that. The homogeneity of the Greek world limited the application of ethnic criteria – malleable to begin with. Even the anti-Persian thrust of Panhellenism was far from a compelling idea; the Greekness – or not – of Macedonia was far less important than its actions. Religious wars in the modern sense were unknown among the culturally and religiously similar Greek city-states; Athens was ill favored to compete in the religious politics that did arise and thus religious factors play less of a role in its foreign policy than in that of some other states. An egalitarian ideal coexisted with and, to some extent, mitigated the vast differences in power and size between Greek city-states. States' political systems provided one way of making judgments about them. Athens professed – as does the United States today – to support democracies; in neither case is this a full or fair explanation of their foreign policy. The issue of intervention in another state's internal affairs evoked an ambivalence similar to that it evokes today.

The Athenians structured their feelings about foreign relations in terms of domestic analogies derived from slavery and from family structures and gender relations that were quite unlike those that characterize societies after the abolition of slavery, the demographic revolution, and Women's Liberation. Nevertheless, war rhetoric invoking freedom, manliness, and living up to the ancestors – like those in Tom Brokaw's *The Greatest Generation* – is common throughout the world and far from incomprehensible.[2] Nor when the most powerful nation on earth has a Department of Homeland Security and fights supposedly pre-emptive wars can we regard any of the ancient extensions and abuses of the right to defend the home and family as something distant and unfamiliar.

---

[2] Brokaw 1998. President Lyndon Johnson was afraid he would be mocked as "unmanly" if he lost Vietnam (Karnow 1984: 485).

The calculations of interest that the Athenians took account of in their foreign relations are just as central to policy decisions today. One can also detect the same equivocations about the course to follow when interest and justice seem to point in different directions. As in the Athenian assembly, Realist arguments are less common today as part of an overall ethical position – which would have to approve of advantageous genocide, for example – than as a way to unmask specious moralizing and to curb the emotional force of hate and anger in foreign policy. Indeed, the elimination of disadvantageous wars would be a great step forward for world peace.

The modernity of interest and Realism will arouse little objection; in contrast, the proponents of reciprocity and honor as the guiding principles of Athenian foreign relations take a resolutely primitivist stand. There are, admittedly, differences of degree between the prominence of honor in ancient thinking about the relations of states and in policy discussions today. But too stark a contrast cannot be maintained. Reciprocity and honor played their part in ancient thinking, but they provided but one system of judgment among several. The relationship of honor and interest was as often complementary as opposed – and was seen as such. So too today, states act and statesmen talk as if honor were still alive and well.[3] States still seek to repay harm and benefits, aware of the long-term advantages of reciprocity as well as guided by moral feeling and basic emotions.[4]

Greece knew no unified body of international law such as exists today; the interstate laws of the Greeks consisted of unwritten rules guiding the conduct of diplomacy and war and of the written and sworn terms of treaties. No permanent organizations such as the United Nations claimed to represent the Greeks and impose its judgments on them, although Common Peace conferences included many Greek states and often acted as if their decisions were binding upon all Greek states. These differences notwithstanding, two commonalities are striking: as in the classical period, so today people look to the application of law among states as an alternative to violence; second, the lack of authoritative sanctions among states is an unfortunate defect manifestly shared by modern and ancient legalism.

A professed preference for peace in general was as characteristic of Athens as it is common today and was equally ineffectual as a curb on specific wars. Anti-war and anti-militarist pronouncements are attested, especially among wealthy intellectuals, but the Athenians never produced the principled and compelling condemnation of all wars seen today in pacifist thinking. Whether this is a good or bad thing is a matter of opinion;

---

[3] Amply demonstrated in O'Neill 1999.   [4] Axelrod and Keohane 1985.

the reader may already have gleaned that my sympathies lie with just-war theory as propounded by Michael Walzer rather than with pacifism.[5] Nevertheless, many scholars who emphasize the foreignness of ancient Greek foreign policy also insist on its bellicosity. But condemnation of the "the squabbling cities of old Greece" ignores the obvious.[6] They were succeeded by the warring Hellenistic kingdoms, and after more than two thousand years are being dismissed in a twenty-first century that shows few signs of abandoning war, which is perhaps not such an easy matter.

[5] Walzer 1977.
[6] Davidson 1997: 106. This contemptuous attitude is particularly common among historians of Macedon, e.g. Errington 1990: 70–1, 74, and Hammond 1994: 77, but it is also found in general treatments, e.g. Demand 1996: 285.

Speeches and texts

Scholars agree that our nineteen core speeches were written by fourth-century orators. But do they reflect what the orators actually said in the assembly? A strong prejudice against written speeches meant that Athenian speakers did not read from a text either at a trial or in the assembly – nor did stenographers record their words as they spoke.[1] A perfect fit between our texts and the words of a speaker is improbable. In addition, several scholars have suggested the possibility that the texts of speeches were revised after they had been delivered.[2] These issues make the relationship of our oratorical texts and the actual words spoken a complex and disputed one. A full treatment is fortunately not necessary here. The crucial issue is not whether our texts are different from actual speeches, but whether they are systematically different in such a way that would jeopardize our use of them as evidence for popular Athenian thinking – both topics treated by a variety of scholars.

Professional speech-writers drafted law-court speeches for clients to memorize. These drafts were close to what was actually said – insofar as the client succeeded in memorizing them.[3] Written versions of these speeches were circulated as advertisements for the speech-writer and some have survived to this day. Such texts may have contained revisions and thus not have duplicated exactly the client's pre-trial version, but the goal of such revision was not to appeal to a different audience. It was rather to show to better advantage how skilled the author was at persuading an Athenian jury. For example, the readers of forensic speeches, potential litigants or students of oratory, were typically rich. Some of them probably despised the

---

[1] Hudson-Williams 1951: 68.

[2] Some prose works, although never intended to be delivered, were written in speech form: for example, Isocrates' *On the Peace* and *Archidamus*.

[3] Although Dover 1968 and Usher 1976 disagree about the relationship of clients and writers of forensic speeches, such speeches must have been composed by somebody beforehand for a client to practice. The issue of imperfect memorization has occasioned little discussion, mainly because we have no useful evidence on the subject.

majority of Athens' citizens as low-born, uneducated, fickle, and gullible. The last thing, however, that they would have considered desirable in a speech to an Athenian jury would have been an honest expression of this contempt.

When the author and speaker were identical, forensic speeches need not have been written out in full beforehand, but they probably often were. In particular, the oratorical art of Demosthenes involved precise wording, prose rhythm, and a host of linguistic features such as the restriction of hiatus.[4] Such a speech would be better worked up in a full draft than in outline.[5] Scholars agree that four speeches (Demosthenes, *On the False Embassy*, *On the Crown*; Aeschines, *On the False Embassy*, *Against Ctesiphon*) were probably drafted as part of the antagonists' own preparations for these trials – and more was prepared than could actually be spoken in the limited time available to the litigants.[6]

Other factors governed the circulation of deliberative speeches: politicians did not normally publish the texts upon which their speeches were based – if they wrote out their speeches at all.[7] So what are our texts? Scholars have proposed three basic theories: our texts may be political pamphlets in the form of speeches; they may be drafts written as preparation for giving a speech; they may be radical revisions of preparatory drafts or re-creations of actual speeches given without the benefit of a draft.

The pamphlet theory implies texts addressed to the concerns of a reading audience, probably elite and possible non-Athenian, rather than to those of the assembled Athenians. Since elite opinions on war and peace could differ significantly from popular views, pamphlets composed for an exclusively elite audience might well not represent the thinking of the average Athenian in the assembly.[8] But Charles Adams long ago pointed out the flaws in the pamphlet theory.[9] Demosthenes, in particular, with his excellent delivery, his access to the assembly, and his interest in immediate, practical effects on foreign policy, had little reason to concentrate his energy on writing for a small group of readers – and he certainly would not publish unpopular opinions at the risk of alienating the voters in the assembly.[10] Pamphlets seem to be the work of rhetoricians and intellectuals rather than active politicians. For example, Isocrates was apparently incapable of speaking

---

[4] E.g. Pearson 1975; Wooten 1977; Slater 1988; and Yunis 2001: 17–26.   [5] *Pace* Tuplin 1998: 297.
[6] E.g. MacDowell 2000: 22–6.   [7] Hudson-Williams 1951: 68–9. See also Hansen 1984.
[8] See pp. 256–64.   [9] Adams 1912 followed by Trevett 1996b: 33–5 and Fox 1997: 198.
[10] Most of the speeches seem too strictly Athenian in their appeals to have been originally designed or extensively revised for circulation to other cities (Adams 1912: 9). The thesis of Hansen 1984: 70 that Demosthenes published speeches when his policies were not adopted and enshrined in decrees still faces the objections to the use of political pamphlets by a frequent speaker.

before a large audience. He was more interested in his influence on an educated elite than in an immediate impact on the decisions of the Athenian assembly. He advocated unpopular ideas. He did this in political pamphlets addressed to an elite readership.[11]

Despite the prejudice against written assembly speeches, Demosthenes prepared some of his speeches in writing – and some of them so extensively that they "smelt of the lamp."[12] His experience as a speech-writer for the law courts, an unusual background for a prominent Athenian statesman, and his initial difficulties with delivery – his famous stutter – probably recommended the practice of writing out full drafts of his speeches. And, indeed, the majority of our extant deliberative speeches are by Demosthenes; very few other deliberative speeches seem ever to have been in circulation.[13] Thus, the surviving texts of assembly speeches were probably based on drafts written in anticipation of oral presentation. Jeremy Trevett, in particular, argues that many of the peculiarities of the deliberative speeches can be explained on the hypothesis that they are drafts, found among Demosthenes' papers after his death and published.[14] Such a theory implies that our speeches are close to what Demosthenes said in the assembly – or what he planned to say, which is just as good.

Several challenges to the reliability of our texts have focused on the possibility of extensive revisions to a text after a speech was given. On the one hand, evidence exists for some revision: for example, a speaker sometimes refers to an event which took place during a trial and which could not have been known or guessed at before.[15] Other speeches provide evidence of an essentially unrevised draft written before giving a speech: Demosthenes' *On the False Embassy* preserves references to Philocrates as present in Athens, although he had fled before the trial took place. This part of our text must have been written before the trial and not revised.[16] Most arguments for revision are more subjective and depend on a scholar's sense of whether a speech-writer could anticipate an adversary's arguments or the level of organization and the style we would expect in an oral presentation. Accordingly the extent of revision is controversial.[17]

---

[11] See pp. 21–2.

[12] Hudson-Williams 1951: 73. Dorjahn 1947 collects the evidence for written preparation, but also shows that Demosthenes must have been able to extemporize on occasion. See also Tuplin 1998: 293 and Trevett 1996b: 433.

[13] Hansen 1984: 60–8.   [14] Trevett 1996b contra Tuplin 1998. See also Yunis 1996: 241–7.

[15] E.g. MacDowell 2000: 24 on Aeschin. 2.4, 153.   [16] MacDowell 2000: 24–6.

[17] Worthington 1991a is most extravagant: "any resemblance between the Stage One product (the speech) and the Stage Two product (the publication) may be little more than coincidental" (68). Most scholars emphasize the essential congruence between the written and oral speech: Edwards 1995:

The goal of an orator's revision of his speeches is more crucial to this study than its extent. Such revision may have aimed at a more polished and tightly organized speech. It may have served to make the speaker of a law-court speech look better after the fact.[18] But only a systematic reworking of a speech for a different audience or a different goal would undermine the use of deliberative oratory as evidence for popular thinking.[19] Several considerations persuade me that the revision of deliberative orations did not distort the actual arguments used to this extent. Stylistic features suggest that our surviving texts were designed as orations.[20] More telling, oratory presents a populist version of history with an anti-intellectual slant – in striking contrast to Thucydides, for example, who did write for an elite readership.[21] The attitudes of oratory, both forensic and deliberative, parallel those in Aristophanes' comedies, plays patently aimed at a general audience.[22] So, if our speeches were rewritten with elite readers in mind, their goals may have been parallel to those of texts of trial speeches: they must have aimed not to persuade those elite readers, but rather to demonstrate to them how an orator should persuade the Athenian assembly.

This would be quite sufficient for our purposes. The position is probably better than that. It is a reasonable assumption that Demosthenes already put forth his best persuasive efforts when it counted, when the assembly voted. If Demosthenes wanted to circulate his assembly speeches – which he may or may not have[23] – and devoted any time to revision, it was probably to accommodate better the attitudes and prejudices of his audience in cases when he had perceived that some arguments had fallen flat.[24] Thus, the

---

4, 108 on Andocides, *On the Peace*; MacDowell 2000: 24–6 on Demosthenes, *On the False Embassy*; Yunis 2001: 26–7 on Demosthenes, *On the Crown*. Other scholars countenance the possibility of significant revision in specific cases: Sealey 1993: 132–3 on the *First Philippic*; Usher 1999: 242–3 on the *Fourth Philippic*, a special case to be examined below.

[18] Todd 1990: 167.

[19] Usher 1999: 192, 215 n. 155 posits such reworking in some cases, but his argument is stronger for *Against Leptines* than for the deliberative speech *For the Liberty of the Rhodians*.

[20] Pearson 1975 presents the most decisive evidence for this: the different levels of speaking ability assumed by different speeches. The early deliberative speeches and speeches written for private persons avoid long, unbroken sections that would require a trained speaker to pronounce effectively. Only when Demosthenes wrote for himself in his maturity as a speaker, did he compose these "virtuoso passages."

[21] Dover 1974: 11 and Pearson 1941. Cf. Milns 1995: 11.   [22] Dover 1974: 9–10.   [23] Trevett 1996b.

[24] Demosthenes could have revised his speeches to show himself as possessing more foresight than he actually possessed – see p. 181 on Demosthenes' pride in his forecasts – or, in general, to show himself in a better light. There is little sign of this and several contrary indications. Critics of Demosthenes harp on his failure to see Philip as a threat before 350: in particular, a sentence added to *On the Liberty of the Rhodians* 24, in which Demosthenes refers in passing to Philip, would have put this speech in line with Demosthenes' self-image as a prophet. In the light of Thebes' later alliance with Athens, Demosthenes could also have added some hints of this possibility or, at least, not attacked

most likely changes to our texts – and I believe that even these are rare and minor – are these revisions that make the texts better represent popular views.[25]

NOTES ON SPECIFIC SPEECHES

Andocides, On the Peace

I accept the arguments of Edwards 1995: 107–8 in favor of the authenticity of Andocides, *On the Peace*; contra Harris 2000.

Demosthenes 13

The authenticity of Demosthenes 13, *On Organization*, is controversial: Sealey 1967: 251–3, 1993: 235–7 rejects this work as most likely composed by a later rhetorician, but Trevett 1994 argues that Demosthenes was its author and Usher 1999: 215–16 agrees though less definitely. On account of its disputed status, I have not included it among my core speeches and have only occasionally adduced evidence from it, only to support arguments based on other evidence.

Demosthenes 9

The *Third Philippic* is undoubtedly Demosthenes' work, but it survives in a long and a short form. At issue are the sections that are only in the longer version: were these additions the work of Demosthenes or a later editor? Sealey 1993: 234–5 argues persuasively for the Demosthenic authorship of both versions – and holds that the longer one was delivered in the assembly and then revised for distribution throughout the Greek world – now supported by Wooten 2008: 167–73. Nevertheless, I have alerted the reader in the two cases where I cite material that is only in the longer version.

Demosthenes 8 and 10

Two long sections are common to the *Fourth Philippic* (Dem. 10) and *On the Chersonese* (Dem. 8), but both seem to be by Demosthenes – although

---

Thebes (e.g. Dem. 20.109 and 9.34). See also Fox 1997: 200 "Above all the misplaced advice to keep Thrace weak between three kings could have been edited out of Speech 23 when Philip promptly exposed its folly. None of these opportunities was taken."

[25] *Pace* Tuplin 1998.

Dem. 10 has been called unfinished and rough. Various scholars have proposed explanations for this oddity: Adams 1938; Daitz 1957; Worthington 1991b; Trevett 1996b: 439; Usher 1999: 241–3, Sealey 1993: 232–3, Hajdú 2002: 44–9, 451–71. Although the *Fourth Philippic* seems to have been the original speech from which material was borrowed for use in *On the Chersonese*, we cannot be sure which, if either, text formed the basis of a speech delivered in the assembly. This is a case where the thesis of Trevett 1996b, that our texts are rough drafts prepared in advance, is particularly apt (see also Hajdú 2002: 49). And as long as Demosthenes wrote these two speeches in preparation for speaking in the assembly, we can still use their arguments as evidence for popular conceptions.

[Demosthenes] 7 and 17

These speeches are not by Demosthenes, but most scholars believe that they are contemporary texts and derive from the speeches of other anti-Macedonian politicians, possibly Hegesippus and Hyperides respectively. Thus, they provide evidence for the types of arguments that might be expected to convince the assembly and are particularly valuable precisely because they are not by Demosthenes. They have not attracted much scholarly attention, but Ryder 2000: 73–4 accepts the attribution of [Dem.] 7 to Hegesippus as does Sealey 1993: 177–8. Schäffer 1885–7: III.206–10; Sealey 1993: 240; and Cawkwell 1961 all agree that *On the Treaty with Alexander*, [Dem.] 17, is a contemporary speech.

Plato and Aristotle on the causes of war

In the *Republic* Plato argues for a purely materialist and internal explanation for war: states attack their neighbors to gain their possessions, especially their land. He can imagine a city fighting such a war to escape poverty: the people in the *Republic*'s original, self-sufficient city will not have too many children "lest they fall into either poverty or war."[1] But the main thrust of his argument is that the "unlimited acquisition of wealth, disregarding the limit set by our necessary wants" drives cities to war."[2] In the *Phaedo* Plato specifies the reason why people want "wealth and luxuries" and sums up the entire causal chain:

It [the body] fills us with wants, desires, fears, all sorts of illusions and much nonsense . . . Only the body and its desires cause war, civil discord and battles, for all wars are due to the desire to acquire wealth, and it is the body and the care of it, to which we are enslaved, which compels us to acquire wealth, and all this makes us too busy to practice philosophy.[3]

Plato thus attributes the drive to war to the desires of the body and links it with a deplorable lack of individual self-restraint. These attitudes find parallels among critics of Athenian foreign policy such as Isocrates.[4]

Aristotle does not provide an overarching theory of the cause of war, but he too mentions material motivations for war. To begin with, he emphasizes the role that competition for food or carnivorous behavior plays in what he describes as war among animals, either of different species or within a species.[5] More significant, he emphasizes the acquisition of slaves as a goal

---

[1] Pl. *Resp.* 2.372b–c.
[2] Pl. *Resp.* 2.372e–374a. See also Pl. *Resp.* 8.547b–c.   [3] Pl. *Phd.* 66b–d.
[4] Davidson 1990: 29 characterizes Isocrates' *On the Peace* as "a highly moralising characterisation of imperialism, directly comparable to an individual's relationship to his pleasures and desires." Cf. Men. *Dys.* 745; Menander seems to have been opposed to an active Athenian foreign policy and, perhaps, sympathetic to Macedonia (Major 1997).
[5] Garlan 1989: 27 on Arist. *Hist. an.* 608b–610b.

of war. Although slaves were not the only possible profit in warfare, their acquisition attracts Aristotle's particular attention:

Now if nature makes nothing incomplete, and nothing in vain, the inference must be that she has made all animals for the sake of man. And so, from one point of view, the art of war is a natural art of acquisition, for the art of acquisition includes hunting, an art which we ought to practise against wild beasts, and against men who, though intended by nature to be governed, will not submit: for war of such a kind is naturally just.[6]

Although Aristotle's view of the motivation of warfare, like Plato's, includes material factors, two distinctions between Aristotle and Plato are striking.[7] First and most obviously, Plato's description of war is manifestly a blanket condemnation: the acquisitiveness that leads to wars is a deplorable effect of the body's insatiable desires. Aristotle, on the other hand, considers the enslavement of natural slaves a just reason for war since such wars lead to the imposition of a natural hierarchy. Second, Aristotle's materialism is not as all-encompassing as Plato's: material gain is only one motive for warfare. The phrase "from one point of view" in the passage above is a translation of the Greek particle, *pōs*: this is a significant hedge.[8] And necessarily so, for, as we have seen, Aristotle elsewhere suggests other just motives for war – not to mention unjust ones – and does not reduce all motivations for war to the quest for slaves.[9]

In contrast to Plato's view, wars were a source of pride for most Athenians. Not only did the Athenians celebrate their success, but also their motivations, such as the defense of liberty or the succor of the weak and unjustly treated. Plato's argument that the origins of war lay in greed and the needs of the body calls all these motivations into question: its result would be the "unmasking" of all these pretensions and would reveal the true and ignoble motivations underneath.

Plato's hostility to material motivations is not the only reason for his dismissal of the grounds advanced in the assembly for Athenian wars. Plato's hostility to the democracy and the oratory upon which its decisions were based are well known. Plato, indeed, uses the same images of gross or infantile sensuality to condemn the Athenians for their execution of Socrates and for their military victories and consequent acquisition of empire. In the *Gorgias* Socrates predicts how he will fare if he is brought to trial:

---

[6] Arist. *Pol.* 1.1256b20–26; see also 1.1255b37–39 with Garlan 1989: 28. Cf. Pl. *Soph.* 222c, another Platonic criticism of warfare.

[7] Ostwald 1996: 105; contra Garlan 1989: 31.

[8] Schütrumpf 1991–2005: 1.315. Cf. Ostwald 1996: 105, 113–16.   [9] Pp. 74–5.

"For I'll be judged the way a doctor would be judged by a jury of children if a pastry cook were to bring accusations against him."[10]

The decisions of the fifth-century empire, even those that resulted in the famous victories of which the Athenians were most proud, were flawed in the same way. Plato attacks Athens' fifth-century democratic leaders such as Pericles, Cimon, Miltiades, and Themistocles, men famous for their military victories.[11] He depicts the leadership of these men in negative terms:

For they filled the city with harbors and dockyards, walls, and tribute payments and such trash as that, but did so without justice and self-control.[12]

He compares what these leaders did for the city with the activities of well-known purveyors of luxuries, who did not deserve to be called good caretakers of the body just because they provided wonderful bread, pastry, and wine.[13] The accusation of sensuality is used against the democracy both in the decisions of its jury-courts and in the foreign policy and wars determined by the assembly. For his part, Aristotle's ties with the Macedonian royal family gave him no reason to favor the policies of a Demosthenes or, more generally, an Athens that fought three wars with Macedonia in a generation. During the last of these, the Lamian War, he fled the country, in part out of fear that his Macedonian connections would get him into trouble.[14]

Plato's and Aristotle's dismissal of the stated grounds of war, then, does not spring entirely from a materialist theory of war's origins at odds with the terms of assembly debates. Rather, an elitist contempt for the masses and democratic deliberations made such a theory more attractive. Particular disagreements with the specific alignment of Athenian foreign policy also contributed to their hostility.

---

[10] Pl. *Grg.* 521e.   [11] Pl. *Grg.* 515c–d. Cf. Pl. *Grg.* 502e.
[12] Pl. *Grg.* 519a. See also *Grg.* 503c, 517b–519b; Pl. *Resp.* 4.422c–d.
[13] Pl. *Grg.* 518b.   [14] Strauss 1991b: 229–32.

Claims of service

TWO CONCLUSIONS

(1) References to military service to the state were as common as those to financial contributions in Athenian law-court speeches: with remarkable consistency over time, approximately the same fraction of speeches discuss financial contributions and military service. Both could show character or establish a debt of gratitude – although the latter claim was always a prickly subject and there were standard rebuttals to such claims.

(2) Neither claim was *de rigueur*: more than half of our extant speeches contain no such reference. Such claims play little role in deliberative or epideictic speeches. If we subtract these speeches (approximately 25) from our total, we still find that claims of service are mentioned in 58/120 law-court speeches, that is, less than 50 percent of them.

METHODOLOGY

The largest group of passages comprises those in which a litigant talks about his own services, but derogatory remarks about an opponent are also common. I have counted such references even when they may be merely informational, for example "I happened to be out of the country serving as a trierarch when he died," on the assumption that skillful speechwriters reveal why somebody was out of the country or not depending on the impression the reason will make. I have also included sundry other passages where claims of service are discussed, but not with direct application to either the plaintiff or defendant or their families. These references indicate the relative prominence of financial and military service in the Athenian consciousness. Their inclusion, however, tends to inflate the number of speeches which I describe as including a claim of service. This means that my second conclusion above is actually stronger than it appears; had I not included such references the proportion of speeches including claims of service would have be even smaller. The corpus of orations is large and this list is probably not comprehensive – and I did not count references in fragments.[1] Nevertheless, I would be surprised if any omission I have made would substantially change the picture.

THE DATA

1 Totals by period and grand totals

| Period | Speeches with claims | Breakdown of claims | | |
		Financial contributions[a]	Military service[b]	Trierarchy[c]
450–404	4/8 (50%)	3/4 (75%)	3/4 (75%)	1/4 (25%)
403–378	21/46 (46%)	16/21 (76%)	17/21 (81%)	10/21 (47%)
377–356	8/22 (36%)	7/8 (87.5%)	5/8 (62.5%)	3/8 (37.5%)
355–338	12/40 (30%)	9/12 (75%)	10/12 (83%)	7/12 (58%)
337–322	9/17 (53%)	7/9 (78%)	7/9 (78%)	3/9 (33%)
Undated	4/15 (27%)	4/4 (100%)	1/4 (25%)	1/4 (25%)
Totals	58/148 (39%)	46/58 (79%)	43/58 (74%)	25/58 (43%)

[a] Financial contributions include personal outlay, but not the administration of state moneys.
[b] Military service does not include financial contributions even for warfare; it does include service as a general.
[c] Trierarchies always count as financial contributions; I only count them as military service if the passage makes it clear that the person commanded his ship in person as well as outfitting it.
Source: I used the speech lists and dates in Ober 1989: 341–9 and especially in 349 nn. a–f. I did not canvass or count the nine speeches embedded in Thucydides, Plato's *Menexenus*, Demosthenes 11–13, 61, *Letters*, *Exordia*, or Isocrates 19.

2 Passages and totals by period

(A) 450–404 BC

Speech	Financial contributions	Military service	Trierarchy
Andoc. 2	11, 17–18	12, 17–18	
Antiph. 2	2.2.12		2.12
Antiph. 3		2.3	
Lys. 20	23, 24	14, 23, 24–5	
Total	3 (75%)	3 (75%)	1 (25%)

[1] E.g. military service in Dinarchus fr. C 14 from *Against Proxenus*.

(B) 403–378 BC

Speech	Financial contributions	Military service	Trierarchy
Pl. *Apol.*		28e	
Andoc. 1		101, 147	
Isae. 5	36–8, 41–2, 44, 45	42, 46	36, 41, 45
Isae. 11	50	(11.50?)[a]	
Isoc. 16	35	15, 17, 21, 28, 29,	35
Isoc. 18	59–62	59–62	59–62
[Lys.] 6	46–7	46	46
Lys. 7	31	41	31
Lys. 10		21–2, 27–8	
Lys. 12	20, 38	38–40, 42	38
Lys. 14		7–8, 15, 17, etc.	
Lys. 16	14	13–18	
Lys. 18		24–7	
Lys. 19	22–3, 42–3, 62–3		42, 62
Lys. 21	1–10	9–11, 20, 24–5	2, 5–10
Lys. 25	4, 12–13	4, 12	12
Lys. 26	3–4, 22	21	
Lys. 27	9–10		
Lys. 29	3		3
Lys. 30	15–16, 26	26	
Lys. 31	15–16	14	
Total	16 (76%)	17 (81%)	10 (47%)

[a] Section numbers in parenthesis refer to passages that I found it hard to categorize. For example, serving as a general is a military service, but does Demosthenes' role in acquiring allies and bringing together a great army count? Or does *erga* parallel to *leitourgia* suggest military action? I did not count such passages in my totals.

(C) 377–356 BC

Speech	Financial contributions	Military service	Trierarchy
Dem. 22	(8), (42), 63		
Dem. 28	24		
[Dem.] 49	46		
Dem. 50	9, 11–13, 52, 58–9, etc.	11–13, 52, 58–9, etc.	11–13, 58–9, etc.
Dem. 51	1, 5–6, etc.	11, 18, etc.	1, 5–6, 11, 18, etc.
Isae. 4	27, 29	27, 29	
Isae. 6	(1) 5, 60	1, 5, 9	(1), 5, 60
Isae. 10		20, 25	
Total	7 (87.5%)	5 (62.5%)	3 (37.5%)

(D) 355–338 BC

Speech	Financial contributions	Military service	Trierarchy
Aesch. 2		147–51, 167–70	
Dem. 8	70–1		
Dem. 19	166–72, 229–30	113	230
Dem. 20	30–5, 41–5, 149, 151, etc.	59, 68, 76–83, etc.	26–8, 151
Dem. 21	13–14, 151–67	95, 143–6, 148, 162–3, 171–2	151–7
Dem. 23	211	196–9, 212, 214	
Dem. 45	66, 85		85
[Dem.] 46	20	20	20
Dem. 57		37–8, 64	
Isae. 2		6, 42	
Isae. 7	32, 35, 37–40	35, 41	32, 35, 38
Isoc. 15	145	107–13 (101–2)	145
Total	9 (75%)	10 (83%)	7 (58%)

(E) 337–322 BC

Speech	Financial contributions	Military service	Trierarchy
Aesch. 3	17, 19, 23	175–6, 181, 187, 184–8, 212, 243, 253	19
Dem. 18	112–13, 257, 268, 311–13	285–6 (229–31, 237, 248, 299–300)	257
Dem. 25	76–8	(76)	
Dem. 34	38–9		
Din. 1	(96)	12, 16–17, 71, 81–2	
Din. 2	17–18	17–18	
Din. 3		12, 17	
Hyp. 1	col. 16	cols. 16–18	
Lyc. 1	139–40	8, 37–8, 46, 51, 57, etc.	139–40
Total	7 (78%)	7 (78%)	3 (33%)

(F) Undated speeches

Speech	Financial contributions	Military service	Trierarchy
Dem. 36	39–42, 57		
Dem. 38	25–6		
Dem. 52	26		
Dem. 53	5	5	5
Total	4 (100%)	1 (25%)	1 (25%)

Source: As listed in Ober 1989: 349 n. f – except that I did not consider the *Menexenus*.

References

Abbreviations of journal titles correspond to those used in *L'Année philologique*.

Adams, C. D. (1912) "Are the Political Speeches of Demosthenes To Be Regarded as Political Pamphlets?," *TAPhA* 43: 5–22.
    (1938) "Speeches VIII and X of the Demosthenic Corpus," *CPh* 33: 129–44.
Adcock, S. F. and D. J. Mosley (1975) *Diplomacy in Ancient Greece*. London.
Adkins, A. W. H. (1960) *Merit and Responsibility: A Study in Greek Values*. Oxford.
    (1972) *Moral Values and Political Behavior in Ancient Greece: From Homer to the End of the Fifth Century*. London.
    (1997) "Homeric Ethics," in *A New Companion to Homer*, ed. I. Morris and B. Powell. Leiden: 694–713.
Ager, S. L. (1993) "Why War? Some Views on International Arbitration in Ancient Greece," *EMC/CV n.s.* 12: 1–13.
    (1996) *Interstate Arbitrations in the Greek World, 337–90 BC*. Berkeley.
Ahrensdorf, P. J. (1997) "Thucydides' Realistic Critique of Realism," *Polity* 30: 231–65.
Allen, D. S. (2000) *The World of Prometheus: The Politics of Punishing in Democratic Athens*. Princeton.
Alonzo, V. (2007) "War, Peace and International Law in Ancient Greece," in *War and Peace in the Ancient World*, ed. K. Raaflaub. Malden, MA: 206–25.
Anderson, C. A. and T. K. Dix (2004) "Small States in the Athenian Empire: The Case of the Eteokarpathioi," *Syll Class* 15: 1–31.
Aron, R. (1964) "War and Industrial Society," in *War: Studies from Psychology, Sociology, Anthropology*, ed. L. Bramson and G. W. Goethals. New York: 351–94.
Ashton, N. G. (1984) "The Lamnian War – *stat magni nominis umbra*," *JHS* 104: 152–7.
Atkinson, J. E. (1981) "Macedon and Athenian Politics in the Period 338 to 323 BC," *AClass* 24: 37–48.
Austin, M. (1993) "Alexander and the Macedonian Invasion of Asia: Aspects of the Historiography of War and Empire in Antiquity," in *War and Society in the Greek World*, ed. J. Rich and G. Shipley. London: 197–223.
Axelrod, R. (1984) *The Evolution of Cooperation*. New York.

Axelrod, R. and R. O. Keohane (1985) "Achieving Cooperation under Anarchy: Strategies and Institutions," *World Politics* 38: 226–54.

Badian, E. (1982) "Greeks and Macedonians," in *Macedonia and Greece in Classical and Early Hellenistic Times*, ed. B. Barr-Sharrar and E. Borza. Washington, DC: 33–53.

(1995) "The Ghost of Empire: Reflections on Athenian Foreign Policy in the Fourth Century BC," in *Die athenische Demokratie im Jahrhundert v.Chr.: Vollendung oder Verfall einer Verfassungsform*, ed. W. Eder. Stuttgart: 79–106.

(2000) "The Road to Prominence," in *Demosthenes: Statesman and Orator*, ed. I. Worthington. London: 9–44.

Bakewell, G. (2007) "Agamemnon 437: Chrysamoibos Ares, Athens and Empire," *JHS* 127: 123–32.

Balot, R. K. (2007) "Subordinating Courage to Justice: Statecraft and Soulcraft in Fourth-century Athenian Rhetoric and Platonic Political Philosophy," *Rhetorica* 25: 35–52.

(forthcoming) "Democratizing Courage in Classical Athens," in *War, Cutlture, and Democracy in Classical Athens*, ed. D. Pritchard. Cambridge.

Baltrusch, E. (1997) "Review of Martin Jehne, *Koine Eirene*: Verträge zur Besserung der Welt oder: War die koine Eirene zum Scheitern verurteilt?," *GGA* 249: 30–42.

Barnes, J., ed. (1984) *The Complete Works of Aristotle: The Revised Oxford Translation*. Vol. ii. Princeton.

Barron, J. P. (1964) "Religious Propaganda of the Delian League," *JHS* 84: 35–48.

Baynes, N. H. (1955) "Isocrates," in *Byzantine Studies and Other Essays*. London: 144–67.

Beal, R. H. (2007) "Making, Preserving, and Breaking the Peace with the Hittite State," in *War and Peace in the Ancient World*, ed. K. Raaflaub. Malden, MA: 81–97.

Bearzot, C. (1985) "Da Andocide ad Eschine: motivi ed ambiguità del pacifismo ateniese nel IV secolo a.C.," *Contributi dell' Istituto di storia antica* 11: 86–107.

Beckby, H. (1958–65) *Anthologia Graeca*. Munich.

Bederman, D. J. (2001) *International Law in Antiquity*. Cambridge.

Behrwald, R. (2005) *Hellenika von Oxyrhynchos*. Darmstadt.

Bengtson, H. (1962) *Die Staatsverträge des Altertums*. 2 vols. Munich and Berlin.

Bertman, S., ed. (1976) *The Conflict of Generations in Ancient Greece and Rome*. Amsterdam.

Bettali, M. (1992) "Isocrate e la Guerra," *Opus* 11: 37–56.

Blainey, G. (1973) *The Causes of War*. New York.

Blass, F. (1877) *Die Attische Beredsamkeit*. Leipzig.

Blassingame, J. W. (1979) *The Slave Community*. Oxford.

Bloedow, E. F. (1975) "Corn Supply and Athenian Imperialism," *AC* 44: 20–9.

Blundell, M. W. (1989) *Helping Friends and Harming Enemies: A Study in Sophocles and Greek Ethics*. Cambridge.

Boardman, J. (1995) *Greek Sculpture: The Late Classical Period and Sculpture in Colonies and Overseas*. London.

Boegehold, A. L. (1982) "A Dissent at Athens, *ca.* 424–421," *GRBS* 23: 147–56.

Boehm, C. (1984) *Blood Revenge: The Enactment and Management of Conflict in Montenegro and Other Tribal Societies*. Lawrence, KS.

Bolmarcich, S. (2007) "The Afterlife of a Treaty," *CQ* 57: 477–89.

Borza, E. (1990) *In the Shadow of Olympus: The Emergence of Macedon*. Princeton.

(1995) "The Philhellenism of Archelaus," in *Makedonika*, ed. C. G. Thomas. Claremont, CA: 125–33.

Bosworth, A. B. (1996) *Alexander and the East: The Tragedy of Triumph*. Oxford.

Bourdieu, P. (1977) *Outline of a Theory of Practice*. Cambridge.

Bowden, H. (2005) *Classical Athens and the Delphic Oracle: Divination and Democracy*. Cambridge.

Briant, P. (2002) "Guerre et succession dynastique chez les Achéménides: entre 'coutume perse' et violence armée," in *Army and Power in the Ancient World*, ed. A. Chaniotis and P. Ducrey. Stuttgart: 39–49.

Brock, P. (1991) *Freedom from War: Nonsectarian Pacifism 1814–1914*. Toronto.

Brock, P. and N. Young (1999) *Pacifism in the Twentieth Century*. Syracuse, NY.

Brokaw, T. (1998) *The Greatest Generation*. New York.

Brown, D. E. (1991) *Human Universals*. New York.

Bruce, I. (1967) *An Historical Commentary on the "Hellenica Oxyrhynchia."* Cambridge.

Brunt, P. A. (1969) "Euboea in the Time of Philip II," *CQ* n.s. 19: 245–65.

Brzezinski, Z. (2007) *Second Chance: Three Presidents and the Crisis of American Superpower*. New York.

Buchanan, J. J. (1962) *Theorika: A Study of Monetary Distributions to the Athenian Citizenry during the Fifth and Fourth Centuries* BC. Locust Valley, NY.

Buckler, J. (1980) *The Theban Hegemony: 371–362* BC. Cambridge.

(1989) *Philip II and the Sacred War*. Leiden.

(1996) "Philip II's Designs on Greece," in *Transitions to Empire: Essays in Greco-Roman History, 360–146* BC, *in honor of E. Badian*, ed. R. W. Wallace and E. M. Harris. Norman: 77–97.

(2000) "Demosthenes and Aeschines," in *Demosthenes: Statesman and Orator*, ed. I. Worthington. London: 114–58.

Bull, H. (2002) *The Anarchical Society: A Study of Order in World Politics*. New York.

Burckhardt, L. A. (1996) *Bürger und Soldaten: Aspekte der politischen und militärischen Rolle athenischer Bürger im Kriegswesen des 4 Jahrhunderts v. Chr.* Stuttgart.

Burke, E. M. (1977) "*Contra Leocratem* and *De Corona*: A Political Collaboration," *Phoenix* 31: 330–40.

(1984) "Eubulus, Olynthus, and Euboea," *TAPhA* 114: 111–20.

(1990) "Athens after the Peloponnesian War: Restoration Efforts and the Role of Maritime Commerce," *ClAnt* 9: 1–13.

(2002) "The Early Political Speeches of Demosthenes: Elite Bias in the Response to Economic Crisis," *ClAnt* 21: 165–94.

Burstein, S. (1978) "I.G. II² 653: Demosthenes and Athenian Relations with Bosporus in the Fourth Century BC.," *Historia* 27: 428–36.

Burtt, J. O., trans. (1954) *Minor Attic Orators*, vol. II: *Lycurgus, Dinarchus, Demades, Hyperides*. Cambridge, MA.

Byrne, L. (1997) "Fear in the *Seven against Thebes*," in *Rape in Antiquity*, ed. S. Deacy and K. F. Pierce. London: 143–62.

Caldwell, W. E. (1919) *Hellenic Conceptions of Peace*. New York.

Carey, C. (1989) *Lysias: Selected Speeches*. Cambridge.

    ed. (1992) *Apollodorus against Neaira: [Demosthenes] 59*. Greek Orators. Warminster.

    (1994) "Rhetorical Means of Persuasion," in *Persuasion: Greek Rhetoric in Action*, ed. I. Worthington. London: 26–45.

    (2005) "Propaganda and Competition in Athenian Oratory," in *The Manipulative Mode. Political Propaganda in Antiquity: A Collection of Case Studies*, ed. K. A. E. Enenkel and I. L. Pfeizffer. Leiden: 65–100.

Carey, C. and R. A. Reid (1985) *Demosthenes: Selected Private Speeches*. Cambridge.

Carey, C., M. Edwards, Z. Farkas *et al.* (2008) "Fragments of Hyperides' *Against Diondas* from the Archimedes Palimpsest," *ZPE* 165: 1–19.

Cargill, J. (1981) *The Second Athenian League: Empire or Free Alliance?* Berkeley and Los Angeles.

    (1985) "Demosthenes, Aeschines, and the Crop of Traitors," *Ancient World* 11: 75–85.

Carr, E. H. (1946) *The Twenty Years' Crisis. 1919–1939: An Introduction to the Study of International Relations*. London.

Cartledge, P. (1981) "Spartan Wives: Liberation or License?," *CQ* n.s. 31: 84–105.

    (1987) *Agesilaos and the Crisis of Sparta*. Baltimore.

    (1990) "Review of Yvon Garlan, *Guerre et économie en Grèce ancienne*," *Gnomon* 62: 464–6.

    (1998a) "The Machismo of the Athenian Empire – or the Reign of the Phaulus?," in *When Men Were Men: Masculinity, Power and Identity in Classical Antiquity*, ed. L. Foxhall and J. Salmon. London: 54–67.

    (1998b) "War and Peace," in *The Cambridge Illustrated History of Ancient Greece*, ed. P. Cartledge. Cambridge: 167–92.

Cawkwell, G. L. (1960) "Aeschines and the Peace of Philocrates," *REG* 73: 416–38.

    (1961) "A Note on Ps. Demosthenes 17.20," *Phoenix* 15: 74–8.

    (1962a) "Aeschines and the Ruin of Phocis in 346," *REG* 75: 453–9.

    (1962b) "The Defence of Olynthus," *CQ* n.s. 12: 122–40.

    (1963a) "Demosthenes' Policy after the Peace of Philocrates. I," *CQ* n.s. 13: 120–38.

    (1963b) "Demosthenes' Policy after the Peace of Philocrates. II," *CQ* n.s. 13: 200–13.

    (1963c) "Eubulus," *JHS* 83: 47–67.

    (1963d) "Notes on the Peace of 375/4," *Historia* 12: 84–95.

    (1969) "The Crowning of Demosthenes," *CQ* n.s. 19: 163–80.

(1973) "The Foundation of the Second Athenian Confederacy," *CQ* n.s. 23: 47–60.

(1978a) *Philip of Macedon.* Boston.

(1978b) "The Peace of Philocrates Again," *CQ* n.s. 28: 95–104.

(1981) "Notes on the Failure of the Second Athenian Confederacy," *JHS* 101: 40–55.

(1982) "Isocrates," in *Ancient Writers: Greece and Rome*, ed. T. J. Luce. New York: 313–29.

Ceadel, M. (1996) "Ten Distinctions for Peace Historians," in *The Pacifist Impulse in Historical Perspective*, ed. H. L. Dyck. Toronto: 17–35.

Ceccarelli, P. (1993) "Sans thalassocratie, pas de démocratie?: Le rapport entre thalassocratie et démocratie à Athènes dans la discussion du Ve et IVe siecle av. J.-C.," *Historia* 42: 444–70.

Chambers, J. T. (1975) "The Fourth-century Athenians' View of their Fifth-century Empire," *PP* 30: 177–91.

Chaniotis, A. (2004) "Justifying Territorial Claims in Classical and Hellenistic Greece: The Beginnings of International Law," in *The Law and Courts in Ancient Greece*, ed. E. M. Harris and L. Rubinstein. London: 185–213.

(2005) *War in the Hellenistic World: A Social and Cultural History.* Oxford.

Chatfield, C. (1996) "Thinking about Peace in History," in *The Pacifist Impulse in Historical Perspective*, ed. H. L. Dyck. Toronto: 36–51.

Chiron, P. (2007) "The Rhetoric to Alexander," in *A Companion to Greek Rhetoric*, ed. I. Worthington. Malden, MA: 90–106.

Christ, M. R. (1990) "Liturgy Avoidance and *antidosis* in Classical Athens," *TAPhA* 120: 147–69.

(2001) "Conscription of Hoplites in Classical Athens," *CQ* 51: 398–422.

(2006) *The Bad Citizen in Classical Athens.* Cambridge.

Cobet, J. (1986) "Herodotus and Thucydides on War," in *Past Perspectives: Studies in Greek and Roman Historical Writing*, ed. I. S. Moxon, J. D. Smart, and A. J. Woodman. Cambridge: 1–18.

Cohen, A. (1996) "Portrayals of Abduction in Greek Art: Rape or Metaphor?," in *Sexuality in Ancient Art*, ed. N. B. Kampen. Cambridge: 117–35.

Cohen, D. (1984) "Justice, Interest, and Political Deliberation in Thucydides," *Quaderni Urbinati* n.s. 16: 35–60.

(1991) *Law, Sexuality, and Society: The Enforcement of Morals in Classical Athens.* Cambridge.

(1993) "Consent and Sexual Relations in Classical Athens," in *Consent and Coercion to Sex and Marriage in Ancient and Medieval Societies*, ed. A. E. Laiou. Washington: 5–16.

(1995) *Law, Violence and Community in Classical Athens.* Cambridge.

(2005) "Crime, Punishment, and the Rule of Law in Classical Athens," in *The Cambridge Companion to Ancient Greek Law*, ed. M. Gagarin and D. Cohen. Cambridge: 211–35.

Cohen, E. (1992) *Athenian Economy and Society: A Banking Perspective.* Princeton.

(2000) *The Athenian Nation.* Princeton.

(2005) "Commercial Law," in *The Cambridge Companion to Ancient Greek Law*, ed. M. Gagarin and D. Cohen. Cambridge: 290–304.

Collier, J. G. (1991) "Legal Basis of the Institution of War," in *The Institution of War*, ed. R. A. Hinde. London: 121–32.

Collins, A. and D. Gentner (1987) "How People Construct Mental Models," in *Cultural Models in Language and Thought*, ed. N. Quinn and D. Holland. Cambridge: 243–65.

Connor, W. R., ed. (1966) *Greek Orations*. Ann Arbor.

 (1984) *Thucydides*. Princeton.

Cook, M. L. (1990) "Timocrates' 50 Talents and the Cost of Ancient Warfare," *Eranos* 88: 69–97.

Cooper, J. and D. S. Hutchinson, eds. (1997) *Plato: Complete Works*. Indianapolis.

Crane, G. (1996) *The Blinded Eye: Thucydides and the New Written Word*. Lanham, MD.

 (1998) *Thucydides and the Ancient Simplicity: The Limits of Political Realism*. Berkeley.

Croally, N. T. (1994) *Euripidean Polemic: The Trojan Women and the Function of Tragedy*. Cambridge.

Daitz, S. G. (1957) "The Relationship of the *De Chersoneso* and the *Philippica Quarta* of Demosthenes," *CPh* 52: 145–62.

Daly, M. and M. Wilson (1988) *Homicide*. New York.

Davidson, J. (1990) "Isocrates against Imperialism: An Analysis of the *De Pace*," *Historia* 39: 20–36.

 (1997) *Courtesans and Fishcakes: The Consuming Passions of Classical Athens*. Hammersmith.

Dawson, D. (1996) *The Origins of Western Warfare: Militarism and Morality in the Ancient World*. Boulder, CO.

Dean-Jones, L. (1994) "Medicine: The Proof of Anatomy," in *Women in the Classical World: Image and Text*, ed. E. Fantham, H. P. Foley, N. B. Kampen, S. B. Pomeroy, and H. A. Shapiro. Oxford: 183–205.

DeBrohun, J. B. (2007) "The Gates of War (and Peace): Roman Literary Perspectives," in *War and Peace in the Ancient World*, ed. K. A. Raaflaub. Oxford: 256–78.

Degler, C. (1959) "Starr on Slavery," *Journal of Economic History* 19: 271–7.

Demand, N. (1996) *A History of Ancient Greece*. United States.

Denyer, N. (2001) *Plato: Alcibiades*. Cambridge.

Develin, R. J. (1994) *Epitome of the Philippic History of Pompeius Trogus*. Atlanta.

Dickinson, E. D. (1920) *The Equality of States in International Law*. Cambridge.

Diels, H. and W. Kranz (1952) *Die Fragmente der Vorsokratiker*. Berlin.

Dillery, J. (1993) "Xenophon's *Poroi* and Athenian Imperialism," *Historia* 42: 1–11.

 (1995) *Xenophon and the History of his Times*. London.

Dodds, E. R. (1951) *Greeks and the Irrational*. Berkeley and Los Angeles.

Donlan, W. (1997) "The Homeric Economy," in *A New Companion to Homer*, ed. I. Morris and B. Powell. Leiden: 649–67.

Dorjahn, A. P. (1940) "Demosthenes' Reply to the Charge of Cowardice," *PhQ* 19: 337–42.

(1947) "On Demosthenes' Ability to Speak Extemporaneously," *TAPhA* 78: 69–76.

Dover, K. J. (1968) *Lysias and the Corpus Lysiacum*. Los Angeles.

(1972) *Aristophanic Comedy*. Berkeley.

(1974) *Greek Popular Morality in the Time of Plato and Aristotle*. Oxford.

(1978) *Greek Homosexuality*. London.

(1993) *Aristophanes: Frogs*. Oxford.

Doyle, M. W. (1991) "Thucydides: A Realist?," in *Hegemonic Rivalry: From Thucydides to the Nuclear Age*, ed. R. N. Lebow and B. S. Strauss. Boulder, CO: 169–88.

duBois, P. (1991) *Torture and Truth*. London and New York.

Ducrey, P. (1968) *Le traitement des prisonniers de guerre dans la Grèce antique*. Paris.

(1971) "Remarque sur les causes du mercenariat dans la Grèce ancienne et la Suisse moderne," in *Buch der Freunde für J. R. von Salis*. Zurich: 115–23.

Dunkel, H. B. (1938) "Was Demosthenes a Panhellenist?," *CPh* 33: 291–305.

Eckstein, A. M. (2000) "Review Article: Brigands, Emperors, and Anarchy," *International History Review* 22: 862–79.

(2006) *Mediterranean Anarchy, Interstate War, and the Rise of Rome*. Berkeley.

Edmunds, L. (1975) *Chance and Intelligence in Thucydides*. Cambridge.

Edwards, M. (1995) *Greek Orators*, vol. iv: *Andocides*. Warminster.

Ehrenreich, B. (1997) *Blood Rites: Origins and History of the Passions of War*. New York.

Ellis, J. R. (1982) "Philip and the Peace of Philokrates," in *Philip, Alexander the Great and the Macedonian Heritage*, ed. W. L. Adams and E. N. Borza. Washington: 43–59.

Erhrard, C. T. H. R. (1995) "Speeches before Battle?," *Historia* 44: 120–1.

Errington, R. M. (1990) *A History of Macedonia*. Berkeley.

Fearon, J. D. (1995) "Rationalist Explanations for War," *International Organization* 49: 379–414.

Ferguson, N. (1999) *The Pity of War: Explaining World War I*. New York.

Ferguson, R. B. (1997) "Violence and War in Prehistory," in *Troubled Times: Violence and Warfare in the Past*, ed. D. L. Martin and D. W. Frayer. Australia: 321–55.

Fernandez, J. W., ed. (1991) *Beyond Metaphor: The Theory of Tropes in Anthropology*. Stanford.

Fiala, A. (2007) "Pacifism," *The Stanford Encyclopedia of Philosophy*, from http://plato.stanford.edu/archives/sum2007/entries/pacifism/.

Figueira, T. J. (1990) "Aigina and the Naval Strategy of the Late Fifth and Early Fifth Centuries," *RhM*: 15–51.

(1995) "KHRĒMATA: Acquisition and Possession in Archaic Greece," in *Social Justice in the Ancient World*, ed. K. D. Irani and M. Silver. Westport, CT: 41–60.

Finley, J. (1967) *Three Essays on Thucydides*. Cambridge.

Finley, M. I. (1978a) *The World of Odysseus*. London.

(1978b) "Empire in the Greco-Roman World," *Greece and Rome* n.s. 25: 1–15.

(1985a) *The Ancient Economy*. Berkeley.

(1985b) "War and Empire," in *Ancient History: Evidence and Models*. New York: 67–87.

Finnegan, W. (2000) "A Slave in New York: From Africa to the Bronx, One Man's Long Journey to Freedom," *New Yorker*: 50–61.

Fisher, N. R. E. (1992) *Hybris: A Study in the Values of Honour and Shame in Ancient Greece*. Warminster.

(1993) *Slavery in Classical Greece*. London.

(1998) "Violence, Masculinity and the Law in Classical Athens," in *When Men Were Men: Masculinity, Power and Identity in Classical Antiquity*, ed. L. Foxhall and J. Salmon. London: 68–97.

(2000) "Hybris, Revenge and Stasis in the Greek City-States," in *War and Violence in Ancient Greece*, ed. H. van Wees. London: 83–123.

Fornara, C. W. (1983) *Translated Documents of Greece and Rome*, vol. 1: *Archaic Times to the End of the Peloponnesian War*. Cambridge.

Forrest, W. G. (1975) "An Athenian Generation Gap," *YClS* 24: 37–52.

Fox, R. L. (1997) "Demosthenes, Dionysius and the Dating of Six Early Speeches," *C&M* 48: 167–203.

French, A. (1991) "Economic Conditions in Fourth-century Athens," *G&R* 38: 24–40.

Fritz, K. v. (1973–4) "Influence of Ideas on Greek Historiography," in *Dictionary of the History of Ideas: Studies of Selected Pivotal Ideas*, ed. P. P. Wiener. New York: 499–511.

Fuks, A. (1972) "Isokrates and the Social-Economic Situation in Greece," *Ancient Society* 3: 17–44.

Gabrielsen, V. (1994) *Financing the Athenian Fleet: Public Taxation and Social Relations*. Baltimore.

Gagarin, M. (1996) "The Torture of Slaves in Athenian Law," *CPh* 91: 1–18.

Garlan, Y. (1975) *War in the Ancient World: A Social History*. London.

(1989) *Guerre et économie en Grèce ancienne*. Paris.

(1995) "War and Peace," in *The Greeks*, ed. J.-P. Vernant, trans. C. Lambert and T. L. Fagan. Chicago: 53–85.

(1999) "War, Piracy, and Slavery in the Greek world," in *Classical Slavery*, ed. M. I. Finley. London: 7–21.

Garland, R. (1985) *The Greek Way of Death*. Ithaca, NY.

Garnsey, P. (1988) *Famine and Food Supply in the Graeco-Roman World*. Cambridge.

(1998) *Cities, Peasants and Food in Classical Antiquity*. Cambridge.

Gaubatz, K. T. (1999) *Elections and War: The Electoral Incentive in the Democratic Politics of War and Peace*. Stanford.

Gauthier, P. (1976) *Un commentaire historique des Poroi de Xénophon*. Paris.

Gehrke, H.-J. (1987) "Die Griechen und die Rache: Ein Versuch in historischer Psychologie," *Saeculum* 38: 121–49.

Gellner, E. (1991) "An Anthropological View of War and Violence," in *The Institution of War*, ed. R. A. Hinde. London: 62–79.

Gera, D. (1997) *The Anonymous Tractatus De Mulieribus*. Leiden.

Gibbon, E. (1952) *The Portable Gibbon: The Decline and Fall of the Roman Empire*. New York.

Gibert, J. (2002) "The Sophists," in *The Blackwell Guide to Ancient Philosophy*, ed. C. Shields. Oxford: 27–50.

Gill, C., N. Postlethwaite, and R. Seaford (1998) *Reciprocity in Ancient Greece*. Oxford.

Gillis, D. (1970) "The Structure of Arguments in Isocrates' *De Pace*," *Philologus* 114: 195–210.

Gilpin, R. G. (1986) "The Richness of the Tradition of Political Realism," in *Neorealism and its Critics*, ed. R. O. Keohane. New York: 301–21.

Goodman, M. D. and A. J. Holladay (1986) "Religious Scruples in Ancient Warfare," *CQ* 36: 151–71.

Goossens, R. (1962) *Euripides et Athènes*. Brussels.

Gottschall, J. (2008) *The Rape of Troy: Evolution, Violence, and the World of Homer*. Cambridge.

Gouldner, A. W. (1965) *Enter Plato: Classical Greece and the Origins of Social Theory*. New York.

Gourevitch, P. (1998) *We Wish to Inform You That Tomorrow We Will Be Killed with our Families*. New York.

Grant, J. R. (1965) "A Note on the Tone of Greek Diplomacy," *CQ* n.s. 15: 261–6.

Green, P. (1996) "The Metamorphosis of the Barbarian: Athenian Panhellenism in a Changing World," in *Transitions to Empire: Essays in Greco-Roman History, 360–146 BC, in Honor of E. Badian*, ed. R. W. Wallace and E. M. Harris. Norman: 5–36.

(1999) "War and Morality in Fifth-century Athens: The Case of Euripides' Trojan Women," *AHB* 13: 97–110.

Greenspan, A. (2007) *The Age of Turbulence*. London.

Greenwood, C. (1991) "In Defense of the Laws of War," in *The Institution of War*, ed. R. A. Hinde. London: 133–47.

Griffith, G. T. (1978) "Athens in the Fourth Century," in *Imperialism in the Ancient World*, ed. P. D. A. Garnsey and C. R. Whittaker. Cambridge: 127–44.

Grimaldi, W. (1980) *Aristotle, Rhetoric*, vol. 1: *A Commentary*. New York.

Grossman, L. C. D. (1995) *On Killing: The Psychological Costs of Learning to Kill in War and Society*. Boston.

Grotius, H. (1925) *The Law of War and Peace*. Indianapolis.

Hahn, I. (1983) "Foreign Trade and Foreign Policy in Archaic Greece: Cambridge Philological Society Supplementary Volume 8," in *Trade and Famine in Classical Antiquity*, ed. P. Garnsey and C. R. Whittaker. Cambridge: 30–6.

Hajdú, I. (2002) *Kommentar zur 4. Philippischen Rede des Demosthenes*. Berlin.

Hall, J. M. (1997) *Ethnic Identity in Greek Antiquity*. Cambridge.

(2001) "Contested Ethnicities: Perceptions of Macedonia within Evolving Definitions of Greek Identity," in *Ancient Perceptions of Greek Ethnicity*, ed. I. Malkin. Cambridge, MA: 159–86.

(2002) *Hellenicity: Between Ethnicity and Culture*. Chicago.

(2007) *A History of the Archaic Greek World, ca. 1200–479 BCE*. Malden, MA.

Hallpike, C. R. (1973) "Functionalist Interpretations of Primitive Warfare," *Man* 8: 451–70.

Hamel, D. (1995) "*Strategoi* on the *Bema*: The Separation of Political and Military Authority in Fourth-century Athens," *AHB* 9: 25–39.

(1998) *Athenian Generals: Military Authority in the Classical Period*. Leiden.

Hamilton, C. D. (1979) "Greek Rhetoric and History: The Case of Isocrates," in *Aktouros: Hellenic Studies Presented to Bernard M. W. Knox on the Occasion of his 65th Birthday*, ed. G. Bowersock, W. Burkert, and M. C. J. Putnam. Berlin: 290–8.

(1980) "Isocrates, IG II² 43, Greek Propaganda and Imperialism," *Traditio* 36: 83–109.

Hammond, N. G. L. (1986) *A History of Greece to 322 BC*. Oxford.

(1994) *Philip of Macedon*. Baltimore.

Hammond, N. G. L. and G. T. Griffith (1972–88) *A History of Macedonia: 550–336 BC*. Vol. II. Oxford.

Hansen, M. H. (1976) "The Theoric Fund and the *graphe paranomon* against Apollodorus," *GRBS* 17: 235–46.

(1984) "Two Notes on Demosthenes' Symbouleutic Speeches," *C&M* 35: 57–70.

(1985) *Demography and Democracy: The Number of Athenian Citizens in the Fourth Century BC*. Herning.

(1987) *The Athenian Assembly in the Age of Demosthenes*. Oxford.

(1991) *The Athenian Democracy in the Age of Demosthenes: Structure, Principles, and Ideology*. Oxford.

(1993) "The Battle Exhortation in Ancient Historiography. Fact or Fiction?," *Historia* 42: 161–80.

(2006) *The Shotgun Method: The Demography of the Ancient City-State Culture*. Columbia.

Hansen, M. H. and T. H. Nielsen (2004) *An Inventory of Archaic and Classical Poleis*. Oxford.

Hanson, V. D. (1989) *The Western Way of War: Infantry Battle in Classical Greece*. New York.

(1998) *Warfare and Agriculture in Classical Greece*. Berkeley.

(2000) "The Classical Greek Warrior and the Egalitarian Military Ethos," *Ancient World* 31.2: 111–26.

Harding, P. (1974) "The Purpose of Isokrates' *Archidamos* and *On the Peace*," *California Studies in Classical Antiquity* 6: 137–49.

(1979) "Review of George Cawkwell, *Philip of Macedon*," *Phoenix* 33: 173–8.

(1985) *Translated Documents of Greece and Rome*, vol. II: *From the End of the Peloponnesian War to the Battle of Ipsus*. Cambridge.

(1987) "Rhetoric and Politics in Fourth-century Athens," *Phoenix* 41: 23–39.

(1988) "Athenian Defensive Strategy in the Fourth Century," *Phoenix* 42: 61–71.

(1995) "Athenian Foreign Policy in the Fourth Century," *Klio* 77: 105–25.

(2006) *Didymos: On Demosthenes*. Oxford.

Harris, E. (1990) "Did the Athenians Regard Seduction as a Worse Crime than Rape," *CQ* n.s. 40: 370–7.

(1994) "Law and Oratory," in *Persuasion: Greek Rhetoric in Action*, ed. I. Worthington. London: 130–50.

(1995) *Aeschines and Athenian Politics*. Oxford.

(1996) "Demosthenes and the Theoric Fund," in *Transitions to Empire: Essays in Greco-Roman History, 360–146 BC, in Honor of E. Badian*, ed. R. W. Wallace and E. M. Harris. Norman: 57–76.

(2000) "The Authenticity of Andocides' *De Pace*: A Subversive Essay," in *Polis and Politics: Studies in Ancient Greek History Presented to Mogens Herman Hansen on his Sixtieth Birthday*, ed. P. Flensted-Jensen, T. Nielsen, and L. Rubinstein. Copenhagen: 479–505.

(2004) "Antigone the Lawyer or the Ambiguities of *Nomos*," in *The Law and the Courts in Ancient Greece*, ed. E. Harris and L. Rubinstein. London: 19–56.

Harris, M. (1977) *Cannibals and Kings: The Origins of Cultures*. New York.

Harris, W. V. (1997) "Lysias III and Athenian Beliefs about Revenge," *CQ* n.s. 47: 363–6.

Harrison, A. R. W. (1971) *The Law of Athens: Procedure*. Oxford.

Haslam, J. (2002) *No Virtue Like Necessity: Realist Thought in International Relations since Machiavelli*. New Haven.

Havelock, E. A. (1972) "Heroism and History," in *Valeurs antiques et temps modernes*, ed. E. Gareau. Ottawa: 19–52.

Heath, M. (1996) "Justice in Thucydides' Athenian Speeches," *Historia* 39: 385–400.

Heller, J. (1994) *Catch-22*. New York.

Henderson, J. (1991) *The Maculate Muse: Obscene Language in Attic Comedy*. Oxford.

Herman, G. (1987) *Ritualised Friendship and the Greek City*. Cambridge.

(1993) "Tribal and Civic Codes of Behavior in Lysias I," *CQ* n.s. 43: 406–19.

(1994) "How Violent Was Athenian Society?," in *Ritual, Finance, Politics: Athenian Democratic Accounts Presented to David Lewis*, ed. R. Osborne and S. Hornblower. Oxford: 99–117.

(1995) "Honour, Revenge and the State in Fourth-century Athens," in *Die athenische Demokratie im Jahrhundert v.Chr.: Vollendung oder Verfall einer Verfassungsform*, ed. W. Eder. Stuttgart: 43–60.

(1996) "Ancient Athens and the Values of Mediterranean society," *MHR* 11: 5–36.

(1998a) "Reciprocity, Altruism, and the Prisoner's Dilemma: The Special Case of Classical Athens," in *Reciprocity in Ancient Greece*, ed. C. Gill, N. Postlethwaite, and R. Seaford. Oxford: 199–225.

(1998b) "Review of David Cohen, *Law, Violence and Community in Classical Athens*," *Gnomon* 70: 605–15.

(2000) "Athenian Beliefs about Revenge: Problems and Methods," *PCPhS* 46: 7–27.

Herrman, J., ed. (forthcoming) *Hyperides: Funeral Oration. Edited with Introduction, Translation, and Commentary*, American Philological Association.

Hirsch, S. W. (1985) *The Friendship of the Barbarians: Xenophon and the Persian Empire*. Hanover, NH.

Hobson, J. A. (1938) *Imperialism: A Study*. London.

Hornblower, S. (1991–2009) *A Commentary on Thucydides*. 3 vols. Oxford.

(1992) "The Religious Dimension to the Peloponnesian War, or What Thucydides Does Not Tell Us," *HSPh* 94: 169–97.

(2000) "The *Old Oligarch* (Pseudo-Xenophon's *Athenaion Politeia*) and Thucydides. A Fourth-century Date for the *Old Oligarch*?," in *Polis and Politics: Studies in Ancient Greek History Presented to Mogens Herman Hansen on his Sixtieth Birthday*, ed. P. Flensted-Jensen, T. H. Nielsen, and L. Rubinstein. Copenhagen: 363–84.

Howard, M. (2000) *The Invention of Peace*. New Haven.

Hudson-Williams, H. L. (1951) "Political Speeches in Athens," *CQ* n.s. 1: 68–73.

Humphreys, S. C. (2007) "Social Relations on Stage: Witnesses in Classical Athens," in *The Attic Orators*, ed. E. Carawan. Oxford: 140–213.

Hunt, P. (1998) *Slaves, Warfare, and Ideology in the Greek Historians*. Cambridge.

(2007) "Military Forces," in *The Cambridge History of Greek and Roman Warfare*, ed. P. Sabin, H. V. Wees, and M. Whitby. Cambridge: 108–46.

(forthcoming) "Athenian Militarism and the Recourse to War," in *War, Culture, and Democracy in Classical Athens*, ed. David Pritchard. Cambridge.

Hunter, V. (1994) *Policing Athens: Social Control in the Attic Lawsuits, 420–320 BC*. Princeton.

Isaacson, W. (2004) "Colin Powell's Redeeming Failures," *New York Times* (November 16): Op-Ed Page.

Isager, S. and M. H. Hansen (1975) *Aspects of Athenian Society in the Fourth Century BC*. Odense.

Jackson, A. H. (1991) "Hoplites and the Gods: The Dedication of Captured Arms and Armour," in *Hoplites: The Classical Greek Battle Experience*, ed. V. Hanson. London: 228–49.

(1993) "War and Raids for Booty in the World of Odysseus," in *War and Society in the Greek World*, ed. J. Rich and G. Shipley. London: 64–76.

Jameson, M. H. (1991) "Sacrifice before Battle," in *Hoplites: The Classical Greek Battle Experience*, ed. V. Hanson. London: 197–227.

(1992) "Agricultural Labor in Ancient Greece," in *Proceedings of the Seventh International Symposium at the Swedish Institute at Athens*, ed. B. Wells. Stockholm: 135–46.

(2006) "The Family of Herakles in Attika," in *Herakles and Hercules*, ed. L. Rawlings and H. Bowden. Swansea: 15–36.

Jehne, M. (1994) *Koine Eirene: Untersuchungen zu den Befriedungs- und Stabilisierungsbemühungen in der griechischen Poliswelt des 4. Jahrhunderts v. Chr.* Stuttgart.

Johnson, D. P. (2004) *Overconfidence and War: The Havoc and Glory of Positive Illusions.* Cambridge, MA.

Johnson, G. R. (1986) "Kin Selection, Socialization, and Patriotism: An Integrating Theory," *Politics and the Life Sciences* 4: 127–40.

   (1987) "In the Name of the Fatherland: An Analysis of Kin Term Usage in Patriotic Speech and Literature," *International Political Science Review* 8: 165–74.

Jones, A. H. M. (1957) *Athenian Democracy.* Oxford.

Jones, C. P. (1999) *Kinship Diplomacy in the Ancient World.* Cambridge.

Jordan, B. (1986) "Religion in Thucydides," *TAPhA* 116: 119–47.

Jost, K. (1936) *Das Beispiel und Vorbild der Vorfahren bei den attischen Rednern und Geschichtschreibern bis Demosthenes.* Paderborn.

Joyal, M. (2003) "Review of Nicolas Denyer, *Plato: Alcibiades*," *BMCRev* January 28.

Julien, J.-M. and H. L. De Péréra, eds. (1902) *Eschine: Discours sur l'ambassade.* Paris.

Just, R. (1989) *Women in Athenian Law and Life.* London.

Kagan, D. (1961) "The Economic Origins of the Corinthian War (395–387 BC)," *PP* 16: 321–41.

Kallet, L. (2001) *Money and the Corrosion of Power in Thucydides: The Sicilian Expedition and its Aftermath.* Berkeley and Los Angeles.

Kallet-Marx (1994) "Money Talks: Rhetor, Demos, and the Resources of the Athenian Empire," in *Ritual, Finance, Politics: Democratic Accounts Presented to David Lewis*, ed. R. Osborne and S. Hornblower. Oxford: 227–51.

Kant, I. (1983) "Perpetual Peace," in *Perpetual Peace and Other Essays on Politics, History, and Morals.* Indianapolis, IN.

Kaplan, L. F. (2001) "Colin Powell," *Prospect Magazine* 60 (February): www.prospect-magazine.co.uk/article_details.php?id=3392.

Karavites, P. (1982a) *Capitulations and Greek Interstate Relations: The Reflection of Humanistic Ideals in Political Events.* Göttingen.

   (1982b) "Ἐλευθερία and Αὐτονομία in Fifth-century Interstate Relations," *RIDA* 29: 145–62.

   (1984) "Greek Interstate Relations and Moral Principles in the Fifth Century," *PP* 39: 161–92.

Karnow, S. (1984) *Vietnam: A History.* Harmondsworth.

Keegan, J. (1976) *The Face of Battle.* New York.

Keil, B. (1916) *EIPHNH: Eine philologisch-antiquarische Untersuchung.* Leipzig.

Kelly, D. H. (1980) "Philip II of Macedon and the Boeotian Alliance," *Antichthon* 14: 64–83.

Kennan, G. F. (1947) "The Sources of Soviet Conduct," *Foreign Affairs* 25: 566–82.

Kennedy, G. (1959) "Focusing of Arguments in Greek Deliberative Oratory," *TAPhA* 90: 131–38.

   (1963) *The Art of Persuasion in Greece.* Princeton.

   (1996) "The Composition and Influence of Aristotle's *Rhetoric*," in *Essays on Aristotle's Rhetoric*, ed. A. O. Rorty. Berkeley and Los Angeles: 416–24.

(1986) "Theory of World Politics: Structural Realism and Beyond," in *Neorealism and its Critics*, ed. R. O. Keohane. New York: 158–203.

Kinder, D. and J. Weiss (1978) "In Lieu of Rationality: Psychological Perspectives on Foreign Decision Making," *Journal of Conflict Resolution* 22: 707–38.

Kissinger, H. (1994) *Diplomacy*. New York.

Klees, H. (1998) *Sklavenleben im Klassischen Griechenland*. Stuttgart.

Knippschild (2002) *Drum bietet zum Bunde die Hände: Rechtssymbolische Akte in zwischenstaatlichen Beziehungen im orientalischen und griechisch-römischen Altertum*. Stuttgart.

Knock, T. J. (1992) *To End All Wars: Woodrow Wilson and the Quest for a New World Order*. Oxford.

Knox, B. (1957) *Oedipus at Thebes*. New Haven, CT.

Knox, R. A. (1989) "Review of *Phocion the Good*, by Lawrence A. Tritle," *CR* 39: 79–80.

Kock, T., ed. (1880–8) *Comicorum atticorum fragmenta*. Leipzig.

Konstan, D. (1997a) *Friendship in the Classical World*. Cambridge.

(1997b) "Defining Ancient Greek Ethnicity," *Diaspora* 6: 97–110.

(1998) "Reciprocity and Friendship," in *Reciprocity in Ancient Greece*, ed. C. Gill, N. Postlethwaite, and R. Seaford. Oxford: 279–301.

(2007) "War and Reconciliation in Greek Literature," in *War and Peace in the Ancient World*, ed. K. Raaflaub. Malden, MA: 191–205.

Kraut, R. (2002) *Aristotle: Political Philosophy*. Oxford.

Kroll, J. (2000) "Review of Leslie Kurke, *Coins, Bodies, Games, and Gold: The Politics of Meaning in Archaic Greece*," *CJ* 96: 85–90.

Krüger, T. (2007) " 'They Shall Beat their Swords into Plowshares': A Vision of Peace through Justice and its Background in the Hebrew Bible," in *War and Peace in the Ancient World*, ed. K. Raaflaub. Malden, MA: 161–71.

Kurke, L. (1999) *Coins, Bodies, Games, and Gold: The Politics of Meaning in Archaic Greece*. Princeton.

Laforse, B. (1998) "Xenophon, Callicratidas and Panhellenism," *Ancient History Bulletin* 12: 55–67.

Laistner, M. L. W., ed. (1927) *Isocrates, De Pace and Philippus*. Cornell Studies in Classical Philology. New York.

Lakoff, G. and M. Johnson (1980) *Metaphors We Live By*. Chicago.

Lambert, S. D. (2001) "The Only Extant Decree of Demosthenes," *ZPE* 137: 55–68.

Lanni, A. (2005) "Relevance in Athenian Courts," in *The Cambridge Companion to Ancient Greek Law*, ed. M. Gagarin and D. Cohen. Cambridge: 112–28.

Laurenti, R. (1987) "Polemologia del Corpus Aristotelicum," *GIF* 39: 19–38.

Lavelle, B. M. (1986) "The Nature of Hipparchos' Insult to Harmodius," *AJPh* 107: 318–31.

Lawton, C. L. (1995) *Attic Document Reliefs*. Oxford.

Leader, R. E. (1997) "In Death Not Divided: Gender, Family, and State on Classical Athenian Grave Stelae," *AJA* 101: 683–99.

Lebow, R. N. (2001) "Thucydides the Constructivist," *American Political Science Review* 95: 547–60.

Lembcke, J. (1998) *The Spitting Image: Myth, Memory, and the Legacy of Vietnam.* New York.

Lendon, J. E. (2000) "Homeric Vengeance and the Outbreak of Greek Wars," in *War and Violence in Ancient Greece*, ed. H. van Wees. London: 1–30.

(2005) *Soldiers and Ghosts: A History of Battle in Classical Antiquity.* New Haven.

(2006) "Xenophon and the Alternative to Realist Foreign Policy: Cyropaedia 3.1.14–31," *JHS* 126: 82–98.

(2007) "Athens and Sparta and the Coming of the Peloponnesian War," in *Cambridge Companion to the Age of Pericles*, ed. L. J. Samons. Cambridge: 258–80.

Lenin, V. I. (1939) *Imperialism: The Highest Stage of Capitalism. A Popular Outline.* New York.

Leopold, J. W. (1981) "Demosthenes on Distrust of Tyrants," *GRBS* 22: 227–46.

(1987) "Demosthenes' Strategy in the First Philippic, 'An Away Match with Macedonian Cavalry?,'" *Ancient World* 16: 59–69.

Lewis, S. (1996) *News and Society in the Greek Polis.* Chapel Hill, NC.

Loman, P. (2004) "No Woman No War: Women's Participation in Ancient Greek Warfare," *Greece and Rome* 51: 34–54.

Long, T. (1986) *Barbarians in Greek Comedy.* Carbondale, IL.

Lonis, R. (1980) "La valeur du serment dans les accords internationaux en Grèce classique," *Dialogues d'historie ancienne* 6: 267–86.

Loraux, N. (1986) *The Invention of Athens: The Funeral Oration in the Classical City.* Cambridge.

Low, P. (2007) *Interstate Relations in Classical Greece: Morality and Power.* Cambridge.

Lynn, J. A. (2003) *Battle: A History of Combat and Culture.* Boulder, CO.

MacDowell, D. M. (1978) *The Law in Classical Athens.* London.

ed. (2000) *Demosthenes: On the False Embassy (Oration 19).* Oxford.

MacMullen, R. (1963) "Foreign Policy for the Polis," *G&R* n.s. 10: 118–22.

Mactoux, M.-M. (1980) *Douleia: esclavage et pratique discursive dans l'Athènes classique.* Paris.

Major, W. E. (1997) "Menander in a Macedonian World," *GRBS* 38: 41–73.

Manning, J. G. and I. Morris, eds. (2005) *The Ancient Economy: Evidence and Models.* Stanford.

Markle, M. M. (1974) "The Strategy of Philip in 346 BC," *CQ* n.s. 24: 253–68.

(1976) "Support of Athenian Intellectuals for Philip: A Study of Isocrates' *Philippus* and Speusippus' *Letter to Philip*," *JHS* 96: 80–99.

(1981) "Demosthenes' *Second Philippic*: A Valid Policy for the Athenians against Philip," *Antichthon* 15: 62–85.

Mattern, S. P. (1999) *Rome and the Enemy: Imperial Strategy in the Principate.* Berkeley and Los Angeles.

McCauley, C. (1990) "Conference Overview," in *The Anthropology of War*, ed. J. Haas. Cambridge: 1–25.

McCullagh, C. B. (1991) "How Objective Interests Explain Actions," *Social Science Information* 30: 29–54.

Mearsheimer, J. J. (2001) *The Tragedy of Great Power Politics*. New York.

Meiggs, R. and D. Lewis (1988) *A Selection of Greek Historical Inscriptions to the End of the Fifth Century* BC. Rev. edn. Oxford.

Mikalson, J. D. (1991) *Honor thy Gods: Popular Religion in Greek Tragedy*. Chapel Hill.

Miller, H. F. (1984) "The Practical and Economic Background to the Greek Mercenary Explosion," *G&R* 31: 153–60.

Miller, M. C. (1997) *Athens and Persia in the Fifth Century* BC: *A Study in Cultural Receptivity*. Cambridge.

Millett, P. (1989) "Patronage and its Avoidance in Classical Athens," in *Patronage in Ancient Society*, ed. A. Wallace-Hadrill. London: 15–47.

(2000) "The Economy," in *Short Oxford History of Europe: Classical Greece*, ed. R. Osborne. Oxford: 23–51.

Milns, R. D. (1995) "Historical Paradigms in Demosthenes' Public Speech," *Electronic Antiquity* 2.5.

Mirhady, D. (1996) "Torture and Rhetoric in Athens," *JHS* 116: 119–31.

Missiou, A. (1992) *The Subversive Oratory of Andokides: Politics, Ideology, and Decision-making in Democratic Athens*. Cambridge.

(1993) "Doulos tou basileos: The Politics of Translation," *CQ* 43: 377–91.

(1998a) "Reciprocal Generosity in the Foreign Affairs of Fifth-century Athens and Sparta," in *Reciprocity in Ancient Greece*, ed. C. Gill, N. Postlethwaite, and R. Seaford. Oxford: 181–97.

Missiou-Ladi, A. (1987) "Coercive Diplomacy in Greek Interstate Relations (with Special Reference to *presbeis autokratores*)," *CQ* n.s. 37: 336–45.

Mitchell, L. G. (1996) "New for Old: Friendship Networks in Athenian Politics," *G&R* 43: 11–21.

(1997) *Greeks Bearing Gifts: The Public Use of Private Relationships in the Greek World, 435–323*. Cambridge.

(2007) *Panhellenism and the Barbarian*. Swansea.

Momigliano, A. (1966) "Some Observations on Causes of War in Ancient Historiography," in *Studies in Historiography*, ed. A. Momigliano. London: 112–26.

(1978) "Greek Historiography," *History and Theory* 17: 1–28.

Moreno, A. (2007) *Feeding the Democracy: The Athenian Grain Supply in the Fifth and Fourth Centuries*. Oxford.

Morrison, J. V. (2006) "Interaction of Speech and Narrative in Thucydides," in *Brill's Companion to Thucydides*, ed. A. Rengakos and A. Tsakmakis. Leiden: 251–77.

Mosley, D. J. (1973) *Envoys and Diplomacy in Ancient Greece*. Wiesbaden.

(1974) "On Greek Enemies Becoming Allies," *AncSoc* 5: 43–50.

Mossé, C. (1973) *Athens in Decline 404–86* BC. London.

Moysey, R. A. (1982) "Isokrates' *On The Peace*: Rhetorical Exercise or Political Advice," *AJAH* 7: 118–27.

(1987) "Isocrates and Chares: A Study in the Political Spectrum of Mid-fourth-century Athens," *Ancient World* 15: 81–6.

Müller, C. W. (1989) "Der schöne Tod des Polisbürgers oder 'Ehrenvoll ist es, für das Vaterland zu sterben,' " *Gymnasium* 9: 317–40.

Munn, M. (1997) "Thebes and Central Greece," in *The Greek World in the Fourth Century*, ed. L. Tritle. London: 66–106.

(2006) *The Mother of the Gods, Athens, and the Tyranny of Asia*. Berkeley.

Murray, G. (1944) "Reactions to the Peloponnesian War in Greek Thought and Practice," *JHS* 64: 1–9.

Nauck, A., ed. (1889). *Tragicorvm graecorvm fragmenta*. Leipzig.

Nestle, W. (1938) *Der Friedensgedanke in der Antiken Welt*. Leipzig.

Newman, W. L. (1887–1902) *The Politics of Aristotle*. 4 vols. Oxford.

O'Neill, B. (1999) *Honor, Symbols and War*. Ann Arbor.

Ober, J. (1978) "View of Sea Power in the Fourth-century Attic Orators," *The Ancient World* 1: 119–30.

(1989) *Mass and Elite in Democratic Athens: Rhetoric, Ideology, and the Power of the People*. Princeton.

(1991) "National Ideology and Strategic Defense of the Population from Athens to Star Wars," in *Hegemonic Rivalry: From Thucydides to the Nuclear Age*, ed. R. N. Lebow and B. S. Strauss. Boulder, CO: 251–67.

(2001) "Thucydides Theoretikos/Thucydides Histor: Realist Theory and the Challenge of History," in *War and Democracy: A Comparative Study of the Korean War and the Peloponnesian War*, ed. D. R. McCann and B. S. Strauss. Armonk, NY: 273–306.

Ostwald, M. (1982) *Autonomia: Its Genesis and Early History*. Chico, CA.

(1996) "Peace and War in Plato and Aristotle," *Scripta classica Israelica* 15: 102–18.

Parke, H. W. (1977) *Festivals of the Athenians*. London.

Parker, R. (1996) *Athenian Religion: A History*. Oxford.

(2000) "Sacrifice and Battle," in *War and Violence in Ancient Greece*, ed. H. van Wees. London: 299–314.

(2005) *Polytheism and Society at Athens*. Oxford.

Patterson, C. B. (1998) *The Family in Greek History*. Cambridge.

Patterson, O. (1971) "Quashee," in *The Debate over Slavery: Stanley Elkins and his Critics*, ed. A. J. Lane. Chicago: 210–17.

(1982) *Slavery and Social Death: A Comparative Study*. Cambridge, MA.

(1991) *Freedom in the Making of Western Culture*. New York.

Paulus, C. G. (2007) "Arbitration," in *Brill's New Pauly Online*, ed. H. Cancik and H. Schneider. Leiden.

Pearson, L. (1941) "Historical Allusions in the Attic Orators," *CP* 36: 209–29.

(1964) "The Development of Demosthenes as a Political Orator," *Phoenix* 18: 95–109.

(1975) "The Virtuoso Passages in Demosthenes' Speeches," *Phoenix* 29: 214–30.

Pecirka, J. (1982) "Athenian Imperialism and the Athenian Economy," *Eirene* 19: 117–25.

Perlman, S. (1963) "The Politicians in the Athenian Democracy of the Fourth Century BC," *Athenaeum* n.s. 41: 327–55.

(1968) "Athenian Democracy and the Revival of Imperialistic Expansion at the Beginning of the Fourth Century BC," *CP* 63: 257–67.

(1976) "Panhellenism, the Polis and Imperialism," *Historia* 25: 1–30.

(1985) "Greek Diplomatic Tradition and the Corinthian League of Philip of Macedon," *Historia* 34: 153–74.

Pew (2003) The 2004 Political Landscape: Evenly Divided and Increasingly Polarized. Washington, Pew Research Center for People and the Press: http://people-press.org/reports/display.php3?PageID=751.

Phillipson, C. (1911) *The International Law and Custom of Ancient Greece and Rome*. 2 vols. London.

Pierce, K. F. (1998) "Ideals of Masculinity in New Comedy," in *Thinking Men: Masculinity and its Self-Representation in the Classical Tradition*, ed. L. Foxhall and J. Salmon. London: 130–47.

Pinker, S. (2002) *The Blank Slate: The Modern Denial of Human Nature*. Harmondsworth.

Podlecki, A. J. (1971) "Cimon, Skyros, and 'Theseus' Bones,'" *JHS* 91: 141–3.

Pomeroy, S. B. (1994) *Xenophon, Oeconomicus: A Social and Historical Commentary*. Oxford.

Powell, C. A. (1979) "Religion and the Sicilian Expedition," *Historia* 28: 15–31.

Powell, R. (2002) "Bargaining Theory and International Conflict," *Annual Review of Political Science* 5: 1–30.

Pownall, F. S. (1998) "What Makes a War a Sacred War?," *Échos du monde classique/Classical Views* n.s. 17: 35–55.

Price, S. (1999) *Religions of the Ancient Greeks*. Cambridge.

Pritchard, D. (1998) " 'The Fractured Imaginary': Popular Thinking on Military Matters in Fifth-century Athens," *Ancient History: Resources for Teachers* 28: 38–61.

(1999) "The Fractured Imaginary: Popular Thinking on Citizen Soldiers and Warfare in Fifth-century Athens." Doctoral dissertation: Department of Ancient History, Macquarie University (Sydney, Australia).

(2007) "How Do Democracy and War Affect Each Other? The Case Study of Ancient Athens," *Polis* 24: 328–53.

Pritchett, W. K. (1971–91) *The Greek State at War*. 5 vols. Berkeley.

(2002) *Ancient Greek Battle Speeches and a Palfrey*. Amsterdam.

Quinn, N. and D. Holland (1987) "Culture and Cognition," in *Cultural Models in Language and Thought*, ed. N. Quinn and D. Holland. Cambridge: 3–42.

Raaflaub, K. (1983) "Democracy, Oligarchy and the Concept of the 'Free Citizen' in Late Fifth-century Athens," *Political Theory* 11: 517–44.

(1985) *Die Entdeckung der Freiheit*. Munich.

(1994) "Democracy, Power, and Imperialism in Fifth-century Athens," in *Athenian Political Thought and the Reconstruction of American Democracy*, ed. P. Euben, J. R. Wallach, and J. Ober. Ithaca: 103–46.

(1997) "Politics and Interstate Relations in the World of Early Greek *Poleis*: Homer and Beyond," *Antichthon* 31: 1–27.

(2001) "Father of All, Destroyer of All: War in Late Fifth-century Athenian Discourse and Ideology," in *War and Democracy: A Comparative Study of the Korean War and the Peloponnesian War*, ed. D. R. McCann and B. S. Strauss. Armonk, NY: 307–56.

(2004) *The Discovery of Freedom in Ancient Greece*. Chicago.

ed. (2007a) *War and Peace in the Ancient World*. Malden, MA.

(2007b) "Introduction: Searching for Peace in the Ancient World," in *War and Peace in the Ancient World*, ed. K. Raaflaub. Malden, MA: 1–33.

Rackham, H. (1937) *Aristotle's Problems II; Rhetorica ad Alexandrum*. Cambridge.

Radicke, J. (1995) *Die Rede des Demosthenes für die Freiheit der Rhodier*. Stuttgart.

Rankin, D. I. (1988) "The Mining Lobby at Athens," *AncSoc* 19: 189–205.

Rawlings, H. R. (1977) "Thucydides on the Purpose of the Delian League," *Phoenix* 31: 1–8.

Rhodes, P. J. (1978) "On Labelling 4th-century Politicians," *LCM* 3: 207–11.

(1992) *A Commentary on the Aristotelian Athenaion Politeia*. Oxford.

(2004) "Keeping to the Point," in *The Law and the Courts in Ancient Greece*, ed. E. Harris and L. Rubenstein. London: 137–58.

(2007) "Democracy and Empire," in *The Cambridge Companion to the Age of Pericles*, ed. L. J. Samons. Cambridge: 24–45.

(2008) "Making and Breaking Treaties in the Greek World," in *War and Peace in Ancient and Medieval History*, ed. Philip de Souza and John France. Cambridge: 6–27.

Rhodes, P. J. and R. Osborne (2003) *Greek Historical Inscriptions 403–323*. Oxford.

Richardson, R. B., ed. (1889) *Aeschines: Against Ctesiphon (On the Crown)*. College Series of Greek Authors. Boston.

Robert, L. (1977) "Une fête de la paix à Athènes au IVe siècle," *Archaiologike Ephemeris*: 1–8.

Roberts, J. T. (1982) "Dorians and Ionians," *JHS* 102: 1–14.

Roebuck, D. (2001) *Ancient Greek Arbitration*. Oxford.

Rogers, B. B., ed. (1902–16) *The Comedies of Aristophanes*. 5 vols. London.

Roisman, J. (2005) *The Rhetoric of Manhood: Masculinity in the Attic Orators*. Berkeley.

(2006) *The Rhetoric of Conspiracy in Ancient Athens*. Berkeley.

Romilly, J. de (1954) "Les modérés Athéniens vers le milieu du IVe siècle: échos et concordances," *REG* 67: 327–54.

(1958) "Eunomia in Isocrates or the Political Importance of Creating Good Will," *JHS* 78: 92–101.

(1992) "Isocrates and Europe," *G&R* 39: 2–13.

Rosenberg, S. D. (1993) "The Threshold of Thrill: Life Stories in the Skies over Southeast Asia," in *Gendering War Talk*, ed. M. Cooke and A. Woollacott. Princeton: 43–66.

Rosivach, V. (1994) *The System of Public Sacrifice in Fourth-century Athens*. Atlanta.

(1999) "Enslaving *Barbaroi* and the Athenian Ideology of Slavery," *Historia* 48: 129–57.

Rowe, G. O. (1966) "The Portrait of Aeschines in the *Oration on the Crown*," *TAPhA* 97: 397–406.

(1968) "Demosthenes' First Philippic: The Satiric Mode," *TAPhA* 99: 361–74.

Runciman, W. G. (1990) "Doomed to Extinction: the *Polis* as an Evolutionary Dead-end," in *The Greek City from Homer to Alexander*, ed. O. Murray and S. Price. Oxford: 347–68.

(1998) "Greek Hoplites, Warrior Culture, and Indirect Bias," *Journal of the Royal Anthropological Institute* 4: 731–51.

Ruschenbusch, E. (1979) "Die Einführung des Theorikon," *ZPE* 36: 303–8.

Russell, B. (1916) *Justice in War-Time*. Chicago.

(1951) *The Autobiography of Betrand Russell, 1914–1944*. Boston.

Ryder, T. T. B. (1965) *Koine Eirene: General Peace and Local Independence in Ancient Greece*. Oxford.

(1976) "Demosthenes and Philip's Peace of 338/7 BC," *CQ* n.s. 26: 85–7.

(2000) "Demosthenes and Philip II," in *Demosthenes: Statesman and Orator*, ed. I. Worthington. London: 45–89.

Sage, M. M. (1996) *Warfare in Ancient Greece: A Sourcebook*. London.

Sager, E. W. (1980) "The Social Origins of Victorian Pacifism," *Victorian Studies* 23: 211–36.

Saïd, S. (2001) "The Discourse of Identity in Greek Rhetoric from Isocrates to Aristides," in *Ancient Perceptions of Greek Ethnicity*, ed. I. Malkin. Cambridge, MA: 275–99.

Saller, R. (2002) "Framing the Debate over Growth in the Ancient Economy," in *The Ancient Economy*, ed. W. Scheidel and S. von Reden. New York: 251–69.

Salmond, P. D. C. N. (1996) "Sympathy for the Devil: Chares and Athenian Politics," *G&R* 43: 43–53.

Samons, L. J. (2004) *What's Wrong with Democracy? From Athenian Practice to American Worship*. Berkeley.

Sandys, J. E. (1897) *The First Philippic and the Olynthiacs of Demosthenes*. London.

(1900) *Demosthenes: On the Peace, Second Philippic, On the Chersonese, and Third Philippic*. New York.

Santoni, R. E. (1991) "Nurturing the Institution of War: 'Just War' Theory's 'Justifications' and Accommodations," in *The Institution of War*, ed. R. A. Hinde. London: 99–120.

Sawada, N. (1996) "Athenian Politics in the Age of Alexander the Great: A Reconsideration of the Trial of Ctesiphon," *Chiron* 26: 57–84.

Scafuro, A. (1997) *The Forensic Stage: Settling Disputes in Graeco-Roman New Comedy*. Cambridge.

Scala, R. von (1890) *Die Studien des Polybios*. Stuttgart.

Schäfer, A. D. (1885–7) *Demosthenes und seine Zeit*. 4 vols. Leipzig.

Schaps, D. (1982) "The Women of Greece in Wartime," *CPh* 77: 193–213.

(1998) "Review of David Tandy, *Warriors into Traders: The Power of the Market in Early Greece*," *BMCRev* November 1.

Scheidel, W. and S. von Reden, eds. (2002) *The Ancient Economy*. London.

Schelling, T. C. (1960) *The Strategy of Conflict*. Cambridge.

Schmookler, A. B. (1995) *The Parable of the Tribes: The Problem of Power in Social Evolution*. Albany.

Schofield, M. (1998) "Political Friendship and the Ideology of Reciprocity," in *Kosmos: Essays in Order Conflict and Commnitiy in Classical Athens*, ed. P. Cartledge, P. Millett, and S. von Reden. Cambridge: 37–51.

Schumpeter, J. A. (1951) "The Sociology of Imperialisms," in *Imperialism and Social Classes*. New York: 3–130.

Schütrumpf, E. (1991–2005) *Aristoteles, Politik*. 4 vols. Berlin.

(1993) "Aristotle's Theory of Slavery – a Platonic Dilemma," *AncPhil* 13: 111–23.

(1995) "Discussion of G. Herman, Honour, Revenge and the State in Fourth-century Athens," in *Die athenische Demokratie im Jahrhundert v.Chr.: Vollendung oder Verfall einer Verfassungsform*, ed. W. Eder. Stuttgart: 65–6.

Seager, R. (1974) "The King's Peace and the Balance of Power in Greece, 386–362 BC," *Athenaeum* 52: 36–63.

Sealey, R. (1955) "Athens after the Social War," *JHS* 75: 74–81.

(1956) "Callistratos of Aphidna and his Contemporaries," *Historia* 5: 178–203.

(1957) "Thucydides, Herodotus, and the Causes of War," *CQ* n.s. 7: 1–12.

(1966) "The Origin of the Delian League," in *Ancient Society and Institutions: Studies Presented to Victor Ehrenberg on his 75th Birthday*, ed. E. Badian. Oxford: 233–55.

(1967) "Pseudo-Demosthenes XIII and XXV," *REG* 80: 250–5.

(1993) *Demosthenes and his Time: A Study in Defeat*. Oxford.

(1994) *The Justice of the Greeks*. Ann Arbor, MI.

Seaman, M. G. (1997) "The Athenian Expedition to Melos in 416 BC," *Historia* 46: 385–418.

Sekunda, N. V. (1992) "Athenian Demography and Military Strength," *ABSA* 87: 311–35.

Shapiro, H. A. (1993) *Personifications in Greek Art: The Representation of Abstract Concepts 600–400 BC*. Zurich.

Shay, J. (1994) *Achilles in Vietnam: Combat Trauma and the Undoing of Character*. New York.

Sheehan, M. (1996) *The Balance of Power: History and Theory*. London.

Sheets, G. A. (1994) "Conceptualizing International Law in Thucydides," *AJPh* 115: 51–73.

Shinozaki, M. (1980) "Abstract: The Position of the Mercenaries in Isokrates' Social View," *Seiyåo-kotengaku kenkyåu* 28: 160–1.

Shrimpton, G. S. (1991) *Theopompus the Historian*. Montreal.

Siewert, P. (1977) "The Ephebic Oath in Fifth-century Athens," *JHS* 97: 102–11.

Silverthorne, M. (1973) "Militarism in the Laws," *SO* 49: 29–38.

Simon, E. (1986) "Eirene," in *Lexicon Iconographicum Mythologiae Classicae*. Zurich: 700–5.

Sinclair, R. K. (1978) "The King's Peace and the Employment of Military and Naval Forces 387–378," *Chiron* 8: 29–54.

Slater, W. J. (1988) "The Epiphany of Demosthenes," *Phoenix* 42: 126–30.

Snell, B. (1953) *The Discovery of the Mind in Greek Philosophy and Literature*. New York.

Soesberber, P. G. von (1982–3) "Colonisation as a Solution to Socio-economic Problems in Fourth-century Greece," *AncSoc* 13–14: 131–45.

Sosin, J. (2004) "An Endowed Peace," *MH* 61: 2–8.

Ste. Croix, G. E. M. de (1964) "Review of James J. Buchanan, *Theorika. A Study of Monetary Distributions for the Athenian Citizenry during the Fifth and Fourth Centuries BC*," *CR* n.s. 14: 190–2.

(1972) *The Origins of the Peloponnesian War*. London.

(1983) *The Class Struggle in the Ancient Greek World: From the Archaic Age to the Arab Conquests*. Ithaca, NY.

Stafford, E. (2000) *Worshipping Virtues: Personification and the Divine in Ancient Greece*. London.

Steele, D. R. (1981) "Review of Geoffrey Blainey, The Causes of War," *Free Life: The Journal of the Libertarian Alliance* 2: 3–7.

Stewart, F. H. (1994) *Honor*. Chicago.

Strauss, B. S. (1984) "Philip II of Macedon, Athens, and Silver Mining," *Hermes* 112: 418–27.

(1985) "The Cultural Significance of Bribery and Embezzlement in Athenian Politics: The Evidence of the Period 403–386 BC," *AncW* 11: 67–74.

(1986) *Athens after the Peloponnesian War: Class, Faction and Policy 403–386 BC*. Ithaca, NY.

(1991a) "Of Balances, Bandwagons, and Ancient Greeks," in *Hegemonic Rivalry: From Thucydides to the Nuclear Age*, ed. R. N. Lebow and B. S. Strauss. Boulder, CO: 189–210.

(1991b) "On Aristotle's Critique of Athenian Democracy," in *Essays of the Foundation of Aristotelian Political Science*, ed. C. Lord and D. K. O'Connor. Berkeley and Los Angeles: 212–33.

(1993a) *Fathers and Sons in Athens: Ideology and Society in the Era of the Peloponnesian War*. Princeton.

(1993b) "Andocides' *On the Mysteries* and the Theme of the Father in Late Fifth-century Athens," in *Nomodeiktes: Greek Studies in Honor of Martin Ostwald*, ed. R. Rosen and J. Farrell. Ann Arbor: 255–68.

(2000) "Perspectives on the Death of Fifth-century Athenian Seamen," in *War and Violence in Ancient Greece*, ed. H. von Wees. London: 261–83.

Stroud, R. S. (1971) "Greek Inscriptions. Theozotides and the Athenian Orphans," *Hesperia* 40: 280–301.

(1998) *The Athenian Grain-Tax Law of 374/3 BC*. Princeton.

Struckmeyer, F. R. (1971/2) "The 'Just War' and the Right of Self-Defense," *Ethics* 82: 48–55.

Suganami, H. (1978) "The 'Peace through Law' Approach: A Critical Examination of its Ideas," in *Approaches and Theory in International Relations*, ed. T. Taylor. New York: 100–21.

Sumner, W. G. (1964) "War," in *War: Studies from Psychology, Sociology, Anthropology*, ed. L. Bramson and G. W. Goethals. New York: 205–27.

Tandy, D. W. (1997) *Warriors into Traders: The Power of the Market in Early Greece*. Berkeley and Los Angeles.

Teichman, J. (1986) *Pacifism and the Just War*. Oxford.

Temes, P. S. (2003) *The Just War: An American Reflection on the Morality of War in our Time*. Chicago.

Theweleit, K. (1989) *Male Fantasies: Psychoanalyzing the White Terror*. Minneapolis.

Thomas, C. G. (1979) "The Territorial Imperative of the Polis," *AncW* 2: 35–9.

Thomas, R. (1989) *Oral Tradition and Written Record in Classical Athens*. Cambridge.

   (2005) "Writing, Law, and Written Law," in *The Cambridge Companion to Ancient Greek Law*, ed. M. Gagarin and D. Cohen. Cambridge: 41–60.

Thür, G. (1996) "Reply to D. C. Mirhady: Torture and Rhetoric in Athens," *JHS* 116: 132–4.

   (2005) "The Role of the Witness in Athenian Law," in *The Cambridge Companion to Ancient Greek Law*, ed. M. Gagarin and D. Cohen. Cambridge: 146–69.

   (2007) "Diaitetai," in *Brill's New Pauly Online*, ed. H. Cancik and H. Schneider. Leiden.

Tod, M. N. (1913) *International Arbitration amongst the Greeks*. Oxford.

   ed. (1946–8) *Greek Historical Inscriptions: From the Sixth Century* BC *to the Death of Alexander the Great in 323* BC. Oxford.

Todd, S. (1990) "The Use and Abuse of the Attic Orators," *G&R* 37: 159–78.

   (1993) *The Shape of Athenian Law*. Oxford.

   (2007) "Lady Chatterley's Lover and the Attic Orators: The Social Composition of the Athenian Jury," in *The Attic Orators*, ed. E. Carawan. Oxford: 312–58.

Trevett, J. (1994) "Demosthenes' Speech *On Organization* (Dem. 13)," *GRBS* 35: 179–93.

   (1996a) "Aristotle's Knowledge of Athenian Oratory," *CQ* 46: 371–9.

   (1996b) "Did Demosthenes Publish his Deliberative Speeches?," *Hermes* 124: 425–41.

Tritle, L. (1988) *Phocion the Good*. New York.

   (1992a) "Continuity and Change in the Athenian *Strategia*," *AHB* 7.4: 125–9.

   (1992b) "Virtue and Progress in Classical Athens: The Myth of the Professional General," *AncW* 23: 71–89.

   (1996) "Review of Edward M. Harris, *Aeschines and Athenian Politics*," *BMCRev* October 12: 1–7.

   (2000) *From Melos to My Lai: War and Survival*. London.

   (2007) "Laughing for Joy: War and Peace among the Greeks," in *War and Peace in the Ancient World*, ed. K. Raaflaub. Malden, MA: 172–90.

Tucker, R. W. (1977) *The Inequality of Nations*. New York.

Tuplin, C. (1998) "Demosthenes' *Olynthiacs* and the Character of the Demegoric Corpus," *Historia* 47: 276–320.

Turner, M. (1987) *Death Is the Mother of Beauty: Mind, Metaphor, Criticism.* Chicago.

Usher, S. (1976) "Lysias and his Clients," *GRBS* 17: 31–41.

(1999) *Greek Oratory: Tradition and Originality.* Oxford.

Ussher, R. G. (1973) *Aristophanes: Ecclesiazusae.* Oxford.

Vagts, A. (1959) *A History of Militarism.* London.

van Wees, H. (1992) *Status Warriors: War, Violence and Society in Homer and History.* Amsterdam.

(1995) "Politics and the Battlefield: Ideology in Greek Warfare," in *The Greek World*, ed. A. Powell. London: 153–78.

(1998a) "Greeks Bearing Arms: The State, the Leisure Class, and the Display of Weapons in Archaic Greece," in *Archaic Greece: New Approaches and New Evidence*, ed. N. Fisher and H. van Wees. London: 333–78.

(1998b) "The Law of Gratitude: Reciprocity in Anthropological Theory," in *Reciprocity in Ancient Greece*, ed. C. Gill, N. Postlethwaite, and R. Seaford. Oxford: 13–49.

(2004) *Greek Warfare: Myths and Realities.* London.

Vattel, E. de (1793) *The Law of Nations; or, Principles of the Law of Nature; Applied to the Conduct and Affairs of Nations and Sovereigns.* London.

Versnel, H. S. (1987) "Wife and Helpmate: Women of Ancient Athens in Anthropological Perspective," in *Sexual Asymmetry: Studies in Ancient Society*, ed. J. Blok and P. Mason. Amsterdam: 59–86.

Vidal-Naquet, P. (1986a) "Slavery and the Rule of Women in Tradition, Myth, and Utopia," in *The Black Hunter: Forms of Thought and Forms of Society in the Greek World.* Baltimore: 205–23.

(1986b) "The Tradition of the Athenian Hoplite," in *The Black Hunter: Forms of Thought and Forms of Society in the Greek World.* Baltimore: 85–105.

Viola, L. (2008). "Diplomacy and the Origins of the Membership System." Doctoral dissertation: Program on International Politics, Economics, and Security, University of Chicago (Chicago).

Vlastos, G. (1941) "Slavery in Plato's Thought," *PhR* 50: 289–304.

Walbank, F. W. (1951) "The Problem of Greek Nationality," *Phoenix* 5: 41–60.

Walt, S. M. (1987) *The Origins of Alliances.* Ithaca, NY.

Waltz, K. N. (1979) *Theory of International Politics.* Reading, MA.

(1986) "Reflections on *Theory of International Politics*: A Response to My Critics," in *Neorealism and its Critics*, ed. R. O. Keohane. New York: 322–45.

Walzer, M. (1977) *Just and Unjust Wars: A Moral Argument with Historical Illustrations.* New York.

(2004) "The Triumph of Just War Theory (and the Dangers of Success)," in *Arguing about War.* New Haven: 3–22.

Wankel, H., ed. (1976) *Demosthenes: Rede für Ktesiphon über den Kranz.* Wissenschaftliche Kommentare zu griechischen und lateinischen Schriftstellern. Heidelberg.

Waterfield, R. A. H. (1982) "Double Standards in Euripides' *Troades*," *Maia* n.s.
34: 139–42.

Wehrli, F., ed. (1949) *Demetrios von Phaleron*. Die Schule des Aristoteles: Text und
Kommentar. Basel.

Weißenberger, M. (2007) "Isocrates," in *Brill's New Pauly Online*, ed. H. Cancik
and H. Schneider. Leiden.

Wells, D. A. (1969) "How Much Can the 'Just War' Justify?," *JPh* 64: 819–29.

Wendt, A. (1992) "Anarchy in What States Make of It: The Social Construction
of Power Politics," *International Organization* 46: 391–425.

West, M. L. (1989) *Iambi et Elegi Graeci ante Alexandrum cantati*. Oxford.

Wheeler, E. L. (1984) "Sophistic Interpretation and Greek Treaties," *GRBS* 25:
253–74.

(1991) "The General as Hoplite," in *Hoplites: The Classical Greek Battle Experience*, ed. V. D. Hanson. London: 121–70.

Whitehead, D. trans. and ed. (1990) *Aeneias the Tactician: How to Survive under
Siege*. Oxford.

Whitman, C. H. (1974) *Euripides and the Full Circle of Myth*. Cambridge.

Williams, B. (1993) *Shame and Necessity*. Berkeley.

Winkler, J. J. (1990) "Laying down the Law: The Oversight of Men's Sexual
Behavior in Classical Athens," in *The Constraints of Desire: The Anthropology
of Sex and Gender in Ancient Greece*. London: 45–70.

Winter, J. M. (1995) *Sites of Memory, Sites of Mourning: The Great War in European
Cultural History*. Cambridge.

Wolff, H. J. (2007) "Demosthenes as Advocate: The Functions and Methods of
Legal Consultants in Classical Athens," in *The Attic Orators*, ed. E. Carawan.
Oxford: 91–115.

Wolpert, A. (2001) "The Genealogy of Diplomacy in Classical Greece," *Diplomacy
and Statecraft* 12: 71–88.

Wooten, C. (1977) "A Few Observations on Form and Content in Demosthenes,"
Phoenix 31: 258–61.

(2008) *A Commentary on Demosthenes' Philippic I: With Rhetorical Analyses of
Philippics II and III*. Oxford.

Worthington, I. (1991a) "Greek Oratory, Revision of Speeches and the Problem of
Historical Reliability," *C&M* 42: 55–74.

(1991b) "The Authenticity of Demosthenes' Fourth Philippic," *Mnemosyne* 44:
425–7.

(1992) *A Historical Commentary on Dinarchus; Rhetoric and Conspiracy in Later
Fourth-century Athens*. Ann Arbor.

(1994) "History and Oratorical Exploitation," in *Persuasion: Greek Rhetoric in
Action*, ed. I. Worthington. London: 109–29.

(2000) "Demosthenes' (In)activity during the Reign of Alexander the Great,"
in *Demosthenes: Statesman and Orator*, ed. I. Worthington. London: 90–113.

Wyse, W. (1904) *The Speeches of Isaeus*. Cambridge.

Yates, R. (2007) "Making War and Making Peace in Early China," in *War and
Peace in the Ancient World*, ed. K. Raaflaub. Malden, MA: 34–52.

Yunis, H. (1996) *Taming Democracy: Models of Political Rhetoric in Classical Athens.* Ithaca, NY.

(2000) "Politics as Literature: Demosthenes and the Burden of the Athenian Past," *Arion* 8: 97–118.

(2001) *Demosthenes: On the Crown.* Cambridge.

(2005) "The Rhetoric of Law in Fourth-century Athens," in *The Cambridge Companion to Ancient Greek Law*, ed. M. Gagarin and D. Cohen. Cambridge: 191–208.

Zampaglione, G. (1973) *The Idea of Peace in Antiquity.* Notre Dame.

Zelnick-Abrahmovitz, R. (2000) "Did Patronage Exist in Classical Athens?," *AC* 69: 65–80.

Index